OXFORD IB PREPARED

ECONOMICS

IB DIPLOMA PROGRAMME

Peter Dumortier

Series Editors:
Constantine Ziogas
Marily Apostolakou

IB PREPARED

OXFORD
UNIVERSITY PRESS

OXFORD
UNIVERSITY PRESS

Great Clarendon Street, Oxford, OX2 6DP, United Kingdom

Oxford University Press is a department of the University of Oxford. It furthers the University's objective of excellence in research, scholarship, and education by publishing worldwide. Oxford is a registered trade mark of Oxford University Press in the UK and in certain other countries

First published in 2022

British Library Cataloguing in Publication Data

Data available

978-1-38-203389-3

10 9 8 7 6 5 4 3

Paper used in the production of this book is a natural, recyclable product made from wood grown in sustainable forests. The manufacturing process conforms to the environmental regulations of the country of origin.

Printed in Great Britain by Ashford Colour Press Ltd.

Acknowledgements

We would like to thank Rafaela Antezana Suárez for her contribution to this book.

The publisher would like to thank the International Baccalaureate for their kind permission to adapt questions from past examinations and content from the subject guide.

The publisher and authors would like to thank the following for permission to use photographs and other copyright material:

Cover: Evis Disha / EyeEm / Getty Images. **Photos: piv:** Southtownboy Studio/Shutterstock; **p1:** Bernhard Richter/Shutterstock; **p11:** Rawpixel.com/Shutterstock; **p78:** Thanwa photo/Shutterstock; **p140:** Herr Petroff/Shutterstock; **p170(t):** Globe Turner/Shutterstock; **p170(b):** charnsitr/Shutterstock; **p194:** Anton Veselov/Shutterstock; **p202:** Herr Petroff/Shutterstock; **p213:** Rawpixel.com/Shutterstock; **p221:** Thanwa photo/Shutterstock; **p236:** Southtownboy Studio/Shutterstock.

Artwork by Integra Software Services, Aptara, General Statistics Office of Viet Nam (p110), and OPHI (2018). Global Multidimensional Poverty Index 2018: The Most Detailed Picture to Date of the World's Poorest People. Report. Oxford Poverty and Human Development Initiative, University of Oxford (p114).

The author and publisher are grateful to those who have given permission to reproduce the following extracts and adaptations of copyright material:

Tess McClure: An extract from the article - *'New Zealand unveils $8,600 subsidy for electric vehicles to reduce emissions'*; published by The Guardian, 14 June 2021. Copyright © Guardian News & Media Ltd 2022. Used by permission; **Tabita Diela**: An extract from reuters.com – 'Indonesia parliament tells government to tax a wider range of plastic products'; published by Reuters, FEBRUARY 19, 2020. Copyright © 2020 Reuters.com 2020. All rights reserved. Used under license from PARS International; **MAP**: From the article – 'One of China's poorest provinces wants to be a tech hub'; published by The Economist, June 2nd 2018. Reprinted by permission from The Economist Group Limited.

Every effort has been made to contact copyright holders of material reproduced in this book. Any omissions will be rectified in subsequent printings if notice is given to the publisher.

Links to third party websites are provided by Oxford in good faith and for information only. Oxford disclaims any responsibility for the materials contained in any third party website referenced in this work.

Contents

Answers to questions and exam papers in this book can be found on your free support website. Access the support website here:

www.oxfordsecondary.com/ib-prepared-support

INTRODUCTION

This book provides coverage of the IB diploma syllabus in economics and offers support to students preparing for their examinations. The book will help you revise the study material, consolidate the essential concepts and models, understand the assessment criteria and improve your approach to IB examinations.

All topics are illustrated by annotated examples of student answers to sample examination questions, explaining why and how marks may be achieved or missed.

Overview of the book structure

The first four units of the book focus on content-specific guidance, following the structure of the IB DP economics syllabus:

- **Unit 1**: Introduction to economics
- **Unit 2**: Microeconomics
- **Unit 3**: Macroeconomics
- **Unit 4**: The global economy.

Each of these four units is divided into sub-units with summaries of the key syllabus content, useful advice and related question practice.

Subsequent units examine the modes of assessment for this course.

All standard level (SL) and higher level (HL) students must complete the internal assessment and take papers 1 and 2 as part of their external assessment. HL students have an additional external assessment, paper 3.

- **Unit 5**: paper 1 requires extended responses. You need to answer *one* question from a *choice of three*. The questions are each subdivided into two parts, (a) and (b) and are drawn from the four units of the syllabus. This unit unpacks the mark bands used by examiners to award marks for parts (a) and (b). You may want to refer to the descriptors for each mark band (on pages 194 and 195) as you go through the sample paper 1 question across Units 1–4. This unit includes a sample question based on Unit 2 content and a sample student answer.
- **Unit 6**: paper 2 requires responses that use the text/data provided. You need to answer *one* question from a *choice of two*. The questions are each subdivided into seven parts, (a), (b), (c), (d), (e), (f) and (g). Unlike paper 1 questions, where parts (a) and (b) of any one question tend to focus on the content from the same unit, paper 2 questions may cover contents from all four units within the same question. A sample question is included along with a sample student answer. Parts (a) to (g) of that sample question are drawn from the four units of the syllabus, so you might need to complete all content-based units to attempt this sample question or any sample paper 2 question. However, sample parts (a) to (f) are included throughout Units 1–4.
- **Unit 7**: paper 3 requires calculations and responses that use the text/data provided. You must answer *two compulsory questions*. The questions are subdivided into parts (a) and (b) where part (a) has subparts. These are drawn from the four units of the syllabus. A sample question is included with a sample response. This question draws on Units 2 and 3 of the syllabus. Sample part (a) questions are also included throughout Units 1–4. Paper 3 is not included in the SL mode of assessment.
- **Unit 8**: this section focuses on the internal assessment (IA) task, which requires candidates to write three commentaries based on news articles. This unit addresses the difficulties commonly encountered by students while carrying out the IA task. The specific elements of each assessment criteria will be examined. Two sample IA portfolios are provided, each related to content from Unit 2 of the syllabus.
- **Unit 9**: (practice exam papers) includes examples of IB-style practice questions like those found in papers 1, 2 and 3, written exclusively for this book. These examples give you the opportunity to test yourself before the examination, as they provide additional practice problems for the material featured in all the units. The answers and solutions are given online at: www.oxfordsecondary.com/ib-prepared-support.

Concepts

Nine concepts underpin the DP economics course. They are:

- scarcity
- choice
- sustainability
- change

- efficiency
- interdependence
- equity
- intervention
- economic well-being.

There is no universally accepted definition of these concepts; you are not expected to memorize the definitions included in Unit 1 (page 2); what matters is your understanding of these concepts, both in general and in economics.

Assessment overview

The internal and external assessment marks are combined, as shown in the following table, to give your overall DP economics grade, from 1 (lowest) to 7 (highest).

Assessment	Task	Weight	Task	Weight
Paper 1	1 hour and 15 minutes examination	30%	1 hour and 15 minutes examination	20%
Paper 2	1 hour and 45 minutes examination	40%	1 hour and 45 minutes examination	30%
Paper 3 (HL)	—	—	1 hour and 45 minutes examination	30%
Internal assessment (IA)	3 written commentaries	30%	3 written commentaries	20%

Command terms

In the examination questions, command terms are the words that tell you how to approach the question, especially in terms of depth. It is crucial that you understand these terms correctly.

Before you answer a question, you should:

- underline the command term
- look at the mark weighting of that question
- match your answer to the depth required for the command term.

Some candidates do not achieve high marks because they do not pay sufficient attention to the command terms and therefore do not fully address the requirements of the question.

Command terms fall into four categories, as follows.

Knowledge and understanding

Some command terms assess your ability to demonstrate knowledge and understanding of the subject—the ability to recall previously learned concepts. These are the most accessible questions such as definitions, which tend to be worth 2 marks.

Command term	IB definition	Sample question and marks	Note the following
Define	Give the precise meaning of a word, phrase, concept or physical quantity.	Define the term *economic growth*. [2]	You should know how to define all the terms in the four units of the syllabus. You should also be familiar with the functions of institutions listed in the syllabus.
List	Give a sequence of brief answers with no explanation.	List two responsibilities of a country's central bank. [2]	
Describe	Give a detailed account.	Using information from Table 1, describe the changes in the business cycle. [4]	The questions may seem easy, yet many candidates do not achieve full marks because: they write answers that are too theoretical (without referring to the text/data); or their answers are too superficial (the answer is too short and does not provide detail, or the answer just repeats a sentence from the text without adding value).
Outline	Give a brief account or summary.	Outline one difficulty in measuring poverty. [2]	
State	Give a specific name, value or other brief answer without explanation or calculation.	State two characteristics of a monopolistic market structure. [2]	Your answer may be very brief, just a few words or bullet points.

Application and analysis

Some command terms assess your ability to demonstrate application and analysis. Application refers to the ability to use learned concepts and models in new and concrete situations. Analysis refers to the ability to break down economic theory into its parts to explain its essential features. These command terms come with more demanding tasks where questions are worth more marks and require longer responses.

Command term	IB definition	Sample question and marks	Note the following
Explain	Give a detailed account including reasons or causes.	Explain two possible causes of a fall in the demand for a good. [10]	This command term is frequently used across all three papers. A common reason why candidates do not achieve high marks is that they tend to *describe* rather than *explain* theory. For instance, listing the non-price determinants of demand is *describing* theory. Establishing the link between the change in a non-price determinant and a fall in demand using, for example, a diagram is *explaining* theory.
Distinguish	Make clear the differences between two or more concepts or items.	Distinguish between positive and normative economics. [4]	One common reason why many candidates do not achieve high marks is that they *describe* one concept and then the other and they do not focus on the difference(s) between the two.
Analyse	Break down in order to bring out the essential elements or structure.	Analyse the impact of asymmetric information on the allocation of resources. [4]	Analysis requires a rigorous and systematic approach, as you must pay attention to all variables involved and their relationships with one another.
Apply	Use an idea, equation, principle, theory or law in relation to a given problem or issue.	Apply the concept of price elasticity of demand (PED) to the changes in consumption illustrated in Table 1. [4]	Applying means making explicit links between "theory" and the text/data. In this example, the concept of PED may be used to determine the relative elasticity of the demand for a good.
Comment	Give a judgment based on a given statement or result of a calculation.	Comment on the significance of the value of the price elasticity of demand. [2]	Your judgment must have economic value. For instance, you should state that "demand is price-inelastic" and not "PED is low".

Synthesis and evaluation

Some command terms assess your ability to demonstrate synthesis and evaluation. Synthesis refers to the ability to connect different outcomes or viewpoints to provide an overview of an argument or discussion. Evaluation refers to the ability to formulate judgments supported by sound rationale and theory. These questions are worth 10 marks or 15 marks.

Command term	IB definition	Sample question and marks	Note the following
Discuss	Offer a considered and balanced review that includes a range of arguments, factors or hypotheses. Opinions or conclusions should be presented clearly and supported by appropriate evidence.	Using information from the text/data and your knowledge of economics, discuss the possible economic effects of Peru's trade protection policies on the domestic market for agricultural products. [15]	These command terms are frequently used in paper 1 and paper 2 questions. There are two main reasons why many candidates do not achieve high marks. Some candidates do not present balanced arguments, focusing either on the advantages or disadvantages (for "discuss"), or on strengths or limitations (for "evaluate"). Some candidates do not clearly present a conclusion after presenting a balanced range of arguments.
Evaluate	Make an appraisal by weighing up the strengths and limitations.	Using real-world examples, evaluate the consequences of a price ceiling. [15]	

Command term	IB definition	Sample question and marks	Note the following
Recommend	Present an advisable course of action with appropriate supporting evidence or reason in relation to a given situation, problem or issue.	Using the data provided and your knowledge of economics, recommend a policy that could be introduced by the government of Norway to reduce inflation. [10]	This command term is used in paper 3 questions and will be examined in greater detail in Unit 7.
Compare	Give an account of the similarities between two (or more) items or situations, referring to both (all) of them throughout.	Compare adverse selection and moral hazard as sources of asymmetric information. [4]	*Compare* requires you to focus on similarities. *Contrast* focuses on the differences. Candidates sometimes do not score high marks because they describe one concept and then the other, without pointing out the similarities or differences.
Contrast	Give an account of the differences between two (or more) items or situations, referring to both (all) of them throughout.	Contrast deflation and disinflation. [4]	
Compare and contrast	Give an account of similarities and differences between two (or more) items or situations, referring to both (all) of them throughout.	Using information from Table 1, compare and contrast GDP per capita and GDP per capita at purchasing power parity (PPP). [4]	Candidates may not score high marks if they provide a descriptive response or either compare or contrast (which is only half of the requirements of the command term).
Examine	Consider an argument or concept in a way that uncovers the assumptions and interrelationships of the issue.	Using real-world examples, examine the consequences of the lack of a pricing mechanism for common access resources. [15]	Candidates may not achieve high marks if they do not consider the consequences on all stakeholders or parties involved.
To what extent	Consider the merits or otherwise of an argument or concept. Opinions and conclusions should be presented clearly and supported with appropriate evidence and sound argument.	To what extent does the unequal income distribution impact economic development in China? [15]	You are advised to: • consider a range of perspectives and viewpoints • write a balanced answer • reach a precise, explicit conclusion.

Quantitative skills

Some other command terms assess your quantitative skills (ability to draw adequate diagrams and calculate relevant economic figures).

Command term	IB definition	Sample question and marks	Note the following
Calculate	Obtain a numerical answer showing the relevant stages in the working.	Calculate the producer revenue following the imposition of a $1 tax. [2]	Candidates may not achieve full marks if they forget to include their workings or units (in this case, dollars).
Construct	Display information in a diagrammatic or logical form.	Using the information, construct the Lorenz curve. [2]	Some candidates do not achieve full marks because they do not fully and correctly label their diagram.
Determine	Obtain the only possible answer.	Determine the size of the decrease in monthly corn consumption following the imposition of the price floor. [1]	Candidates often forget to provide the unit (such as $) or misinterpret the data (for example some figures are expressed in thousands but the final answer fails to recognize that).

Command term	IB definition	Sample question and marks	Note the following
Draw	Represent by means of a labelled, accurate diagram or graph, using a pencil. A ruler (straight edge) should be used for straight lines.	On the diagram above, draw the firm's demand curve following the introduction of subsidy of US$2 per unit of the product. [2]	Just as for "construct", the main reason candidates do not achieve full marks is due to missing or incorrect labels.
Identify	Provide an answer from a number of possibilities.	Identify the level of output at which the firm would maximize profits. [2]	These command terms are often used in paper 3 questions (refer to Unit 7).
Label	Add labels to a diagram.	Label the welfare loss resulting from the imposition of a tariff. [1]	
Plot	Mark the position of points on a diagram.	Using the data provided, plot the demand curve for fuel. [2]	Plotting is often done on graph paper or a grid.
Sketch	Represent by means of a labelled diagram or graph. The sketch should give a general idea of the required shape or relationship and should include relevant features.	Sketch a short-run Phillips curve. [2]	This command term should not be confused with "plot", which requires curves to accurately reflect the data provided.

Key features of the book

Summaries focus on the main points of each sub-unit's topic. They cover all the key contents on which you may be examined.

Annotated student answers show you real answers written by IB candidates, which mark they achieved and why. Positive or negative feedback from examiners about these answers is given in the green and red pullout boxes. These comments will help you understand how marks may be achieved or missed.

Content link

Link to your IA

Links to your IA (internal assessment) help you connect your IA and your examination revision, as your IA consists of commentaries in which you show application of economic concepts.

Link to other sub-units

Content links to other sub-units connect different sub-units that you could revise together, as they offer complementary perspectives on the same topic.

QUESTION PRACTICE

An **examination paper icon** indicates that the question has been taken from a past IB paper.

Assessment tip

Assessment tips give advice to help you optimize your examination techniques, warning against common errors and showing how to approach particular questions and command terms.

Concept link

Concept links connect the contents of the sub-unit to the concepts of scarcity, choice, efficiency, equity, economic well-being, sustainability, change, interdependence and intervention.

Test yourself

Test yourself features contain questions relating to the main text, which invite students to consolidate their learning.

Revision tip

Revision tips give advice to help you structure your revision.

1 INTRODUCTION TO ECONOMICS

1.1 WHAT IS ECONOMICS?

You should be able to:

- ✔ define the terms
  - ✔ scarcity, choice, efficiency, equity, economic well-being, sustainability, change, interdependence and intervention (the nine central key concepts)
  - ✔ the factors of production—land, labour, capital and entrepreneurship (entrepreneurs)
  - ✔ opportunity cost
  - ✔ economic goods and free goods
- ✔ explain that economics is a social science, which is divided into two branches—microeconomics and macroeconomics
- ✔ explain that economics studies the ways that scarce (finite) resources (factors of production) are allocated to meet the unlimited needs and wants of individuals
- ✔ explain how different economic systems answer the three basic economic questions
- ✔ explain that as a result of scarcity, choices have to be made, resulting in an opportunity cost
- ✔ explain how a production possibilities curve (PPC) model may be used to illustrate the concepts of scarcity, choice, opportunity cost and a situation of unemployed resources and inefficiency
- ✔ distinguish, using a PPC model, between actual (short-term) and potential (long-term) growth
- ✔ explain, using a circular flow of income model, how the economic decision-makers interact and make choices in an economy.

This sub-unit introduces economics, a social science that studies the behaviour and social relationships of individuals using scientific methods (such as data collection and analysis, hypothesis testing).

Summary

Microeconomics studies particular markets and segments of the economy. For example, the increase in the price of surgical masks in early 2020 is a microeconomic issue as it is related to the market for a specific good. **Macroeconomics** studies the whole economy and looks at "aggregate" variables such as GDP, unemployment and inflation. For instance, the impact of the Australian Central Bank's decision to decrease the interest rate in 2020 is a macroeconomic issue, since the implications of such a policy would affect all consumers (households) and producers (firms) in the Australian economy).

There are nine key concepts that are central to economics. You will need to draw links to a different key concept for each of your internal assessment (IA) commentaries. There is more on this in Unit 8 and you will also find regular "Concept link" boxes in relevant units of this book.

- **Scarcity**—also known as "the central problem of economics", scarcity refers to the limited availability of resources relative to society's unlimited wants and needs. Economics is the study of how to make the best possible use of limited (scarce) resources to satisfy those unlimited human wants and needs.
- **Choice**—the scarcity of resources means that not all economic wants can be fulfilled. Choices must thus be made. Economic decision-makers continually make choices between competing alternatives, and economics studies the consequences of these choices, both present and future.
- **Efficiency**—(scarce) resources must be used with minimal wastage to produce combinations of goods and services to satisfy the many wants of members of society. This is known as allocative efficiency.
- **Equity**—this refers to the concept of fairness. Policies that seek to achieve equity often aim for a more equal distribution of income, wealth or human opportunity. As fairness is a normative concept, it means different things to different people and there is thus much debate on the degree to which governments should intervene in markets to redistribute income and/or wealth.
- **Economic well-being**—this refers to the living standards (quality of life) of residents and citizens in a country. The dimensions of economic well-being include:
  - present and future financial security
  - the ability to meet basic needs
  - the ability to make economic choices to achieve personal satisfaction
  - the ability to maintain adequate income levels over the long term.
- **Sustainability**—this is the ability to use scarce resources without compromising their availability for future generations. Economic activities are sustainable when they do not incur environmental damage, resource depletion or degradation that will negatively affect future generations.
- **Change**—the world is in a continual state of flux. Economic theory does not focus on the value of the variables it investigates, but on their change from one situation to another. Economists study continuous change at institutional, structural, technological, economic and social levels.
- **Interdependence**—the economic agents of governments, firms, households and consumers are not self-sufficient. They interact with each other within and across nations. Decisions by certain economic agents are likely to generate many, and often unintended, economic consequences for other agents. A consideration of possible economic consequences of interdependence is essential to economic analysis
- **Intervention**—governments need to intervene in markets when they fail to achieve certain societal goals, such as equity, economic well-being or sustainability. There is often disagreement among economists and policymakers on the need for, and extent of, government intervention. There is a considerable debate about the merits of intervention versus the free market.

At the heart of economic theory is the problem of **scarcity**. Resources (factors of production) are finite (limited). The **factors of production** needed to produce goods and services are classified into four categories.

- **Land**—this includes the natural resources (gifts of nature) used for production. Some are renewable (e.g. wheat); some are non-renewable (e.g. crude oil).
- **Labour**—this is the human contribution (physical and mental) to production.
- **Capital**—this refers to the stock of manufactured resources (e.g. factories, equipment, tools, refined oil) needed for production.
- **Entrepreneurs**—these are the people willing to take risks to make business decisions and organize the other three factors of production in the production process.

Scarcity implies that societies cannot fulfil the unlimited human needs and wants and so choices must be made. Every time an entrepreneur allocates resources to the production of a particular good, these resources are no longer available to the production of other goods. For example, in deciding to produce wheat, a farmer (the entrepreneur) dedicates a plot of land, deploys workers (labour), uses fertilizer (capital), which will not be available to produce another crop such as corn. In choosing to produce wheat, the farmer has sacrificed the production of corn. This sacrifice (the alternative forgone) is the opportunity cost of that choice. The **opportunity cost** is the value of the next best alternative forgone when an economic decision is made. In the farming example, the opportunity cost of producing wheat is the production of corn that was sacrificed.

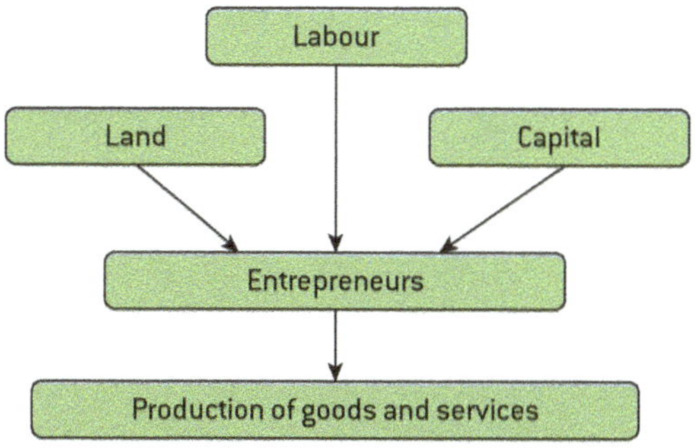

▲ Figure 1.1.1 The factors of production

Economic goods are produced using scarce resources, so they come with an opportunity cost. In contrast, **free goods** such as air and seawater are not produced using scarce resources and thus have a zero opportunity cost of production. The production of economic goods is sustainable if it does not lead to resource depletion or degradation, or environmental damage.

Since not all needs and wants can be satisfied, societies must decide on how scarce resources are to be used answer the **three fundamental economic questions**.

- What to produce?
- For whom to produce?
- How to produce?

Three systems allocate resources and answer these three questions.

- **The free market economy** is an economy where the factors of production are privately owned. The market forces (demand and supply) determine what and how much to produce, how to produce and for whom to produce.
- **The planned economy** exists where factors of production are owned by the state (except labour). The state determines what and how much to produce, how to produce and for whom to produce.
- **The mixed economy** has elements of planned and free market economies. In reality, all economies are mixed. What differs is the degree of state intervention from country to country.

A production possibilities curve (PPC) is an economic model showing the maximum combinations of two goods that an economy can produce in a given time period, if all the resources are being used fully and efficiently and the state of technology is fixed. A PPC diagram illustrates the concepts of scarcity, choice, opportunity cost and efficiency.

The PPC on Figure 1.1.2 illustrates the choices available to an economy that devotes all of its resources to the production of two goods: X and Y. (X and Y can be any goods or services such as corn and rice, or education and national defence.) The economy can produce at A where it only produces good Y or point B where it only produces good X, or any other combination of X and Y in between points A and B, such as points, C, D or E. Figure 1.1.2 illustrates the concept of opportunity cost. Due to the scarcity of resources, producing more of one good, for example X, implies that resources must be diverted away from the production of other goods, in this case Y. A movement from point C to point D implies that to produce an additional 100 units of X, resources need to be reallocated from the production of Y and thus 40 fewer units of Y will be produced. The opportunity cost of 100 units of X is thus 40 units of Y.

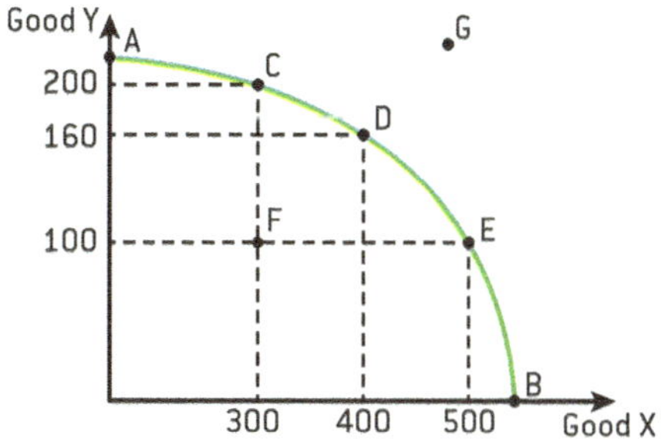

▲ Figure 1.1.2 The PPC

Note that the shape of the PPC is concave, implying that the **opportunity cost is increasing** as the economy increases the production of X. Going from point D to point E, the opportunity cost of another 100 units of X is now 60 units of Y. This means that to produce more of one good, an economy must sacrifice increasing amounts of the other good. The reason for increasing opportunity costs is that resources are not equally suited for producing different goods. Going from points C to D and eventually to E means that the economy concentrates more on producing X, diverting resources such as labour from the production of Y. At first, the workers who are more suitable for the production of X will be redeployed. Eventually, producing more X implies using more workers who might be more suitable for the production of Y and less productive in producing X. This means that increasingly more resources must be used to produce additional equal amounts of X. Consequently, increasing amounts of Y are given up to produce additional amounts of X.

Point F lies below the PPC and thus represents a combination of goods and services that is attainable, but the economy does not make full use of the resources available. For instance, point D (which is on the PPC) comes with more of both Y and X. **Any point below the PPC reflects inefficiency in the allocation of resources** since the economy is producing less than the maximum it can—**the PPC represents the productive capacity of the economy**. Moving from a point below the PPC (such as F) towards a point closer or on the PPC represents an increase in the production of goods and services, also known as **actual (short-term) economic growth**. This may occur when unemployed workers are given jobs producing goods and services.

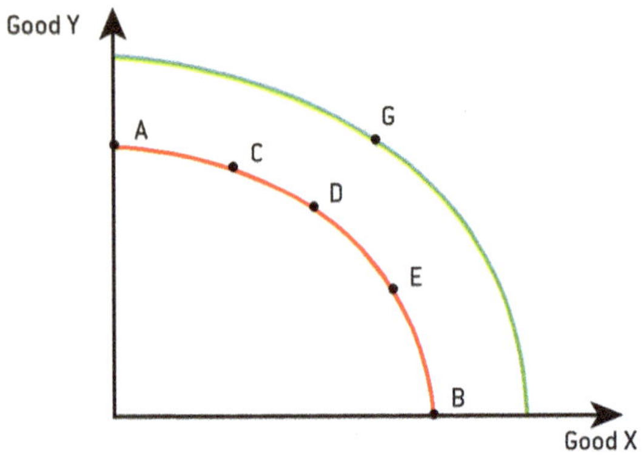

▲ Figure 1.1.3 Potential (long-term) growth

Point G lies beyond the PPC and is thus a combination of Y and X that is unattainable with the current level of resources and technology. **Potential (long-term) economic growth**, which occurs when the amount and/or quality of resources increases or with technological improvements, would allow for greater production combination of the two goods. Potential (long-term) economic growth is represented by an outward shift of the PPC (Figure 1.1.3). Combinations of goods that were previously unattainable, such as point G, may now be achieved.

The circular flow of income is an economic model representing the interaction between economic agents (governments, firms, households, the foreign sector) in an economy. Households own the factors of production (capital, land, labour and entrepreneurship) and they provide these to firms. In exchange, firms offer payments and so households receive rents (for land owners), wages (for labour/workers), interest (for capital owners) and profits (for entrepreneurs). The sum of these factor payments makes up **national income.** The factors of production, which are provided by households, are used by firms to produce goods and services. Households use their income to purchase these goods and services and so household expenditure on goods and services is received by firms.

There are two types of flows. These are:

- the real flows (factors of production, goods and services)
- monetary flows (income from factor payments, expenditure on goods or services).

This model demonstrates an important principle: the value of goods and services (total output produced) must be equal to the income received by households and the expenditure on goods and services. In short: output = income = expenditure.

Not all income will be spent on goods and services within the circular flow, some income will leave the circular flow as **leakages** (withdrawals), including **savings, taxes** and **imports** (since the payment for imported goods will be received by firms in other countries). Similarly, some spending on domestic goods and services may not originate from households. These are called **injections** and consist of **exports, government spending** and **investment** (spending by firms on capital goods, to produce other goods and services).

QUESTION PRACTICE

This question is adapted from the November 2021 examination paper.

Using a production possibilities curve (PPC) diagram, explain how the importing of new technology and capital equipment might affect Thailand's production possibilities (potential output). [4]

SAMPLE STUDENT ANSWER

Response 1

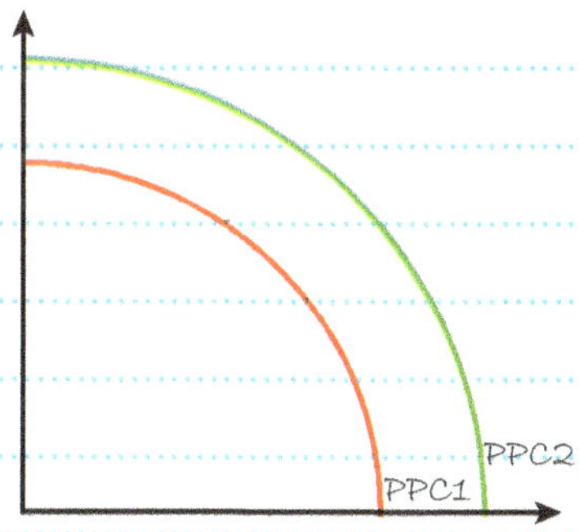

The additional capital goods allow Thailand to produce more so there is an increase in productive capacity.

▼ The diagram illustrates an outward shift of the PPC but there are no labels for the axes. As this is a 4-mark question, 2 marks are usually awarded for the diagram and another 2 marks for the explanation. Since it is not fully labelled, the diagram can only be awarded 1 mark.

▼ The explanation identifies the correct change in productive capacity (an increase) but does not provide a justification. There is also no reference to the diagram. Therefore, only 1 mark can be awarded to the explanation.

This response could have achieved 2/4 marks.

Response 2

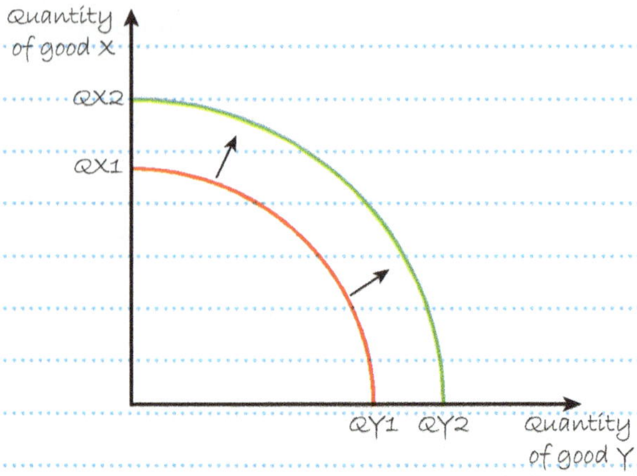

The imported capital equipment imply a greater amount of capital goods and hence a higher amount of factors of production. The access to imported technology would also lead to greater efficiency. The combined impact of more factors of production and technology would then lead to an increase in the maximum that Thailand can produce, which is reflected by the outward shift of the PPC from QX1QY1 to QX2QY2.

▲ The diagram is fully and correctly labelled. The arrows clearly indicate the direction of the shift of the PPC.

▲ There is an adequate justification for the outward shift of the PPC (the increase in factors of production and access to technology). There is also an adequate reference to the diagram.

This response could have achieved 4/4 marks.

QUESTION PRACTICE

This question is adapted from the May 2016 examination paper.

Using a production possibilities curve (PPC) diagram, explain the effects of the violence in Timor-Leste on production possibilities (potential output). [4]

SAMPLE STUDENT ANSWER

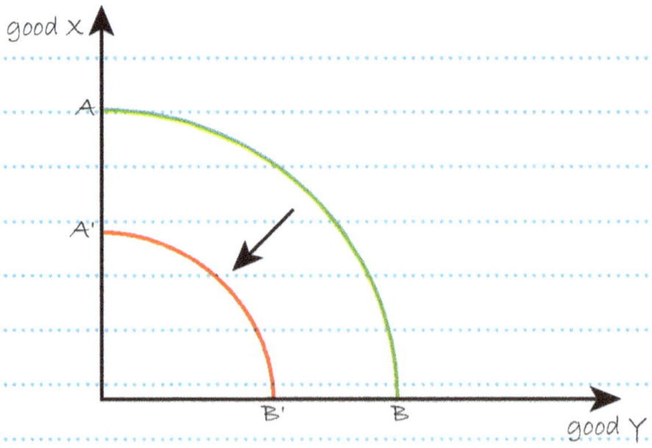

▲ The diagram is fully and correctly labelled and the direction of the shift of the PPC is clearly indicated by an arrow.

SAMPLE STUDENT ANSWER

The violence has resulted in death and many workers leaving the country. This has resulted in a reduction in quantity of labour, a factor of production. This led to a fall in production possibilities (potential output) which is reflected by an inward shift of the PPC from AB to AB'.

This response could have achieved 4/4 marks.

▲ The response explains that the potential output decreases due to a decrease in the quantity of factors of production. Reference is also made to the diagram.

QUESTION PRACTICE

This question is adapted from the November 2016 examination paper.

Using a production possibilities curve (PPC) diagram, explain why choices have to be made in all economies. [10]

SAMPLE STUDENT ANSWER

Response 1

Economies have scarce resources and thus must decide on what must be produced. So there is a choice to be made.

This can be shown on a PPC diagram.

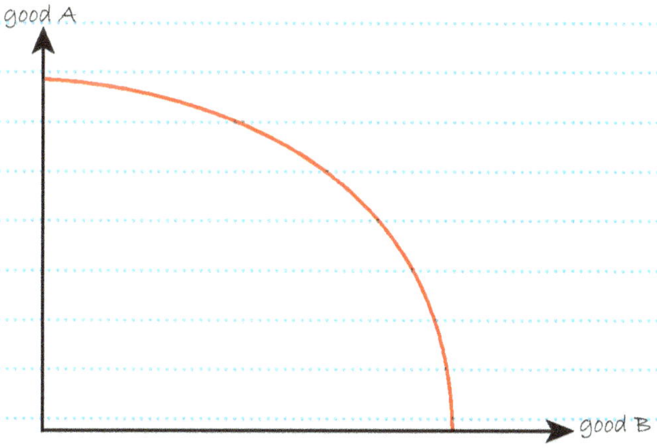

As we can see, an economy can produce either good A or good B. When they produce more good B, they produce less good A and hence they must make a choice to produce more good B at the expense of the production of good A or more good A and less good B.

▼ The candidate is alluding to the problem of scarcity, which is the central theme of this essay question. This could be better explained. What are the resources that are scarce? Economic theory must be fully explained for essay questions. Here the issue of scarcity is not well developed.

▼ The diagram the candidate has included is correctly labelled, but it is not sufficiently explained (the response makes no reference to it).

▼ There is some understanding that the choice has to be made because economies cannot produce all goods, but the candidate does not adequately link this to the issue of scarcity, so the demands of the question are only partially addressed.

A paper 1 question also tests your use of economic terminology. The choice being referred to involves an **opportunity cost** but that term is not mentioned.

This is a paper 1 style of question. Marks are awarded based on a set of descriptors. This response meets some of the descriptors of the second mark band (3–4) and some of the third mark band (5–6).

- The specific demands of the question are understood but partially addressed.
- Relevant economic theory is mostly described rather than explained.
- Only some economic terms are included.
- A diagram is included but not explained.

This response could have achieved 5/10 marks. Refer to Unit 5 (pages 194–195) for a full explanation of the paper 1 level descriptors.

Response 2

All economies face the problem of scarcity, also known as the central problem of economics. Resources are finite but individual wants and needs are infinite. Since there is a limited amount of land, labour and capital (the factors of production) which entrepreneurs can use to produce goods and services, it follows that not all wants and needs can be fulfilled.

▲ The issue of scarcity (of resources) is introduced and clearly explained (with reference to unlimited human wants and needs). The candidate also explains the related concept of resources (capital, land and labour).

The factors of production are limited but they have alternative use. Every time resources are allocated to the production of one good, they cannot be allocated to another. This can be illustrated by a production possibilities curve (PPC) diagram below. The PPC shows the maximum combination of two goods which can be produced when all resources available in the economy are fully employed.

▲ The paragraph explains how the PPC diagram illustrates the issue of scarcity. The candidate also mentions that resources have alternative uses.

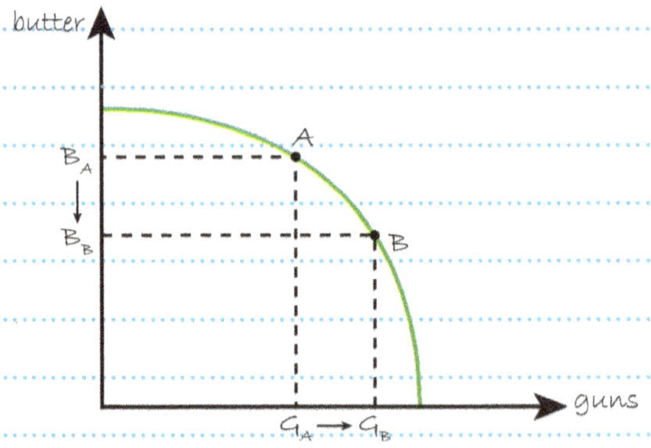

This economy faces the choice of producing agricultural goods (referred to as butter) or military goods (guns). At point A, they produce a certain amount of butter and guns. Moving from point A to B, more guns are produced. However, since the resources are scarce, to produce more military goods, some of the workers were transferred from farming production to factories. This meant that less agricultural goods can be produced. B_AB_B is the amount of butter sacrificed in order to produce G_AG_B. This sacrifice is known as the opportunity cost.

▲ The diagram is fully explained. Making references to the diagram helps the candidate to establish a link between the choices made due to scarcity and the PPC. The concept of opportunity cost is also introduced.

Economies face scarcity and this implies that they must choose what to produce. Every time they allocate more scarce resources to the production of one good, they forgo the production of another good—and so the PPC is downward sloping. Because all choices involve an opportunity cost, economies must decide on which wants and needs to fulfil.

▲ This is a good summary statement showing that the demands of the question are fully addressed—economies must make choices because of scarcity, since not all goods can be produced.

This response meets all the descriptors of the top mark band (9–10).

- The specific demands of the question are understood and addressed.
- Relevant economic theory is fully explained.
- Relevant economic terms are used appropriately throughout the response.
- Where appropriate, relevant diagrams are included and fully explained.

This response could have achieved 10/10 marks.

1.2 HOW DO ECONOMISTS APPROACH THE WORLD?

You should be able to:

- ✔ distinguish between positive and normative economics
- ✔ explain the evolution of economic thought in an historical context.

This sub-unit distinguishes between positive and normative economics and presents a brief history of economic thought.

Summary

Economic methodology uses "scientific methods" to formulate theories (consideration of data including statistics, observation of patterns and prediction of results). Economists distinguish between "positive" and "normative" economics.

Positive economic statements are objective and verifiable (they can be proven right or wrong). For instance, "actions by the central bank will bring inflation below 2% by the end of this year" is a hypothesis that can be verified. Positive economics uses *logic* to formulate *hypotheses*, which are then tested against *empirical evidence* (information that is acquired by observation or experimentation) before being formulated into economic *models* and *theories*. These models and theories are open to *refutation*, meaning they may be rejected or modified if they are not supported by the empirical evidence. An important part of testing positive economic statements is the assumption of **ceteris paribus**, which means "other things equal" or "all else constant" in Latin. In order to examine a possible relationship between two economic variables, economists assume that no other variable changes.

Normative economic statements are opinions, points of view or value judgments (about what ought to be, about whether something is desirable or undesirable). For example, take the idea that taxes on high income earners should be increased to finance goods and services for low income individuals. If this cannot be tested so that it can be refuted or accepted, then it is open to interpretation. Normative economics deals with the issue of equity. Equitable means fair, it does not mean equal. However, different people have different ideas of what is fair. Going back to the idea of increasing taxes on high income earners to provide more for low income individuals—many would argue that this would create disincentives to work among low income individuals and that it is unfair to deprive high income earners of the full rewards of their hard work. Equity is therefore a normative concept.

The evolution of economic thought is set out below.

18th century: Adam Smith—laissez-faire

- Adam Smith (1723–1790) saw individual behaviour as self-interested. Since individuals behave in a self-interested way, they try to do the best for themselves and this leads to orderly results. Smith believed that markets should be allowed to operate with minimal government intervention. This approach is often referred to as the "invisible hand" or laissez-faire (French for "let it be") approach.

19th century: Classical economics

- Alfred Marshall (1842–1924) introduced diagrams to illustrate the workings of competitive markets.
- William Stanley Jevons (1835–1882) contributed the utility theory and the concept of the margin—what matters is not total utility (satisfaction) but the additional utility from consuming one more unit of the good. The concept of the margin was later extended to supply: marginal productivity and marginal cost.
- Jean-Baptiste Say (1767–1832) claimed that production is the source of demand, meaning that households will purchase goods and services as long as households are engaged in the production of other goods and services, which provides them with an income to finance their expenditure.
- Classical economic thought's biggest critique came from Karl Marx (1818–1883), who predicted that the tension between capital and labour would eventually bring about the collapse of the modern economic system. His book *Das Kapital* (also known as *Capital*) inspired a political movement calling for social, economic and political change.

20th century: After the Great Depression

- John Maynard Keynes (1889–1946) challenged the notion that governments should keep their involvements in markets to a minimal role. He advocated that it is expenditure on goods and services that determines the level of production. If spending is insufficient to reach full employment, the government should intervene.
- Milton Friedman (1912–2006) led the monetarist school of thought. This mostly opposed Keynesian ideals and championed deregulation and a return to free markets.

21st century

- There is an increasing dialogue with other disciplines. Behavioural economists challenge the conventional rational decision-making approach, considering the effects of psychological, cultural and other social factors on economic decisions.
- There is a growing awareness of the need for sustainability due to the interdependence between the economy and the environment.

2 MICROECONOMICS

You should know about:

- ✔ demand
- ✔ supply
- ✔ competitive market equilibrium
- ✔ the maximizing behaviour of consumers and producers
- ✔ elasticities of demand
- ✔ elasticity of supply
- ✔ the role of government in microeconomics
- ✔ different types of market failure
- ✔ the market's ability to achieve equity.

2.1 DEMAND

You should be able to:

- ✔ define the terms
  - ✔ market
  - ✔ demand
- ✔ explain the negative causal relationship between the price and quantity demanded, as stated by the law of demand
- ✔ describe the relationship between an individual consumer's demand and the market demand
- ✔ distinguish, using a diagram(s), between a change in demand and a change in quantity demanded
- ✔ explain how changes in non-price determinants of demand may change the demand for a good.

This sub-unit introduces the concept of *competitive markets*. To analyse how markets function, we need to examine first the factors that affect choices made by consumers in competitive markets.

HL In addition to the points above, for HL you should be able to:

- explain the assumptions behind the law of demand
  - the income and substitution effects
  - the law of diminishing marginal utility.

> **Content link**
> **Link to other sub-units**
> Refer to sub-unit 1.2. In order to focus on the relationship between the two economic variables price and quantity demanded, we need to assume ceteris paribus—that no other variable (e.g. income) is changing.

Summary

Economists use the term **market** to refer to the interaction of consumers (buyers) and producers (sellers) that determines the price for goods and services.

The **demand** for a good is the quantity that consumers are willing and able to buy at various prices per period of time, ceteris paribus.

The **law of demand** states that there is an inverse (negative) relationship between the price and the quantity demanded for a good, meaning that if the price of the good increases ceteris paribus, then the quantity demanded for that good will decrease.

HL The negative relationship between price and quantity demanded is supported by the following factors.

- **The substitution and income effects**—the substitution effect states that if the price of good X increases then other goods become relatively cheaper, so consumers may switch away from X towards other goods. The income effect states that if the price of good X rises then the real income (the purchasing power) of consumers decreases, so they typically buy less of good X.
- **The law of diminishing marginal utility**—the word "marginal" in economics means additional, while "utility" refers to the satisfaction someone gains by consuming a good. The law of diminishing marginal utility states that as a person consumes more of a good per period of time, the (additional) utility derived diminishes with additional units of the good consumed. If this law holds then a consumer will be willing to pay less to consume additional units per period.

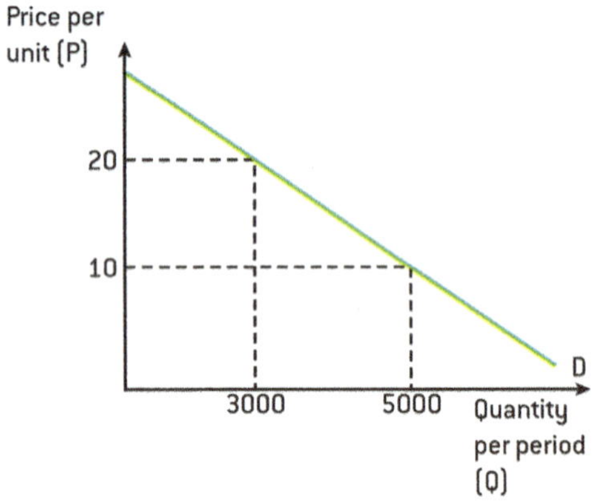

▲ Figure 2.1.1 The demand curve

An **individual consumer's demand curve** examines the willingness and ability of one consumer to purchase a good at various prices. The **market demand curve** is the sum of the quantity demanded by all consumers in the market at each price.

The demand for a product is influenced by both the **price** of the good itself and the **non-price determinants** of demand.

A **change in the price** of a good, ceteris paribus, **leads to a change in quantity demanded**. This change is represented by a **movement along the demand curve**. Figure 2.1.1 shows that the increase in the price of the good from \$10 to \$20 led to a decrease in quantity demanded from 5000 to 3000 units per period.

A **change in a non-price determinant of demand** leads to a **shift of the demand curve**—at each price, more or less quantity is demanded per period. The main non-price determinants of demand ("shift" factors) are listed below.

- **Number of consumers**—a change in the number of consumers for a good would lead to a shift of the market demand for the good. For example, when the number of residents in a town increases, it typically increases the demand for utilities such as water. The quantity demanded for water per period increases at each price. This is illustrated by a shift of the demand curve to the right from D0 to D1 on Figure 2.1.2. If, on the other hand, people are moving out of the town then the market demand for water will decrease (a shift to the left from D0 to D2 on Figure 2.1.2).
- **Income**—as income increases, the demand for most goods will rise. Such goods are called normal goods. For some goods, known as inferior goods, an increase in income will lead to a decrease in demand. Inferior goods are usually goods of poor quality for which there are better quality substitutes.
- **The price of related goods**—substitutes and complements—affects demand.
  - **Substitutes** are goods that satisfy similar wants or needs (e.g. Nike running shoes and Adidas running shoes, Pepsi and Coke). The increase in the price of one good will lead to an increase in the demand for a substitute.
  - Two goods are considered **complements** if they are consumed together (e.g. coffee and milk). The increase in

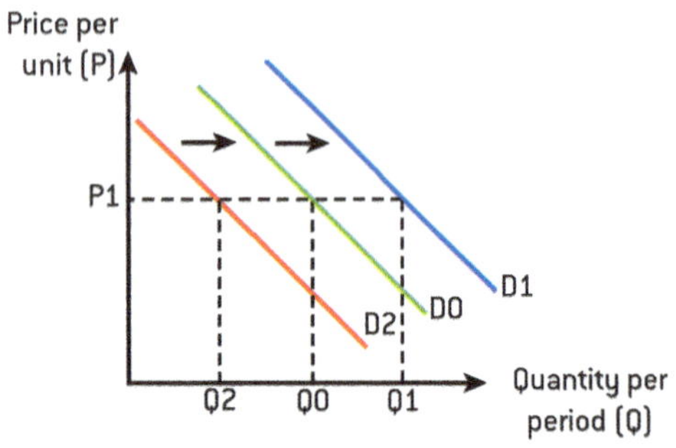

▲ Figure 2.1.2 Shifts of the demand curve

the price of a good may lead to a decrease in the demand for its complements.

- Changes in **tastes and preferences** affect the willingness of consumers to purchase a good. The release of the 2003 animation movie *Finding Nemo* made clownfish popular aquarium pets, and this led to an increase in the demand for clownfish at pet stores.
- **Future price expectations**—if consumers expect the price of a good to increase in price, they are likely to buy more of it now and this will increase the demand for the good. Similarly, if they expect the price to decrease soon, they will probably delay purchases and the demand will decrease.

QUESTION PRACTICE

This question is adapted from the May 2018 examination paper.

A demand curve is drawn under the assumption of *ceteris paribus*. Using an example, outline why the assumption of ceteris paribus is necessary when analysing the effect of a change in price on the quantity demanded of a product. [2]

SAMPLE STUDENT ANSWER

Response 1

It is necessary because "ceteris paribus" means "all other things remaining constant".

▼ The candidate understands the meaning of ceteris paribus but does not explain why the assumption is necessary in this case—that is, to isolate the impact of the change in price on quantity demanded from other variables that could also affect quantity demanded.

This response could have achieved 1/2 marks.

Response 2

There are many variables which could affect a consumer's decision to purchase a product besides the price. For example, if the price of coffee increases, we expect quantity demanded for coffee to decrease but if, at the same time, there are reports that researchers discovered that drinking coffee daily prevents heart failure then quantity demanded might not decrease despite the higher price. To isolate the impact of the change in the price of the good itself on quantity demanded, we need to assume "ceteris paribus", which means "other things equal". So that everything else that could have affected quantity demanded has remained the same and the change in quantity demanded is purely attributed to a change in price.

▲ This response clearly explains that a change in any of the non-price determinants, such as a change in taste and preferences, may distort the effect of the change in price, meaning that the impact of the change in price alone cannot be determined if we do not assume that everything else remains the same.

This response could have achieved 2/2 marks.

▲The candidate identifies income as a non-price determinant of demand.

QUESTION PRACTICE

This question is adapted from the November 2021 examination paper.

Distinguish between the effect of an increase in income and an increase in the price of a good on the demand for the good. [10]

SAMPLE STUDENT ANSWER

The demand for a good refers to the quantities of a good that consumers are willing and able to purchase at various prices, ceteris paribus. There are two main causes for a change in the quantity that consumers may demand—a change in the price of the good itself and a change in a non-price determinant of demand, such as the consumer's income.

The following diagram depicts a demand curve (D), which is a graphical representation of the demand for a good. The demand curve is downward sloping due to the law of demand, which states that there is an inverse relationship between the price and the quantity demanded for the good, ceteris paribus. For example, an increase in the price of the good from $8 to $10 led to a fall in quantity demanded from 20 to 15. An increase in the price of a good leads to a movement along the demand curve from point A to point B where we have a higher price but lower quantity demanded. As we move along the demand curve, we assume ceteris paribus or "everything else is constant" so the only variable affecting quantity demanded is the price of the good.

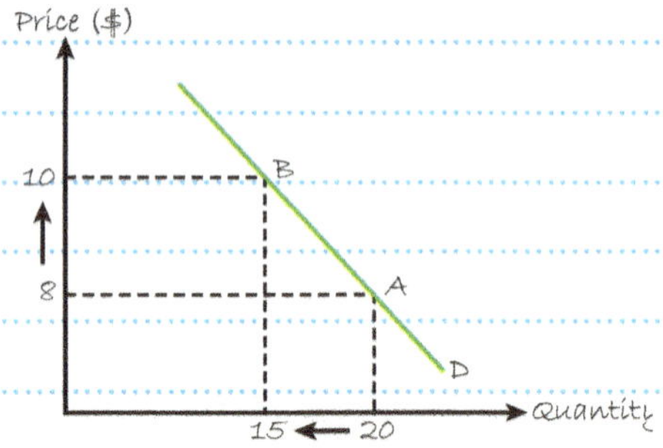

▲Relevant theory is explained—the law of demand. Relevant terms such as "quantity demanded" and "ceteris paribus" are used appropriately throughout the paragraph. The diagram is used effectively to illustrate the impact of a change in price.

On the other hand, an increase in income is a change in a non-price determinant of demand. As income increases, the consumers' willingness and ability to purchase goods and services change as well. For most goods, also known as normal goods, an increase in income would lead to an increase in the demand for the good as consumers have a greater purchasing power. This is reflected by the shift of the demand curve from D0 to D1 on the next diagram. Assuming once again ceteris paribus, the increase in income implies at the same price of $8, the consumer is willing and able to consume more so quantity demanded has increased from 20 to 25. We can see that the increase in income, a non-price determinant of demand has led to a rightward shift of the demand curve—the quantity demanded has increased at every price point. It is possible that the increase in income may lead to a decrease in demand for what economists call inferior goods. For example, when consumers get higher income, they buy less of unbranded running shoes and more of branded running shoes such as Adidas and Nike shoes.

▲The rest of the relevant theory is explained. The candidate continues to make effective use of diagrams to illustrate the response. As the candidate has now explained both the impact of an increase in price and an increase in income, the requirements of the question have been met. While examples are not required for part (a), the hypothetical example provided helps illustrate the concept of inferior goods.

Therefore, a change in price leads to a movement along the demand curve as only the quantity demanded changes while a change in income leads to a shift of the demand curve where the quantity demanded at every price point has changed.

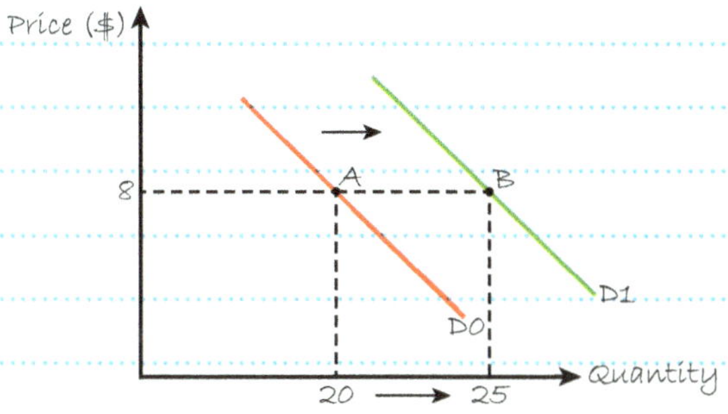

▲ The candidate provides a brief summary of the response.

This response met all the descriptors of the top mark band (9–10).

- The specific demands of the question were understood and addressed.
- Relevant economic theory was fully explained.
- Relevant economic terms were used appropriately throughout the response.
- Where appropriate, relevant diagrams were included and fully explained.

This response could have achieved 10/10 marks.

Refer to Unit 5 (pages 194–195) for a full explanation of the paper 1 level descriptors.

2.2 SUPPLY

You should be able to:

- ✔ define the terms
  - ✔ supply
  - ✔ indirect taxes
  - ✔ subsidies
- ✔ explain the positive causal relationship between the price and quantity supplied, as stated by the law of supply
- ✔ describe the relationship between an individual producer's supply and the market supply
- ✔ distinguish between a change in supply and a change in quantity supplied
- ✔ explain how changes in non-price determinants of supply may change the supply of a good.

This sub-unit examines the factors that affect the choices made by producers (firms) in competitive markets.

HL In addition to the points above, for HL you should be able to:

- explain the assumptions behind the law of supply
- the law of diminishing marginal returns
- increasing marginal costs.

Summary

The **supply** of a good is the quantity that producers (firms) are willing and able to offer at various prices per period of time, ceteris paribus.

The **law of supply** states that there is a direct (positive) relationship between the price and the quantity supplied for a good, meaning that if the price of the good increases ceteris paribus, then the quantity supplied for that good will also increase per period.

Content link

Link to other sub-units

Refer to sub-unit 1.2 In order to focus on the relationship between the two economic variables price and quantity supplied, we need to assume ceteris paribus—that no other variable (e.g. a tax or subsidy) is changing.

HL Producers (firms) are assumed to be profit-maximizers, implying that they would produce more if the additional quantity produced can be sold at a price high enough to at least cover the cost of producing the additional units of the good. Firms have fixed capacity in the short run, so producing increasing quantities of a good per period may become more difficult and thus costly. This is the result of two factors.

- **The law of diminishing marginal returns**—in the short run, firms are unable to access more or all factors of production. Some will be easily varied (variable factors) and some may not be changed (fixed factors). Consider a bakery as a firm producing breads and pastries. The bakery may easily increase production of breads and pastries by procuring more flour, sugar and eggs and might easily find new workers to increase production—those factor inputs and the workers are the variable factors. The bakery would not be able to get more kitchen space and additional machines at short notice, so the capital equipment is the fixed factor.
  In the short run, firms may only produce more goods per period by adding more of the variable factors to the fixed factors—the baker may hire more workers and get more supplies of sugar, flour and eggs (the variable factors) but the workers will need to produce breads and pastries in the same kitchen space and share the existing equipment (the fixed factors). *The law of diminishing marginal returns states that as more and more units of a variable factor are used with a fixed factor, there is a point beyond which the total quantity produced will continue to rise, but at a decreasing rate.* In short, the additional variable factors (newly hired workers) contribute less to the production of goods (breads and pastries).
- **Increasing marginal costs**—marginal cost is the cost of producing an additional unit of the good. If an additional unit of variable factors leads to fewer and fewer additional units of the good being produced (as it was the case in our previous example of a bakery), then a greater number of those variable factors will be needed to produce equal additional numbers of the good. It follows that the marginal cost will increase and thus firms will only be willing and able to produce a higher quantity at a higher price.

An **individual firm's supply curve** examines the willingness and ability of one firm to offer a good at various prices. The **market supply curve** is the sum of the quantity supplied by all firms in the market at each price.

The supply of a product is influenced by both the **price** of the good itself and the **non-price determinants** of supply.

A **change in the price** of a good, ceteris paribus, **leads to a change in quantity supplied**. This change is represented by a **movement along the supply curve**. Figure 2.2.1 shows that the increase in the price of the good from $20 to $40 led to an increase in quantity supplied from 3000 to 5000 units per period.

A **change in a non-price determinant of supply** leads to a **shift of the supply curve**—at each price, more or less quantity is supplied per period. A decrease (fall) in supply is reflected by a leftward shift of the supply curve as illustrated on Figures 2.2.2 and 2.2.3. This may be interpreted as producers offering a lower quantity for the same price (Figure 2.2.2) or producers offering the same amount per period at a higher price (Figure 2.2.3).

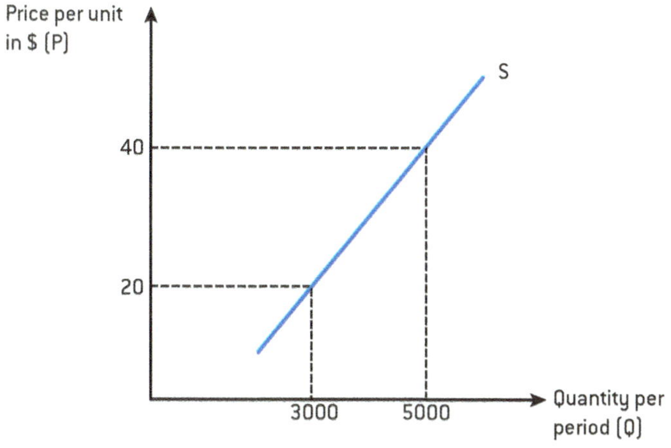

▲ **Figure 2.2.1** The supply curve

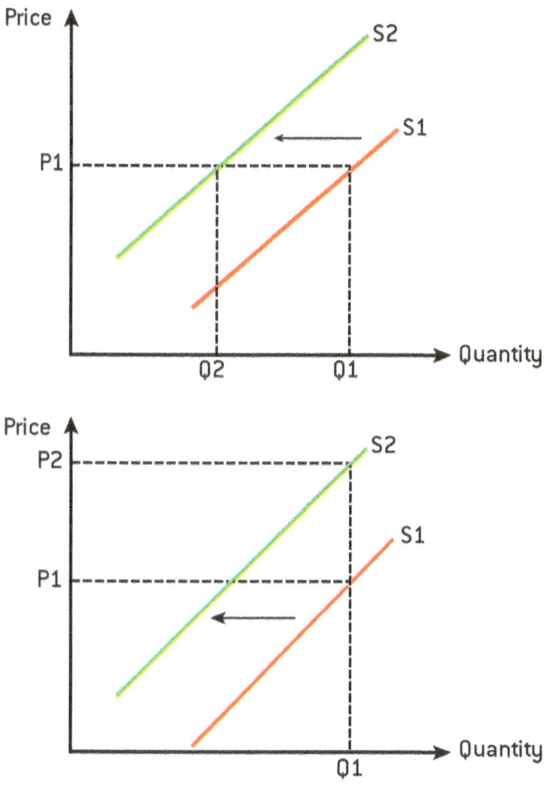

▲ **Figures 2.2.2 and 2.2.3** Decrease (leftward shift) of the supply curve

These are the main non-price determinants of supply ("shift" factors).

- **Number of firms**—if the number of firms in the market increases, this will lead to an increase in the market supply for the good.
- **Changes in prices of factors of production (FOPs)**—increases in wages, the prices of raw materials and other FOPs will result in a higher unit cost of production. Firms will thus offer the same quantity of a good at higher prices (as shown on Figure 2.2.3).
- **Prices of related goods**
  - Goods in **joint supply** are goods that are produced together. For instance, cattle farms may produce both beef and leather. If the price of beef increases, there is higher incentive for farmers to increase their beef production (a movement along the supply of beef). As more cows are slaughtered to meet the increase in beef production, more of their skins can be used to produce leather and there is therefore an increase in the supply of leather.
  - Goods in **competitive supply** are goods that are produced using the same resources (e.g. potato chips and frozen fries). If the price of potato chips increases, firms may allocate more resources to the production of potato chips (a movement along the supply of potato chips) and as such, those resources can no longer be used to produce frozen fries. The supply of frozen fries will decrease.
- **Indirect taxes** and **subsidies**
  - **Indirect taxes** are a government levy on expenditure. They increase the cost of production of a good or service and this leads to a decrease in supply as producers offer the same quantities per period at higher prices (as shown on Figure 2.2.3).
  - **Subsidies** are financial aid per unit produced given to firms by the government. Subsidies help absorb parts of the firms' cost of production and so they increase supply.
- **Future price expectations**—if the price of a good is expected to increase, producers may temporarily withhold production and accumulate stocks. They would only release stocks once the price has increased. The supply of the good would therefore decrease in anticipation of the higher market price.
- **Technological improvements** lead to increases in efficiency and hence an increase in supply since a higher quantity will be produced per period with the same amount of FOPs.

QUESTION PRACTICE

This question is adapted from the May 2019 examination paper.

Outline the reason why the quantity supplied increases as the price rises. [2]

SAMPLE STUDENT ANSWER

Response 1

Because of the law of supply.

▼ The law of supply states that the quantity supplied will increase when the price rises but it does not in itself provide a reason for the direct relationship between price and quantity supplied.

This response could have achieved 1/2 marks.

Response 2

Since marginal costs of producing goods rise due to the firms facing diminishing marginal returns, producers will only be willing to offer more units per period at a higher price.

▲ This response identifies the increasing marginal costs as the justification for firms requiring a higher price to produce more (increase quantity supplied).

This response could have achieved 2/2 marks.

QUESTION PRACTICE

This question is adapted from the May 2018 examination paper.

Two products are in competitive supply. Using an example, outline how the supply for one of them is likely to be affected by an increase in the price of the other. [2]

SAMPLE STUDENT ANSWER

Wheat and corn are two goods in competitive supply since they both can be produced with the same resources such as land, tractors, workers.

▲ A valid example is given, showing that the candidate understands that both goods are produced using the same resources.

A farmer with a fixed plot of land and a fixed number of workers and tractors may allocate those resources between the productions of wheat and corn. An increase in the price of wheat will cause an increase in the quantity supplied of wheat as the farmer is incentivized to produce more wheat due to the possibility of higher profits. To produce more wheat, more of the farmer's resources are allocated to the production of wheat. Since those resources are no longer available to produce corn, the supply of corn decreases. The farmer is thus less willing and able to produce corn at the current price of corn.

▲ The candidate has clearly explained how the reduced amount of resources for corn would lead to a fall in the supply of corn.

This response could have achieved 2/2 marks.

2.3 COMPETITIVE MARKET EQUILIBRIUM

You should be able to:

- ✔ define the terms
  - ✔ excess demand (shortage)
  - ✔ excess supply (surplus)
  - ✔ market equilibrium
  - ✔ consumer surplus
  - ✔ producer surplus
  - ✔ social (community) surplus
  - ✔ allocative efficiency
- ✔ explain, using diagrams, how demand and supply interact to produce a market equilibrium
- ✔ explain, using diagrams, how changes in the determinants of demand and/or supply result in a new market equilibrium
- ✔ explain, using diagrams, that price serves a signalling function and an incentive function, which result in a reallocation of resources
- ✔ explain that the best allocation of resources from society's point of view is at the competitive market equilibrium, where social (community) surplus is maximized (where marginal benefit = marginal cost).

This sub-unit outlines the role of competitive markets in allocating scarce resources.

HL In addition to the points above, for HL you should be able to:

- calculate the consumer surplus and producer surplus from a diagram.

Summary

The price of a good and the quantity transacted are determined by the interaction between consumers (demand) and producers (supply) in a competitive market. The **market equilibrium** is determined where the demand curve intersects the supply curve (where quantity demanded equals quantity supplied) and there is no tendency for the price to change (PeQe on Figure 2.3.1).

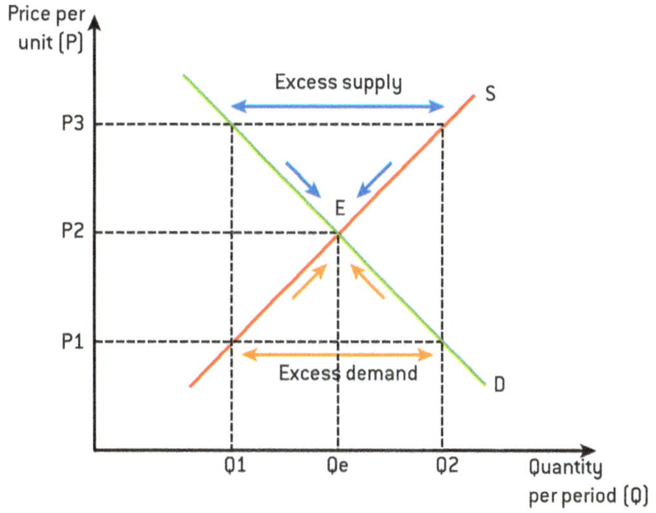

▲ Figure 2.3.1 Market equilibrium

Consider the demand and supply diagram on Figure 2.3.1. If the price of the good is below the market (equilibrium) price, for example P1, then the quantity demanded for the good (Q2) will exceed the quantity supplied of the good (Q1) at that price, leading to **excess demand** (shortage), Q1Q2. The excess demand puts pressure on the price to rise, resulting in a greater quantity supplied and lower quantity demanded (as stated by the laws of supply and demand) until the market reaches the equilibrium, E.

If the price of the good is above the market (equilibrium) price, for example P2, then the quantity supplied for the good (Q2) will exceed the quantity demanded of the good (Q1) at that price, leading to **excess supply (surplus)**, Q1Q2. As a result of the excess supply, there is pressure on the price to decrease, resulting in a decrease in quantity supplied and increase in quantity demanded until the market clears at the equilibrium, E.

Content link

Link to other sub-units

Refer to:

- sub-unit 2.1 for more on the changes in non-price determinants of demand
- sub-unit 2.2 for more on the changes in non-price determinants of supply.

As prices are determined by the intersection of demand and supply in a competitive market, changes in prices are due to changes in demand and/or changes in supply.

Consider the market diagram Figure 2.3.2, where the initial equilibrium price and quantity are Pe and Qe respectively. Assuming that the good traded is a normal good, an increase in income (a non-price determinant of demand) would lead to a shift of the demand curve to the right, D1 to D2. There will be an excess demand at the previous equilibrium price, Pe. This will cause the price to rise to Pe′ and quantity to increase from Qe to Qe′. A new equilibrium is attained at E2 with a higher equilibrium price, Pe′ and a higher equilibrium quantity, Qe′. Similarly, a decrease in demand would create an excess supply, which would lead to fall in equilibrium price and equilibrium quantity.

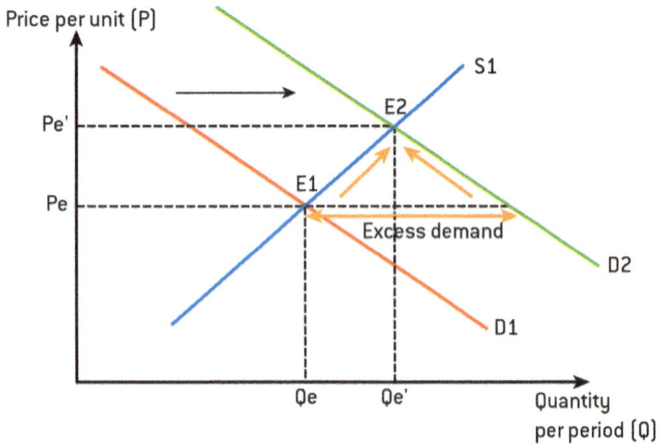

▲ Figure 2.3.2 Increase in demand

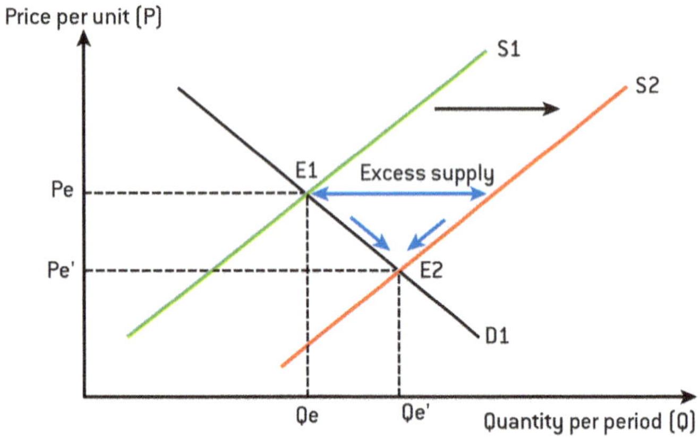

▲ Figure 2.3.3 Increase in supply

An increase in supply would also lead to changes to equilibrium price and equilibrium quantity. If, for instance, the cost of a factor of production (a non-price determinant of supply) decreases, supply will increase—as reflected as the shift of the supply curve to the right from S1 to S2 on Figure 2.3.3. There is an **excess supply** at Pe and this will cause the price to fall. As the price falls, the quantity demanded increases and quantity supplied decreases until both are equal at Qe′. The equilibrium is once again restored at E2 with a lower equilibrium price, Pe′ and a higher equilibrium quantity, Qe′. Similarly, a decrease in supply would lead to excess demand, resulting in an increase in equilibrium price and decrease in equilibrium quantity.

You learned in sub-unit 1.1 that scarcity forces societies to make choices in allocating resources. In competitive markets, those choices are made by consumers and producers. The interaction between consumers and producers determines the quantity of goods and services produced and hence the resources allocated to the production of those goods and services. Changes in demand and/or supply result in changes in resource allocation. Changes in price provide **signals** and **incentives** to consumers and producers. As signals, prices communicate information to consumers and producers. For example, a higher price may be a signal to consumers that they can afford less of the good, to the firms that the good is in greater demand. As incentives, higher prices motivate consumers and producers to respond to the information. For example, firms allocate more resources to the production of the good attracted by higher profits, consumers respond by looking for cheaper substitutes.

In any market, there are consumers who are willing to pay more than the market price. The **consumer surplus** is the additional benefit or utility received by consumers by paying a price that is lower than the highest price they are willing to pay. Similarly, there are producers who are willing to provide the good at a lower price than the market price. The **producer surplus** is the additional benefit received by producers by receiving a price that is higher than the lowest price they are willing to receive. The consumer surplus and producer surplus measure the welfare of consumers and producers respectively. The sum of consumer and producer surpluses represents society's welfare, also known as **social (community) surplus**.

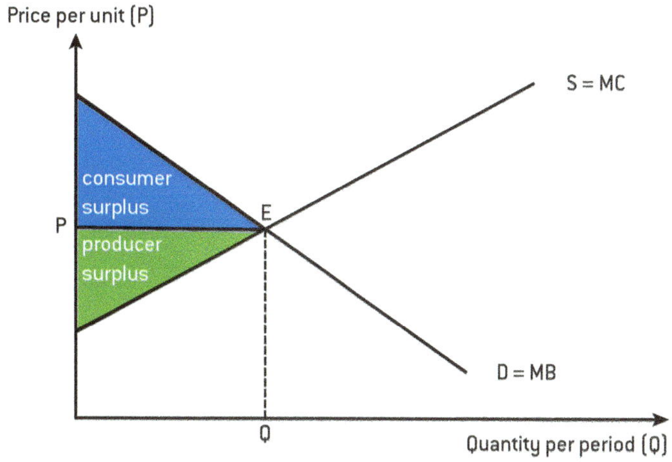

▲ Figure 2.3.4 Consumer, producer and society (community) surpluses

Competitive markets are said to be **allocatively efficient** as they achieve the best allocation of resources for society. Allocative efficiency takes place when social (community) surplus is maximized. Since consumers are willing to pay according to how much utility (benefit) they derive from consuming the good, the demand curve shows the benefit derived from consuming one more unit of the good, which is the marginal benefit (MB). The supply curve is also the marginal cost (MC) (the cost of producing one more unit of the good since firms are only willing to offer more units of a good if the price covers the cost of producing those additional units). When MB > MC, the production and consumption of additional units of the good bring more benefits than costs. When MB = MC, allocative efficiency is achieved.

QUESTION PRACTICE

This question is adapted from the November 2017 examination paper.

Using a demand and supply diagram, explain how the market for coffee in Papua New Guinea could be affected by improved irrigation. [4]

SAMPLE STUDENT ANSWER

Response 1

The supply will increase and this would lead to a lower price, as shown on my diagram.

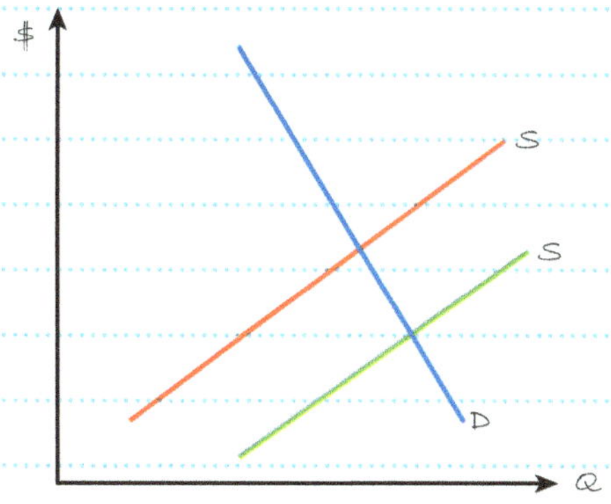

This response could have achieved 1/4 marks.

▲ The candidate identifies the correct change in supply (an increase) and price (a decrease).

▼ No reason is given for the increase in supply. The change in market quantity is not indicated. For questions about the impacts of a market, you need to comment on changes in price and in quantity. The candidate cannot make effective references to the diagram because it lacks labels.

▼ The supply curves have identical labels and there is no arrow to indicate the direction. The candidate has also not projected the prices and quantities along the axes and "$" is not a valid label for the vertical axis of a demand and supply diagram. No mark can be awarded for this diagram.

Response 2

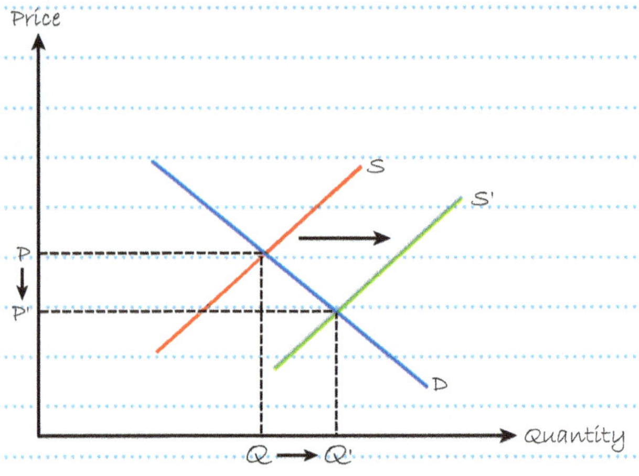

▲ This diagram is fully and correctly labelled. The labels for both axes are correct. The direction of the shift in supply and changes in price and quantity are clearly indicated with arrows.

Improved irrigation systems would represent a "technological improvement" for farmers. It would make their land more fertile, and this would increase the supply of coffee. This increase in supply would lead to a lower market price (P') and higher market quantity (Q').

▲ The response provides an adequate reason for the increase in supply. The candidate also identifies the decrease in price and increase in quantity, with effective references to the diagram.

This response could have achieved 4/4 marks.

QUESTION PRACTICE

Using a demand and supply diagram, explain how an increase in population size would affect the market for rice in Thailand. [4]

SAMPLE STUDENT ANSWER

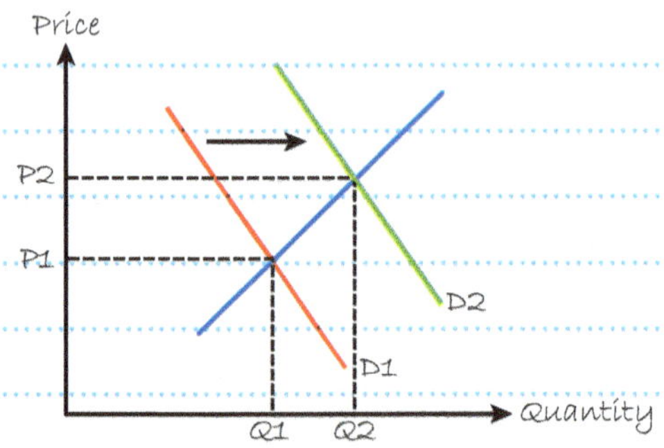

▲ The diagram illustrates the correct shift in demand. There are no arrows to illustrate the changes in price and quantity, as was the case in the previous response, but the labels (P1, P2, Q1 and Q2) clearly indicate the changes.

▼ Unfortunately, the supply curve is not labelled. The diagram can only be awarded 1 mark.

As the number of consumers is a non-price determinant of demand, we should expect an increase in the demand for rice in Thailand should the population increase. This would lead to a higher price (P2 instead of P1) and a greater quantity demanded and supplied (Q2 instead of Q1).

▲ The explanation provides a valid reason for the increase in demand. The changes in price and quantity are correctly identified, with reference to the diagram.

This response could have achieved 3/4 marks.

Test yourself

Demand and supply diagrams, also known as market diagrams, are used to explain real-world price changes. In the past two practice questions, we have examined impacts of changes in either demand or supply on markets. When either demand or supply changes, the impact on both price and quantity is certain. If the demand increases, we know the equilibrium price and quantity will both increase. If the supply decreases, the equilibrium price will increase, and the equilibrium quantity will fall (as shown on Figures 2.3.2 and 2.3.3). However, you may come across news articles describing a situation where both demand and supply change at the same time. In early 2020, an outbreak of swine flu (a disease affecting pigs) led to a significant drop in the supply of pork in China. At the same time, the upcoming lunar new year celebrations caused an increase in demand for pork, which is used in many traditional dishes during the festivities. We know that a decrease in supply and an increase in demand both put upward pressures on price but have different impacts on quantity. The overall impact on quantity will depend on the magnitude of the shifts of demand and supply. When both demand and supply shift, the impact on either price or quantity will be uncertain. Test yourself by drawing diagrams with both curves shifting to identify all possible outcomes—be sure to check that all labels, curves and intercepts along the axes are appropriately labelled. Be mindful that your selected internal assessment article may depict changes in both demand and supply so make sure to aptly reflect the magnitude of both shifts to illustrate the changes in price and quantity described in the article.

	Equilibrium price	Equilibrium quantity
↑ **Demand** (demand curve shifts right)	↑	↑
↓ **Demand** (demand curve shifts left)	↓	↓
↑ **Supply** (supply curve shifts right)	↓	↑
↓ **Supply** (supply curve shifts left)	↑	↓
↑ **Demand** and ↑ **Supply**	uncertain	↑
↓ **Demand** and ↓ **Supply**	uncertain	↑
↑ **Demand** and ↓ **Supply**	↑	uncertain
↓ **Demand** and ↑ **Supply**	↓	uncertain

QUESTION PRACTICE

This question is adapted from the November 2018 examination paper.

The following figure illustrates the market for cotton in the country of San Marcus. Quantity is in thousands of kilograms (kg).

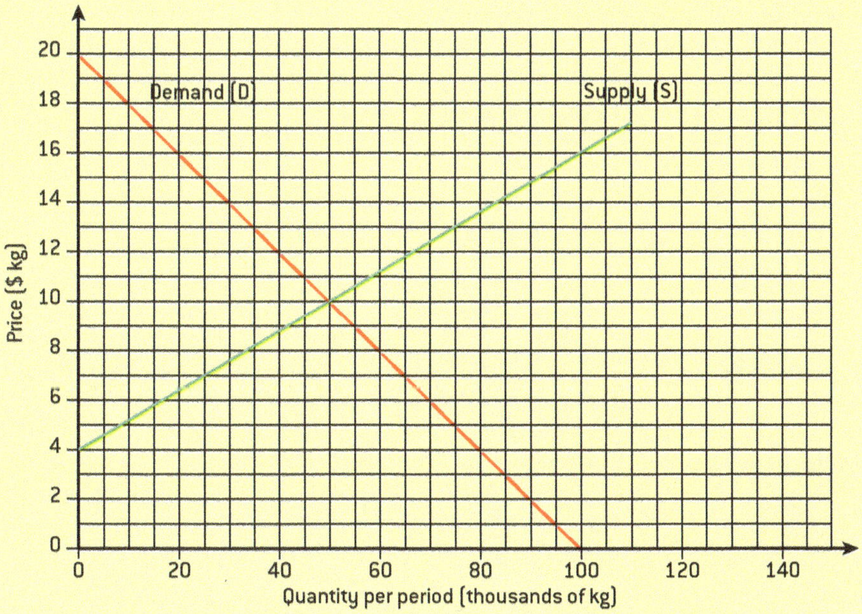

(i) Define the term consumer surplus. [2]

SAMPLE STUDENT ANSWER

Response 1

The consumer surplus is the benefit that consumers receive from consuming a good.

▼ The consumer surplus is not the entire benefit or utility derived from consuming the good (it is not the entire area below the demand curve).

This response could have achieved 1/2 marks.

Response 2

The consumer surplus is the additional benefit received by consumers by paying a price that is lower than they are willing to pay.

▲ This is an adequate definition. Unlike the previous response, this one clearly identifies the consumer surplus as the difference between the price consumers are willing to pay and the price they end up paying (the market price).

This response could have achieved 2/2 marks.

QUESTION PRACTICE

(Question adapted from the November 2018 examination paper continued.)

(ii) Calculate the social (community) surplus in the market for cotton in San Marcus. [2]

SAMPLE STUDENT ANSWER

Response 1

Consumer surplus:

$$\frac{10 \times 50}{2} = 250$$

Producer surplus:

$$\frac{6 \times 50}{2} = 150$$

Social surplus: $250 + 150 = \$400$

▲ The candidate understands that the social (community) surplus is the sum of consumer and producer surpluses. Workings are provided. The unit for the social (community) surplus is also correct ($).

▼ Unfortunately, the candidate did not interpret the quantities correctly. Quantities are in thousands of kilograms so the answer should be $400,000.

This response could have achieved 1/2 marks.

Response 2

$$\frac{16 \times 50000}{2}$$

$= \$400\ 000$

▲ This candidate has chosen a different approach and has calculated directly the area of the combined consumer and producer surpluses. This approach is valid as it reflects an understanding of the concept. Workings are provided and the unit is correct ($).

This response could have achieved 2/2 marks.

Content link

Link to your IA

Your article may describe changes in the price of one or more products. Make sure to identify the reason(s) for the change (the correct non-price determinant of demand and/or supply). If both demand and supply factors are responsible for the change in market forces, try to identify the more significant factor. For example, your article may mention a significant increase in wages (increase in the cost of resources) and a slight increase in population. In such a case, your diagram and analysis should acknowledge the varying magnitude in changes in demand and supply. This would make your analysis more effective, helping you achieve a higher mark on criterion C: Application and analysis.

Concept link

- **Change**—your article may describe how a change in a non-price determinant of demand or supply (technology, taste and preference, the weather, for instance) might have significant impacts on stakeholders. For example, a news story on better use of fertilizers for wheat production and the resulting changes in income of farmers and nutritional status of the population could allow for a rich discussion on the impact on society of a change in production.
- **Choice**—changes in price force consumers and producers to alter their choices. Look out for indications that producers have switched to the production of other products and/or consumers have had to change their consumption patterns.

2.4 CRITIQUE OF THE MAXIMIZING BEHAVIOUR OF CONSUMERS AND PRODUCERS

You should be able to:

- ✔ define the terms
  - ✔ imperfect information
  - ✔ consumer nudges
  - ✔ choice architecture
- ✔ evaluate the assumptions of consumer rationality, utility maximization and perfect information
- ✔ discuss the limitations of the assumptions of rational consumer choice established in behavioural economics
- ✔ discuss the significance of organizing the context in which consumers make decisions (choice architecture) to improve the choices they make
- ✔ evaluate the effectiveness of nudges in altering consumer choices
- ✔ compare and contrast the business objective of profit maximization and alternative goals of businesses, including corporate social responsibility, market share, growth maximization and satisficing.

HL This sub-unit provides an overview of behavioural economics that challenges rational choice theory.

Summary

HL Most mainstream economic assumptions and theories are based on rational choice theory. The **assumptions underlying rational choice theory** are as follows.

- **Consumer rationality**— consumers make purchasing decisions based on the following assumptions.
  - Completeness—consumers make choices that can be made with certainty. When presented with two baskets of goods, A and B, it is assumed that consumers can state whether they prefer basket A to basket B, basket B to basket A or whether they are indifferent when choosing between the two baskets.
  - Transitivity—if basket A of goods and services is preferred to basket B and basket B preferred to basket C, then basket A must be preferred to basket C (consumers make consistent choice decisions).
  - Non-satiation—more of a good is always better.
- **Utility maximization**—consumers choose baskets of goods and services that maximize their utility (benefit) within their budget (income).
- **Perfect information**— consumers have all the information they need about their alternatives.

According to behavioural economists, rational choice theory faces some limitations.

- Consumer decisions are subject to **biases** and these lead to choices that may not be optimal.
  - **Rules of thumb** are decision-making shortcuts that help people make a quick and simplified choice, which may be satisfactory but not optimal. For example, a common health recommendation is to consume 2½ cups of vegetables and 2 cups of fruit daily. However, consumers may have differing understanding of what a cup of fruit and/or vegetables entails. Also, not all fruits and vegetables have the same nutritional value.
  - **Anchoring** occurs when consumers rely on pre-existing but irrelevant or obsolete information, or the first information they come across, in the decision-making process. For example, if your classmate gets a job paying $10 an hour and you subsequently get offered $12 an hour for a similar job, you may think you landed a high-paying job. However, the average wage for such a job may be $12 or more.
  - **Framing** bias occurs when consumer choices are influenced by how options are presented. A yoghurt brand with a "99% fat free" label may seem more appealing than one with a "1% fat" label although both contain the same amount of fat.
  - **Availability** bias occurs when consumer decisions are influenced by recent, significant or convenient information. Smokers may continue buying cigarettes at the risk of developing lung cancer because they know of an elderly person who is a long-time smoker and whose health does not seem to have been affected by this.
- **Bounded rationality** is the idea that individuals satisfice (a combination of satisfy and suffice) rather than maximize their utility (benefit). Consumers do not have ready access to information, they face time constraints in obtaining information and they do not have an unlimited capacity to process information (the complexity of some products makes choice difficult—for example, few people understand the full range of investment products available to them). Consumers may thus be rational but within limits.
- According to rational choice theory, consumers maximize utility (benefit) by consuming a good as long as the price of the good exceeds the marginal benefit they derive from consuming an additional unit of that good—rational consumers stop consuming when P = MB. In reality, consumers have **bounded self-control** and often do not stop consuming even when it is sensible to stop (they consume even though the price of the good is greater than the marginal benefit they gain from consumption). Examples are over-eating and excessive drinking. They often make decisions that they come to regret later.
- Rational choice theory assumes that individuals act in their best self-interest to maximize the satisfaction they expect to receive from their economic decisions. Behavioural economists have proposed that utility maximization may be limited by **bounded selfishness**—individuals are selfish only within limits. For example, consumers may continue to purchase goods from a neighbourhood shop out of friendship or loyalty even if the good is cheaper if purchased online.

- Rational consumer choice theory is based on the assumption of perfect information. In practice, consumers do not have all the information about prices and available products. Markets are subject to **imperfect information** as stakeholders cannot have at their disposal all the necessary information to make decisions.

Choice architecture suggests that the decisions we make are affected by the layout, sequencing and range of choices that are available. Choice architects are individuals or organizations that arrange the context in which choices are made, with the intention to alter those choices to achieve socially desirable outcomes. Three main methods are available to choice architects.

- **Default choice** is a choice made by default (the option that results when one does nothing). Individuals tend to follow the default choice—even if that is not their preferred choice. For example, in some countries everyone is registered as an organ donor. To opt out of the scheme, a person needs to start an official procedure. This default choice has helped address the lack of organ donors.
- **Restricted choice**—too many choices can result in bad decisions due to imperfect information, so options can be restricted to encourage people to make choices resulting in a better outcome. For example, all Singaporean residents must contribute to a compulsory savings scheme, where a portion of an individual's monthly salary is set aside for retirement. Singapore residents have the option to see their retirement funds grow at a risk-free interest rate or invest their savings in financial products with the hope of greater disbursement upon retirement. However, to mitigate the risk of excessive losses, the choice of financial products is restricted.
- **Mandated choice** is a choice between alternatives that is made mandatory (compulsory). Individuals are still free to choose which option they like, but what is mandatory is for the person to make a choice. In the US state of Illinois, in order to get a driver's license renewed, it is mandatory to answer a question on whether one wishes to be registered as an organ donor.

Behavioural economists also propose the use of nudges to help individuals make better choices. **Consumer nudges** are positive reinforcement and indirect suggestions used to influence the behaviour and decision-making of consumers. Nudges do not restrict consumer choices and do not offer a financial incentive. As such, they are an inexpensive tool to achieve socially desirable outcomes. To attend to the growing incidence of obesity, the New York City authorities have made it compulsory for restaurants to display calorie information on their menus. The information nudges consumers to opt for meals with a lower calorie count.

Standard economic theory assumes that rational businesses are driven by self-interest and seek to **maximize profits** (there is more on this in sub-unit 2.11). However, firms may have other objectives.

- **Corporate social responsibility**—the self-interest behaviour of firms that comes with the pursuit of profit maximization often leads to negative consequences for society. Examples are pollution, unsustainable use of resources and use of child labour. Corporate social responsibility is a business objective in which companies make a commitment to ethical and environmentally responsible production methods, even if there are more cost-effective ways to produce.
- **Market share** refers to the percentage of total sales in a market that is earned by a single firm. Seeking a greater market may increase a firm's market power and long-term profits (there is more on this in sub-unit 2.11).
- **Growth maximization**—businesses may wish to grow the size of their firm to enjoy more economies of scale. Firms may also wish to diversify into other products to reduce their dependence on a narrow range of goods. Firms often seek greater market share or growth by cutting price to increase sales, which leads to lower profits in the short term.
- **Satisficing**—given the informational constraints faced, businesses may not try to maximize profits or sales but instead seek a satisfactory level of profits.

QUESTION PRACTICE

Define the term *consumer nudges*. [2]

SAMPLE STUDENT ANSWER

Response 1

▼ This definition is vague. It could also apply to many economic policies (e.g. taxes, subsidies). For example, a higher tax on cigarettes is an incentive for consumers to reduce consumption of cigarettes.

It is an incentive for consumers to behave differently, in a better way.

This response could have achieved 1/2 marks.

Response 2

▲ This is a precise definition.

It is a positive reinforcement which leads consumers to make better decisions without restricting their choice.

This response could have achieved 2/2 marks.

QUESTION PRACTICE

Explain the methods by which choice architecture may impact consumer choice. [10]

SAMPLE STUDENT ANSWER

▲ The candidate introduces the concept of "choice" then identifies the main methods used by choice architects.

Consumers make choices such as what goods to purchase given their budget constraints. Those choices may be influenced through choice architecture, which we may define as the structuring or presentation of choices in a certain form or manner to influence consumer choices. The three main methods available to choice architects are "Default choice", "Restricted choice" and "Mandated choice".

▲ The candidate explains how default choice may impact consumer behaviour. The choice affected is clearly identified. While real-world examples are not required for 10-mark essay questions, they may be used to illustrate answers.

Default choice may change or influence market outcomes as consumers are often predisposed to opt for the "easy option" (the pre-determined choice made for them by the choice architect), believe that the "default" option is the best one, or may not even know there are other options available to them. An example of default choice in action is fast food chain KFC supporting Singapore's No Straw Initiative. The initiative tries to affect consumption of disposable plastic straws, which have caused damage to marine life. Under the initiative, consumers are neither given nor offered a plastic straw for their beverages at check out. Unless consumers make a request for one, no straw is the default choice for all KFC consumers.

Choice architecture in the form of a restricted choice impacts consumer decisions by limiting the options available to them and thus not offering the options that the choice architect believes will result in less-than-optimal outcomes. Many takeaway salad shops that believe in healthy living have offered options for salad dressing—"regular dressing", "reduced dressing" or "no dressing" on order forms. There is no "extra dressing" option, to prevent consumers from overindulging in salad dressings, which can be high in fats. This shows how offering a restricted choice impacts the demand for unhealthy food, by simply removing options that the choice architect determines to be undesirable. Finally, a mandate choice forces consumers to make a choice between alternatives. In some countries, to attend to the low number of organ donors, the authorities made it mandatory to answer a question on joining the organ donor programme when renewing or registering a driver's license. If applicants do not make a choice between "opting in" or "opting out" of an organ donor programme, they will not have their request for a driving license processed. In this case, individuals are forced to think about the option and make a choice. This shows how having choice architecture in the form of a mandated choice impacts consumer choice by resulting in consumers making choices that they do not typically consider. While they remain free to choose between either options, consumers are forced to consider choices that come with a moral or ethical dimension.

▲ The second method available to choice architects is clearly explained using an example.

▲ Another example illustrates use of the third method in influencing consumer choice. While the previous two examples were less precise than the first (there was no name or brand for the salad shop and no country name), they remain effective in explaining the relevant economic theory for part (a) questions.

This response meets all the requirements of the top mark band [9–10]. Note that no diagrams were drawn for this question. Diagrams should only be included *where appropriate*. It is important that candidates only include diagrams when they enrich the economic analysis.

This response could have achieved 10/10 marks.

Content link

Link to your IA

It is unlikely that you could sustain a full commentary on this unit alone. However, consumer nudges and choice architecture are often used to address market failure (which will be the focus of sub-unit 2.8). You may consider a news article on the use of nudges or choice architecture to reduce the consumption of plastic bags, electricity or tobacco, for example.

Concept link

- **Economic well-being**—nudges and choice architecture help individuals to make choices that lead to better outcomes. We saw earlier that restricted choices protect Singapore residents from significant loss of their retirement income. This assures their future financial stability. Restaurants with all-you-can-eat options have also started providing diners with smaller plates to prevent overeating and promote healthier living. However, nudges and choice architecture have also been used extensively by businesses to convince consumers to make decisions that are not in their best interest.
- **Sustainability**—nudges and choice architecture help consumers to make more optimal choices. Often nudges are used to address environmental degradation. Consider how any choices affected by nudges or choice architecture mentioned in the article help us satisfy our current needs without compromising the needs of future generations.

2.5 ELASTICITIES OF DEMAND

You should be able to:

- ✔ define the terms
  - ✔ price elasticity of demand (PED)
  - ✔ income elasticity of demand (YED)
- ✔ explain the determinants of PED
- ✔ explain, using diagrams, the relationship between PED and total revenue
- ✔ discuss the significance of PED for firms and government decision-making
- ✔ explain the significance of the sign of YED
  - ✔ distinguish between normal goods (YED > 0) and inferior goods (YED < 0)
  - ✔ distinguish between necessity goods (0 < YED <1) goods and luxury goods (YED > 1)
- ✔ explain, using an Engel curve, that the demand for services and luxury goods tend to be income elastic while the demand for necessities tend to be income inelastic.

This sub-unit introduces the concepts of price elasticity of demand and income elasticity of demand, and their calculations.

HL In addition to the points above, you should be able to:

- explain how and why the value of PED changes along a linear demand curve
- explain why the PED for primary commodities is generally lower than the PED for manufactured products
- discuss the significance of YED for firms
- discuss the significance of YED in explaining the sectoral structure of an economy.

Summary

The **price elasticity of demand (PED)** is a measure of the responsiveness of the quantity demanded of a good to a change in its price. It is calculated as:

$$PED = \frac{\%\,\Delta\,quantity\ demanded}{\%\,\Delta\,price} = \frac{\frac{Q2 - Q1}{Q1}}{\frac{P2 - P1}{P1}} = \frac{Q2 - Q1}{P2 - P1} \times \frac{P1}{Q1}$$

Since the law of demand states that price and quantity demanded are inversely related, PED is always a negative number. As such, the negative sign is often omitted (except in calculations).

Magnitude	Interpretation	Diagram
PED > 1	Demand is **price elastic.** A change in price results in a *more than proportionate* change in quantity demanded. For example, PED = 3 implies that a 10% increase in price results in a 30% decrease in quantity demanded. The demand curve for a good with PED > 1 has a gentler slope, because the quantity demanded responds significantly to a change in price. The more price elastic the demand (the higher the value of PED), the gentler the slope of the demand curve.	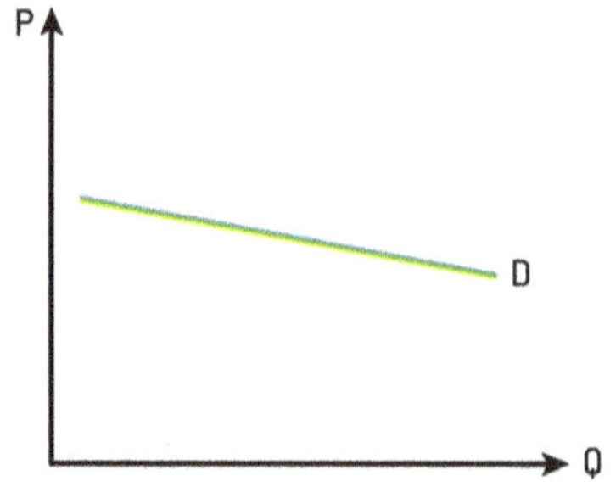

Magnitude	Interpretation	Diagram
PED < 1	Demand is **price inelastic**—a change in price results in a *less than proportionate* change in quantity demanded. For example, PED = 0.5 implies that a 20% decrease in price results in a 10% increase in quantity demanded. The demand curve for a good with PED < 1 appears to be steeper, because the quantity demanded will not change much in response to a change in price. The more price inelastic the demand is (the closer PED is to 0), the steeper the slope is.	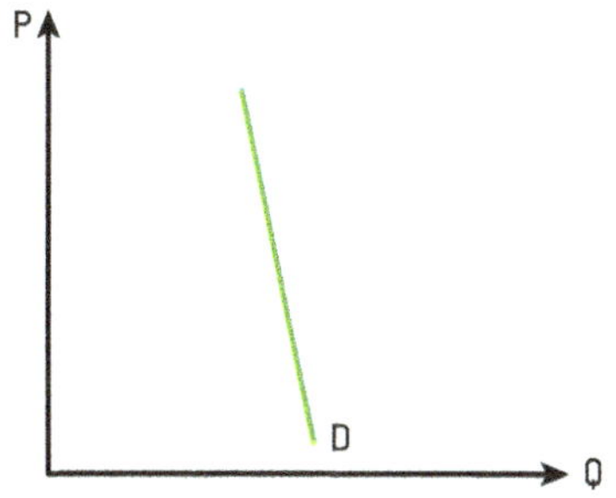
PED = 1	Demand is **unit-price elastic**—a change in price leads to a proportionately equal change in quantity demanded (a demand curve of unitary elasticity is a rectangular hyperbola).	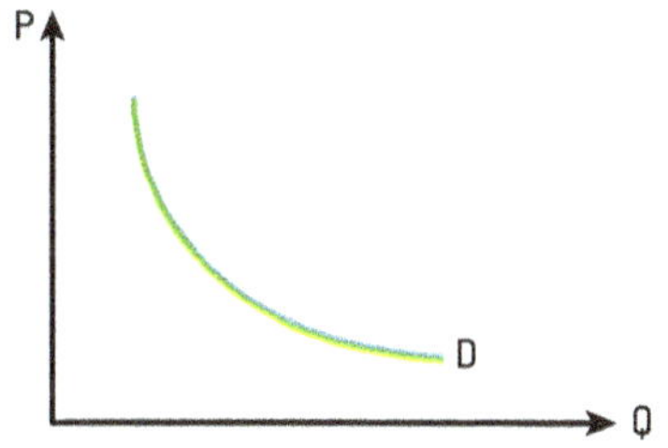
PED = 0	Demand is **perfectly price inelastic**—a change in price does not result in a change in quantity demanded.	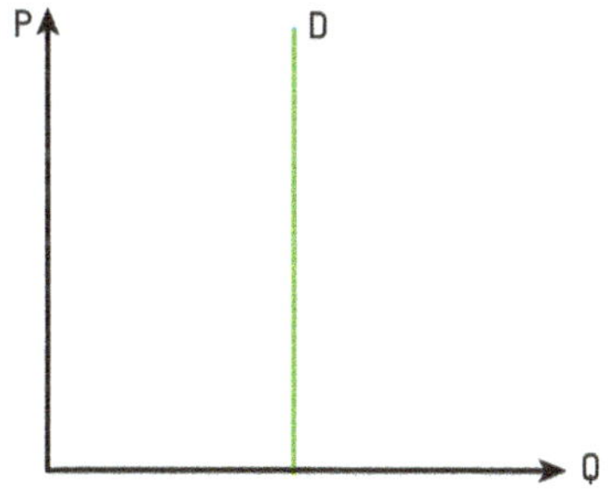
PED = ∞	Demand is **perfectly price elastic**—any change in price would result in an infinitely large change in quantity demanded.	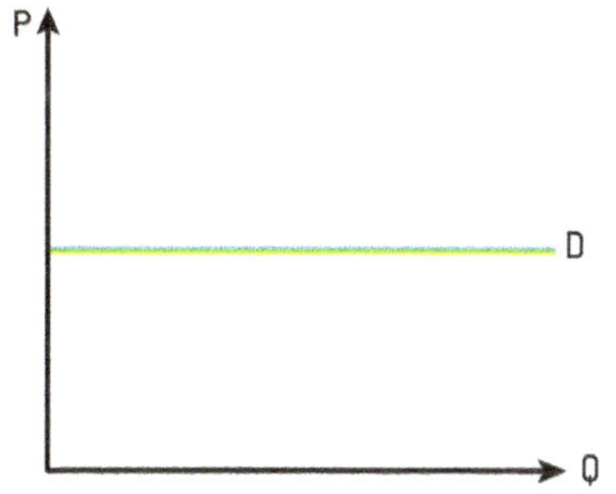

The main **determinants** of PED are as follows.

- **The number and closeness of substitutes**—consumers are likely to respond more to a change in price if there are substitutes for the good, especially if there are close substitutes. For example, the demand for a specific brand of rice is expected to be rather price elastic because an increase in its price would probably result in consumers easily switching to other brands—most consumers do not see noticeable differences between different brands of rice so they consider most brands to be close substitutes. Note that if we defined the good more broadly as "rice", rather than a "specific brand of rice", it is likely that demand for it would be inelastic since many consumers would not see other staple foods such as maize, bread or pasta as close substitutes for rice.
- **The nature of the good**—consumers are unlikely to alter their consumption of **necessities** due to price changes. For instance, an increase in the price of oil is likely to result in a less than proportionate fall in quantity demanded (demand is inelastic) since oil is necessary for cars, industrial engines and central heating systems. Some goods, such as cigarettes, are **addictive** and consumers might have difficulty cutting down their consumption in response to an increase in price, making demand price inelastic.
- **The proportion of income spent on the good**—a change in price is unlikely to affect consumers' spending if they only spend a small proportion of their income on the good. The PED for salt is likely to be very low because most consumers spend a negligible share of their income on salt. They might not even notice an increase in price. The demand for most goods and services is thus more price inelastic for higher income individuals, as the expenditure on a good accounts for a smaller proportion of their higher income.

- **Time**—consumers take time to adjust their consumption following a change in price. They may need time to gather information on substitutes available or may be bound by contracts in the short term. Demand is likely to be more price elastic over a longer time period. For instance, the price of petrol cars has increased in many countries in a bid to push drivers to more environmentally friendly electric cars. In most cases, consumers need time to find out more about the ease of charging, driving range and models of electric cars available before they switch from a petrol car to an electric one. The demand for petrol cars remained relatively price inelastic after the increase in price.

HL The price elasticity of a downward sloping straight-line demand curve varies from infinity when it meets the price axis (point A), to zero where the demand curve reaches the quantity axis (point B). At the midpoint, demand is unit-price elastic (point M). Mathematically, this can be explained by the formula for PED:

$$PED = \frac{\Delta Q}{\Delta P} \times \frac{P1}{Q1}$$

The first component of the equation, $\frac{\Delta Q}{\Delta P}$ is the inverse of the slope of the demand curve and hence a constant throughout a straight line.

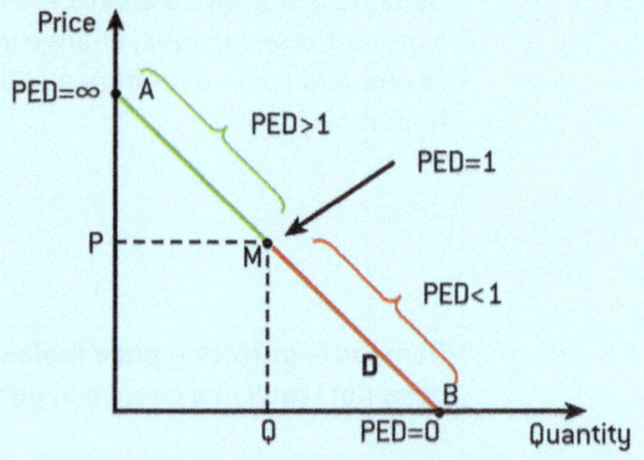

▲ Figure 2.5.1 PED along a demand curve

The second part, $\frac{P1}{Q1}$, will go from 0 if the price is zero all the way to ∞ as quantity approaches 0 (dividing a number by 0 results in ∞). Another way to justify the varying PED along a full demand curve is to go back to one of the determinants of PED, the proportion of income spent on the good. The smaller the price, the more price inelastic the demand because a change in price is insignificant to consumers. If the price rose so high that consumers could barely afford the good, the demand would be highly price elastic.

Total revenue (TR) is the revenue gained by a firm from the sale of a particular quantity of a good. It is calculated as:

$$TR = P \times Q$$

PED	Price	TR
PED > 1	↑	↓
	↓	↑
PED < 1	↑	↑
	↓	↓

If PED > 1, a decrease in price would result in a more than proportionate increase in quantity demanded and hence total revenue would increase. For example, PED = 3 would imply that a 10% decrease in price would result in a 30% increase in quantity demanded and hence an increase in TR since it is P × Q.

If PED < 1, an increase in price would result in a less than proportionate decrease in quantity demanded and thus total revenue would increase. For example, PED = 0.5 would imply that a 10% increase in price would result in quantity decreasing by 5% and this would thus increase TR.

The importance of PED for firms and for government decision-making

Firms with knowledge of PED are able to predict the impact a change in price would have on total revenue. As we saw earlier, firms that estimate the demand for their good to be price inelastic may increase their prices to increase revenue. Those who expect the demand for their good to be price elastic should decrease prices if they seek higher revenues. Firms may also use PED data to determine the proportion of an indirect tax they can pass on to consumers. The more price inelastic the demand, the higher the share of an indirect tax that can be transferred to consumers. For example, the demand for tobacco-related products is highly inelastic because consumers are addicted to them. As such, tobacco companies are unlikely to expect significantly lower revenue or reduce production in anticipation of an increase in tax. They know that they may increase the price of cigarettes without fear of a significant drop in quantity demanded. However, a significant tax on cigarettes could make the demand price elastic for low income consumers as the proportion of income spent on cigarettes may become prohibitively high.

HL Primary commodities are goods derived directly from the earth and include both agricultural products (e.g. corn, rice, wheat) and non-agricultural products (e.g. coal, copper, oil). Manufactured goods (e.g. laptops, cars, textiles) are produced by the application of labour and capital to raw materials and other intermediate factors of production. The PED of primary products is relatively low because they are necessities without close substitutes—if the price of corn increases, producers of cereals such as Kellogg's would continue purchasing corn since wheat cannot be used to produce cornflakes.

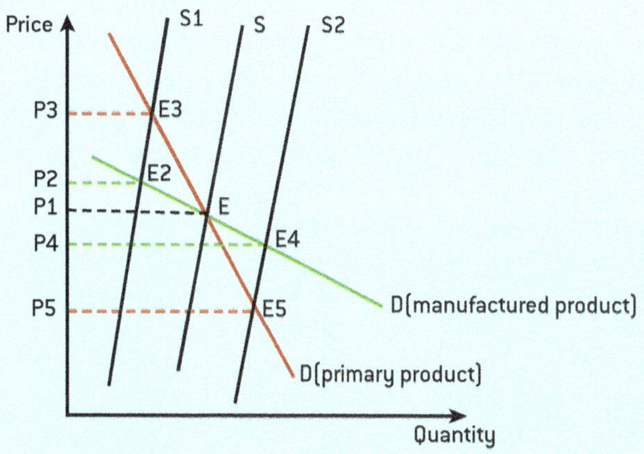

▲ Figure 2.5.2 Primary versus manufactured products

In contrast, the PED of manufactured products tends to be higher because of the presence of substitutes and their purchase may often be delayed (consumers may wait to replace a laptop or car, for example). Expenditure on primary products such as fruits and vegetables also take a smaller proportion of the typical consumer's income compared to the expenditure on manufactured goods such as laptops. Agricultural products are often subject to variations in supply due to weather conditions. Using Figure 2.5.2, a bad harvest would lead to a reduction in supply (S1) and a good harvest to a higher supply (S2). Those changes in supply, coupled with a low PED, result in significant fluctuations in price (P3 to P5). In contrast, the supply of manufactured goods is less prone to changes and even when supply changes, the higher PED results in smaller variations in price (P2 to P4).

Content link

Link to other sub-units

Refer to sub-unit 2.1. Income is one of the main non-price determinants of demand. An increase in income may lead to an increase in demand for normal goods and a decrease in demand for inferior goods.

The **income elasticity of demand (YED)** is a measure of the responsiveness of demand for a good or service to a change in the income of consumers. It is calculated as:

$$YED = \frac{\%\ \Delta\ quantity\ demanded}{\%\ \Delta\ income} = \frac{\frac{Q2 - Q1}{Q1}}{\frac{Y2 - Y1}{Y1}} = \frac{Q2 - Q1}{Y2 - Y1} \times \frac{Y1}{Q1}$$

While PED values are usually negative and the sign is often ignored, YED values may be either positive (normal goods) or negative (inferior goods).

The magnitude of the coefficient is also of significance.

Sign and magnitude	Interpretation
YED < 0	An inferior good—as income increases, consumers turn to "better substitutes" (see sub-unit 2.1).
0 < YED < 1	Demand is **income inelastic**—a change in income results in a *less than proportionate* change in quantity demanded. For example, YED = 0.2 implies that a 10% increase in income results in a 2% increase in quantity demanded. The necessity goods (e.g. milk, bread, rice) fall in this category as consumers are unlikely to make significant changes to their consumption in response to a change in income.
YED > 1	Demand is income elastic—a change in **income leads** to more than proportionate change in quantity demanded. For example, YED = 2 implies that a 10% increase in income results in a 20% increase in quantity demanded. Luxury goods (e.g. sports cars, jewellery) and most services (e.g. movie screenings, cruises, gym memberships) have high YED.

Engel curves are shown on Figures 2.5.3a, b and c. These diagrams illustrate the relationship between income (Y) and the quantity demanded (Qd) for a good or service. If the Engel curve is negatively sloped (E1 on Figure 2.5.3a) then the good is an inferior good (YED < 0). This may be the case for home (generic) brand peanut butter, for example—a 50% increase in income may result in a decrease in quantity demanded from Q to Q1 as consumers switch to branded peanut butter of higher quality. Engel curves that are positively sloped (E2 and E3 on Figures 2.5.3b and 2.5.3c) indicate normal goods (YED > 0). For goods with an income inelastic demand (0 < YED < 1), the Engel curve (E2) will cut the horizontal axis—as those goods are necessities such as bread, consumers will buy them even at very low (or no) income—a 50% increase in income would lead to a less than proportionate increase in quantity demanded for bread, from Q to Q2. The Engel curve cuts the vertical axis for goods with an income elastic demand (YED > 1) as they are consumed when consumers reach a certain threshold level of income. For households on a limited budget, an increase in income might, for example, allow for foreign holidays for the first time—a 50% increase in income would lead to a more than proportionate increase in quantity demanded from Q to Q3.

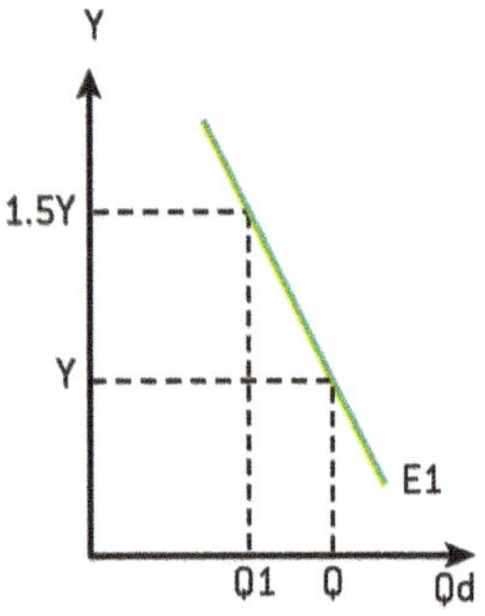

▲ Figure 2.5.3a

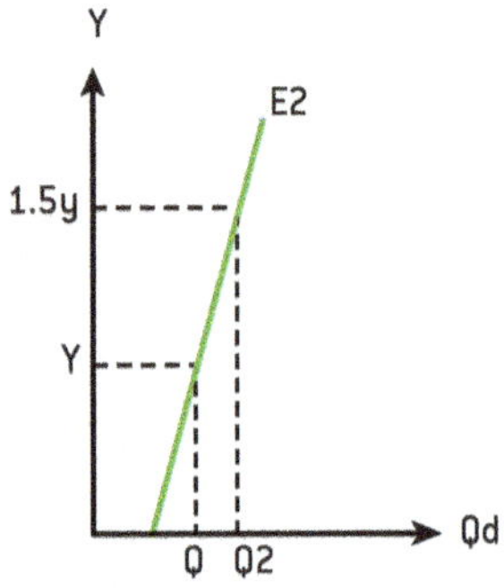

▲ Figure 2.5.3b

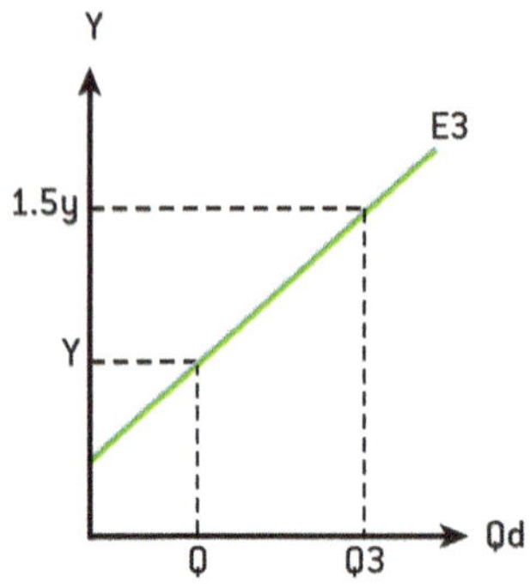

▲ Figure 2.5.3c

HL

The importance of YED for firms

Household income fluctuates based on the state of the economy—economic growth brings an increase in income for most households while recessions come with decreases in income. Knowledge of YED allows firms to forecast changes in demand for their products and reallocate production from normal goods to inferior goods during recessions. Consider, for instance, car manufacturers who usually offer a wide range of models from entry-level cars to sports model, SUVs and other lifestyle cars that are usually expensive—YED would differ across the range of models. Car manufacturers would be likely to shift more of their production to entry-level models during recessions.

The significance of YED in explaining sectoral change in an economy

Economic activities are organized into three sectors—primary sector (agriculture, forestry, fishing and mining), secondary sector (manufacturing) and tertiary sector (services). As countries experience economic growth and incomes increase, the demand for normal goods increases. Producers of goods and services with higher YED will see the expansion of their industries. Agricultural goods tend to have a low YED, so the demand for agricultural products does not grow as fast as income increases over time. In contrast, manufactured products tend have a YED that is greater than 1 and services have even higher YED. As countries go from low income to middle income, they typically see their primary sector lose importance in relation to the production of goods and services. High income countries tend to have the highest share of their economic activities in the tertiary sector.

Revision tip

Elasticity terminology is often a source of confusion. Candidates often forget that elasticity is measured using proportional or percentage changes (relative values). An income or price elastic demand is a case of a change in income or price leading to a "less than proportionate" and **not** a "small" or "smaller" change in quantity demanded. The terms "small" or "smaller" do not capture the notion of proportions. Absolute changes do not convey the significance of the change. A $10 price change might be significant for the price of a cup of coffee because it is could signify a 200% change in price, but insignificant if it is applied to the price of a car, where it might not even represent a 0.1% change. As such, economists always consider relative rather than absolute changes.

QUESTION PRACTICE

This question is adapted from the May 2021 examination paper.

Define the term *income inelastic demand*. [10]

SAMPLE STUDENT ANSWER

Response 1

The quantity demanded of the product does not change a lot when income changes, meaning it's probably a necessity.

▼ "The quantity does not change a lot" is not as precise as "the quantity changes by a less than proportionate amount". Elasticity is measured using proportional or percent changes (relative values).

This response could have achieved 1/2 marks.

Response 2

Income inelastic demand is when the quantity demanded changes by a smaller percentage change than the change in income. It happens when YED is more than zero but less than one.

▲ The candidate understands that YED measures relative changes. Adding that $0 < YED < 1$ adds precision to the definition.

This response could have achieved 2/2 marks.

QUESTION PRACTICE

This question is adapted from the November 2014 examination paper.

The following table provides data on the price and quantity demanded (per month) of two goods in Zestria.

	Good A		**Good A**	
	Price ($ per unit)	Quantity demanded	Price ($ per unit)	Quantity demanded
January 2014	8	160	10	200
February 2014	6	220	12	160

(i) Calculate the price elasticity of demand for Good A when its price falls between January 2014 and February 2014. [2]

(ii) Calculate the price elasticity of demand for Good B when its price increases between January 2014 and February 2014. [2]

SAMPLE STUDENT ANSWER

Response 1

$PED = \frac{37.5\%}{-25\%} = -1.5$

▲ PED = 1.5 (without the negative sign) would also be a correct answer.

This response could have achieved 2/2 marks.

Response 2

PED = 1

▼ Full marks cannot be awarded if no working is provided, even when the final answer is correct.

This response could have achieved 1/2 marks.

QUESTION PRACTICE

This question is adapted from the November 2020 examination paper.

(Explain how knowledge of price elasticity of demand could be used by a firm that is considering changing the price of its product.

(10)

SAMPLE STUDENT ANSWER

The price elasticity of demand (PED) for a good measures the responsiveness of quantity demanded of the good in response to a change in the price of the good, ceteris paribus. It is calculated as:

$$PED = \frac{\% \Delta \text{quantity demanded}}{\% \Delta \text{price}}$$

Because of the law of demand, PED values are usually negative and the sign is ignored. We distinguish between PED < 1 when a change in price will not lead to a significant change in quantity demanded. In such cases the demand is said to be price inelastic. If the PED > 1 then the change in quantity demanded will be significant and demand is said to be price elastic.

▲ This is a good brief introduction to PED.

Knowledge of a good's PED can help firms to anticipate future changes in total revenue. In particular, PED can indicate how firms' total revenues will change when the price of their good increases or decreases. Consider the following diagram in the market for widgets: firm X produces the product at output Q1 and price P1. On this part of the demand curve, PED is more than 1, for example PED = 1.2.

▲ The candidate correctly identifies the concept of total revenue.

Terms used (such as "demand is elastic") are adequate.

A fictitious example is used to illustrate the answer. While examples are not needed for part (a), it is fine to use them for illustration of theoretical concepts.

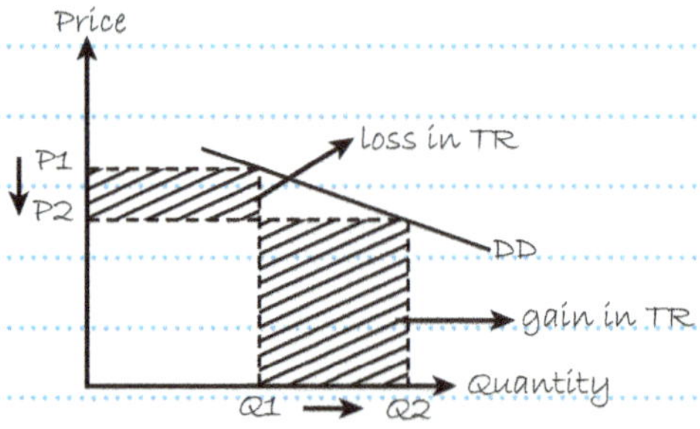

Thus, if widget firms wants to increase revenue, it should decrease the price of widgets. A decrease in price of 10% (from P1 to P2) would lead to a 12% increase in quantity demanded (from Q1 to Q2). Since TR = P × Q, it would lead to an increase in revenues. As you can see on my diagram, the gain in revenue is more than the loss in revenue from the lowered price.

▲ The candidate makes good use of a numerical example and effective referencing to the diagram to illustrate the increase in TR due to a lower price.

Conversely, if the firms know that the demand for widgets is inelastic—maybe PED = 0.8, the effects of changes in price on total revenues would differ. In that case, the firm should increase the price because consumers are less responsive to changes in price. Hence, a 10% increase in price would decrease quantity demanded by only 8% and total revenue would still increase.

▲ The candidate continues to explain the link between PED and TR with appropriate terms and a numerical example.

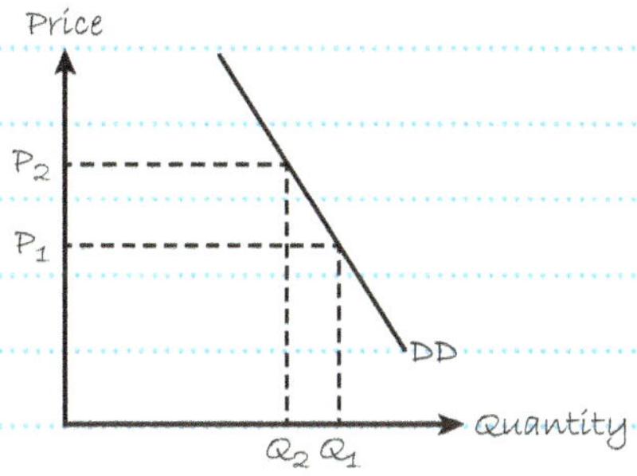

▼ The diagram is not used effectively: no reference is made to points or areas on the diagram.

Consequently, firms must consider the PED of their goods/services in order to predict the impact of price changes on total revenue. For goods with an elastic demand, they should decrease prices and for goods with an inelastic demand, they should increase prices.

▲ This is a brief summary of the response. While a conclusion is not necessary, it does contribute to a good essay structure.

This response meets all the descriptors of the highest mark band (9–10). The candidate addresses the specific demands of the question (there is adequate application of the concept of PED to a firm considering a change in price). The concepts of PED and TR are explained with appropriate use of economic terms. While effective references to the first diagram allow for a full explanation, the second diagram is hardly explained. This keeps the response in the lower range of the (9–10) mark band.

This response could have achieved 9/10 marks.

QUESTION PRACTICE

This question is adapted from the May 2021 examination paper.

Explain why the price elasticity of demand for primary commodities is often relatively low while the price elasticity of demand for manufactured goods is often relatively high. [10]

SAMPLE STUDENT ANSWER

Primary commodities are goods which are extracted from the factor of production, land. Manufactured goods are goods which go through the manufacturing process and therefore have added value, such as cars.

▲ This is a clear distinction between the two types of goods.

▲ The concept of PED is explained using appropriate and precise terminology (such as "demand is inelastic", "smaller percentage change") and effective references to the diagram.

▼ It would be good to provide the formula for PED when explaining the significance of the "low" and "high" values.

Price elasticity of demand (PED) refers to the responsiveness of quantity demanded as a result of a change in price. The demand for primary commodities tends to be more price inelastic, meaning that PED is low. Especially when compared to manufactured goods which come with higher PED and so are more price elastic demand. That may be seen on the following diagram. The demand for primary products is a lot steeper than the demand for manufactured goods. Due the relatively low PED of primary commodities, the percentage increase in price causes a smaller percentage change in quantity demanded from Q1 to Q2 compared to the higher price of P2. On the other hand, manufactured goods have a relatively high PED, they experience a greater percentage drop in quantity demanded (Q1 to Q2) in response to the higher price.

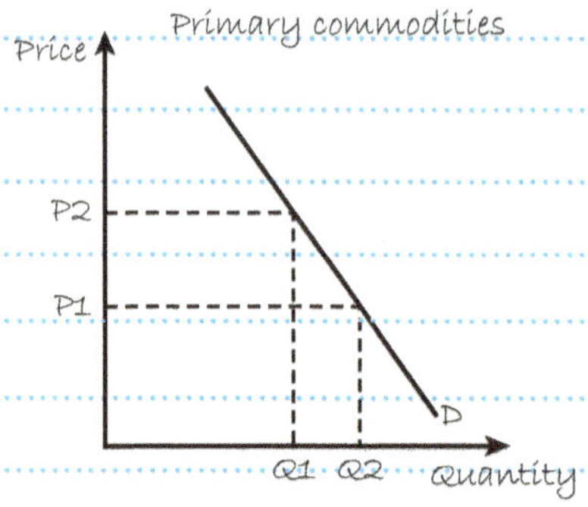

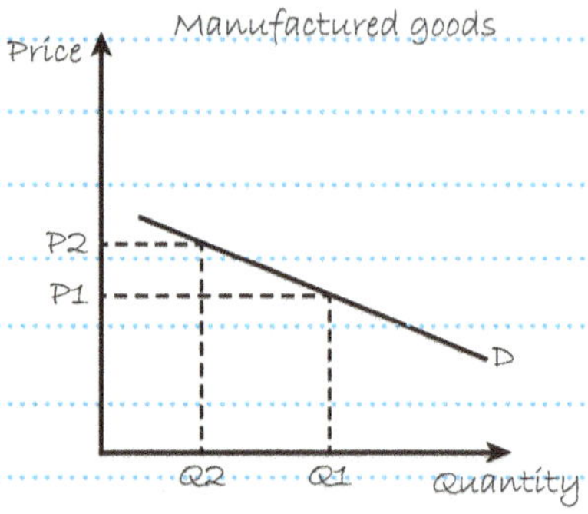

▲ This is an adequate justification for the low PED of primary goods with reference to the relevant determinants of PED.

▲ The higher PED of manufactured goods is justified with references to the determinants of PED. The theoretical examples aptly illustrate the analysis.

▼ There is no consideration of the proportion of income spent on primary commodities versus manufactured goods.

The difference in PED is due to different determinants of PED. Many primary commodities such as oil have limited substitutes. There is solar energy but if the price of oil increases, you can't switch every engine from using oil to solar energy easily. Another reason is due to the degree of necessity of the good. As many primary commodities are agricultural goods, which are essential due to being needed for survival, their PED is rather low. As a result, consumers would be less willing to change to another good, and hence are less sensitive to changes in price.

On the other hand, as manufactured goods tend to have many more substitutes, consumers can change to another good, with more ease. For example, there are many brands of cars so when a brand becomes more expensive, consumers can turn to another. Furthermore, many manufactured goods are not deemed to be as essential, and even seen to be luxuries in some cases such as handbags and televisions. As such, they have a greater PED (demand is more elastic).

This response meets all the descriptors of the highest mark band (9–10). The candidate addresses the specific demands of the question (explaining the differing PED values). The response also demonstrates adequate use of economic terminology and effective use of a diagram. However, the candidate could have better explained the economic theory—there is no mention of the proportion of income spent on agricultural versus manufactured goods (and that plays a significant part in determining the relatively elasticity). As such, the response is kept to the lower end of the (9–10) band.

This response could have achieved 9/10 marks.

2.6 ELASTICITY OF SUPPLY

This sub-unit introduces the concept of price elasticity of supply and its calculation.

You should be able to:

- ✔ define the term
  - ✔ price elasticity of supply (PES)
- ✔ explain the determinants of PES

HL In addition to the points above, you should be able to:

- explain why the PES for primary commodities is generally lower than the PES for manufactured products.

Summary

The **price elasticity of supply (PES)** is a measure of the responsiveness of the quantity supplied of a good to a change in its price. It is calculated as:

$$PES = \frac{\%\,\Delta\,quantity\ supplied}{\%\,\Delta\,price} = \frac{\frac{Q2 - Q1}{Q1}}{\frac{P2 - P1}{P1}} = \frac{Q2 - Q1}{P2 - P1} \times \frac{P1}{Q1}$$

Since the law of supply states that price and quantity supplied are directly (positively) related, PES values are always positive.

Magnitude	Interpretation	Diagram
PES > 1	Supply is **price elastic**. A change in price results in a *more than proportionate* change in quantity supplied. For example, PES = 2 implies that a 10% increase in price results in a 20% increase in quantity supplied. A price elastic supply curve must cut the vertical (price) axis.	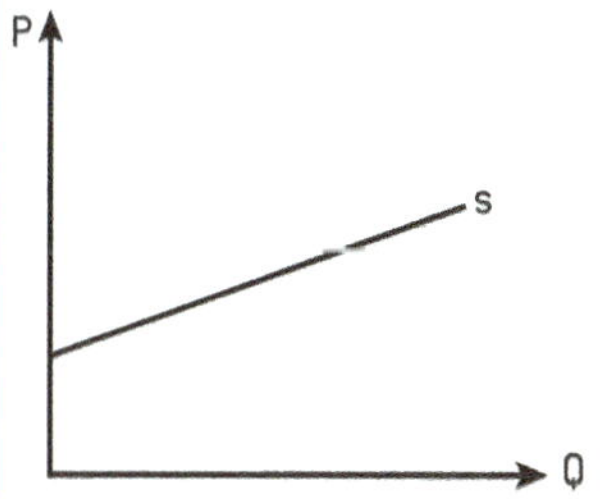

Magnitude	Interpretation	Diagram
PES < 1	Supply is **price inelastic**—a change in price results in a *less than proportionate* change in quantity supplied. For example, PED = 0.4 implies that a 10% decrease in price results in a 4% decrease in quantity supplied. A price inelastic supply curve must cut the horizontal (quantity) axis.	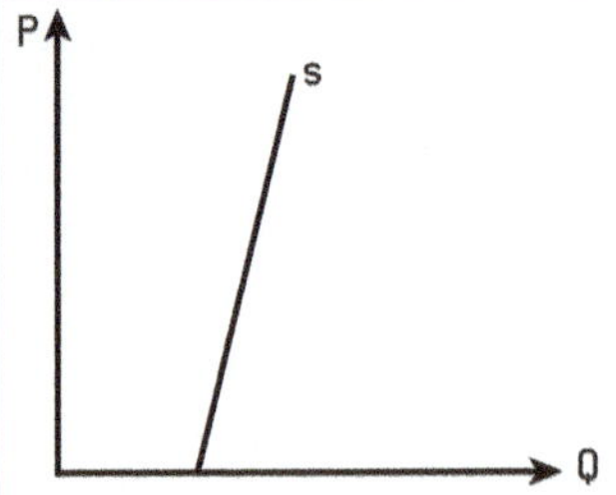
PES = 1	Supply is **unit-price elastic**—a change in price leads to a proportionate change in quantity supplied. Any straight line supply curve passing through the origin (0) has a PES of 1.	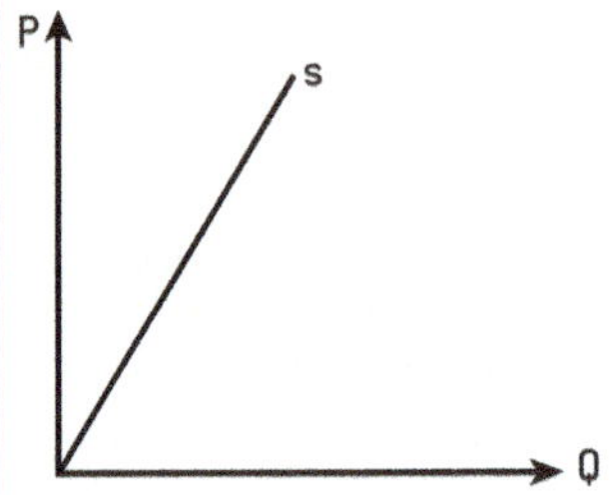
PES = 0	Supply is **perfectly price inelastic**—a change in price does not result in a change in quantity supplied.	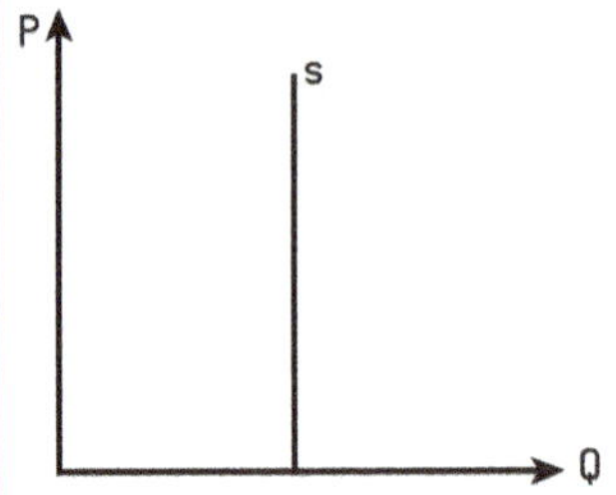
PES = ∞	Supply is **perfectly price elastic**—any change in price would result in an infinitely large change in quantity supplied.	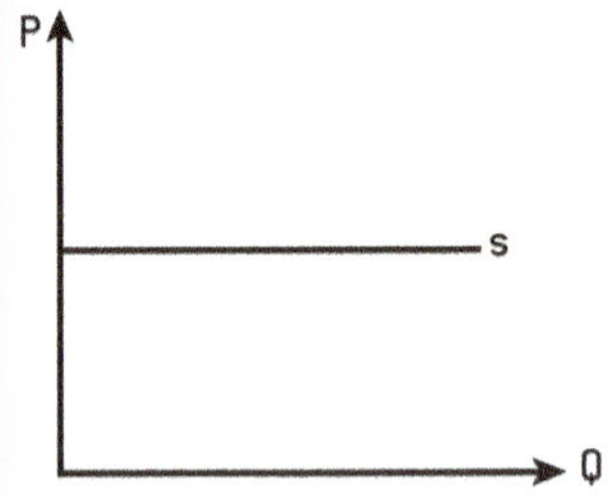

The main **determinants** of PES are as follows.

- **The time period involved**—firms need time to acquire more factors of production to increase output. Economists distinguish between the momentary run (the time period when no change can be made to factors of production (FOPs), so no adjustment to production is possible), the short run (when some but not all FOPs can be increased) and the long run (when all FOPs can be changed). The shorter the time period, the more price inelastic the supply.
- **Mobility of factors of production**—a price elastic supply implies that production can be easily adjusted when demand and thus price increase. When it is easy to reassign resources from the production of one good to another (for example an electronics firm may easily recalibrate machines and redeploy workers from the production of laptops to smartphones), factor mobility is high and the supply is more likely to be price elastic.
- **Unused capacity**—when firms are producing at full capacity, increasing production is difficult. If they have spare capacity, production can increase easily to respond to higher demand and price. The PES of manufactured goods tends to be higher during economic downturns when firms are producing below capacity.

- **Ability to store**—if the good is not perishable and if it can be stored easily, firms are more likely to produce additional units to accumulate stocks that can be released when prices increase. For example, firms can store frozen fish but not fresh fish, so the supply of frozen fish is more price elastic than the supply of fresh fish.
- **The rate at which costs increase**—increasing production might be costly. For instance, mining companies need to use extremely expensive earth-moving equipment so they would be willing to increase output only at a much higher price. The additional cost (marginal cost) to raise output would be very high. In such cases, the supply would be more price inelastic as the price increase needs to be sufficient to cover the high marginal cost.

Content link

Link to other sub-units

Refer to sub-unit 2.3. The supply curve is also the marginal cost (MC).

HL You learned in sub-unit 2.5 that the PED of primary commodities is lower than the PED of manufactured goods. Similarly, **the PES of primary commodities is also lower than the PES of manufactured goods**. To explain this, we need to go back to the determinants of PES. Additional land, labour and capital are needed to increase production. For example, it is very difficult—if not impossible in the short run—to convert non-agricultural land for farming use or find additional sources of minerals for mining. Agricultural production is also subject to long gestation periods as farmers may only harvest crops a certain time after planting. By contrast, the production of manufactured good can be more easily adjusted, sometimes by asking workers living in nearby dormitories to work overtime, and hence supply is more price elastic.

QUESTION PRACTICE

This question is adapted from the May 2019 examination paper.

The time taken to produce goods is an important determinant of the price elasticity of supply. Apart from time, explain **two** factors which influence the price elasticity of supply. [4]

SAMPLE STUDENT ANSWER

Response 1

The existence of spare capacity and the time period involved.

▼ The candidate identifies two determinants of PES but they are not explained. This would be a valid answer for full marks had the command term been "list".

This response could have achieved 2/4 marks.

Response 2

1. Whether the firm has excess capacity available: if it does, then increasing output in response to higher price will be easier so supply will be more price elastic.

2. Mobility of factors of production: the easier it is for a producer to switch resources from one use to another, the easier it will be to increase the quantity supplied in response to an increase in the price of the good, so supply will be more price elastic.

▲ The candidate provides and explains two valid determinants of PES.

This response could have achieved 4/4 marks.

QUESTION PRACTICE

This question is adapted from the November 2014 examination paper.

The final of the 2018 Football World Cup is expected to be held in the Luzhniki stadium, Moscow. The capacity of the stadium is 80,000. The expected cost of holding the final is US$12 million, which is not dependent on the number of people attending the match. All tickets will be sold for the same price.

State the value of the price elasticity of supply (PES) for tickets to the 2018 Football World Cup final. [1]

SAMPLE STUDENT ANSWER

PES = 0

▲ Since the quantity supplied does not change with the price (there is only a fixed quantity available), supply is perfectly price inelastic. As the command word is "state", no workings or justification are required.

This response could have achieved 1/1 mark.

Content link

Link to your IA

Sudden changes in the price of agricultural goods are often reported in the news. You may apply the concepts of demand and supply to explain the cause of the price change and elasticity to explain the magnitude of that price change. If the weather or natural disasters are responsible for a sharp increase in price, then you need to consider a shift of the supply curve and the PED. You may also come across news articles recounting an unexpected increase in the demand for manufactured goods, such as medical supplies, and the resulting increase in price. In such a case, you should consider the increase in demand and the elasticity of supply.

Concept link

Change—the prices of goods and services are constantly affected by changes in non-price determinants of demand and supply. A single occurrence might have a far-reaching impact on stakeholders. Use demand and supply analysis, and elasticity concepts, to explain the extent of a change in one economic variable on stakeholders. Change may affect consumers and producers very differently. It may affect low income consumers differently from how it affects high income consumers and small firms differently from large multinationals. Keeping in mind the low PED of agricultural products, a bad harvest means higher market prices and higher total revenue for farmers of larger farms that might be better equipped to protect their crops. Those running smaller farms may see their production wiped out and be thrown into poverty. The higher prices will incur higher consumer expenditure on the agricultural product, leaving a smaller share of consumers' income to be spent on other goods and services.

2.7 ROLE OF GOVERNMENT IN MICROECONOMICS

You should be able to:

- ✔ define the terms
  - ✔ price controls
  - ✔ price ceiling (maximum price)
  - ✔ price floor (minimum price)
  - ✔ welfare loss
- ✔ explain the reasons for government intervention in markets
- ✔ explain, using diagrams, the impact of government policies, including price controls, taxes and subsidies on market outcomes and stakeholders
- ✔ explain the impact of government policies such as (command and control) regulation and legislation, and the direct provision of services on markets and stakeholders
- ✔ discuss, with the aid of real-world examples, the consequences for markets and stakeholders of government policies.

This sub-unit examines the tools available to governments for intervention in markets.

Content link

Link to other sub-units

Refer to sub-unit 2.2. Changes in non-price determinant of supply such as taxes and indirect taxes lead to shifts of the supply curve.

HL In addition to the points above, you should be able to:

- explain the impact of consumer nudges on markets and stakeholders
- calculate the effects of price ceilings, price floors, indirect taxes and subsidies on:
  - quantity demanded and quantity supplied or equilibrium quantity
  - consumer surplus
  - producer surplus
  - welfare loss
  - consumer expenditure
  - total revenue
  - government expenditure
- discuss, with the aid of real-world examples, the effectiveness of consumer nudges in influencing consumer behaviour and affecting market outcomes.

Summary

Governments intervene in markets to:

- **earn government revenue** through indirect taxes
- **support certain producers**, usually farmers and other small businesses
- **support low income individuals**, by making sure that basic goods and services (e.g. food, housing) are affordable
- **correct market failure** by encouraging the production and/or consumption of socially desirable goods (merit goods) and discouraging the production and/or consumption of socially undesirable goods (demerit goods)—there is more on this in sub-unit 2.8.
- promote **equity** as free market economies tend to lead to growing inequalities (there is more on this in sub-unit 2.12).

There are a few standard microeconomic tools available to government for intervention in specific markets.

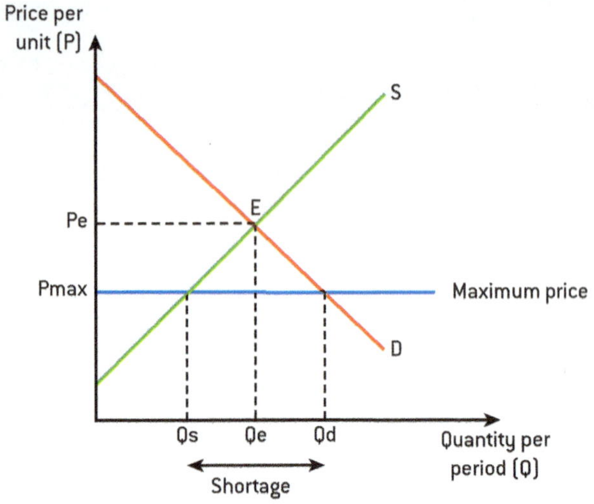

▲ Figure 2.7.1 Impact of a price ceiling (maximum price) on market outcomes

Price controls

A **price ceiling (maximum price)** is the highest price a firm may legally charge for a good. A price ceiling must be set below the market equilibrium for it to be effective. Price ceilings are often used to make necessities (e.g. food, fuel, housing) more affordable. In cities with a high cost of living, authorities may set a maximum price on rental of flats, also known as rent control.

Consider the market shown on Figure 2.7.1. If the government feels that the price of a necessity (e.g. rice) is too high for low income individuals, it may set a price ceiling (maximum price) at Pmax, below the equilibrium price (Pe). At Pmax, the quantity producers are willing and able to offer (Qs) is lower than the quantity consumers are willing and able to buy (Qd). This results in a shortage (QsQd).

These are the consequences and implications of a price ceiling.

- Governments must introduce a non-price rationing mechanism to deal with the shortage, for example as follows.
    - Allocation to resources may be on first come-first served basis. For example, Australia adopts such a system for public housing. Interested applicants are placed on a waiting list.
    - Allocation may be based on sellers' preferences. This often happens when authorities set a maximum rent on rental flats and landlords who receive multiple offers choose tenants based on personal preference (e.g. profession or number of children).
    - Allocation by ballot could be used. For instance, in Singapore where private flats are expensive, most residents buy government flats at controlled prices. Due to the affordability of these properties, there are often more applicants than flats available when new flats are released for sale. The flats are allocated by ballot.
    - For some items, there may be government rationing using coupons. This tends to be done in wartime when food is scarce.
    - A parallel (illegal) market may emerge when producers sell goods at higher prices illegally.
    - Product quality may deteriorate in the long term. This is common in rental housing markets if landlords feel they do not receive sufficient returns to fund renovation or repairs.
    - There may be more severe shortages in the long term as the maximum price deters firms from joining the industry.

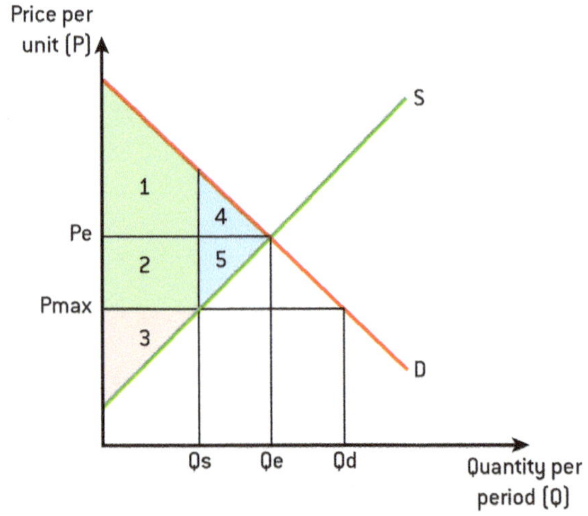

▲ Figure 2.7.2 Welfare impact of a price ceiling (maximum price)

With reference to Figure 2.7.2, the welfare effects of a price ceiling are shown in Table 2.7.1.

▼ Table 2.7.1 Welfare effects of a price ceiling

	Before the price ceiling [A]	After the price ceiling [B]	Net effect ([B]–[A])
Consumer surplus (CS)	1 + 4	1 + 2	2 – 4
Producer surplus (PS)	2 + 3 + 5	3	–(2 + 5)
Social (community) surplus (CS + PS)	1 + 2 + 3 + 4 + 5	1 + 2 + 3	–(4 + 5)

The consumer surplus changes from area (1 + 4) to area (1 + 2). The consumers who are able to find the good at the lower price are better off. Those who end up without the good are worse off.

The producer surplus shrinks to area 3. Revenues decrease as prices are lower and quantity sold falls to Qs. Producers are thus worse off. Social surplus decreases by areas (4 + 5), which represents the **welfare loss** to society—the loss of economic efficiency that can occur when the market for a good does not achieve allocative efficiency (which would only occur at the market equilibrium in this case).

Content link

Link to other sub-units

HL students may want to refer to sub-unit 2.5.

The prices of agricultural products tend to fluctuate due to changes in supply (changes in weather) and a low PED.

A **price floor (minimum price)** is the lowest price a firm may legally charge for a good. To be effective, the price floor must be set above the market equilibrium. Price floors are often imposed on agricultural products to protect farmers against price fluctuations due to changes in weather, which would result in significant decreases in farmers' incomes.

Governments may impose a price floor to discourage the consumption of demerit goods (there is more on this in sub-unit 2.8). For example, a minimum unit price applies to alcohol in some places such as Scotland. A price floor may also apply to labour markets—a minimum wage ensures a socially acceptable level of income for workers.

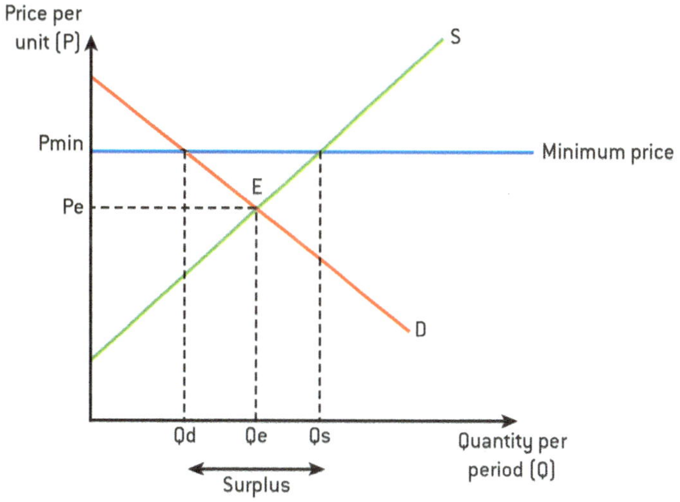

▲ Figure 2.7.3 Impact of a price floor (minimum price) on market outcomes

Consider the market shown on Figure 2.7.3. If the government feels that the price of wheat is too low to generate sufficient income for farmers, it may set a price floor (minimum price) at Pmin, above the equilibrium price (Pe). At Pmin, the quantity that consumers are willing and able to purchase (Qd) is lower than the quantity farmers are willing and able to sell (Qs). This results in a surplus (QdQs).

These are the consequences and implications of a price floor.

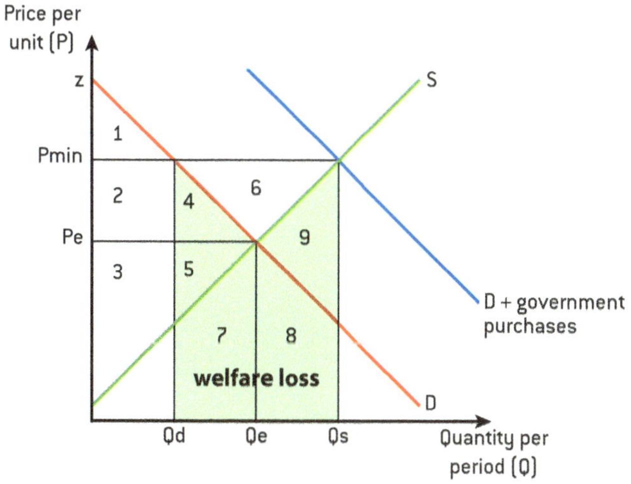

▲ Figure 2.7.4 Welfare impact of a price floor (minimum price)

- To support the minimum price, the government usually buys the surplus. There is an opportunity cost involved as the public funds are no longer available to finance other public services.
- Protecting producers with a high price floor (especially when the government buys the surplus) may lead to inefficiencies. Producers may not feel the need to innovate and find ways to reduce the cost of production, such as using modern farming tools or chemical fertilizers.
- The government must find a way to clear the surplus, either by storing it (for semi-perishable crops such as rice and wheat), destroying it (which represents a huge waste of resources) or selling it abroad (or donating it as foreign aid).

With reference to Figure 2.7.4, the welfare effects of a price floor, assuming the government purchases the surplus, are shown in Table 2.7.2.

▼ Table 2.7.2 Welfare effects of a price floor

	Before the price floor [A]	After the price floor [B]	Net effect ([B]–[A])
Consumer surplus (CS)	1 + 2 + 4	1	–(2 + 4)
Producer surplus (PS)	3 + 5	2 + 3 + 4 + 5 + 6	2 + 4 + 6
Government spending (G)	–	–(4 + 5 + 6 + 7 + 8 + 9)*	–(4 + 5 + 6 + 7 + 8 + 9)
Social (community) surplus (CS+PS+G)	1 + 2 + 3 + 4 + 5	1 + 2 + 3 –(7 + 8 + 9)	–(4 + 5 + 7 + 8 + 9)

*Since government spending occurs an opportunity cost, it represents a loss to society.

A price floor incurs a greater welfare loss than a price ceiling due to the large amount of government spending, which is born by taxpayers.

Indirect taxes and subsidies

Governments impose indirect taxes to:

- raise tax revenue to fund public expenditure
- discourage the consumption of demerit goods or reduce carbon emissions by limiting the production of polluting industries (see sub-unit 4.8)
- reduce the flow of imports and protect domestic producers (such indirect taxes are known as tariffs; see sub-unit 4.2).

On the other hand, subsidies are granted to:

- decrease the price of essential goods and services (just as price ceilings do)
- help certain industries to expand and increase the revenues of producers, usually farmers (in the same way that price floors do)
- encourage the consumption of merit goods (see sub-unit 4.8)
- increase export competitiveness and/or protect local producers from cheaper imports (this will also be examined in sub-unit 4.2).

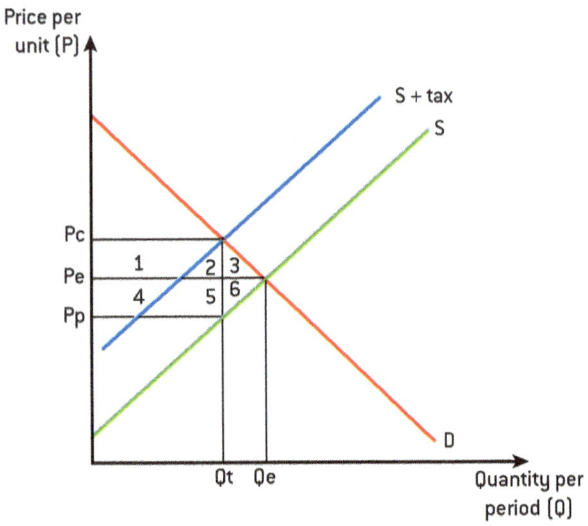

▲ Figure 2.7.5 Impact of an indirect tax on market outcomes

We saw in sub-unit 2.2 that indirect taxes and subsidies are non-price determinants of supply. Imposing an indirect tax results in a leftward shift of the supply curve, while granting a subsidy leads to a rightward shift of the supply curve.

An indirect tax is considered an additional cost of production to producers and thus supply decreases, from S to S + tax on Figure 2.7.5. This results in a higher market price, Pc and lower market quantity, Qt. While consumers pay Pc for each unit purchased, producers only receive Pp per unit since the difference (PpPc) is paid to the government as tax.

Indirect payments have a higher impact on low income consumer. Economists classify such taxes as "regressive" (this concept will be examined in greater detail in sub-unit 3.4).

The tax may also affect the production of other goods if it is imposed on capital goods.

With reference to Figure 2.7.5, the welfare effects of an indirect tax are shown in Table 2.7.3.

▼ Table 2.7.3 Welfare effects of an indirect tax

Consumer surplus decreases [A]	−(1 + 2 + 3)
Producer surplus decreases [B]	−(4 + 5 + 6)
Government revenue increases* [C]	1 + 2 + 4 + 5
Welfare loss incurred as community or society surplus decreases ([A]+ [B]+ [C])	−(3 + 6)

*Since the government revenue may be spent on infrastructure and other public expenditure, it represents a gain to society.

A subsidy decreases costs of production and thus supply increases, from S to S + subsidy on Figure 2.7.6. This results in a lower market price, Pc and higher market quantity, Q1. While consumers pay Pc for each unit purchases, producers receive Pp per unit since they get Pc from consumers and the subsidy (PpPc) from the government.

Other firms may enjoy lower costs of production if the good subsidized is a capital good.

With reference to Figure 2.7.6, the welfare effects of a subsidy are shown in Table 2.7.4.

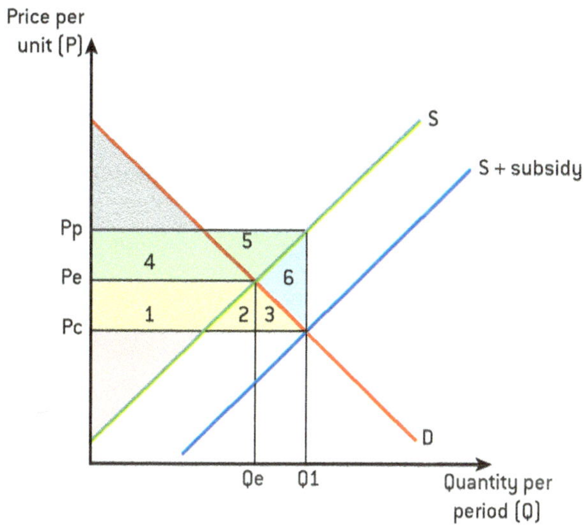

▲ Figure 2.7.6 Impact of a subsidy on market outcomes

▼ Table 2.7.4 Welfare effects of a subsidy

Consumer surplus increases [A]	1 + 2 + 3
Producer surplus increases [B]	4 + 5
Government spending incurred [C]	− (1 + 2 + 3 + 4 + 5 + 6)
Welfare loss incurred as social (community) surplus decreases ([A]+ [B]+ [C])	− 6

You learned in sub-unit 2.3 that competitive markets are allocatively efficient as they achieve the best allocation of resources for society. This is why any deviation from the market equilibrium due to the imposition of any of the four microeconomic tools examined above (price ceiling, price floor, indirect taxes and subsidies) lead to a welfare loss. **However, please note that this welfare loss analysis is based on the assumption that "markets do not fail"** (this is the focus of sub-unit 2.8).

- **(Command and control) regulation and legislation**—intervention in markets may also come in the forms of rules and laws. The consumption of socially desirable goods (e.g. education, vaccines against infectious diseases) may be made compulsory. The production and consumption of undesirable goods (e.g. cigarettes, intoxicating drugs, weapons) may be subject to bans or restrictions. Regulation and legislation are often used to correct market failures (there is more on this in sub-unit 2.8).
- **Direct provision of services**—governments may opt to provide essential services directly (often education and healthcare services through the provision of state schools and national health systems). This ensures that all members of societies have access to those services. A major drawback to this form of intervention is that public enterprises tend to be inefficient and incur avoidable losses due to the lack of profit incentive.

HL

- **Consumer nudges**—consumer nudges may be used to reduce imperfect information and affect market outcomes. In sub-unit 2.4, it was mentioned that New York City restaurants must display calorie information on their menus. This enables consumers to make more informed decisions and the intention is that the demand for high calorie meals will decrease while the demand for dishes with a lower calorie count will increase.

Test yourself

Practise drawing diagrams to illustrate the impacts of indirect taxes, subsidies, minimum price and maximum price on market outcomes and stakeholders. All three examination papers require the use of diagrams to explain an aspect of the theory within a specific context. For paper 1, you will need to provide real-world examples. Search for examples for each government tool and be sure to check the purpose of the policy. For example, Scotland imposed a minimum unit price on alcohol in order to reduce the consumption of low cost alcoholic beverages, which were seen as a source of drinking problems.

In Brazil, the government imposes minimum prices on various agricultural products such as wheat, coffee and oranges and regularly reviews those prices based on changes in farmers' cost of production. In this case, the purpose of the policy is to protect the income of farmers.

QUESTION PRACTICE

This question is adapted from the specimen examination paper.

Draw a demand and supply diagram showing the effect of imposing a minimum price (price floor). [3]

SAMPLE STUDENT ANSWER

Response 1

▲ The candidate has illustrated the surplus. The curves and axes are correctly labelled.

▼ The diagram is not fully labelled—quantity demanded and quantity supplied after the price floor are not projected on the horizontal axis. The minimum price is not labelled on the vertical axis.

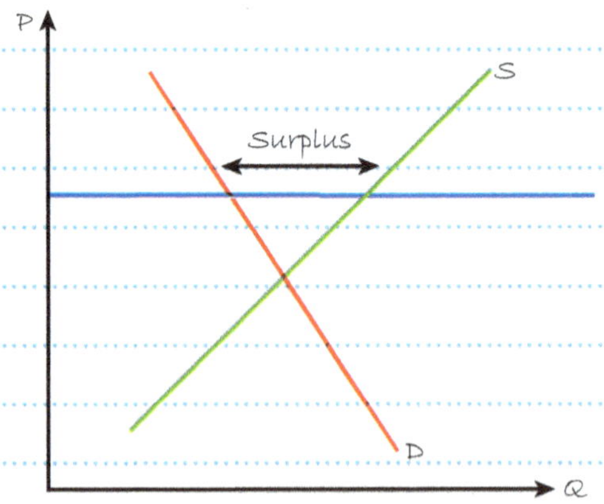

▼ This is a correct explanation but this question does not require an explanation, so this will not be assessed. Always pay attention to command terms—in this case, the command term was "draw".

The minimum price is set above equilibrium and leading to an increase in quantity supplied as producers will be willing to offer more at a higher price. On the other hand, consumers will buy less of the product as it is more expensive since there is an inverse relationship between price and quantity demanded. This results in a surplus or excess supply.

This response could have achieved 1/3 marks.

Response 2

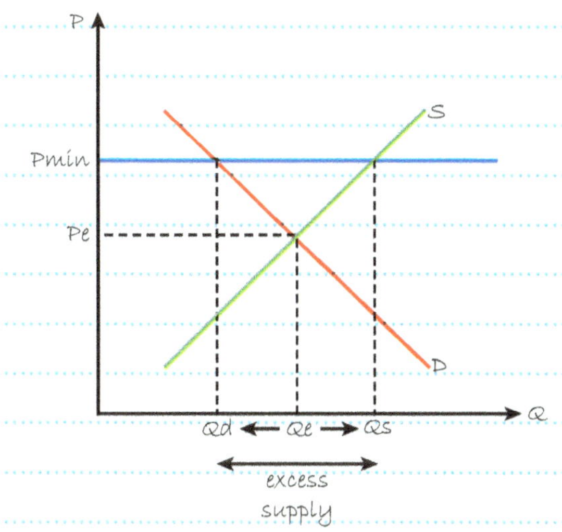

This response could have achieved 3/3 marks.

▲ This diagram is correctly and fully labelled. The impact on quantities and price as well as the resulting excess supply (surplus) are clearly indicated.

QUESTION PRACTICE

This question is adapted from the November 2018 examination paper.

The following diagram illustrates the market for cotton in the country of San Marcus.

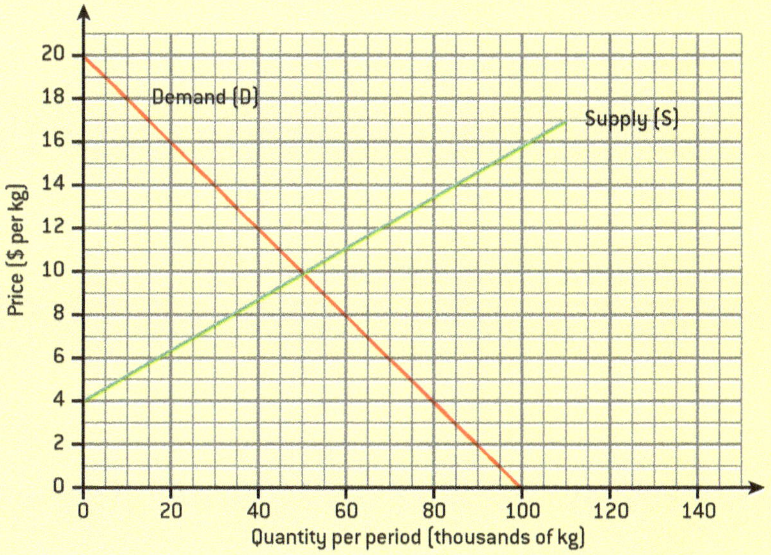

The government of San Marcus decides to provide a subsidy of $8 per kilogram of cotton to producers.

(i) Draw and label the new supply to illustrate the impact of the subsidy to domestic cotton producers. [2]

(ii) Calculate the cost to the government of San Marcus of providing this subsidy to domestic cotton producers. [2]

(iii) Calculate the change in the producer surplus resulting from the subsidy. [2]

▲ The new curve is correctly drawn and labelled. The government expenditure on the subsidy was shaded even though it is not requested in the question and was probably done by the candidate to identify the area to be calculated in (ii). There is no mark penalty for doing this.

▲ The answer is valid and workings are provided (subsidy amount multiplied by the new quantity). The candidate has not forgotten that the figures are expressed in thousands.

SAMPLE STUDENT ANSWER

i)

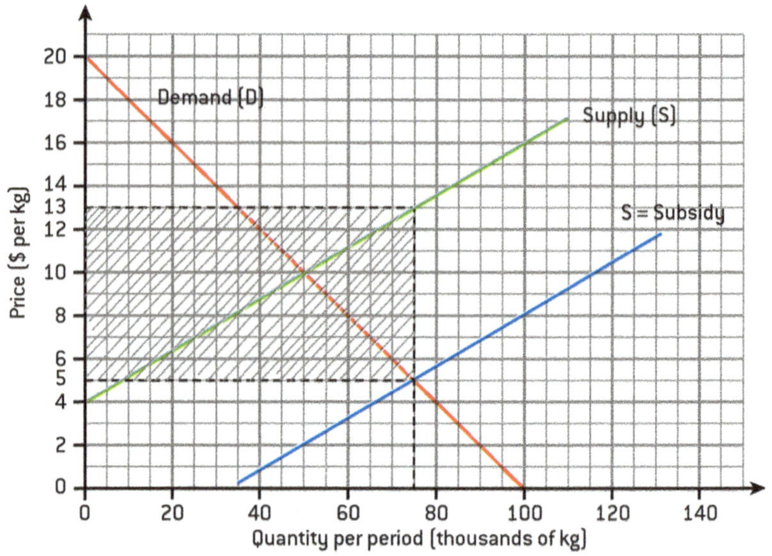

ii) 8 × 75 = $600 000

▲ The answer is correct, full workings are provided. Note that to calculate the producer surplus after the subsidy, the initial supply curve (S) is used and not the new curve (S + subsidy). The producer surplus is the difference between the price received ($5 from consumers and $8 from the government = $13) and **the lowest price producers were willing to receive** (which is reflected by the original supply curve).

SAMPLE STUDENT ANSWER

iii) initial producer surplus = 0.5 × 50 000 × (10 - 4)

= $150 000

new producer surplus = 0.5 × 75 000 × (13 - 4)

= $337 500

change in producer surplus = $337 500 - $150 000

= $187 500

This response could have achieved 6/6 marks.

Assessment tip

For calculation from a diagram (for example the government expenditure incurred in granting a subsidy), shading the relevant areas on the diagram can help minimize the risk of errors. There is no mark penalty for providing additional information on diagrams for paper 3, as long as the required information is clearly provided (that is, the new supply curve for this question).

Check that your calculation results are consistent with economic theory. For example, if you are asked to calculate the change in producer surplus after a subsidy, the theory states that the producer surplus will increase, hence your calculation should give you a positive value. If it does not, then your calculation is incorrect.

2.8 MARKET FAILURE—EXTERNALITIES AND COMMON POOL RESOURCES

This sub-unit examines two types of market failure—externalities and common pool (common access) resources—and the corresponding government responses.

You should be able to:

- ✔ define the terms
  - ✔ market failure
  - ✔ merit goods
  - ✔ externalities
  - ✔ demerit goods
  - ✔ common pool (common access) resources
- ✔ explain the concepts of marginal private benefits (MPB), marginal social benefits (MSB), marginal private costs (MPC) and marginal social costs (MSC).
- ✔ explain, using diagrams, the concept of market failure as a failure of the market to achieve allocative efficiency where MSB equals MSC, resulting in a welfare loss (social (community) surplus is not maximized)
- ✔ explain, using diagrams, the concepts of negative and positive externalities of production and consumption, and the welfare loss associated
- ✔ explain the concept of common pool (common access) resources with reference to the "tragedy of the commons"
- ✔ evaluate, using diagrams and real-world examples, the use of government policies, including taxes (indirect taxes and carbon taxes), subsidies, regulation and legislation, and education (awareness creation) to correct externalities and manage common pool resources
- ✔ evaluate, with the aid of real-world examples, the recourse to tradable permits, international agreements, collective self-governance and government provision to correct externalities and manage common pool resources
- ✔ discuss, using real-world examples, the strength and limitation of international cooperation in fighting threats to sustainability.

HL In addition to the points above, you should be able to:

- calculate the welfare loss associated with externalities from a diagram.

Content link

Link to other sub-units

Refer to sub-unit 2.7 for the consequences of government policies, including indirect taxes and subsidies, (command and control) regulation and legislation, and the direct provision of services for markets and stakeholders.

Summary

In sub-unit 2.3 you learned that competitive markets are **allocatively efficient** as they achieve the best allocation of resources for society (where MB = MC, social (community) surplus is maximized). **Market failure** refers to cases where markets fail to achieve allocative efficiency at equilibrium, leading to either too much or not enough of the good produced and consumed. When this happens, resources are misallocated and social (community) surplus is not maximized.

Externalities are a case of market failure. An externality arises when the production or consumption of a good imposes costs or creates benefits to a **third party** (one who is neither a consumer nor a producer) for which the latter does not get compensated or does not pay for, respectively. As third parties can be positively or negatively affected by the consumption or production of a good or service, there are four types of externalities to consider—negative and positive externalities from consumption, negative and positive externalities from production.

In the market for a good, consumers and producers only consider their own benefits and costs respectively, ignoring any external benefit and/or external cost (those to the third party) that are generated from the consumption or production of the good. The demand curve and supply curve thus only reflect the **marginal private benefit** of consuming a good **(MPB)** and **marginal private cost** of producing a good **(MPC)** respectively (which we simply refer to as MB and MC in the absence of market failure). When externalities are incurred, we can no longer use the criteria MPB = MPC (MB = MC) for allocative efficiency as we need to account for welfare of third parties affected by the market transaction. We therefore consider the **marginal social benefit (MSB)** and **marginal social cost (MSC)**. **MSB** is the extra benefit or utility to society of consuming an additional unit of output, including both the private benefit and the external benefit. **MSC** is the extra cost to society of producing an additional unit of output, including both the private cost and the external costs. The condition for allocative efficiency is thus MSB = MSC.

Only private costs and benefits are considered in a market transaction, so the equilibrium quantity takes place where MPB = MPC. However, the presence of externalities implies a divergence between either MPB and MSB or MPC and MSC. As such, at the market equilibrium, we have either MSB > MSC (positive externalities) or MSC > MSB (negative externalities). Where MSB > MSC, additional production and consumption generate more benefits than costs for society—there is thus an under-allocation of resources since social (community) welfare increases with additional resources allocated to the production of the good. On the other hand, MSC > MSB implies over-allocation of resources since resources were allocated beyond MSC = MSB where allocative efficiency occurs. The under-allocation or over-allocation of resources imply a welfare loss as social (community) surplus is not maximized. It follows that in the absence of externalities, MSB = MPB (or just MB) and MSC = MPC (or just MC), the market equilibrium is then allocatively efficient and so there is no welfare loss.

<table>
<tr><th>Type of externality</th><th>Diagram</th></tr>
<tr><td>

Positive externality from consumption

- For example, the consumption of vaccination generates external benefits for third parties who face a lower probability of falling sick.
- Due to the presence of external benefits from consumption, MSB > MPB. Assuming no externality from production, MSC = MPC.
- At the market equilibrium (Qe), MSB > MSC and thus there is **underconsumption** (QeQs) and a welfare loss (shaded area).

</td><td>

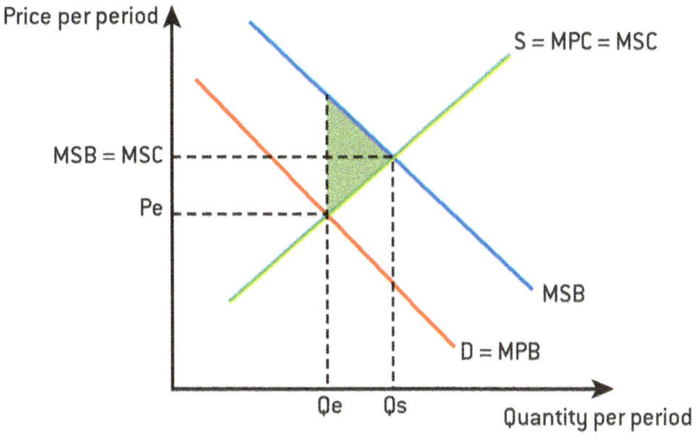

</td></tr>
<tr><td>

Negative externality from consumption

- For example, the consumption of cigarettes leads to external costs on third parties who inhale second-hand smoke.
- Due to the presence of external costs from consumption, MSB < MPB*. Assuming no externality from production, MSC = MPC.
- At the market equilibrium (Qe), MSC > MSB and thus there is **overconsumption** (QsQe) and a welfare loss (shaded area).

</td><td>

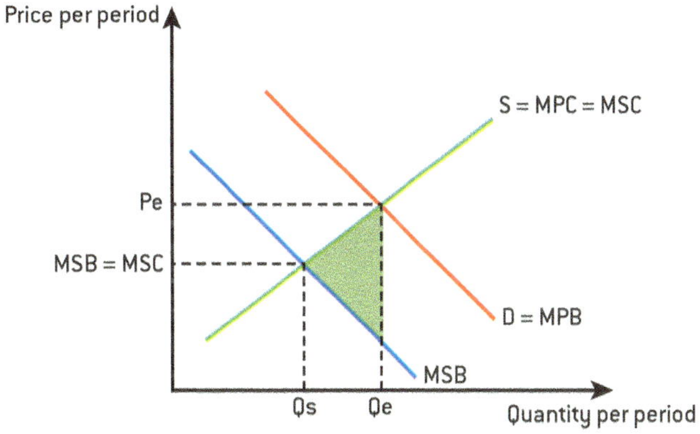

</td></tr>
<tr><th>Type of externality</th><th>Diagram</th></tr>
<tr><td>

Positive externality from production

- For instance, a beekeeper's production of honey may benefit a nearby farmer (a third party) who gains a higher crop yield when bees pollinate plants bearing fruits.
- Due to the presence of external benefits from production, MSC < MPC*. Assuming no externality from consumption, MSB = MPB.
- At the market equilibrium (Qe), MSB > MSC and thus there is **underproduction** (QeQs) and a welfare loss (shaded area).

</td><td>

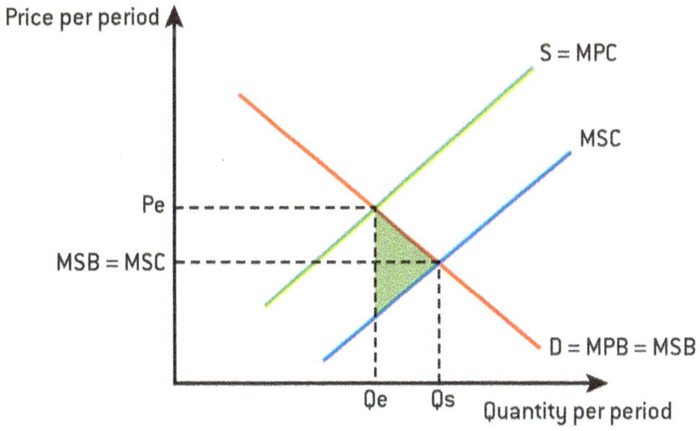

</td></tr>
<tr><td>

Negative externality from production

- Power-plants generate external costs associated with burning fossil fuels. The production of electricity generates external costs in the form of greenhouse gases, which contribute to environmental degradation.
- Due to the presence of external costs from production, MSC > MPC. Assuming no externality from consumption, MSB = MPB.
- At the market equilibrium (Qe), MSC > MSB and thus there is **overproduction** (QsQe) and a welfare loss (shaded area).

</td><td>

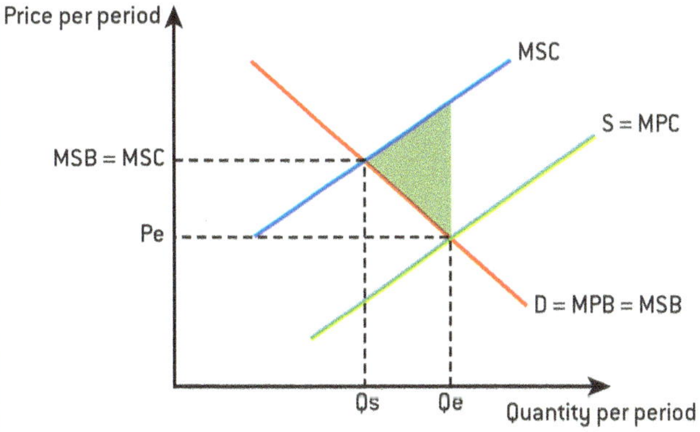

</td></tr>
</table>

* External costs from consumption are not reflected on the cost curves (MPC, MSC) because they are generated from the consumption of the good and hence are independent of the production process. They are reflected as "negative benefits"—society benefits less than consumers. Similarly, positive externalities from production are reflected on the costs curves.

Revision tip

This sub-unit introduces you to four different externalities diagrams. Candidates often confuse the costs and benefits curves, the market equilibrium and social optimum outcome and/or the area corresponding to the welfare loss.

Consider this step-by-step approach in learning and drawing your diagrams.

- Always start by drawing a demand and supply diagram. Add the MPB and MPC labels and project the market equilibrium along the axes (Pe, Qe).
- Identify the origin of the externality; does it arise from consumption or production?
  - If it is from production then D = MPB = MSB assuming no externality from consumption.
  - If it is from consumption then S = MPC = MSC assuming no externality from production.
- Are you illustrating a positive or negative externality? This will determine the position of the MSB (for externalities from consumption) or MSC (for externalities from production).
- Project the social optimum level of output on the horizontal axis (where MSC = MSB).
- Shade the welfare loss.
  - If it is a negative externality, it must be a triangle showing MSC > MSB.
  - If it is a positive externality, it must be a triangle showing MSB > MSC.

As the market fails to achieve allocative efficiency when externalities are generated, the social optimum can only be reached if the government: intervenes to limit consumption or production of goods generating negative externalities; or encourages consumption or production for goods generating positive externalities. The authorities do not intervene in all markets where externalities are incurred. For example, the production of honey does not generate sufficient external benefits to justify subsidies.

Governments intervene in the markets for merit and demerit goods. **Merit goods** are goods or services that generate *significant* positive externalities (e.g. education) and are thus *deemed socially desirable*. **Demerit goods** are goods or services that generate *significant* negative externalities (e.g. tobacco) and are *deemed socially undesirable.*

The overuse of **common pool (common access) resources** is another case of market failure which calls for government intervention. Common pool resources not owned by anyone and are usually available for use without payment. They include fisheries (areas where fish are caught), forests and lakes.

They are resources with these characteristics.

- **Non-excludable**—it is difficult to prevent access to the resources. For instance, fisheries are non-excludable, because it is difficult to prevent people from catching fish.
- **Rival**—the use of the resources by one person diminishes the quantity or quality of the resource available to other people. Using the example of fisheries: the same fish cannot be caught more than once.

As they are non-excludable and subtractable, common pool resources are usually overused, a problem known as the "tragedy of the commons"—a situation in which individuals use the resources for their own short-term gains without considering the long-term costs. As fisheries are common pool resources, overfishing may result when fishermen catch fish faster than the fish can reproduce, leaving fewer fish available for other fishermen to catch. Overfishing damages ecosystems and may lead to the extinction of varieties of fish. The overuse of common pool resources therefore poses a **threat to sustainability**.

A negative externalities diagram may be used to explain the overuse of common access resources where MSC is greater and steeper than MPC. This will show that the external costs increase with production as the common pool resource is depleted.

Here are the common policy responses to the under-provision of merit goods, over-provision of demerit goods and over-use of common access resources.

- **Indirect (Pigouvian) taxes** (e.g. taxes on tobacco products) will result in a leftward shift of the supply curve and thus an increase in the price of a demerit good. If the tax is exactly equal to the external cost, then the market will reach an equilibrium at the social optimum quantity (MSB = MSC). In such a case, the market has "internalized the externality".

- **Carbon taxes** are taxes levied on businesses that burn carbon-based fossil fuels (e.g. coal, oil, natural gas). Carbon taxes are proportionate to the amount of carbon dioxide emitted during production.
- **Subsidies** on merit goods (e.g. education and healthcare services) lead to rightward shift of the supply curve and thus a decrease in price. To reach the social optimum outcome, the subsidy must be equal to the external benefit.
- **Government provision** (e.g. through state schools and national health services) ensure that merit goods are available to all.
- **Legislation and regulation** may be used to make consumption of merit goods compulsory (most countries have mandatory primary school education) and reduce or eliminate the production and/or consumption of demerit goods (examples are restriction on smoking in restaurants and prohibited sale of weapons and intoxicating drugs). Legislation is especially effective in addressing the overuse of common pool resources where imposing a tax is not feasible (since the resources are not traded). For instance, some countries only allow fishing and/or hunting of wildlife during an "open season" so that the fish and wildlife have sufficient time to be replenished.
- **Increasing awareness** through education campaigns involves providing more information to alter consumers' preferences. For instance, recycling and energy efficiency campaigns address the clearing of forests and excessive burning of fossil fuels.
- **Tradable permits** (also known as cap and trade schemes) may be issued to firms, allowing them to emit a specific amount of greenhouse gas. Firms who reduce the greenhouse gas emissions may sell their permits.
- **International agreements** may be required due to the global nature of threats to sustainability. For instance, governments must agree on regulation of fishing in international waters where no single government has authority. The most significant global climate agreement to date is the Paris Agreement, signed by nearly every nation in 2015. By signing the agreement, countries committed to cut their greenhouse gas emissions. The agreement builds on multiple past climate agreements, such as the Kyoto protocol, which were not ratified by the biggest emitters of greenhouse gases—one of which, the USA, briefly withdrew from the Paris agreement in 2020. International agreements require a consensus by governments (who often have different priorities and perspectives on what causes a threat to sustainability) and are therefore difficult to reach.
- **Collective self-governance** is an alternative to intervention by the government where the ownership and regulation of common pool resources is passed on to a group of individuals.

QUESTION PRACTICE

This question is adapted from the November 2021 examination paper.

Using an externalities diagram, explain how coal-fired power plants in the USA might be causing market failure. [4]

SAMPLE STUDENT ANSWER

Response 1

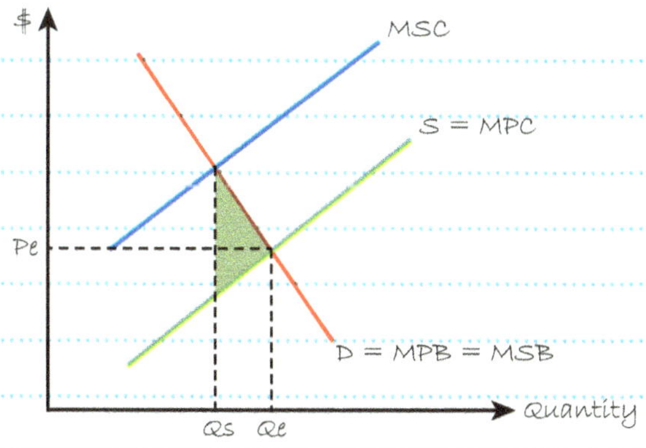

▼ While the diagram clearly illustrates a negative externality from production (MSC > MPC), there are two errors. The label for the vertical axis, "$" is not acceptable—it should be "Price"—and the welfare loss is incorrectly shaded: it is not the area where MSC > MSB. There are too many errors on the diagram for it to be awarded any marks.

▲ The candidate correctly identifies negative externalities from production as the cause of market failure. The external cost is identified (global warming).

▼ Unfortunately, this is only a partial response. The candidate does not make reference to the misallocation of resources or the fact that MSC > MSB, which are needed to explain the concept of market failure (the requirement of the question). There is also no reference to the diagram.

Coal-fired power plants generate negative externalities in the production of electricity. The impact of the burning of fossil fuels leads to global warming, which impacts society and future generations and this causes a threat to sustainability.

This response could have achieved 1/4 marks.

Response 2

▲ The diagram is fully and correctly labelled. The welfare loss is also correctly identified.

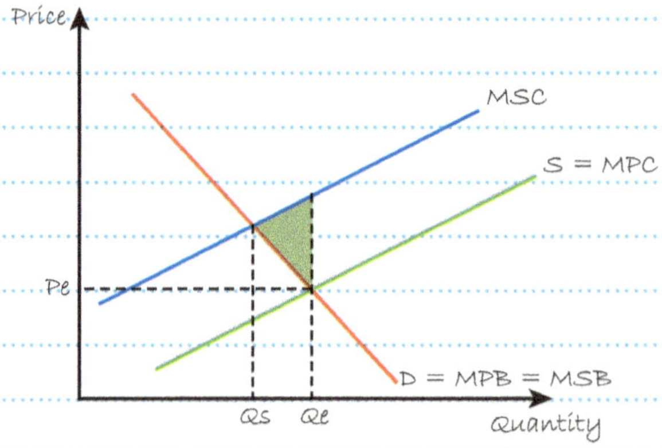

▲ The cause of market failure as a negative externality from production is identified and the misallocation of resources is established. The candidate also specifies that MSC > MSB at the market equilibrium.

The coal-fired power plants are partly responsible for global warming. They burn fossil fuels in producing electricity and emit greenhouse gases in the process. They clearly generate negative externalities in producing electricity. As shown on the diagram, MSC exceeds MPC and this leads to a market equilibrium Qe where MSC > MSB. As such the free market has led to the over-allocation of scarce resources to the production of electricity.

This response could have achieved 4/4 marks.

QUESTION PRACTICE

This question is adapted from the specimen examination paper.

i) Define the term *welfare loss*. [2]

ii) Using the information from the following diagram, calculate the welfare loss resulting from the over-consumption of sugary drinks in New Zealand. [2]

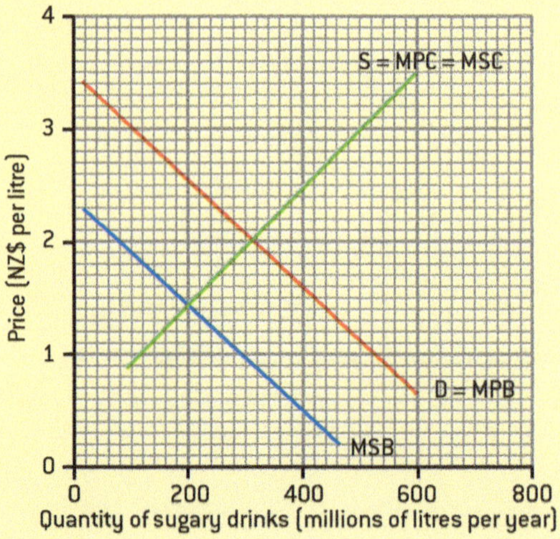

SAMPLE STUDENT ANSWER

i) Welfare loss is the value lost by society from the consumption or production of a good or service does not take place at the socially optimal level of output Qs, which is determined where MSC = MSB.

▲ This is a good definition. It refers to the "social optimal level of output" and "MSB = MSC". It could be awarded 2 marks.

ii) 60 million litres are consumed in excess therefore the welfare loss is 0.5 x 60 million x 1.2 = NZ$ 36 million

▼ The candidate has misinterpreted the diagram. The over-consumption is 120 million not 60 million. The final answer would not be given a mark but the workings are correct, so 1 mark can be awarded.

This response could have achieved 3/4 marks.

Content link

Link to your IA

Externalities are a popular topic for internal assessment. An article with sufficient scope for a commentary is likely to be one that describes a policy to address the associated market failure. You should comment on the effectiveness of the policy in the context set in the article—do not just provide theoretical strengths and limitations of policies. Read the article carefully to identify information that may help you contextualize your evaluation of policies as well as your diagrams. For example, if the article gives an idea of the magnitude of the external cost, illustrate this in your diagram with an adequate gap between the two curves (MSB and MPB or MSC and MPC). Or, if the article suggests that consumers are not responding to a tax, draw a steep demand curve to reflect the low price elasticity of demand.

Concept link

- **Sustainability**—negative externalities associated with polluting activities and the depletion of common access resources represent a threat to sustainability. An article that establishes how action by the present generation may compromise future generations' ability to meet their own needs would be a good link to this key concept.
- **Interdependence**—there is interaction between economic agents (individuals, governments and nations). Market failure shows that individuals are interdependent since their economic choices may impact third parties. The management of common pool resources requires international cooperation since the cost of depletion is shared by all nations (which is another form of interdependence). Yet, such agreements are often hard to reach due to a lack of consensus, which shows that government actions may impact international efforts.

2.9 MARKET FAILURE—PUBLIC GOODS

This sub-unit introduces government responses to the lack of public goods.

You should be able to:

- ✔ define the term
  - ✔ public goods
- ✔ explain, with reference to the free rider problem, how the lack of public goods constitutes a case of market failure
- ✔ discuss, using real-world examples, the implications of government policy responses to the lack of public goods.

Summary

Unlike common pool resources, which are non-excludable but rival, **public goods** (e.g. national defence, streetlights) have the following characteristics.

- **Non-excludable**—once the good is provided, it becomes available to all. For instance, no one can be excluded from enjoying the security that comes with the defence provided by the military. National defence is thus non-excludable.
- **Non-rival**—the consumption by one individual does not decrease the quantity of the good available to others. Going back to the example of national defence, one resident benefiting from the work of the armed forces in preventing foreign attacks does not affect the provision of national defence for the rest of the population.

> **Content link**
> **Link to other sub-units**
> Refer to sub-unit 4.10 on the strengths and limitations of government intervention in contrast to market-oriented approaches to achieve economic growth and economic development.
> Public goods (e.g. sewage systems, roads, national defence) may be necessary for economic activity, so they may lead to economic development.

If individuals cannot be excluded from enjoying a good, they have no incentive to pay for it, allowing them to behave as "free riders". Due to the **free rider problem**, private firms (who usually aim to make the highest possible profits) will not be willing to produce public goods. This represents a case of market failure: the free market will not allocate resources to the production of public goods.

Direct provision is the most common form of intervention to address the lack of public goods. The provision of public goods may increase the government debt if this provision is financed by higher taxes or increased borrowing. As government enterprises tend to be inefficient due to the lack of profit incentives, the authorities may contract out the provision of public goods to the private sector. For instance, military equipment and streetlights are seldom produced by state-owned enterprises and instead the relevant government agencies purchase them from private firms.

> **Revision tip**
> Do not confuse the economic term "public good" with the English word "public" which implies provided by the state, government or authorities. A lot of goods and services preceded by the word "public" are neither non-excludable nor non-rival, so they do not qualify as public goods. Consider *public* schools, *public* swimming pools and *public* libraries. In all three cases, the service provided is rival—an additional student in a classroom implies one place less for others, overcrowding of swimming pools diminishes the enjoyment of other swimmers and a book borrowed needs to be returned before another person can read it. These are also excludable services because entry can be charged for swimming pools, a membership card is required to enjoy a library's full facilities and students need to be registered with a school.

> **QUESTION PRACTICE**
> This question is adapted from the May 2006 examination paper.
> Distinguish between the market failures associated with merit goods and public goods. [10]

SAMPLE STUDENT ANSWER

Merit goods and public goods are sources of market failure, which is the failure of the free market to allocate scarce resources to achieve the highest possible social surplus. That is the failure of the market to achieve a level of consumption and production where marginal social benefits (MSB) is equal to marginal social costs (MSC). The fundamental difference between these two types of market failure is that the market allocates no resources to the production of public goods while market forces allocate insufficient resources to the production of merit goods.

A merit good is one which generates significantly positive externalities and is deemed to be socially desirable. For example, education is under-consumed because consumers do not understand the full benefits of education or they ignore the external benefits borne on third parties. Given that lessons on hygiene and sanitation are taught in most primary schools, students will observe good hygiene and reduce the spread of diseases—this clearly benefits third parties. As such, the MSB is higher than the MPB (which is also the demand curve) and the market equilibrium is where D = S or MPB = MPC, which is less than the allocatively efficient outcome MSB = MSC. Hence the market fails to achieve allocative efficiency by reaching Qe. The underconsumption of education QsQe reflects that resources are under-allocated in this market and that a welfare loss is created.

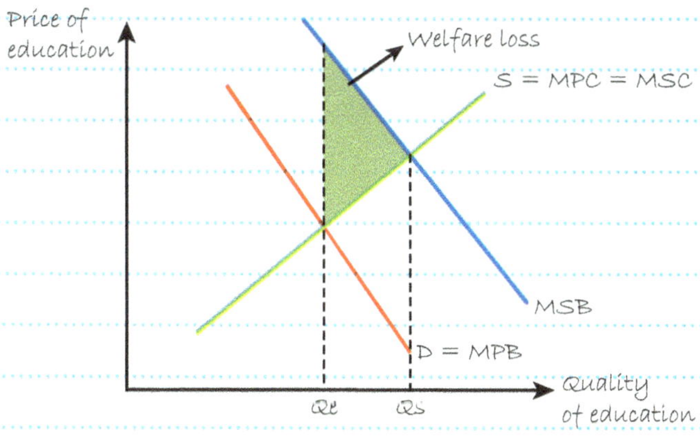

▲ This is an effective introduction. It defines the key concept of market failure and establishes the main difference between merit goods and public goods in terms of resource allocation. As the command term of this question is "distinguish", which requires candidates to *make clear the differences between two or more concepts*, this introduction shows the candidate is addressing the specific demand of the question.

▲ This paragraph clearly explains the concept of a merit good. A fully and correctly labelled diagram is used to explain the resource misallocation. A generic example is provided. While it is not a requirement for 10-mark essay questions, generic and hypothetical examples can help illustrate arguments.

▲ The candidate continues to explain relevant economic theory. This paragraph explains why public goods are a source of market failure.

Public goods are goods that are non-excludable – if the good becomes available to even one consumer, then the good is automatically available for all. An example is streetlights. Public goods are also non-rival – each individual consumption of the good does not decrease the amount available for other users. Using the same example of the streetlights, if an individual can benefit from the light provided by the streetlight so will anyone else nearby. The fact that one person can enjoy the light does not take away the benefit any other individual has. Public goods are a case of market failure as they are goods and services that are not supplied by the market due to the free-rider problem – consumers will not be willing to pay for them since they can enjoy access without paying. Firms have no incentive to produce them as they will not be able to make profits. The market will allocate no resource to their production. There is no diagram to illustrate public goods since producers are not willing to supply them and consumers are not willing to pay for them – so there is neither demand curve nor supply curve.

As such, both merit goods and public goods are cases of market failure. However, they differ from the reasons for their under/lack of provision. For merit goods it is due to consumers ignoring or not understanding the full benefits to the rest of society, whereas for public goods it is the self-interest of individuals who are not willing to pay for them. In terms of resource allocation, they also differ as no resource is allocated to public goods, but insufficient resources are allocated to merit goods.

▲ This paragraph summarizes the main point, making it clear that the candidate has distinguished between the two concepts and so has addressed the question.

This **response meets** all of the descriptors for the highest mark band (9–10) and **could have achieved 10/10 marks.**

2.10 MARKET FAILURE—ASYMMETRIC INFORMATION

You should be able to:

- ✔ define the terms
  - ✔ asymmetric information
  - ✔ moral hazard
  - ✔ adverse selection
- ✔ explain, with reference to the concepts of adverse selection and/or moral hazard, how asymmetric information is a cause of market failure
- ✔ evaluate, using real-world examples, the effectiveness of government policies and private responses to address asymmetric information.

HL This sub-unit examines the problems of adverse selection and moral hazard, which result from asymmetric information.

Summary

HL **Asymmetric information** occurs in an economic transaction when one party (e.g. a producer or consumer) has more or better information than the other party. In such situations, the buyers or sellers make uninformed decisions and the market equilibrium may not lead to an optimum allocation of resources, resulting in market failure. Asymmetric information can lead to two distinct problems: adverse selection and moral hazard.

Adverse selection occurs when the buyer and seller do not have the same information, causing a transaction to take place based on uneven terms.

This might occur in the following situations.

- The buyer has more or better information than the seller. For example, in the market for health insurance, buyers may not disclose their full health history to health insurance companies.
- The seller has more or better information than the buyer. This is common in the second-hand car market where sellers may not disclose all known information about the condition of cars.

Moral hazard occurs when a party changes behaviour after an economic exchange. For instance, some insurance purchasers may drive more recklessly after insuring their car, knowing they will not bear the cost of the damage caused.

The common **government responses** to asymmetric information are as follows.

- **Regulation and legislation** is established to ensure quality standards and quality features that must be maintained by sellers. For instance, businesses may be obligated to repair, replace or provide a refund for a defective good. This forces them to ensure that their products are defect-free.
- **Provision of information to consumers**—governments may provide information or force businesses to provide certain information. For example, in the UK, food businesses are given a food hygiene rating from 5 to 0 by the food standard agency for aspects such as handling of food and cleanliness of facilities. It is a legal requirement for food businesses in Wales and Northern Ireland to display the rating at their premises and online so that consumers can make more informed choices about the businesses they buy from.

The **private responses** to asymmetric information include the following.

- **Signalling** takes place when the party with more information (usually the seller) convinces the buyer that the product being sold is of good quality through methods such as extended warranties.
- **Screening** is done by the party with limited information and consists in inferring additional information from other observable characteristics. For instance, health insurance companies may require a medical check-up or to be granted access to past medical records before quoting the cost of a policy to potential buyers and/or approving an application for health insurance.

Test yourself

Read the following passage and consider the questions that follow.

> Since October 2013, a Chinese law has given car buyers a right to free repair of faults or replacement of defective vehicles. Customers have the right to a full refund or replacement vehicle if serious safety issues, such as problems with steering or brakes, are not resolved after two repairs within a two-year, 50,000 km (30,000 miles) warranty period. Before the law was introduced, car dealers and automakers in China were under no obligation to buy back or replace cars with such defects.

Does the law described in the passage address asymmetric information? Does it help reduce the problem of adverse selection? Most countries have laws protecting consumers from retailers who sell defective goods or misrepresented services. Such laws help reduce the problem of adverse selection. Find out more about the laws in your countries that protect consumers. Those could be good real-world examples.

QUESTION PRACTICE

This question is adapted from the specimen examination paper.

Explain two ways a government might respond to the existence of asymmetric information in a market. [10]

SAMPLE STUDENT ANSWER

Asymmetric information is a situation where, in a market, sellers and buyers do not have equal access to information. As such, either the buyers or the sellers make uniformed decisions, and the market equilibrium may not lead to maximum community welfare. Adverse selection and moral hazard are the two problems that asymmetric information can lead to.

▲ This is a good introduction to the essay. The candidate explains the key concept in the question, asymmetric information, and introduces the issues of adverse selection and moral hazard.

Adverse selection takes place when one party in the transaction has more information than the other party (either the seller has more information than the buyer or the opposite). In the pharmaceutical industry, pharmaceutical companies have more information about the risks involved with the consumption of drugs than the consumers who may not have the medical knowledge to understand the side effects of drugs. While the pharmaceutical companies will definitely make profits from the sale of these drugs (especially if more consumers buy drugs not knowing the full risks), consumers may be seriously affected—if not die. To remedy to this, the government can force firms to provide consumers with more information about new drugs. The government may also make it compulsory for pharmaceutical companies to disclose all possible side effects and this may even have to be mentioned during television advertisements for the drug.

In some countries, the authorities have volunteer schemes for those who wish to help elderlies with their daily tasks, such as understanding the risks associated with their medications. This would ensure the consumers have more information about the product (the drug).

▲ This paragraph clearly shows how the provision of information may help address adverse selection. The use of a generic (theoretical) example helps illustrate the workings of the policy.

Moral hazard takes place when one party does not bear the full of costs of an economic decision and the other party has to bear those costs. The insurance market is one where consumers may not bear the full costs of their decisions. Buyers of car insurance have more information since the insurance companies do not know the buyers' intentions. The buyers may drive recklessly after obtaining car insurance because they think the insurance company will pay for car repairs in the event of an accident. The government may address the problem of adverse selection through regulation such as making co-payment for insurance claims mandatory. In many countries, the person making a claim must pay a certain portion of the repair. Legislation may also be in place to seriously punish reckless driving. These laws and rules force consumers to consider the full costs of their actions.

To address the issues of adverse selection and moral hazard, the government may make use of legislation or the provision of information.

▲ This is a good explanation of legislation and regulation as a form of intervention to address moral hazard. It is good that the first example considered a market where producers have more information than buyers and the second example involves buyers having more information. This demonstrates a full understanding of asymmetric information.

This response meets all of the descriptors for the highest mark band (9-10) and **could have achieved 10/10 marks.**

2.11 MARKET FAILURE—MARKET POWER

HL This sub-unit examines the behaviour of firms and the conditions that lead to firms having market power in their industries. Government responses to the abuse of market power are also discussed.

You should be able to:

- ✔ define the terms
  - ✔ market power
  - ✔ perfect competition
  - ✔ monopoly
  - ✔ oligopoly
  - ✔ monopolistic competition
  - ✔ barriers to entry
  - ✔ economies of scale
  - ✔ normal profits, abnormal profits and losses
- ✔ distinguish between the various levels of economic profits—normal profits, abnormal profits and losses
- ✔ explain that the goal of profit maximization is achieved when the difference between total revenue (TR) and total costs (TC) is maximized or where marginal revenue (MR) = marginal costs (MC)
- ✔ calculate profits, MC, MR, AC (actual costs), AR (actual revenue) from data
- ✔ explain that the condition for allocative efficiency is P = MC or MB = MC
- ✔ draw diagrams illustrating the output and pricing decisions of profit-maximizing firms in perfect competition, monopolistic competition, collusive oligopoly and monopoly
- ✔ explain, using diagrams, that a perfectly competitive firm is a price-taker
- ✔ explain, using diagrams, why, in the short run, a perfectly competitive firm may make abnormal profits or losses but will make normal profits in the long run
- ✔ explain, using a diagram, why a perfectly competitive market is allocatively efficient
- ✔ with reference to economies of scale, and using diagrams and real-world examples, explain the meaning of the term "natural monopoly"
- ✔ explain, using diagrams, why the profit-maximizing choices of a monopoly firm (and collusive oligopoly) lead to allocative inefficiency (welfare loss)
- ✔ using diagrams and real-world examples, compare and contrast a monopoly market with a perfectly competitive market, with reference to factors including efficiency, price and output, research and development (R&D) and economies of scale
- ✔ describe, using examples, types of non-price competition employed by oligopolistic and monopolistically competitive firms
- ✔ discuss the role of interdependence in the dilemma faced by oligopolistic firms—whether to compete or to collude
- ✔ explain how game theory can illustrate strategic interdependence and the options available to oligopolies
- ✔ explain how a concentration ratio may be used to identify an oligopoly
- ✔ explain, using diagrams, why, in the short run, a monopolistically competitive firm may make abnormal profits or losses but will make normal profits in the long run
- ✔ evaluate, using real-world examples, the desirability of large firms having significant market power
- ✔ evaluate, using real-world examples, policy responses to the abuse of significant market power.

Summary

HL In sub-unit 2.4, you learned that economic theory assumes that rational businesses are driven by self-interest and seek to **maximize profits**.

Economic profits, (typically denoted with the Greek letter π) are equal to the difference between the total revenue (TR) and the total costs (TC) incurred in production:

$$\pi = TR - TC$$

You already know from sub-unit 2.5 that TR is calculated as TR = P × Q. The concept of **economic costs** is a little tricky as economists distinguish between explicit and implicit costs.

- **Explicit costs** refer to payments made by firms for the factors of production they use or employ (e.g. wages paid to workers).
- **Implicit costs** refer to the value of firm-owned resources used in the production process that involves no accounting costs, since the firm does need to pay for them, but incur an opportunity cost. For example, if a firm owns a warehouse, the implicit cost is the rent that could have been earned if the warehouse was leased to another firm.

While accounting costs (those normally declared by businesses in financial reports) only include explicit costs, economic costs include both explicit and implicit costs.

Levels of economic profits		
Normal profits	$\pi = 0$ (TR = TC)	This does not imply that the entrepreneur does not get any money out of his or her investment or work. Keep in mind that economic costs include implicit costs such as the forgone rent on premises owned by the firm or entrepreneur and the salary the entrepreneur could have gained if employed by another firm. This makes it the minimum level of profits the entrepreneur requires to continue the business activity.
Abnormal profits	$\pi > 0$ (TR > TC)	In such a case, the total revenue exceeds both explicit and implicit costs. The entrepreneur's returns are higher than they would be in an alternative investment. The chance to make abnormal profits signals to other entrepreneurs that they should join the industry.
Losses	$\pi < 0$ (TR < TC)	This does not necessarily mean that the firm is making accounting losses—the total revenue may be enough to cover explicit costs but not implicit costs. In such a case, a rational entrepreneur would leave the industry and either join another industry or work as an employee of another firm.

Content link

Link to other sub-units

Refer to sub-unit 2.4. Firms may have goals other than profit maximization.

HL You learned in sub-unit 2 that marginal cost (MC) is the cost of producing one more unit of the good. Similarly, marginal revenue (MR) is the revenue from selling one more unit of the good. When MR > MC, the revenue gained from selling additional units of the good exceeds the cost of producing those additional units so profits increase since $\pi = TR - TC$. Firms increase their output until MR = MC when profits are maximized. **MR = MC is thus the profit-maximizing level of output**.

The average revenue (AR) is the revenue per unit sold. The average cost (AC) is the cost per unit of output produced.

Average revenue	$AR = \frac{TR}{Q} = \frac{P \times R}{Q} = P$	**Average cost**	$AC = \frac{TC}{Q}$
Marginal revenue	$MR = \frac{\Delta TR}{\Delta Q}$	**Marginal cost**	$MC = \frac{\Delta TC}{\Delta Q}$

A **firm** is a business that employs factors of production to produce a good or service while an **industry** is a group of firms producing the same or similar goods or services. For example, McDonald's is a firm in the fast-food industry, Nike is a firm in the sports shoe industry. Industries are classified according to the three main characteristics that determine the **market structure**. These are:

- the number of firms in the industry
- the type of product—the products offered can be differentiated or homogeneous (identical)
- how easily firms may enter the industry—the existence of **barriers to entry** such as **economies of scale** (unit-cost advantages that a business may experience from increasing its scale of operations), high start-up costs or technical knowhow may prevent the entry of new firms into an industry.

	Perfect competition	**Monopoly**	**Monopolistic competition**	**Oligopoly**
Number of firms	very many	one	very many	a few
Type of product	homogenous	unique	slightly differentiated	homogenous or differentiated
Entry conditions	no barriers to entry, perfect information and perfect mobility of factors of production	high barriers to entry	low barriers to entry	significant barriers to entry

HL Firms in perfect competition have no **market power**, which refers to the ability of a firm (or *group of firms* in the case of collusive oligopolies) to raise and maintain price above the level that would prevail under perfect competition. The lower the level of competition in the industry, the greater the market power enjoyed by firms. The existence of market power leads to market failure as the market does not achieve allocative efficiency—the ability of firms to charge higher prices means that part of the consumer surplus is absorbed by firms.

Perfect competition

HL

- Firms in perfect competition are small with no market power. They can only accept the market price (Pm on Figure 2.11.1). As they sell a homogeneous product, charging a price above Pm would result in consumers switching to another of the many firms selling the exact same product. They also have no incentive to lower the price as they can sell their entire output at the market price. Perfectly competitive firms are **price-takers**.
- Since the firms must accept the price, Pm, they face a perfectly price elastic demand curve (note that d is the *demand curve faced by the firm*, it is not the *market demand curve*, D).
- Since the additional revenue earned is always the market price, Pm, it follows that d = AR = MR.
- Assuming a firm seeks to maximize profits, it will produce where MC = MR, at Qi. The sum of all firms' output across the industry adds up to Qm.
- Some of the assumptions are unrealistic, so perfect competition does not exist in its pure form. The closest examples are firms selling agricultural products (e.g. fruit and vegetable stalls).

Content link

Link to other sub-units

Refer to sub-unit 2.2 on supply.

- The shape of the MC curve is explained by the law of diminishing marginal returns
- The MC curve is also the firm's supply curve.

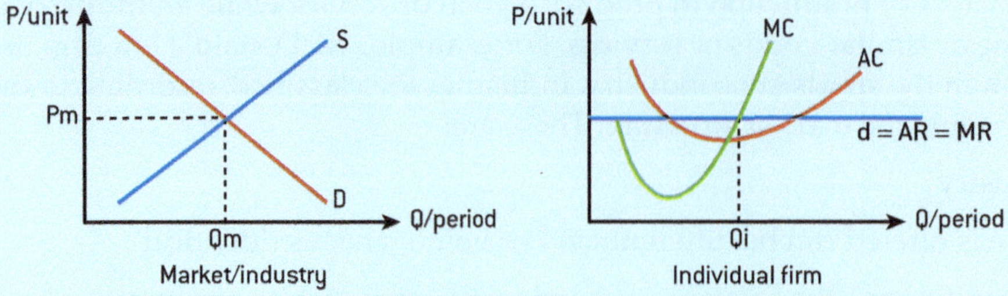

▲ **Figure 2.11.1** A perfectly competitive firm making abnormal profits (short-run equilibrium)

HL The following points explain how firms go from short-run equilibrium to long-run equilibrium in perfect competition.

- A perfectly competitive firm may only enjoy abnormal profits (as shown on Figure 2.11.1) in the short run. Abnormal profits create incentives for new firms to join the industry. As there are no entry barriers, new firms are entering the market, increasing the market supply (S shifts right).
- This puts a downward pressure on the market price, Pm, and abnormal profits are competed away.
- When profits earned are normal there is no longer incentive for any other firm to enter the market.
- Similarly, if perfectly competitive firms are making losses in the short run, this will be an incentive for them to leave the industry. The market supply will decrease, leading to a rise in price. Firms will stop leaving the industry when normal profits are earned.
- Therefore, abnormal profits or losses are never sustained in the long run.

We saw in sub-unit 2.3 that a market is allocative efficient when MB = MC (MB is the market demand curve and MC is the market supply curve—and MB = MC at Qm on Figure 2.11.1). At the firm level, allocative efficiency takes place where P = MC. The price, P, reflects the consumer's willingness to pay for a good based on the derived utility or satisfaction. MC is the producer's value of additional output based on the cost of the additional inputs required. When P > MC, additional units of the good are worth more to consumers than producers. There is under-allocation of resources and production should increase until allocative efficiency is achieved, at P = MC.

Monopoly

HL

- Since there is only one firm in the market, the monopoly firm faces the full (downward sloping) market demand curve (see Figure 2.11.2). The monopoly firm is a price-setter (price-maker) as it can set any price.
- The market power enjoyed by monopoly firms is also referred to as monopoly power.
- Assuming the monopoly firm is a profit-maximizer, it will produce quantity Qm where MC = MR. The firm enjoys abnormal profits equal to:

  (AR – AC) × Q [(Pm – c) × Q]

- As there are strong entry barriers, the monopoly firm (unlike the perfectly competitive firm) will maintain the abnormal profits in the long run.
- For the last unit the monopoly produces Qm, P > MC, hence it is allocatively inefficient, there is a welfare loss (shaded area). Qs is the socially optimum output where social (community) surplus is maximized.

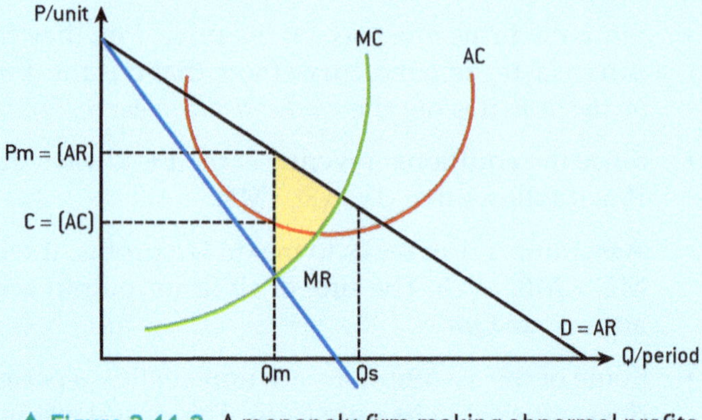

▲ **Figure 2.11.2** A monopoly firm making abnormal profits (short-run and long-run equilibrium)

We have seen that firms in perfect competition do not hold market power while a monopoly enjoys the highest possible market power. Comparing an industry dominated by a monopoly from one in a perfectly competitive market, the main disadvantages of a monopoly (and large firms in general) are as follows.

- There is allocative inefficiency (welfare loss). The loss of consumer surplus to the monopolist may be interpreted as consumer exploitation.
- Monopoly firms restrict output to raise price in order to maximize profits, resulting in higher prices and lower output levels, as compared to a perfectly competitive market (assuming they share the same cost structure—see the counter-argument on economies of scale below).
- Higher inequalities arise as income is transferred from consumers to producers through higher prices.
- There is lack of product variety for consumers.

There are, however, some benefits from a monopoly firm (and other large firms).

- Monopoly firms tend to be large firms, so they can achieve lower unit cost due to the economies of scale they enjoy. Even if monopoly firms restrict output to enjoy higher profits, consumers may still enjoy lower prices than they would in a perfectly competitive market if the cost-saving advantages due to economies of scale are significant.
- Monopolies make abnormal profits, which allows them to invest in research and development (R&D). However, due to the lack of competition, monopolies may not have the incentive to invest in product innovation (oligopolies, in contrast, would feel the need to innovate as part of their non-price competition strategies).
- A **natural monopoly** may emerge if the market is so small that it makes it difficult for two or more firms to be profitable. This is often the case for water and electricity distribution services. A firm in such an industry typically faces very high running costs, such as the cost of maintaining extensive wire and pipe networks from production facilities to each home. It is often impossible for two firms to split the market and remain profitable.

Oligopoly

HL An oligopoly market is dominated by a few large firms. The significant barriers to entry prevent other firms from entering the market. Such barriers to entry include financial start-up costs (e.g. the purchase of planes for airlines, the initial investment for R&D and global distribution network for smartphone producers).

Concentration ratios are used to provide an indication of the extent of competition and so the market power in an industry. For example, CR3 indicates the collective market share held by the three largest firms in the market.

$$\frac{\text{Sales of largest 3 firms in the market}}{\text{Total market sales}} \times 100$$

Since there are only a few firms in the market, each firm must take the potential reaction of its rival(s) in making its own decisions. As such, oligopoly firms are said to be interdependent.

Oligopoly firms are affected by the decisions of their rivals, so they face the **dilemma of whether to collude or compete**.

- Oligopolies may collude to reduce uncertainties and maximize joint profits (in which case they act together as a monopoly and the monopoly diagram on Figure 2.11.2 may be used to illustrate the market). They usually do so by agreeing on price. Collusive agreements are hard to maintain over time as firms face the incentive to cheat on the agreement. Formal collusion is illegal in most countries so oligopolies may resort to tacit collusion (informal agreements).
- Oligopolies may compete to capture a portion of their rivals' market shares and profits. Price competition can lead to a price war, resulting in lower profits for all firms in the oligopoly market. Since this practice is harmful, collusive oligopolies usually adopt **non-price competition** including:
  - heavy advertising
  - branding
  - innovation—developing new products
  - offering volume discounts
  - providing customers with after-sale service
  - offering extended guarantees
  - continuous product differentiation.

Figure 2.11.3 is a "game theory" matrix that illustrates the interdependence of oligopolies and the dilemma of whether to compete or collude. Assume the oligopoly market is made up on two firms, A and B. Each firm may adopt one of two possible strategies. The firm can keep its current price or attempt to compete for market share by reducing price to attract consumers. If the firms are not allowed to communicate (collusion is illegal), there is an incentive to compete and reduce the price since each firm's outcome depends on the decision of the other firm. If firm A thinks that firm B is likely to maintain its current price, it pays off to cut price and enjoy a higher profit of $200 million. If on the other hand, firm A thinks firm B will also reduce its price, firm A will do so as well as the outcome of $50 million is higher. If both firms anticipate the action of their rivals, they will end up reducing their prices. This price war leads to lower profits for both firms. However, the best outcome for both firms is to collude as each get a profit of $150 million and a combined industry profit of $300 million.

Oligopolies face a downward sloping demand curve since they can lower the price of their goods and lose some but not all customers. As such, they will always produce at a point where P > MC and are thus allocatively inefficient.

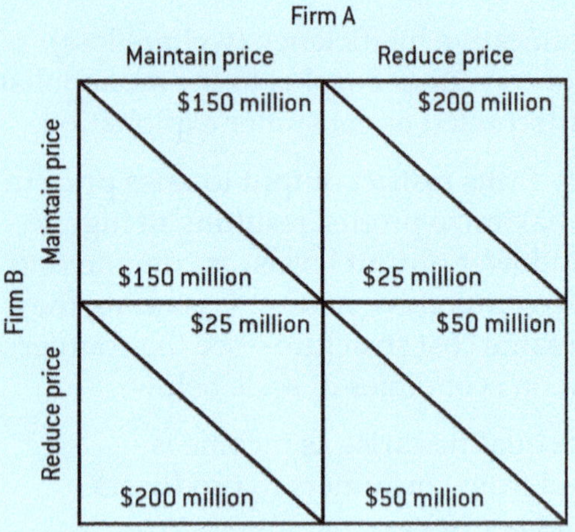

▲ Figure 2.11.3 Matrix showing the dilemma of whether to compete or collude

Monopolistic competition

HL Typical examples of monopolistically competitive markets include hair salons, restaurants, bars and cafés where barriers to entry are low. As firms in such industries sell a slightly differentiated product (a close substitute to other goods in the market), they have some degree of market power. Similarly, to a monopoly, a monopolistically competitive firm faces a downward sloping demand curve (see Figure 2.11.4) since it may increase the price of its differentiated product and lose some but not all customers as some will still show a certain preference for this firm's product (in contrast, a perfectly competitive firm would lose all its customers since all goods in such an industry are homogeneous).

The following points explain how firms go from short-run firm equilibrium to long-run firm equilibrium in monopolistic competition.

- A monopolistically competitive firm making abnormal profits would look a lot like a monopoly firm making abnormal profits (Figure 2.11.2). However, the demand curve faced by a monopolistically competitive firm is likely to be more price-elastic due to the existence of slightly differentiated substitutes.
- Due to the lack of barriers to entry, monopolistically competitive firms that enjoy abnormal profits in the short run will incentivize more firms to enter the market. While this process is similar to the entry of firms in a perfectly competitive market, it is represented as a fall in demand for the monopolistically competitive firm. As entry takes place, the demand faced by each individual firm will:
  - decrease (the demand curve will shift to the left) as each firm's market share is reduced
  - become more price elastic (form a flatter slope) as more substitutes become available.

This process will continue until normal profits are earned by each firm (Figure 2.11.4) and there is no longer an incentive for firms to enter the market.

- Similarly, if monopolistically competitive firms are making losses in the short run, they will have the incentive to exit the market and switch to their next best alternative. The remaining firms' demand curve will increase and be less price elastic. This will continue until firms stop exiting the industry when normal profits are earned.
- Therefore, firms in both monopolistic competition and perfect competition never sustain abnormal profits or losses in the long run.

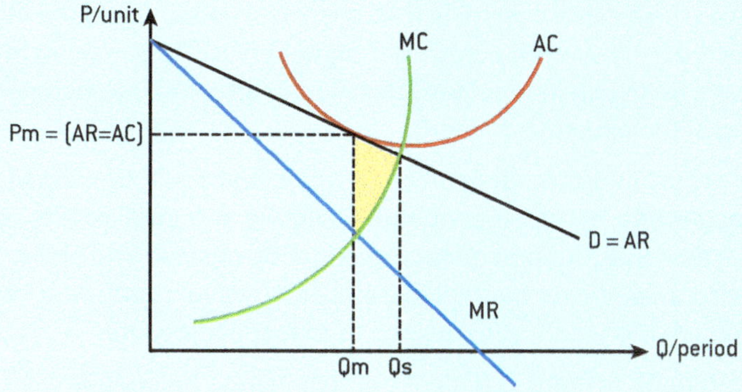

▲ Figure 2.11.4 A monopolistically competitive firm making normal profits (long-run equilibrium)

Monopolistically competitive firms are allocatively inefficient since the socially optimal level, Qs (where P = MC), is greater than the firm's equilibrium, Qm (where P > MC). There is thus under-allocation of resources and a welfare loss (shaded on Figure 2.11.4). However, since consumers in monopolistically competitive markets may easily switch to a close substitute, firms cannot charge a price that is significantly higher than marginal cost. As such, the degree of market power and allocative inefficiency in monopolistically competitive markets is smaller than in oligopoly and monopoly markets.

Government intervention

HL As significant abuse of market power (specifically in monopoly and oligopoly markets) may lead to consumer exploitation (where part of the consumer surplus is absorbed by firms), government intervention is needed to address the market failure. There are a number of tools available to policymakers to ensure that consumers do not pay high prices for (essential) goods and services and to create incentive for firms to innovate.

- Heavy fines for uncompetitive behaviour can be imposed. For example, the Competition and Consumer Commission of Singapore issued a S$27 million (about US$20 million) fine to 13 distributors of fresh chicken in 2018. The firms, which controlled 90% of the fresh chicken sold in Singapore (CR13 = 90%), were found guilty of price fixing and informally agreeing not to compete for a period of seven years.
- Mergers and acquisitions are monitored. In the USA, antitrust laws prohibit firms from colluding or merging to form a monopoly without government approval.
- Prices are regulated (for instance by imposing a maximum price). This is often done for essential services where a private monopoly or oligopoly controls the market. For example, although UK railways were privatized in 1993, the government continues to control the fares.
- Monopolies can be broken up through forcing them to sell off parts of their companies. In 1984, the US telephone service company AT&T was broken up into seven smaller companies. This had benefits for consumers. For example, AT&T service subscribers had to rent phones from AT&T (there was no option to purchase phones) and they were not allowed to connect phones from other manufacturers. The restrictions ended with the break-up.

Assessment tip

You may need to evaluate the desirability of large firms (oligopolies and monopolies) and the need for government intervention as part of a paper 1 question or for your internal assessment commentary. We saw earlier that large firms come with benefits and disadvantages and, as such, it is not easy to decide whether consumers and society benefit from the market being controlled by large firms and/or if those firms' dominant market position justifies intervention.

To answer such a question appropriately and show assessors evidence of evaluation, you need to assess the desirability of monopolies and oligopolies in context (set by your chosen article for a commentary or by the real-world examples you chose in answering part (b) essay questions). Here are some key questions to consider.

What good does the firm/do the firms have control over? Is it an essential good? Could the economic well-being of consumers be significantly affected by restricted output and higher price? Consider, for instance, the earlier example of price fixing in Singapore's fresh chicken market. This clearly affected low income consumers who are likely to spend a significant portion of their income on food.

Does this industry offer sufficient opportunities for economies of scale that could translate into lower prices for consumers? Could the firm be considered a natural monopoly? Could the abnormal profits translate into spending on R&D for product innovation? For example, the presence of economies of scale and ability to invest in fuel-efficient planes could justify allowing an airline to monopolize a specific travel route—especially if the market size is so small it makes the airline a natural monopoly with respect to that specific route.

What is the level of market concentration? Is there sufficient product variety for consumers?

QUESTION PRACTICE

Define the term *monopolistic competition*. [2]

SAMPLE STUDENT ANSWER

Response 1

▼ This definition is too vague because it could also apply to perfect competition.

An industry with many firms.

This response could have achieved 1/2 marks.

Response 2

▲ Listing the characteristics of a market structure is an adequate way to define it.

An industry with the following characteristics:

1. Very many firms
2. Each firm sells a differentiated product
3. Low barriers to entry

This response could have achieved 2/2 marks.

QUESTION PRACTICE

This question is adapted from the November 2020 examination paper.

The following diagrams illustrate a perfectly competitive market and a profit-maximizing firm operating at its short-run equilibrium level of output.

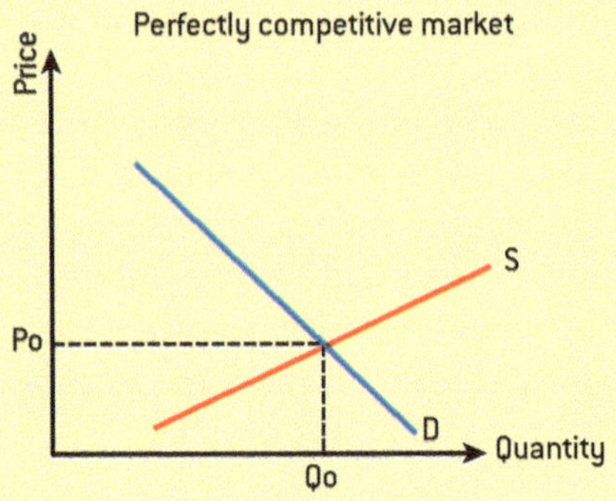

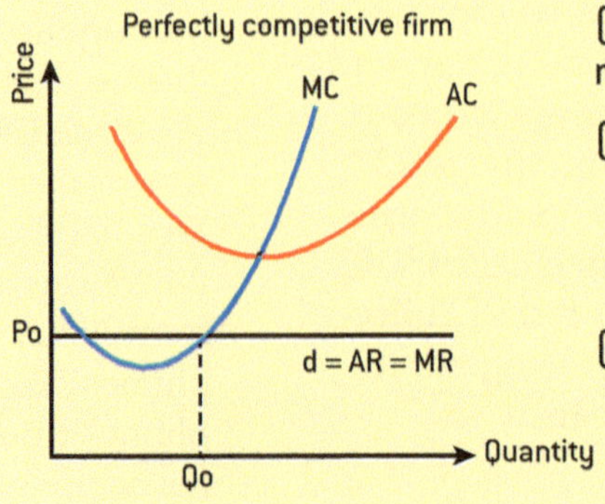

(i) State the level of economic profit made by this firm. [1]

(ii) Draw and label relevant curves to reflect the changes in market condition which bring this firm to a long-run equilibrium. [2]

(iii) Using your answer to part (ii), explain how the market brings a perfectly competitive firm to its long-run equilibrium. [4]

SAMPLE STUDENT ANSWER

(i) The firm is making economic losses.

(ii)

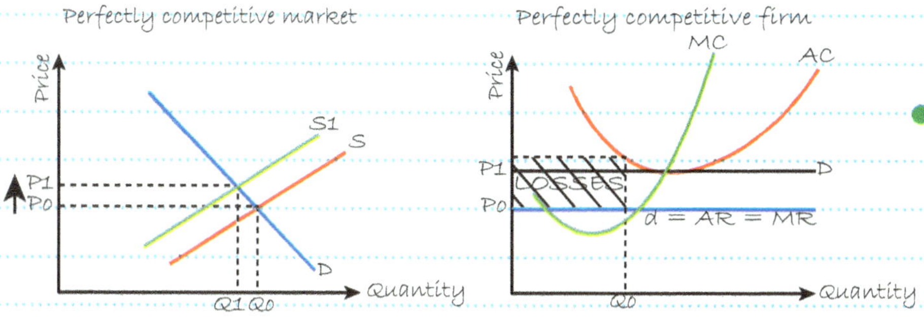

(iii) At P0Q0 the firm is facing losses—total revenue does not cover total costs. For the firms that are facing losses, it is not financially viable to stay in the market so they start leaving the market. As the number of firms leaves the market, supply decreases (shifts to the left from S to S1) as fewer firms are operating in the market. This results in an excess demand that will push gradually prices up from P0 to P1.

Perfectly competitive firms are price-takers, they have no choice but to accept the market price and enjoy a higher price when firms leave the market. When the price reaches P1, AR = AC and normal profits are made. There is no longer an incentive for firms to leave the industry. The market is at its long-run equilibrium.

▲ The correct level of economic profit (economic losses) is identified (AR is lower than AC at Q0). No justification or explanation is needed since the command term is "state".

▲ All the curves are drawn correctly and are fully labelled. Although it was not required, the candidate has shaded the economic losses. There is no penalty for doing so and, on the contrary, you are advised to annotate diagrams for paper 3 if it helps you identify correct answers.

▲ This paragraph clearly establishes the adjustment at the market level. The candidate makes adequate reference to the diagram.

▲ This paragraph clearly explains how the firm will earn normal profits due to the price increasing and hence reach its long-run equilibrium.

This response could have achieved 7/7 marks.

QUESTION PRACTICE

This question is adapted from the May 2017 examination paper.

The following table illustrates the demand conditions faced by a monopolist.

Price per unit ($)	Quantity demanded per week (units)
12	0
10	12
8	24
6	36
4	48
2	60

i) Calculate the marginal revenue resulting from a fall in price from $8 to $6. [2]

ii) State the average revenue when output is equal to 48 units per week. [1]

iii) Calculate the economic profit if output is equal to 12 units per week and average cost is equal to $8. [2]

SAMPLE STUDENT ANSWER

i) $MR = \frac{\Delta TR}{\Delta Q} = \frac{(36 \times 6) - (24 \times 8)}{(36 - 24)} = \frac{24}{12} = 2.$

▼ Workings are provided and valid. Unfortunately, the unit is missing ($).

ii) AR = P = $4

▲ The answer is correct. No calculation is needed since AR is the price, which is given in the table. The unit ($) is provided.

iii) $\pi = TR - TC = (10 \times 12) - (8 \times 12) = \$48$

▲ The answer is correct and workings are provided. Note another way to calculate this: $\pi = (AR - AC) \times Q$

This response could have achieved 4/5 marks.

QUESTION PRACTICE

This question is adapted from the November 2017 examination paper.

Explain why firms in oligopolistic markets may prefer to use non-price competition. [10]

SAMPLE STUDENT ANSWER

An oligopolistic industry is one with the following characteristics: a few large firms control most of the market, the products are slightly differentiated products and there are high barriers to entry preventing the entrance of other firms. Because the firms sell differentiated products, each firm faces downward sloping demand curve. It can choose to decrease the price but obviously it will lose some customers. Those who see the other goods as inferior will continue to buy. As such, oligopolies have some market power and can thus try to increase their market share by decreasing the price of their good (price competition) or by means of non-price competition.

▲ This is a good introduction. It defines the concept of oligopoly and explains that oligopoly may either compete through lower price or by resorting to non-price competition.

The fact that there are only a few firms in the market makes firms interdependent since the outcome of any decision of one firm depends on the reaction of its rivals. A game theory matrix helps to explain the situation of interdependence and the consequences of engaging in price competition.

▲ The candidate has introduced the concept of interdependence, which is the main reason for the lack of price competition in oligopoly.

		Firm A: high price	Firm A: Cut price
Firm B	high price	$200 million (A) / $200 million (B)	$250 million (A) / $30 million (B)
Firm B	Cut price	$30 million (A) / $250 million (B)	$50 million (A) / $50 million (B)

Let's assume we have two firms in this oligopoly market: A and B. Each firm can either maintain the price of its good (maintain a high price) or cut it to attract consumers. As firms are interdependent the outcome of the strategy of one firm will depend on the reaction of the rival. In the pay-off matrix we can see all the possible scenarios and their outcome. The values on the box are the profit each firm would earn in each scenario expressed in millions of dollars. We can see that if either of the firm cuts the price of its good, the rival firm may either maintain its high price and earn a profit of $30 million or also cut the price and get a profit of $50 million. As such, any price cut will be followed by the rivals and a price war will ensue. However, the matrix clearly shows that the best outcome for both firms is to keep their prices high as each firm gets $200 million of profits.

▲ Interdependence and the possibility of price war are clearly explained with reference to the matrix.

Since it is not beneficial for firms to compete by cutting prices, firms have to look for other ways to compete. They do so by engaging in non-price competition, for example by advertising to convince consumers that their product is superior and build brand loyalty. They may also invest in research and development to bring consumers improved products. Or they may offer extended warranty or free after-sales service.

▲ This is a clear explanation of the concept of non-price competition and suitable examples are given.

Like all profit-maximizing firms, oligopoly firms will choose to employ strategies which result in the highest profits. Since price competition leads to price wars, uncertainties and lower profits, they naturally prefer non-price competition.

▲ This is a good conclusion. It sums up the essay and clearly addresses the demands of the question.

This response meets all of the descriptors for the highest mark band [9–10] and **it could have achieved 10/10 marks.**

QUESTION PRACTICE

This question is adapted from the May 2017 examination paper.

Using real- world examples, discuss the view that perfect competition is a more desirable market structure than monopoly. [15]

SAMPLE STUDENT ANSWER

▲ This is a good introduction. It defines both types of market structure and establishes that monopolies and perfectly competitive industries usually operate in different markets. The candidate also provides real-world examples.

Monopoly is one of the four market structures with the following assumed characteristics: single dominant firm, high barriers to entry and unique product with no close substitutes. For example, Paypal has a monopoly over online transactions in many e-platforms like e-bay. Perfect competition (PC) is another market structure with the following assumed characteristics: large number of small firms, homogeneous product and no barrier to entry. PC is a highly theoretical market structure, there is no pure perfectly competitive market in the real world. However, the closer we can get to this model is the market for agricultural products as they tend to be very homogeneous (for example rice) and it is also relatively easy to enter the industry because of relatively low barrier to entry. Therefore, it is clear that the two market structures tend to apply to very different industries and therefore the desirability of either market structure may depend on the product sold in that market.

▲ The candidate explains that a perfectly competitive firm may be more desirable since it is allocatively efficient. This is explained with reference to a diagram.

From the viewpoint of society a monopoly is less desirable than perfect competition as it is allocatively inefficient while the theoretical PC firms are allocatively efficient. This can be seen on figure 1, the demand curve faced by a PC firm is perfectly elastic as firms are price-takers and they accept the price P*. Assuming they are profit-maximizing firms, they will produce at Q* where MR = MC and that leads to an output which is also allocatively efficient since P = MC.

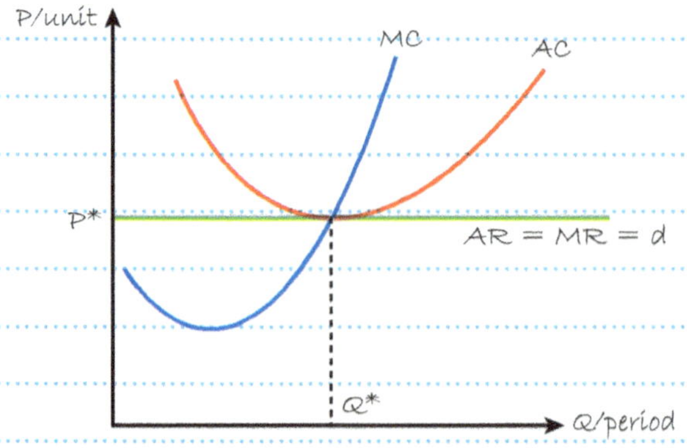

Figure 1– a PC firm in the long run

▲ Comparing the allocative inefficiency in a monopoly with the more desirable outcome in a perfectly competitive industry helps establish the relative desirability of the perfectly competitive model.

Figure 2 illustrates a monopoly which faces a downward sloping demand curve as the firm has the ability to set the price of its product. The monopolist must lower the price to sell additional units of the good hence the marginal revenue (MR) lies below the average revenue (AR) curve. As such, at Qm where MC=MR,

Pm > MC. The monopoly is therefore allocatively inefficient and there is a welfare loss (ABC). If the monopolist was to behave like a PC firm and produce where P = MC, the price would be lower at Ppc and the quantity would be higher, Qpc on figure 2.

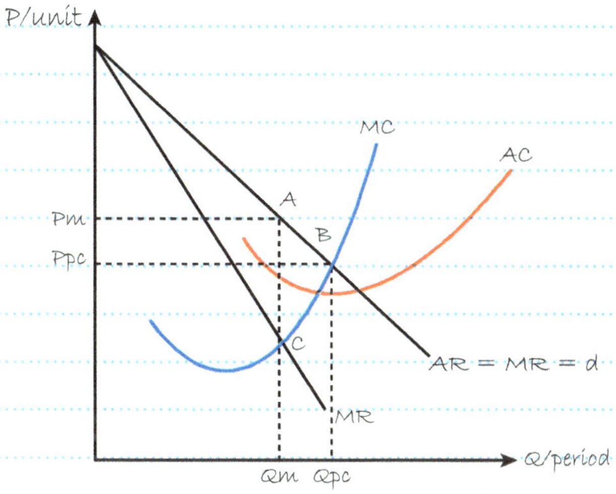

Figure 2- a monopoly firm vs. a PC firm

However, this does not necessarily imply that that a PC firm would charge a lower price and produce a higher quantity than a monopoly. This analysis assumes that the cost structure would be the same across both types of market structure. However, we know that monopolies tend to be large firms and therefore would enjoy economies of scale. A small fruit stall at a local market does not have the potential to reap a lot of economies of scale such as division of labour. However, a large public utilities company has a lot more scope for economies of scale. This translates into lower average costs which can be passed on to consumers, allowing them to enjoy goods at lower prices. In some cases, the large economies of scale do not allow more than one firm into the market. Such cases are natural monopolies. This is why the provision of electricity in small countries is often monopolized by one company.

▲ This is a good counter-argument to the theoretical analysis of a perfectly competitive firm as being more efficient. References to the diagram and real-world examples help illustrate the analysis. The candidate offers a good evaluation point—that the presence of economies of scale is not relevant to all markets.

▲ This is another balanced argument to compare the desirability of both market structures, enriched with real-world examples.

Another advantage of a monopoly is that it can make abnormal profits in the long run unlike a PC firm which can only make normal profits in the long run. The high profits give the ability to monopolies to fund research and development (R&D) projects which result in better quality products and/or a wider range of products for consumers. For example, Microsoft controls most of the market for computer operating systems through Windows and has spent millions of dollars over the years to innovate create different apps such as MS teams, SharePoint, etc. Once again, this argument does not seem to apply to firms we expect to see in PC markets such as fruit and vegetable shops as they have limited scope for product development.

Hence, monopolies and PC firms have different strengths and limitations. It should however but noted that they tend to cater to different markets where economies of scale, scope for R&D... may or may not apply. This being said, some monopolies may enjoy economies of scale and need to innovate but supply essential goods for which the price should not be too high, like Gilead Sciences who has a monopoly over HIV drugs granted by a patent. The ability of a monopoly to charge the highest price for an essential product in order to maximize profits is socially undesirable.

▲ This is an effective conclusion with evidence of synthesis (the main arguments brought forward in the essay) and evaluation (judgment over the danger of monopolies controlling the price of essential goods).

This response meets all of the descriptors for the highest mark band (13–15) and **could have achieved 15/15 marks.**

Content link

Link to your IA

This topic offers some opportunities for economic commentaries. You may choose an article covering a change in the level of competition within an industry. For instance, the COVID-19 pandemic has made some goods and services such as surgical masks and food delivery services more profitable. Evidence of higher profits led to the entry of new firms in such industries. Another possible topic for a commentary is the nature of competition between firms in an oligopoly market—look out for hints of both price (or the absence of price competition) and non-price competition in the article. You may also consider an article covering intervention in oligopoly and monopoly markets to protect the well-being of consumers.

Concept link

- **Change**—we have seen that perfectly competitive and monopolistically competitive markets are subject to constant changes as the entry and exit of firms will bring firms to a long-run equilibrium where normal profits are earned.
- **Efficiency**—this concept was prominent throughout the topic of market failure. Besides the ability of a market to achieve allocative efficiency, you may consider the opportunities for economies of scale in a market. The greater the scope for economies of scale, the more cost-efficient are larger firms.
- **Choice**—the level of choice available to consumers varies greatly depending on the market structure of the industry. In perfectly competitive markets, consumers have a choice of producer or seller but goods are homogeneous so there is no product variety. In monopolistically competitive markets, consumers have a choice of sellers and products since the products are differentiated. However, the opportunity cost of that wide choice is the lack of innovation as firms do not have abnormal profits to invest in R&D. As such, oligopolies may offer limited choice but offer the benefit of improved quality over time.
- **Interdependence**—you have learned in this topic that firms in oligopolistic markets are interdependent. This may explain why extensive non-price competition is employed in some markets. This interdependence may lead to innovation and product variety that benefit consumers. It may also lead to wastage as resources are channelled to advertising to convince consumers that a product they do not need is superior.
- **Intervention**—governments may intervene to address significant abuses of market power. However, intervention might also have created barriers to entry. Examples could be the need for licenses or existence of complex bureaucratic processes that deter the entry of firms, or corruption that maintains the position of dominant firms.

2.12 THE MARKET'S INABILITY TO ACHIEVE EQUITY

HL This sub-unit examines the inequalities that naturally occur in free markets.

You should be able to:

✔ explain, using a circular flow model, that due to unequal ownership of factors of production, the free market economy may not result in an equitable distribution of income.

Content link

Link to other sub-units

Refer to sub-units 1.1 and 1.2 for:

- the circular flow of income model
- the meaning of equity and equality.

Summary

HL The ideas of equality and equity often arise in relation to the distribution of national income (how a nation's total income, often measured by GDP, is distributed across its population). Equality in the distribution of national income would imply that each resident receives the same share of national income (GDP). Equity in the income distribution refers to the national income (GDP) being distributed in a way that is considered to be fair or just.

The circular flow of income model tells us that output = income = expenditure. Households finance their expenditure on goods and services with the income they receive from supplying factors of production in relevant factor markets—rents (from land), wages (from labour services), interest (for capital) and profits (for the entrepreneurs). It is clear that those who own more factors of production or have access to higher valued factors of production will receive more income and will be able to finance greater expenditure on goods and services. Households with less valued skills and those without the means to start a business (become an entrepreneur) will receive lower income and therefore have a lower ability to buy goods and services. Think back to the definition of demand in sub-unit 2.2—it is the quantity that consumers are willing and **able** to buy at various prices per period of time, ceteris paribus. Some households may need and be willing to buy essential goods, but unfortunately be unable to buy them. Free markets may be said to ignore low income individuals. Intervention is often needed as most societies judge that access to essential goods and services should be granted to all, regardless of income. As equity is a normative concept, there is no unique perspective on what is an acceptable level of inequality and thus a desirable degree of intervention.

Content link

Link to your IA

In sub-unit 2.7 you learned about intervention of the government in markets. Such intervention is often done to remedy the inequalities created by market forces. An article on price controls (including minimum wages), taxes or subsidies can be the start point of an economics commentary.

Concept link

- **Intervention**—as free markets lead to inequalities, governments may choose to intervene and influence the workings of markets. News articles often describe policies seeking a more equal distribution of income, but the most interesting articles present opposing views on a policy that may seek more equality but may seem by many not to be fair (equitable).
- **Efficiency**—government intervention distorts market forces, which may lead to inefficiencies. For example, subsidies and minimum prices create disincentives for producers to be cost-efficient. As a result of intervention, resources may be misallocated (as evidenced by the welfare loss) and hence allocative efficiency cannot be achieved.
- **Economic well-being**—Intervention in markets may help low income households to achieve financial security through a minimum wage scheme or result in higher income for farmers who benefit from a price floor (minimum price) on the goods they sell. Subsidies and maximum prices also help vulnerable households to meet basic needs (e.g. housing, food, clothing, education, transportation, healthcare, childcare).

3 MACROECONOMICS

You should know about:

- ✔ measuring economic activity
- ✔ aggregate demand (AD) and aggregate supply (AS)
- ✔ macroeconomic objectives
- ✔ economics of poverty and inequality
- ✔ monetary policy
- ✔ fiscal policy
- ✔ supply-side policies.

3.1 MEASURING ECONOMIC ACTIVITY AND ILLUSTRATING ITS VARIATIONS

You should be able to:

- ✔ define the terms
  - ✔ gross domestic product (GDP) and GDP per capita
  - ✔ gross national income (GNI) and GNI per capita
- ✔ distinguish between the nominal value of GDP and GNI and the real value of GDP and GNI
- ✔ distinguish between the real value of GDP per capita and real GNI per capita and the real value of GDP per capita and GNI per capita at purchasing power parity (PPP)
- ✔ explain, with reference to a circular flow diagram, the equivalence of the output approach, the income approach and the expenditure approach to measuring national income
- ✔ evaluate the appropriateness of the use of national income statistics (GDP per capita or GNI per capita) in comparing economic well-being over time or across countries
- ✔ examine the OECD Better Life Index, the Happiness Index and Happy Planet Index as alternative measures of economic well-being
- ✔ explain the long-term growth trend in the business cycle diagram as the potential output of the economy.

This sub-unit introduces macroeconomic theory. The measures of national income and economic well-being will be discussed.

Content link

Link to other sub-units

Refer to sub-unit 1.1 for the difference between microeconomics and macroeconomics.

The circular flow of income model demonstrates that output = income = expenditure.

Summary

The first macroeconomic concept we will be looking at is national income, the total value of all income made by households in a country. **National income accounting** refers to a set of principles and methods used to measure a country's national income.

The **gross domestic product (GDP)** and **gross national income (GNI)** are the most common measures of national income. GDP is the total value of all final goods and services produced in an economy in one year. In contrast, GNI is the total value of final goods and services *produced by residents of a country, irrespective of whether they are located within the country or abroad*, in one year.

GDP considers all income made by residents of a country while GNI focuses on income earned by nationals of a country.

GNI = GDP + factor income from abroad – factor income sent abroad

For example, Germany's GNI will include profits earned by German companies located in Switzerland (factor income from abroad) but Germany's GDP will not include these since the profits are not made within Germany. On the other hand, Germany's GNI will exclude remittance by Italian citizens working in Germany (factor income sent abroad) but these will be included in Germany's GDP since the Italian workers earned income for producing goods and services in Germany.

Since output = expenditure = income, national income can be measured using the output method, the expenditure method or the income method, defined in Table 3.1.1.

▼ Table 3.1.1 Output, expenditure and income methods of measuring national income

Output method	This method sums up the value of all the final goods and services produced from each industry (e.g. forestry, mining, banking).
Expenditure method	This method sums up the various types of expenditure in an economy, **GDP = C + I + G + (X – M)**: • consumption (C)—expenditure by households • investment (I)—expenditure by firms • government expenditure (G) • net exports (X – M)—expenditure by foreigners on domestically produced goods and services (exports) minus domestic spending on foreign goods and services (imports).
Income method	This method sums up all factor income (wages, interests, rent, profits).

The three approaches should, with some minor adjustments, yield the same result. As we know from the circular flow diagram, what is produced = what is spent = what is being earned.

Nominal GDP is calculated at **current prices**. This value of GDP can increase when the production of goods (output) and/or their prices have increased.

Real GDP is measured output, at **constant prices**, produced in one year. This value of GDP only increases if there is an increase in the production (output) of goods and services.

The GDP deflator is a price index used to convert nominal GDP to real GDP:

$$\text{GDP deflator} = \frac{\text{nominal GDP}}{\text{real GDP}} \times 100$$

$$\text{Real GDP} = \frac{\text{nominal GDP}}{\text{GDP deflator}} \times 100$$

It is essential to isolate the effect of changes in prices to allow for comparison over time and between countries (more on this later).

The real GDP of a country increases over the long term, but this increase is not continuous. The **business cycle** refers to the circular movement of GDP around the potential (long-term) output as it moves from contraction (recession) to expansion. Business cycles are identified as having four distinct phases: peak, contraction (recession), trough and expansion (recovery).

GDP/GNI per capita is obtained by dividing GDP/GNI by the population of a country. As GDP/GNI is a measure of both income and output, GDP/GNI per capita can be used to estimate the basket of goods and services enjoyed by the average resident or citizen of a country (the material standard of living).

For ease of comparison across countries, GDP/GNI per capita data are converted to a common currency, usually the US dollar. Yet, prices of goods and services can vary significantly across countries. For instance, in restaurants a can of Coca Cola may be priced at more than US$4 in Switzerland, about US$2 in Ireland and as little as US$0.5 in India. To account for differences in costs of living, economists use "purchasing power parity" (PPP) exchange rates.

In the hypothetical example shown in the following box, S$2,000 buys the same basket of goods and services as US$1,000 or £500. Hence $1 PPP = S$2 = £0.5 will be the PPP exchange rate used when converting national income statistics to a common currency. The PPP exchange rate accounts for differences in cost of living and makes comparisons across countries more meaningful.

Price of a basket of similar goods and services

price in Singapore = S$2,000	S$2 = $1 PPP
price in the US = US$1,000	£0.5 = $1 PPP
price in the UK = £500	

Real GDP/GNI per capita (and preferably at PPP) allows for comparison of the **economic well-being** of residents or citizens of a country over time. China's real GNI per capita has increased by 83% between 2010 and 2020, implying that the income earned by the average Chinese citizen has almost doubled in 10 years. Since this increase allows for greater financial security and an ability to meet more basic needs and/or access more goods that bring personal satisfaction, it follows that an increase in GNI per capita signifies an improvement in economic well-being.

▼ Table 3.1.2 Real GNI per capita for three countries

Cambodia	China	Switzerland
$4,033	$16,201	$65,011

Real GDP/GNI per capita at PPP is also used to compared economic well-being across countries. Consider the real GNI per capita in 2020 for Cambodia, China and Switzerland shown in Table 3.1.2.

This tells us that the average Chinese citizen enjoys more than four times more goods and services than Cambodian citizens but only a quarter of what a Swiss citizen may enjoy.

Using GDP/GNI statistics as estimators of the economic well-being comes with some limitations.

- Real GDP/GNI per capita is **an average measure** that does not consider income inequality. An increase in real GDP/GNI per capita implies an increase for most or maybe just some residents or citizens. An increase in real GDP per capita may come with an increase in inequality. China's real GNI per capita at PPP in 2020 was $16,201 but China is also home to many billionaires who probably enjoyed a much greater increase in income than the rest of the population.
- An increase in real GDP/GNI per capita **does not reflect changes in the quality of goods and services**. An increase in real GDP/GNI per capita may underestimate improvements in economic well-being in a less developed country if the quality of healthcare services improves concurrently.
- Real GDP/GNI per capita **does not provide information about the composition of output**. An increase in real GDP/GNI per capita may come from greater production of merit goods such as education but it may also come from increased production of goods that bring society fewer benefits.
- The increased production of goods and services may be accompanied by negative externalities from production such as **environmental degradation**. In such cases, the increase in real GDP/GNI is not sustainable and thus the economic well-being of future generations will deteriorate.
- Real GDP/GNI does not reflect **leisure time**—an increase in real GDP/GNI may come from an increase in work hours and stress.
- Real GDP/GNI does not account for **changes in the intangible aspects of economic well-being** such as freedom of expression and civil liberties.

Content link

Link to other sub-units

Refer to sub-unit 1.1 for the meaning of economic well-being.

Given the limitations of GDP/GNI statistics in measuring economic well-being, composite indicators have been proposed to capture the multidimensional nature of economic well-being.

- The **Better Life Index**, developed by the Organisation for Economic Co-operation and Development (OECD) covers 11 topics identified as essential: housing, income, jobs, community, education, environment, civic engagement, health, life satisfaction, safety, and work and life balance.

- The **Happiness Index**, developed by the United Nations Sustainable Development Solutions Network, includes six variables: real GDP per capita, social support, healthy life expectancy, freedom to make life choices, generosity and perceptions of corruption.
- The **Happy Planet Index (HPI)** was introduced by the New Economics Foundation of London. The HPI includes three variables: average life expectancy, average subjective well-being and ecological footprint.

All these indicators provide insights into the qualitative aspects of economic well-being that are not reflected in national income statistics. Critics have pointed out that the three indices are comprehensive but hard to measure and some variables are subjective (e.g. environment, generosity). Some feel that more qualitative indicators should be included such as family time and religion. Data is also not available for all nations—the Better Life Index is only computed for 40 countries.

Test yourself

Figure 3.1.1 is a map of mainland China. As you can see, the GDP per capita varied across provinces from just over 20,000 yuan to over 100,000 yuan in 2016, implying wide regional income inequality. The map also shows the internet penetration rate for each province. While in some provinces less than 40% of residents have access to the internet, in others it is over 80%.

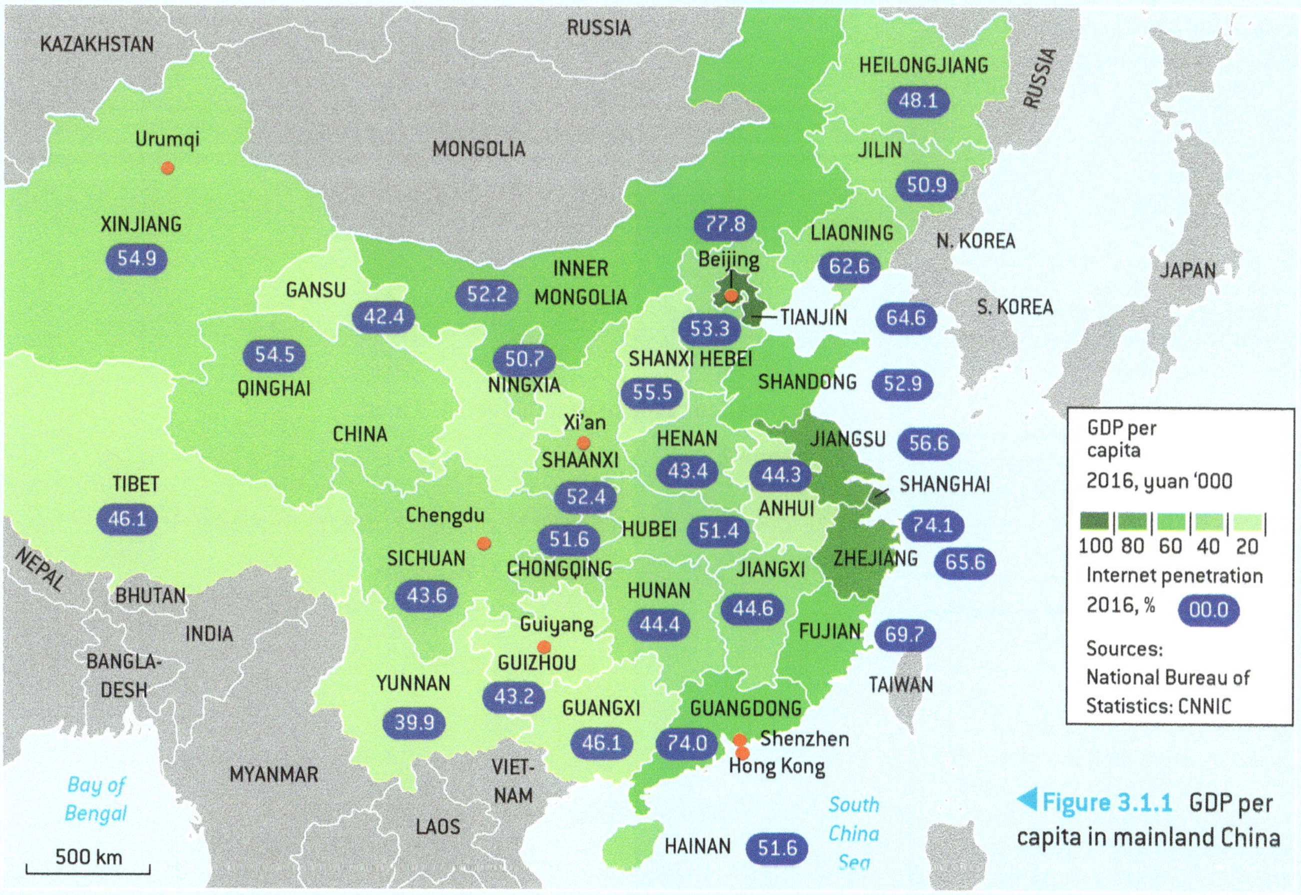

Figure 3.1.1 GDP per capita in mainland China

GDP/GNI per capita is often given for an entire country. Does Figure 3.1.1 illustrate some of the limitations of using the overall GDP per capita to measure economic well-being for the entire population of mainland China?

With some research and with reference to the output method, explain the wide differentials in GDP per capita across mainland China. Consider access to the internet in identifying high value-added industries that may have difficulties operating in provinces with lower internet penetration rate (e.g. industries reliant on e-commerce). Which industries are likely to dominate in these provinces? Find out about the provinces that rely on agricultural production and/or manufacturing. Are those low or high value output industries?

QUESTION PRACTICE

This question is adapted from the May 2014 examination paper.

1. The following table presents national income statistics for selected variables related to Country Z for 2012 and is expressed in millions of dollars.

National Income Statistics	$ (million)
Government spending on goods and services	3300
Wages and salaries	6900
Investment spending	1020
Consumer spending	6520
Direct taxation	4150
Exports	2295
Profits of companies	5475
Imports	2450

(a) Calculate the gross domestic product (GDP) for country Z in 2012. [2]

(b) The population in country Z is 420,000. Calculate per capita GDP for country Z in 2012. [2]

SAMPLE STUDENT ANSWER

Response 1

1) a) C + I + G + (X – M) = GDP

∴ 6520 + 1020 + 3300 + (2295 – 2450)

in millions

= 10685 Answer: $ 10685 million

b) pop: 420000

GDP per capita = GDP / pop

10 685 000 000 / 420 000 = 25440.476 Answer: $ 25440.48 (2dp)

▲ The expenditure approach is used adequately to calculate GDP. Workings are provided and the units are included ($).

This response could have achieved 4/4 marks.

Response 2

(a) C + I + G + (X-M) = 6250 + 1020 + 3300 + (2295 – 2450) = $10,415 million

(b) 10, 415 million/420,000 = 24, 797.62

▼ There is a careless error in copying the value for consumption, so the final answer is incorrect.

▲ As the workings illustrate a correct understanding of the demands of the question, 1 mark can be awarded for part (a).

▲ Due to the error in part (a), the real GDP per capita figure is incorrect. However, IB examiners apply the "own figure rule". If a figure was calculated incorrectly for one part of the question and used for subsequent parts, full marks may be awarded as long as the method used is correct. As a correct calculation method is shown, 2 marks can be given for part (b).

This response could have achieved 3/4 marks.

Assessment tip

No matter how simple the calculation, always provide the workings. Everyone makes arithmetic errors and interprets data incorrectly every now and then. Providing workings for calculation ensures that you may be rewarded for a correct understanding of economic methodology even if the final answer is incorrect.

QUESTION PRACTICE

This question is adapted from the specimen examination paper.

Using a numerical example, explain the importance of presenting "GDP per capita" statistics at purchasing power parity (PPP). [4]

SAMPLE STUDENT ANSWER

Response 1

GDP per capita measures economic well-being and if we do not use purchasing power parity values, we are not considering the cost of living. For example, after conversion to USD, the GDP per capita could be US$ 1200 but if we consider PPP it would only be US$ 1000 because the cost of living in the country is high.

▲ The candidate shows some understanding of the usefulness of using PPP exchange rates to adjust for differences in the cost of living and gives a numerical example.

▼ However, the example and explanation do not highlight the usefulness of PPP values in making comparisons across countries or over time.

This response could have achieved 2/4 marks.

Response 2

GDP per capita measures economic well-being and the purchasing power parity allow for meaningful comparisons across countries because it discounts differences in cost of living in different countries. So, if we want to compare the GDP per capita of different countries it is best to use the GDP per capita at PPP.

Ex: Country A has a GDP per capita of US$ 1000 and country B US$ 1200 we can conclude that country B has higher living standards than country A as – on average – the residents of country B enjoy higher income. However, this could be misleading as we are not considering the cost of living. Let's assume that country B has much higher prices for the same goods sold in country A. So, if we look at the GDP per capita at PPP of each country we have: country A is at US$ 900 while country B is at US$ 800.

▲ Both the explanation and the example highlight the importance of adjusting real GDP for differences in cost of living in order to make meaningful comparisons of economic well-being across countries.

Therefore, one can conclude that country A has better living standards than country B as individuals are able to purchase more goods and services with their income than individuals from country B.

This response could have achieved 4/4 marks.

Content link

Link to your IA

GDP and GNI are fundamental macroeconomic variables that may appear in your chosen article. If you decide to use data provided, do not simply list changes mentioned in the article. For instance, "real GDP increased by 2% in 2019 but only by 1.5% in 2020 and 0.8% in 2021" does not reflect any economic analysis, it simply quotes information from the article. "The continuous decrease in the growth rate of real GDP from 2% in 2019 to 0.8% in 2021 suggests the economy is reaching the peak of a business cycle" is clear evidence of economic analysis.

Concept link

- **Change**—variations in economic activity (GDP) reflect changes in economic variables. For instance, a fall in exports would lead to a fall in GDP, which, in turn, may lead to changes in other variables such as economic well-being. As macroeconomics looks at the entire economy rather than specific markets, groups of firms or consumers, the changes might be wide reaching. You will soon learn how a change in real GDP may affect inflation, unemployment and equity.
- **Sustainability**—the economic performance of a country is often judged based on the increase in real GDP. However, this may come with significant negative externalities from production, especially if the increased production comes from exploiting natural resources. Consider carefully the information given in your article. The industries that have expanded might give a clear indication of the threat to the environment (e.g. mining).
- **Economic well-being**—economic well-being is a multidimensional concept and it should not be measured by national income statistics alone. Consider the limitations of GDP/GNI per capita outlined earlier before reaching a conclusion on changes in economic well-being. However, keep in mind that you are commenting on the contents of the article, do not discuss what is not mentioned or suggested in the text. For instance, you may consider the limitation of national income statistics in reflecting income inequality *only if* your article acknowledges or suggest the presence of inequalities. An example would be an indication that the increase in real GDP comes from the good performance of medical and pharmaceutical industries, which are known to employ highly paid workers.

3.2 VARIATIONS IN ECONOMIC ACTIVITY—AGGREGATE DEMAND AND AGGREGATE SUPPLY

You should be able to:

- ✔ define the terms
  - ✔ aggregate demand (AD)
  - ✔ aggregate supply (AS)
  - ✔ the components/determinants of AD—consumption (C), investment (I), government spending (G), net exports (X – M)
  - ✔ deflationary or recessionary gap
  - ✔ inflationary gap
- ✔ explain, using a diagram, how the AD curve can shift because of changes in consumption, investment, government spending and/or net exports
- ✔ explain, using a diagram, how the short-run aggregate supply (SRAS) curve can shift in the short run
- ✔ explain, using a diagram, the shape of long-run aggregate supply (LRAS) curve in the Monetarist/New Classical model
- ✔ explain, using the Monetarist/New Classical AD/AS model, that the economy may be in a short-run equilibrium at a level of real output below (above) the full employment level of output
- ✔ explain, using a Monetarist/New Classical AD/AS model, while there may be short-term fluctuations in real output, the economy will always return to the full employment level of output in the long run
- ✔ explain, using a diagram, that the Keynesian model of the AS curve has three sections because of "wage/price" downward inflexibility and different levels of spare capacity in the economy
- ✔ explain, using the Keynesian AD/AS model, that the economy may be in equilibrium at any level of real output where AD intersects AS and that, in contrast to the Monetarist/New Classical model, the economy can remain stuck in a deflationary or recessionary gap
- ✔ explain, using a diagram, how the Monetarist/New Classical LRAS and Keynesian AS can shift to the right
- ✔ discuss, with the aid of real-world examples, the limitations of the Monetarist/New Classical and Keynesian models and their implications for government policies.

This sub-unit introduces the aggregate demand and aggregate supply (AD/AS) model used to explain variations in economic activity (national income).

Summary

Aggregate demand (AD) is the total planned spending on domestic goods and services at different price levels per period of time. AD is the sum of *expenditures* by households, firms, the government and the foreign sector, so the components or determinants of AD are the different types of expenditure used in the expenditure method of measuring national income—consumption (C), investment (I), government (G) and net exports (X – M).

$AD = C + I + G + (X - M)$

An increase in AD is represented by a rightward shift of the AD curve (see Figure 3.2.1). Conversely, a decrease in AD corresponds to a leftward shift of the AD curve.

AD will shift when either of the determinants of AD changes. For example, an increase in export revenue would result in an increase in AD—since it is C + I + G + (X – M)—reflected by the rightward shift

Content link

Link to other sub-units

Refer to sub-unit 3.1 for the different types of expenditures in an economy.

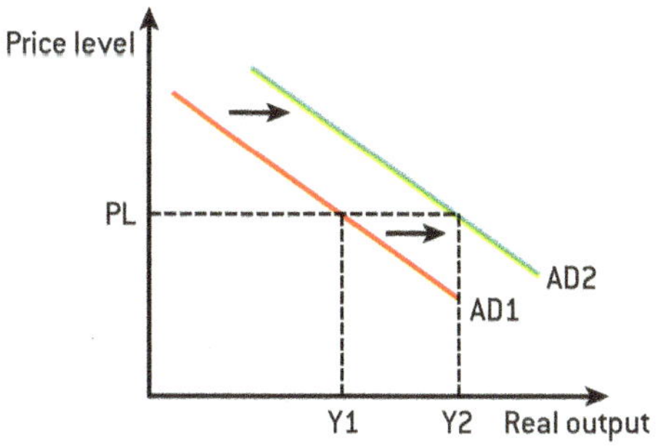

▲ Figure 3.2.1 An increase in AD

from AD1 to AD2 on Figure 3.2.1. This increase in AD implies that total expenditure is higher at every price level.

The main factors affecting the determinants of AD are given in Table 3.2.1.

▼ Table 3.2.1 The main factors affecting AD

Consumption (C)	• Consumer confidence • Interest rates • Wealth • Income taxes • Household indebtedness • Expectations of future price level
Investment (I)	• Interest rates • Business confidence • Technology • Business taxes • Corporate indebtedness
Government spending (G)	• Economic priorities • Political priorities
Net exports (X – M)	• Income of trading partners • Exchange rates • Changes in trade policies

Content link

Link to other sub-units

The impact of changes in exchange rates and trade policies will be the focus of sub-units 4.2 and 4.5.

Aggregate supply (AS) is the planned level of output domestic firms are willing to offer at different price levels per time period.

Although Keynesian and Monetarist/New Classical economists agree on the shape of AD, they have different perspectives on AS. The Monetarist/New Classical model includes a short-run AS (SRAS) and a long-run AS (LRAS).

Content link

Link to other sub-units

Refer to sub-unit 1.2 for the evolution of economic thought in the 20th century.

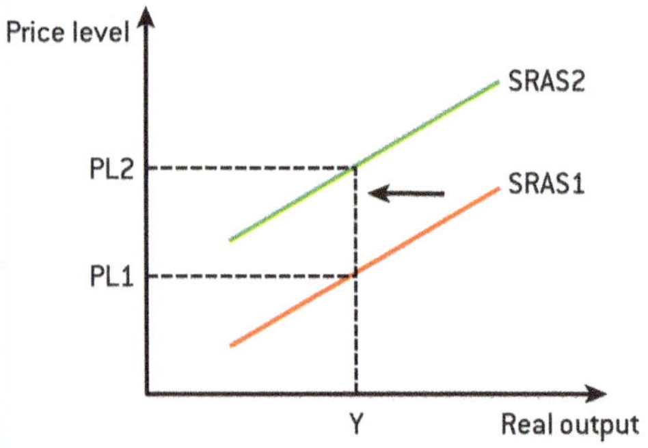

▲ Figure 3.2.2 A decrease in SRAS

The Monetarist/New Classical model

In macroeconomics, the short run is the period of time when the price of factors of production are not responding much to changes in price level. In particular, nominal wages (the cost of labour, which makes up most of the cost of production) are fixed as they do not adjust to match changes in the price level. The **short-run aggregate supply (SRAS)** gives us the real output for each price level in the short run.

The main factors that affect SRAS are given in Table 3.2.2.

▼ Table 3.2.2 The main factors affecting SRAS

Resource prices (costs of production)—for example, an increase in wages leads to higher costs of production for firms and they pass on the higher costs to consumers through higher prices—see Figure 3.2.2, where the higher cost of production leads to a higher price level, PL2 for the same level of real output, Y.
Changes in indirect taxes and subsidies—higher indirect taxes such as the value-added tax (VAT) imposed in all EU countries, or the goods and service tax (GST) implemented in Australia would result in a decrease in SRAS. Similarly, subsidies on essential factors of production such as energy (e.g. oil) would result in a rightward shift (increase) of the SRAS curve.
Supply shocks—sudden changes that reduce the availability of factors of production, or the ability of firms to produce, result in a decrease in SRAS. For instance, a six-day blockage of the Suez Canal in 2021 led to major disruption in international trade as 12% of all goods traded internationally, including barrels of oil and canisters of liquefied natural gas, pass through the Suez Canal. The inability to obtain resources for six days and the resulting backlog led to increases in cost of transportation for many firms, which had to resort to air transportation. For many countries, this supply shock resulted in a leftward shift of the SRAS curve.

According to Monetarist/New Classical economists, nominal wages and the price of other resources are assumed to be flexible in the long-run and always bring the economy to its potential output (full employment output). The **long-run aggregate supply (LRAS)** is vertical at potential output, as shown on Figure 3.2.3. You will learn in sub-unit 3.3 that the potential output, also known as full employment output, is the level of output where the only unemployment present is the natural rate of unemployment (NRU).

A shift to the right of the LRAS curve occurs for these reasons.

- **There is an improvement in the *quantity* of factors of production.** This may happen as a result of an increase in retirement age, which increases the size of the labour force.
- **There is an improvement in the *quality* of factors of production.** Greater access to education and worker retraining schemes make labour more productive.
- **There is an improvement in technology**, which will allow firms to produce more with the same amount of factors of production.
- **Institutional changes occur.** For example, deregulation of economic activities or reduction in bureaucracy (such as introducing an easier process to obtain a business license) and privatization of public enterprises may lead to **an increase in efficiency in the use of factors of production**.

The Monetarist/New Classical model distinguishes between **short-run** and **long-run macroeconomic equilibria** (note that the plural of "equilibrium" is "equilibria"). The short-run macroeconomic equilibrium is determined where AD = SRAS. Any factors affecting AD or SRAS will shift either of the curves, resulting in an adjustment of the economy and thus a new short-run equilibrium. For instance, an increase in government spending would lead to a rightward shift of AD (see Figure 3.2.4). This results in an increase in price level from PL1 to PL2 and an increase in real output from Y1 to Y2.

In the long run, the economy will reach an equilibrium at the potential (full employment) level of output. For instance, an increase in AD might lead to a short-run macroeconomic equilibrium beyond the potential output, as shown on Figure 3.2.5, where the new macroeconomic equilibrium is at real output Y2 and price level PL2. In such a case, the distance between real output and potential output (YPY2) is called an **inflationary gap**—the economy is overheating. Since the price level has increased to PL2 but money wages are constant, the *real* wage of workers decreases. When employment contracts expire and workers adjust their expectations, firms will need to pay workers higher wages, resulting in

Content link

Link to other sub-units

Refer to sub-unit 1.1. The PPC and the LRAS both illustrate the potential output. The factors that affect the PPC are thus also the factors that affect the LRAS.

Refer to sub-unit 3.1 on the theory of business cycles—the potential (long-term) output increases over time.

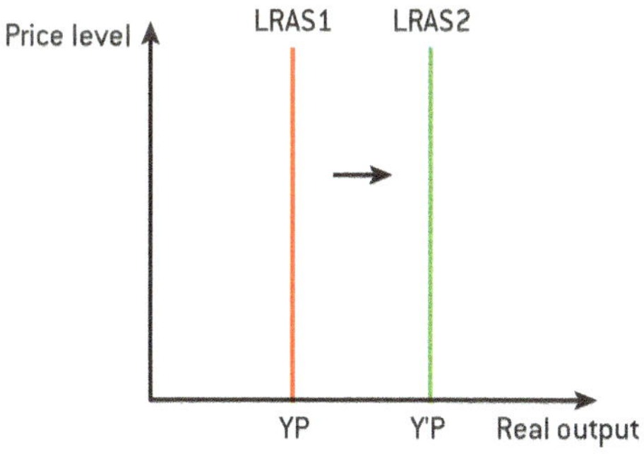

▲ Figure 3.2.3 An increase in LRAS

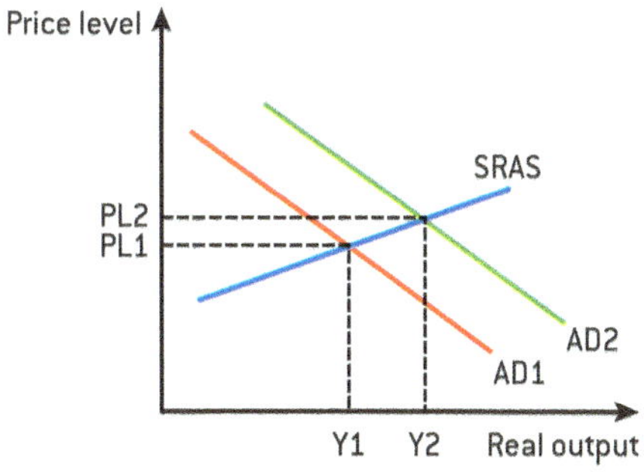

▲ Figure 3.2.4 An increase in real output in the short run

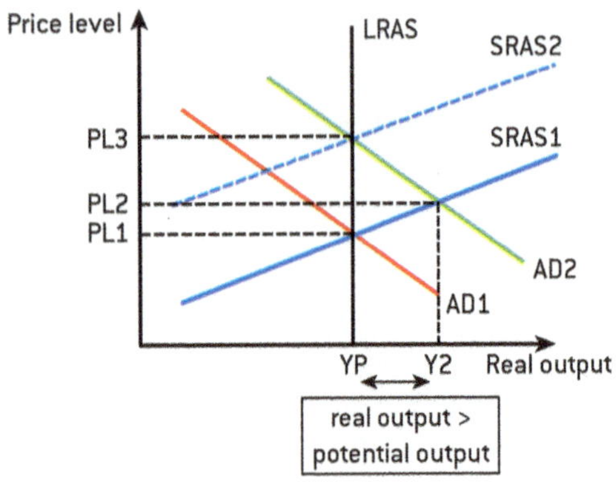

▲ Figure 3.2.5 An inflationary gap

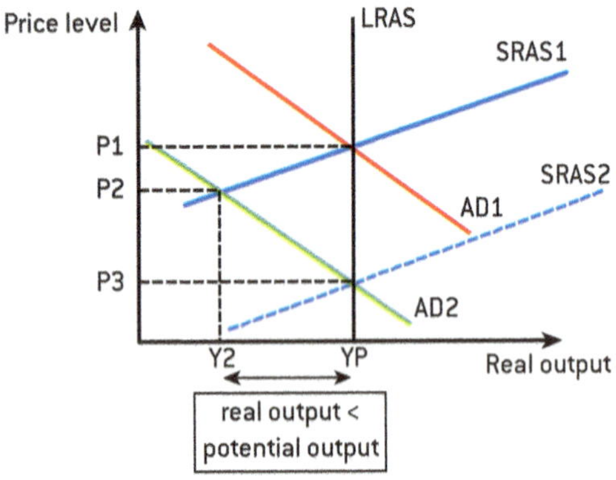

▲ Figure 3.2.6 A deflationary gap

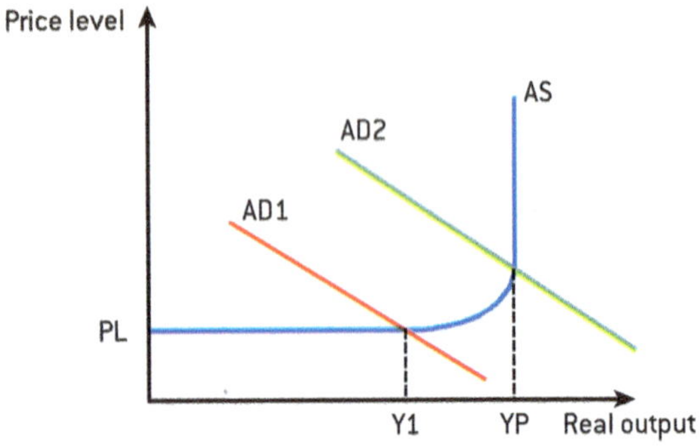

▲ Figure 3.2.7 The Keynesian AS

Content link

Link to other sub-units

Refer to sub-unit 3.1 for the theory of business cycles—the real output of a country fluctuates in the short term around the potential (long-term) output as it moves from contraction (recession) when the economy is a recessionary gap to expansion when the economy goes towards an inflationary gap.

an increase in costs of production and so a decrease of the SRAS. As SRAS slowly shifts to the left, from SRAS1 to SRAS2, the economy reaches its potential output at YP with price level PL3.

Similarly, a decrease in AD might result in a level of output that is less than the potential output and the level of unemployment is greater than the NRU, which is shown on Figure 3.2.6. Here Y2YP is called a **deflationary gap**. As the prices of resources are assumed to be flexible in the long run, the nominal wages and prices of resources will decrease, and the cost of production will fall. This leads to a downward shift of the SRAS from SRAS1 to SRAS2. The economy returns to its potential output. Note that under the Monetarist/New Classical model, the automatism of the market through adjustment in prices implies that government intervention is not required to reach full employment.

The Keynesian AD/AS model

The equilibrium level of real output (real GDP) and price level are determined by the intersection of AD and the Keynesian AS. The model does not adhere to an automatic adjustment. Keynesian economists see wages as "sticky downwards"; that is, they may increase but do not easily decrease. This is for numerous reasons, including the existence of trade unions and employment contracts that prevent a decrease in nominal wages. As such, a deflationary gap would not result in a decrease in wages that would bring the economy back to the potential output. The economy would remain stuck in this deflationary gap.

The Keynesian school of thought sees AS as having three distinct sections based on the level of spare capacity in the economy, as shown on Figure 3.2.7.

- At any level of output below Y1, the AS is horizontal due to excessive spare capacity (a lot of unused resources). Any increase in AD up to AD1 will lead to an increase in output without increasing the price level, PL. Employing more factors of production does not lead to increase in their prices due to their great availability.
- At levels of output between Y1 and Y2, AS slopes upward as resources start to become scarce for some industries which face "bottlenecks" in production (since different industries need different types of factors of production). An increase in AD within that range will lead to an increase in output (from Y1 to Y2) as well as a rise in price level. The closer the increase in AD brings the economy to full employment, the greater the increase in price level.
- Once the economy reaches its potential output of YP, AS is vertical. Increases in AD only result in increases in price level as there is no additional resource for firms to use to increase production. The economy is said to be overheating.

Since the prices of resources do not adjust to bring the economy back to full employment, if follows that it is purely AD that determines the equilibrium level of output. Keynesian economists advocate government intervention to raise AD when real output is below potential output or decrease AD when the economy is overheating.

Note that the analysis for the rightward shift of the LRAS curve in the Monetarist/New Classical model is the same for the Keynesian AS. For example, improvements in technology would result in a rightward shift of the AS curve in the Keynesian model.

In short, in contrast to the Monetarist/New Classical model, the following apply in the Keynesian model.

- Wages are "sticky downwards".
- There is no automatic adjustment to potential output. The economy may remain in an equilibrium where real output is not the potential output.
- The government must try to increase or decrease AD to bring the economy to its potential output and avoid overheating.

QUESTION PRACTICE

This question is adapted from the November 2017 examination paper.

Country Y is currently in a position of long-run equilibrium (assuming a Monetarist/New Classical model). The following diagram illustrates the aggregate demand (AD) and short-run aggregate supply (SRAS) curves for Country Y.

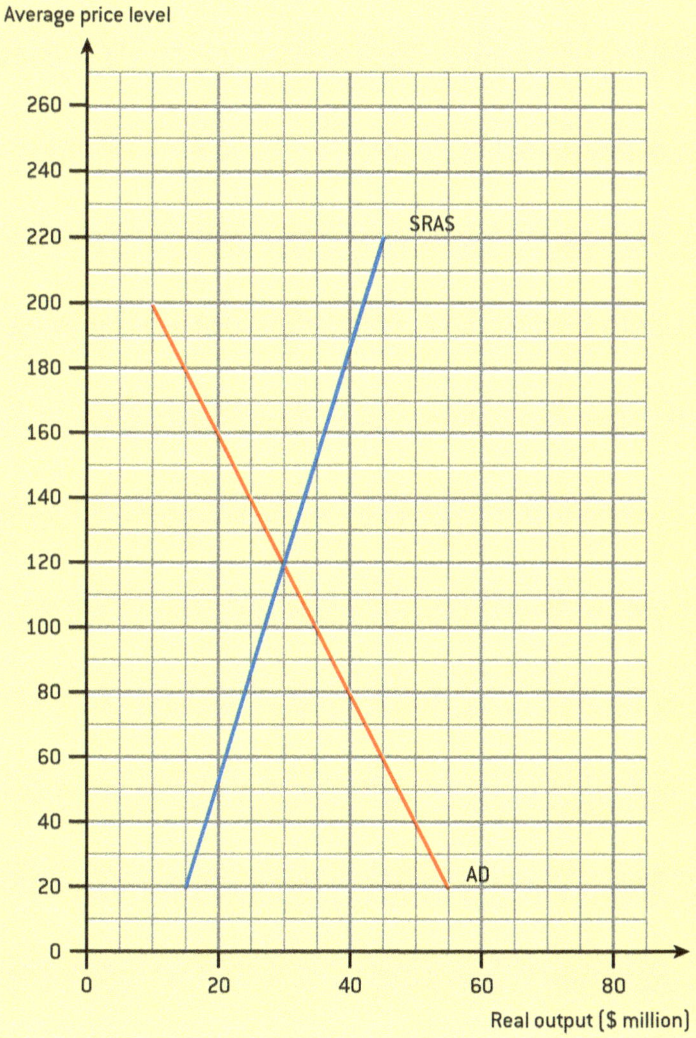

An increase in consumer confidence has caused aggregate demand to increase by $25 million.

(i) On the diagram, draw and label the new aggregate demand curve. [1]

(ii) Determine the average price level once the economy has returned to a position of long-run equilibrium. [1]

(iii) Explain how the economy would move back to this position of long-run equilibrium. [4]

SAMPLE STUDENT ANSWER

Response 1

i)

▲ The diagram shows a clear increase in AD of exactly $25 million and the curve is labelled. Note that the vertical axis is labelled "Average price level", which means the same as "Price level".

(ii) 220

▲ This is correct. Do not hesitate to draw LRAS at Y = $30 million to help you answer the question. Note that a price level is an index so it comes with no unit (that is, it is not expressed in $ or other monetary terms).

(iii) The shift of AD to the right will create an inflationary gap. The economy is above the level of full employment. As wages are flexible in the long run, the shortage of labour will result in an increase in cost of production which in turn will decrease SRAS (shift of the curve to the left) until the economy returns to the full level of employment (US$ 30 million of output) where the average price level is 220.

▲ The question states that the economy was initially in its long-run equilibrium and thus $30 million is the potential output. The SRAS curve will need to shift left to bring back the economy to full employment and this will occur where PL = 220. The answer to part (iii) makes use of the data from the diagram and would be likely to achieve full marks.

This response could have achieved 6/6 marks.

QUESTION PRACTICE

This question is adapted from the November 2015 examination paper.

Explain why, using the Monetarist/New Classical model, the economy will always return to the potential (full employment) output following a recession. [10]

SAMPLE STUDENT ANSWER

Economies go through cycles of expansion and recessions, which is known as business cycles. The Monetarist/New Classical perspective is that the economy will always self-adjust and gravitate towards its long-term output in the long run, a position that is referred to as the full employment level of output. It is not a situation where there is no unemployment but rather that the only unemployment is what is called the natural rate of unemployment (NRU) which happens even when an economy is performing well.

▲ This is a good introduction to the Monetarist/New Classical view that the economy will return to full employment. The concept of full employment output (potential output) is clearly explained.

An economy goes through the recession phase of the business cycle when aggregate demand (AD) decreases and this leads to a fall in real output known and thus a recession. For instance, consumption may decrease following a sudden decrease in the value of real estate, which would decrease the wealth of households. This drop in the consumption expenditure (C) component of AD would result in a lower AD since AD = C + I + G + (X − M). As you can see on my first diagram drawn below, the drop in AD would result in a macroeconomic equilibrium (where AD = SRAS) with lower real output. This is a short-term equilibrium since real output is lower than the full employment output, YP. The distance between real output and full employment output is known as a recessionary gap.

▲ This paragraph is a good explanation of the concept of a recession with reference to the business cycle model learned in sub-unit 3.1. A generic example is used to explain a situation that brings an economy to a recessionary gap.

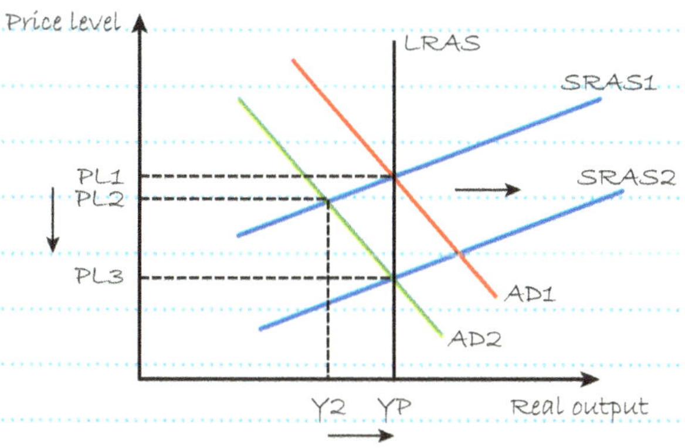

▼ The diagram drawn is correct and fully labelled but more references are needed to explain it. For example, the drop in AD could be described as "a fall in AD from AD1 to AD2", the real output due to the fall in AD is not identified as Y2 and the recessionary gap could be referred to as Y2YP.

▲ This paragraph provides a good explanation of the automatic mechanism that brings the economy back to full employment through a decrease in the price of resources. The candidate has thus addressed the demands of the question.

▼ Again, the candidate should make more references to the diagram, for instance "the SRAS increases from SRAS1 to SRAS2".

When the economy is going through a recessionary gap, there is not enough demand for goods and services so fewer factors of production are needed since firms need to produce fewer goods. This leads to surpluses of resources in the factor market. Over the long term, prices including wages are assumed to be flexible in the Monetarist/New Classical model and thus the prices of resources would start to decrease. This leads to lower costs of production for firms and hence SRAS increases, meaning it shifts to the right as shown on the next diagram.

The real output goes back to the full employment level, YP.

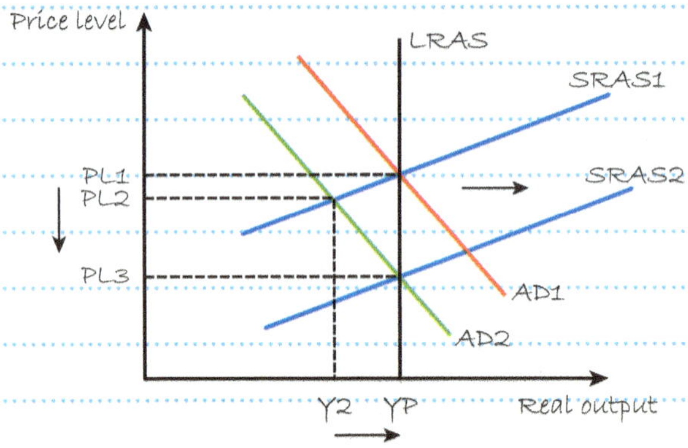

▲ This is a good conclusive statement, highlighting the main assumption of the model (price flexibility in the long run).

As such, in the Monetarist/New Classical model, the economy always goes back to the full employment level of output in the long run. This full automatism of the economy to adjust back to YP is only possible due to the assumption of prices and thus wages being flexible.

This response meets all the descriptors of the highest mark band (9–10). However, the diagrams are not sufficiently explained to be awarded full marks. Refer to Unit 5 pages 194–195) for a full explanation of the paper 1 level descriptors.

This response could have achieved 9/10 marks.

QUESTION PRACTICE

This question is adapted from the May 2016 examination paper

Using the Keynesian AD/AS diagram, explain why an economy may be in equilibrium at any level of real output. [10]

SAMPLE STUDENT ANSWER

Unlike the New Classical economists, the Keynesian economists don't believe in wages being flexible even in the long run. Indeed, John Maynard Keynes once said that "in the long run, we are all dead", meaning that he did not believe the economy will eventually work itself out in any reasonable time. It could take years for the economy to self-adjust.

▲ This is a good introduction to Keynesian belief that prices do not adjust downwards. The quote from John Maynard Keynes is not necessary but it helps explain this central assumption of the model.

The aggregate supply (AS) curve in the Keynesian model has three distinct section depending on the extend of spare capacity, which can be seen on this diagram:

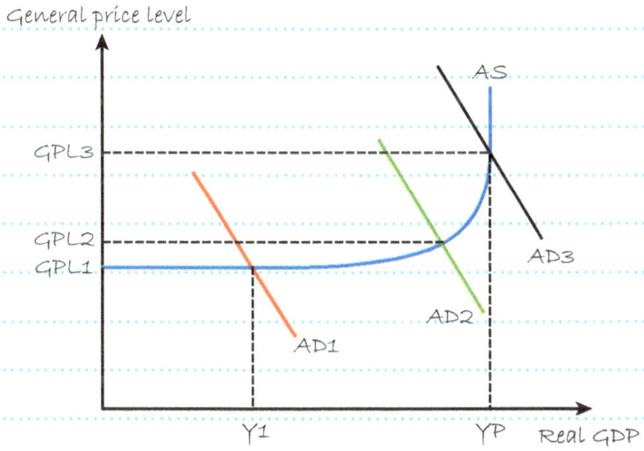

▲ The candidate provides a correct and fully labelled diagram and points out that the shape of the AS curve depends on the level of spare capacity. Note that "general price level" is another commonly used type of price level and "real GDP" is also a valid alternative for "real output".

Adding the aggregate demand (AD) gives us the macroeconomic equilibrium, that is the point where AD = AS, which gives us the equilibrium real GDP. For instance, the economy could be at Y1, where AD1 = AS. At this point, the economy is along the horizontal section of the AS curve where there is a lot of spare capacity, meaning this is insufficient demand for goods and services. At that point a lot of resources are not in use and thus a lot of workers are unemployed. Since the model does not believe that the workers will accept lower wages (a phenomenon called "downward price stickiness"), there is no decrease in price of the labour resource which classical economists believe in. The economy would remain at that position until there is a change in a component of AD.

▲ The concept of macroeconomic equilibrium is explained. The candidate has explained why an economy could remain in a situation of high unemployment. There are also adequate references to the diagram.

On the other hand, the economy could be along the vertical section of the AS curve, which is shaped that way because it represents a stage in the economy where all the resources are employed and hence the real GDP at that point is also the

▲ This paragraph explains that the economy could also remain in another situation where the economy produces at full capacity. The candidate continues to make adequate references to the diagram.

potential GDP, YP – meaning that it is the maximum GDP that can be produced with all resources fully employed. Such a situation may occur where AD is as high as AD3 and the price level is high (GPL3). Unless there is a decrease in one of the components of AD, the economy will remain in this situation of increasing price level.

Ideally, the economy should be near full employment, along the intermediate section of the AS curve, for example where AD 2= AS and real GDP is Y2. At that point, where there are some shortages of resources in some industries, the economy does not experience high price levels and the unemployment is limited. This stage can only be achieved, according to the Keynesian model, if the government intervenes to either boost AD for low AD level such as AD1 or dampen increases in AD when at AD3. Without intervention, the economy could be stuck at any possible level of output.

▲ Stating that the model sees intervention as necessary to bring the economy to an "ideal" level of output is a good way to end this response.

This response meets all of the descriptors of the highest mark band (9–10), so **it could have achieved 10/10 marks.**

Content link

Link to your IA

AD/AS diagrams are often needed for Unit 3 commentaries. They help explain changes in economic activity (often GDP). Make sure you identify both the reason for the change in GDP (that is, a change in AD and/or AS) and the factor(s) causing that change. For example, if an article describes a fall in real GDP due to a reluctance of consumers and firms to spend, identify the *low levels of business or consumer confidence* as the source of the decrease in consumption (C) and investment (I), both of which are components of AD. If the economy sees an increase in AD during a recession as a result of greater government spending, you might want to point out that the authorities are adopting a *Keynesian approach* to management of the economy.

Concept link

- **Intervention**—many governments adopt a Keynesian approach to the management of recessions. You will learn about the policy responses in sub-units 3.5 and 3.6 as well as other forms of intervention in sub-unit 3.7. Some articles may hint to the "downward stickiness" of wages, for instance if they mention tensions with trade unions or frequent worker strikes. These factors would suggest that the economy will not self-adjust, as wages are unlikely to decrease.

3.3 MACROECONOMIC OBJECTIVES

You should be able to:

- define the terms
  - short-term and long-term economic growth
  - recession
  - cyclical (demand-deficient), structural, seasonal and frictional unemployment
  - the natural rate of unemployment (NRU)
  - demand-pull and cost-push inflation
  - deflation
  - disinflation
  - government (national) debt
- explain, using a production possibilities curve (PPC) diagram or an AD/AS diagram, the causes of short-term and long-term economic growth
- calculate the rate of economic growth from a set of data
- discuss, with the aid of real-world examples, the possible consequences of economic growth
- calculate the unemployment rate from a set of data
- explain the difficulties in measuring unemployment
- explain, using a diagram, that the imposition of a minimum wage may result in unemployment
- explain, using a diagram (or diagrams), that cyclical unemployment is caused by a fall in aggregate demand
- explain, using a diagram, that structural unemployment is caused by changes in the demand for particular labour skills, changes in the geographical location of industries and labour market rigidities
- explain the limitations of using the CPI in measuring inflation
- explain, using AD/AS diagrams, the causes of inflation and deflation
- explain the possible consequences of a high inflation rate and deflation
- calculate the inflation rate from a set of data, using quantities purchased as weights in the CPI
- discuss, with the aid of real-world examples, the costs of unemployment versus inflation
- discuss, with the aid of real-world examples, the potential conflicts between the macroeconomic objectives.

This sub-unit introduces the macroeconomic objectives of a government—economic growth, low unemployment, and a low and stable rate of inflation.

HL In addition to the points above, for HL you should be able to:

- construct a weighted price index, using a set of data provided
- explain the importance of a sustainable level of government (national) debt and the costs of a high government (national) debt
- discuss, with the aid of real-world examples and using short-run and long-run Phillips curve diagrams and/or an AD/AS diagram, the view that there is a possible trade-off between the unemployment rate and the inflation rate.

Summary

Economic growth

Economic growth refers to an increase in real output (real GDP) over time. It is the percentage change in real GDP between two years. For example, the economic growth rate for an economy between 2021 and 2022 would be:

$$\frac{rGDP_{22} - rGDP_{21}}{rGDP_{21}} \times 100$$

Short-term economic growth (actual growth) results from the greater use of existing resources. This may be illustrated using a PPC model or an AD/AS model.

Content link

Link to other sub-units

Refer to:

- sub-unit 1.1—a PPC may be used to illustrate both short-term and long-term economic growth
- sub-unit 3.2—an increase in potential output (LRAS/Keynesian AS) represents long-term economic growth
- sub-unit 3.2—an increase in AD may result in an increase in real output and hence short-term economic growth.

Long-term growth (potential growth) results from an increase in potential output (productive capacity of the economy). This may also be illustrated using the PPC and AD/AS models.

Economic growth may have the following results.

- **It may lead to an improvement in living standards (economic well-being).** The increase in real output may lead to an increase in real GDP per capita if real output grows faster than the population as it implies, on the average, greater access to goods and services for the population. As you learned in sub-unit 3.1, there are limitations to using real output per capita to measure changes in economic well-being over time.
- There may be negative and positive **impacts on the environment**. The increase in output may come from increased production of goods that may generate negative externalities, posing a threat to sustainability. On the other hand, in high

income countries, rising real incomes have given society the ability to devote resources to protect the environment and combat the threat to sustainability.

- There may be decreases and increases in **income inequality**. Economic growth may be driven by increased production in some industries or regions, resulting in regional inequalities (refer to Figure 3.1.1, page 81, the map of mainland China for an illustration). In the industries or regions where production rises faster, this is likely to be accompanied by faster increases in wages, widening income inequality—as you learned in sub-unit 2.12, the free market leads to inequalities due to differences in ownership of factors of production. However, economic growth implies higher tax revenue (both from sales taxes and income or business taxes) for the authorities, which enables them to finance redistribution policies.

The opposite of short-term economic growth is a **recession**, which refers to a decrease in real output (real GDP) over time. A recession is often the result of a decrease in AD.

Low unemployment

Unemployment occurs when those who are actively looking for work do not have a job. The unemployment rate is the number of unemployed workers expressed as a percentage of the total labour force (which refer to the active population, the sum of the employed and unemployed):

$$\text{Unemployment rate} = \frac{\text{Number of unemployed}}{\text{Total labour force}} \times 100$$

There are many difficulties in measuring unemployment. Official figures may underestimate the true unemployment rate for these reasons.

- Discouraged workers—those who have stopped looking for a job but would be happy to accept one—are not captured in official statistics.
- Official figures do not take *underemployment* into account. Some workers in part-time jobs are actively looking for full-time employment. As they have a job, they are not considered unemployed. Underemployment also includes individuals in jobs for which they are overqualified.

  "Hidden (disguised)" unemployment includes the underemployed and discouraged workers.

  The unemployment rate may also be overestimated when:

  - workers are employed in illegal or unofficial activities
  - individuals do not reveal that they are employed, in order to claim unemployment benefits or avoid paying income tax.

The **economic costs** of unemployment include:

- loss of real output (real GDP) as unemployment implies that the economy is operating below its potential output (below the PPC)
- a reduction in tax revenue for the government
- higher government expenditures to finance unemployment benefits and retraining programmes
- in the case of prolonged unemployment, widened inequalities and increased poverty.

The **personal and social costs** include:

- psychological stress from being unable to finance daily expenses
- loss of health insurance for people in countries where there is no national healthcare system, and individuals have health insurance provided by their employer
- greater social problems such as increased homelessness, alcoholism and drug abuse, and higher crime rates (e.g. thefts).

Four categories are used to reflect different types of unemployment and their causes. These categories are described below. Governments identify the type of unemployment to adopt appropriate policies.

Cyclical unemployment (also known as demand-deficient unemployment) results from a decrease in AD that decreases the demand for labour. This type of unemployment takes place during recessions when the economy is not producing at the potential output. Since the demand for labour is derived from the demand for goods and services the workers produce, Figure 3.3.1 shows the demand for labour decreasing from D(L)1 to D(L)2, as a result of AD decreasing from AD1 to AD2 during a recession.

Assuming that wages are "sticky downwards" (due to employment contracts, trade unions, for example), the labour market will not reach an equilibrium at W2. At W1, the number of workers willing to work (supply of labour) is greater than the number of jobs offered (demand for labour) and there is a disequilibrium (surplus) in the labour market. This surplus is the number of workers in cyclical unemployment.

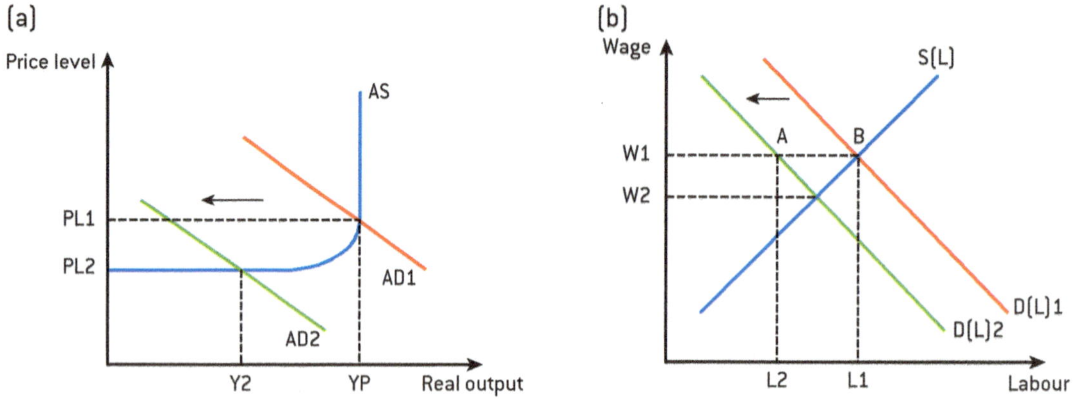

▲ **Figure 3.3.1** Cyclical (demand-deficient) unemployment

You learned in sub-unit 3.2 that even when an economy has reached its potential output, some members of the labour force are part of the **natural rate of unemployment (NRU)**. The NRU is the sum of three types of equilibrium unemployment—seasonal unemployment, frictional unemployment and structural unemployment.

Seasonal unemployment occurs when individuals are out of work because their usual job is "out of season". For example, some farm workers may be without work for a few weeks in winter when cold weather makes it impossible to harvest crops.

Frictional unemployment refers to the members of the labour force who are between jobs. It arises because it takes time for individuals who enter the labour force or who have left their existing jobs to find employment. Job seekers may remain temporarily in frictional unemployment as they need time to gather information on job vacancies. Similarly, employers may not fill a vacancy immediately in hope of finding a better-qualified person. As both frictional unemployment and seasonal unemployment are short term in nature, they do not represent a significant concern to governments.

Structural unemployment is due to skills mismatch and labour market rigidities. The pattern of demand and production methods change in the long term, resulting in a permanent fall in the demand for a particular type of skills. Outsourcing and cheaper labour cost in foreign markets may also lead to a permanent drop in demand for labour. Workers who are unable to adjust to the new requirements of the industry and/or are unable to join other industries find that their skills have become obsolete. This is illustrated on Figure 3.3.2, which shows the labour market for a specific type of worker. For instance, developments in artificial intelligence now allow for the use of robots as waiters in restaurants. These robots can take orders from customers, serve meals and return dirty dishes to the kitchen. The adoption of this technology would probably result in a permanent drop in the demand for restaurant staff from D(L)1 to D(L)2. Figure 3.3.2 may look like Figure 3.3.1b, which shows cyclical unemployment. However, structural unemployment is a long-term problem that lasts longer than recessions and thus the wage may adjust over time, to W2 (while a disequilibrium remains for cyclical unemployment). The means that the workers with this skillset will need to accept a lower wage to remain employed. L2L1 reflects those who are structurally unemployed.

Structural unemployment may be the result of labour market rigidities (laws and regulations that make it difficult for the labour market to adjust to changes in the demand for labour and/or supply of labour).

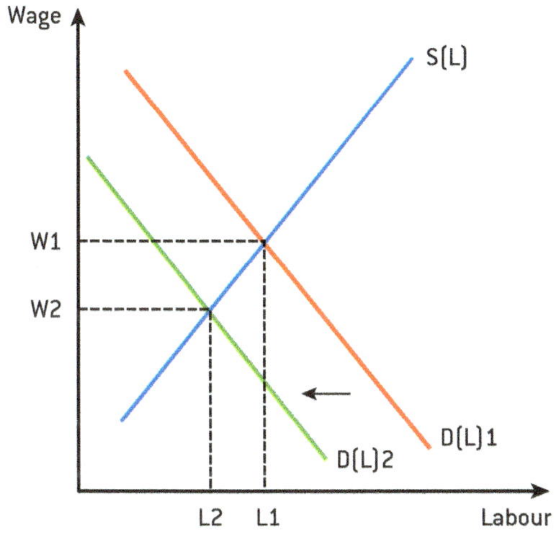

▲ Figure 3.3.2 Structural unemployment due to a permanent drop in the demand for specific skills

Content link

Link to other sub-units

A minimum wage legislation is an application of the price floor analysis you learned in sub-unit 2.7.

The minimum wage, if above the market equilibrium (W2 on Figure 3.3.3) would result in more workers being willing to work than firms are willing to hire. The market disequilibrium in affected labour markets leads to structural unemployment of L2L1.

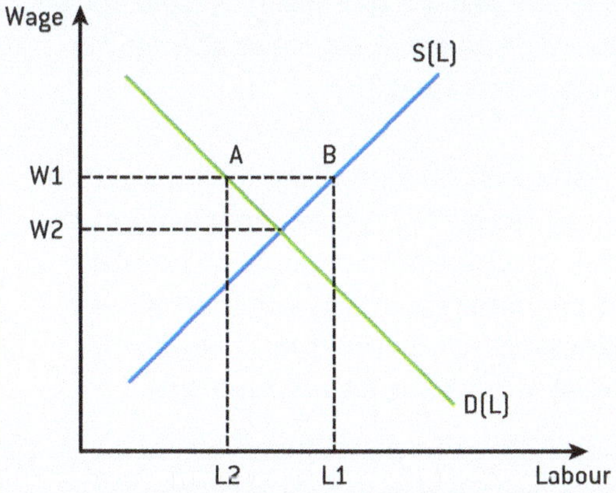

▲ Figure 3.3.3 Structural unemployment due to minimum wage legislation

Low and stable rate of inflation

Inflation is the increase in price level over time. It is usually measured using the **consumer price index (CPI)**, which is the weighted average of the prices of a basket of goods and services bought by the typical consumer in a country. For instance, the inflation rate in a country in 2019 can be calculated as:

$$\text{Inflation rate 2019} = \frac{CPI_{19} - CPI_{18}}{CPI_{18}} \times 100$$

So, if the inflation rate in 2019 was 5%, it means that prices, on the average, increased in 2019 by 5% compared to 2018.

HL Calculating the CPI for a particular year involves summing up the weighted price of each item in the representative basket of goods and services. The weights, which represent the relative importance of a good to households, are the quantities bought of each good in the basket.

So, the CPI for a particular year is:

$\Sigma w_n P_n$

where P is the price of a good and w the weight assigned to that good in the basket.

$$w = \frac{\text{expenditure on the good}}{\text{total household expenditure}}$$

Using the CPI to measure inflation has some limitations.

- The basket of goods and services—that is, the items included and the weight given to each item—represents the typical household expenditure. A "typical household" may not exist, though, due to wide variation in consumption habits, especially in large countries. For example, in the USA the consumption of fuel for heating is much greater in arctic Alaska than in tropical Florida, so an increase in the price of fuel may affect US households differently—the weights may not be representative of all households. Staple foods (rice, bread, pasta) may differ in multicultural societies such as Australia, Canada and Singapore, making it hard to identify the items that represent "the typical household".
- The CPI captures changes in the price of goods included in the basket without consideration for improvements in quality. For instance, smartphones may become more expensive, but they also offer more functions.

- The basket of goods and services needs to be reviewed over time as consumption patterns of the "average household" changes. For instance, in 2021, the UK's office for national statistics (ONS) added hand weights and hand sanitizers to the basket of goods and services used to measure inflation to reflect the greater purchase of home gym equipment and other goods that became common household items because of the COVID-19 pandemic. However, new products may take time to be included or old items time to be removed, making changes in the CPI a less reliable measure of changes in the cost of living—hi-fi systems were only replaced by streaming portable speakers by the ONS in 2019, for example.
- The growing number of online purchases makes it difficult to select representative prices for goods in the basket due to significant differences between online and high-street prices.

Test yourself

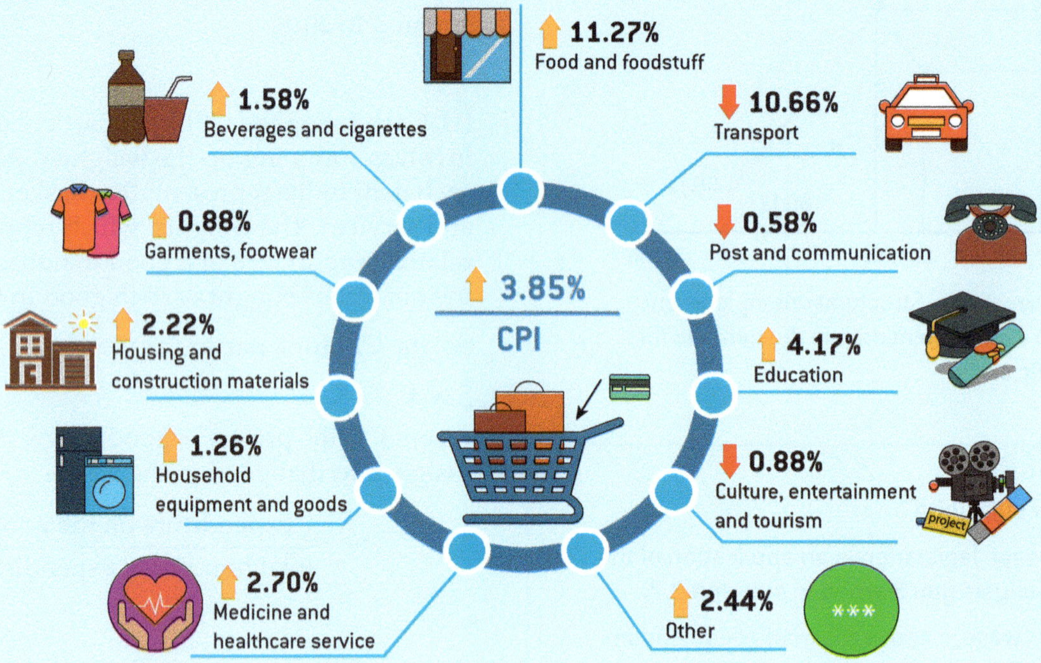

▲ Figure 3.3.4 The CPI in Vietnam 2020

Figure 3.3.4 illustrates the increase in Vietnam's CPI in 2020. The broad categories of the goods included in the basket are provided. While the CPI increased by 3.85%, the increase was not uniform across all categories. How does this graphic help illustrate some of the limitations of the CPI mentioned above? Are all consumers likely to be equally affected? Do you foresee that some households would be concerned about the cost of education while others would not be affected? Is transportation equally important to those living in urban centres and those living in rural areas?

A high rate of inflation comes with these costs.

- Inflation increases uncertainty as it makes it difficult for businesses to determine whether an investment project will be profitable.
- Income inequality may increase as the purchasing power (real income) of fixed income earners (wage earners, pensioners) decreases while variable income earners (professionals such as architects or lawyers, entrepreneurs) see their earnings increase with prices.
- High inflation leads to a loss of export competitiveness, especially when the inflation rate at home is higher than it is in other economies producing similar goods for exports.
- Inflation distorts the signalling and incentive function of prices. If all prices are rising at the same time, producers are unable to identify which price increases are due to a relatively greater demand from consumers, and which they should allocate more resources to.
- Inflation may lead to panic buying when households fear continued high increases in prices.

Inflation may come from increases in any of the components of AD. The closer the economy is to its potential output (YP on Figure 3.3.5), the higher the increase in the price level resulting from an increase in AD. Figure 3.3.5 shows that the initial increase in AD (AD1 to AD2) leads to an increase in the price level from PL1 to PL2. A subsequent increase in AD of an equal magnitude (AD2 to AD3) brings about a significantly higher increase in price level, PL2 to PL3—you learned in sub-unit 3.2 that firms face "bottlenecks" in production as the economy approaches full employment. The increase in price level from PL1 to PL3 is due to increases in AD and is called **demand-pull inflation**.

Note that only high demand-pull inflation is a concern. A mild rate of inflation (averaging 2%) is a sign that the economy is growing. Figure 3.3.5, where AD increases from AD1 to AD2, shows that the increase in price level is accompanied by a significant increase in real output (Y1 to Y2).

Inflation may also arise when all firms face increases in the cost of production, resulting in a decrease in SRAS. In Figure 3.3.5 this is reflected as SRAS1 shifting left to SRAS2, resulting in a higher price level, PL2. This type of inflation is called **cost-push inflation** and often occurs due to a rise in the price of oil, which is used in most industries for transportation and manufacturing, and/or wages increasing faster than labour productivity. An increase in the price of agricultural crops because of a bad harvest also causes cost-push inflation since crops are used in food production.

A decrease in the price level (CPI) over time is a phenomenon called **deflation**. It usually follows a period of **disinflation** that takes place when the inflation rate decreases, which means that the price level is still increasing but at a decreasing rate. Deflation usually comes from prolonged decreases in AD.

It is argued that deflation is a greater problem than inflation for an economy. The costs of deflation are as follows.

- There is uncertainty as firms are unwilling to commit to investment projects if they fear that the price of their goods will continue to decrease.
- The bigger risk associated with deflation is deferred consumption as consumers put on hold the purchase of houses, cars and other consumer durables in anticipation of lower prices in the future. This could start a deflationary spiral as the AD curve continues to shift left, resulting in high levels of cyclical unemployment and bankruptcies.
- The real value of household and corporate debt increases and this limits the ability of consumers and firms to borrow, limiting increases in AD.
- There is inefficient resource allocation as prices lose their signalling power.
- Deflation may worsen inequalities—some households will enjoy an increase in the real value of their savings.
- Deflation may also make monetary policy ineffective as households and firms may not respond to the lower interest rates due to high business and consumer pessimism and interest rates cannot easily be negative. The workings of monetary policy will be examined in greater detail in sub-unit 3.5.

Content link

Link to other sub-units

Refer to sub-unit 3.2 for the factors that affect the components of AD. The main causes of **demand-pull** inflation tend to be:

- excessive increases in government spending (G), sometimes to gain popular support or as part of fiscal policy (which will be examined in sub-unit 3.6)
- excessive increases in the money supply by government—what Monetarist economists see as a situation of "too much money chasing after too few goods"; (monetary policy and quantitative easing will be examined in sub-unit 3.5)
- high increases in C and I due to high consumer and business confidence when the economy is doing well
- a sudden increase in exports
- expectations of high inflation, which result in households bringing forward expenditure on durable goods.

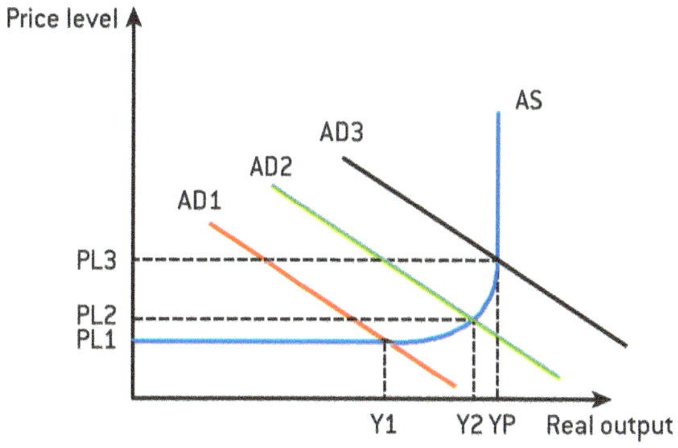

▲ Figure 3.3.5 Demand-pull inflation

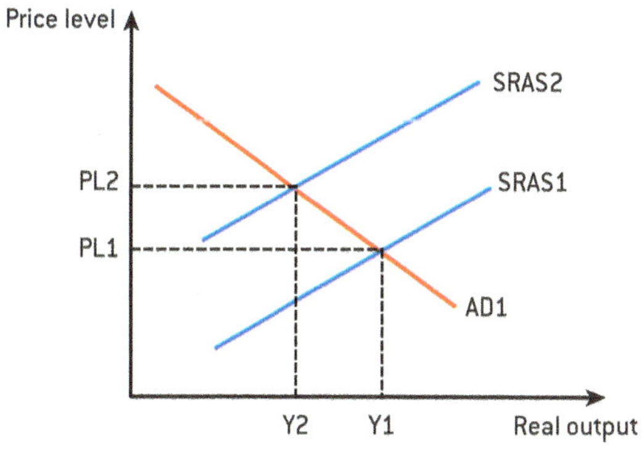

▲ Figure 3.3.6 Cost-push inflation

Assessment tip

Government intervention is needed to achieve a low unemployment rate and a low and stable rate of inflation. As you learned earlier in this sub-unit, inflation and unemployment are complex issues—there are two types of inflation (cost-push and demand-pull inflation) and four types of unemployment (cyclical, structural, seasonal and frictional). The policy responses to high inflation and unemployment will be covered in sub-units 3.5–3.7 but, as you might have guessed, some policies are more suitable for specific types of inflation and/or unemployment. For example, fiscal policy (the focus of sub-unit 3.6) may reduce cyclical unemployment but is unlikely to affect other types of unemployment. A common mistake of candidates is to evaluate the effectiveness of policies in addressing overall unemployment or inflation without considering the impact of the policy on each type of unemployment or inflation separately. Very often, part (b) of paper 1 questions that test on inflation or unemployment require you to distinguish between the types of inflation or unemployment. Failing to do so may result in your response "*partially* addressing the demands of the question" and this will keep you in the (7–9) mark band of the 15-mark question.

The relationship between unemployment and inflation

You have learned that there are costs to both (high) inflation and unemployment. You might have noticed that if AD is so low that the economy is in a recessionary gap, some individuals will fall into cyclical unemployment (Figure 3.3.1, page 98). On the other hand, if AD is so high that the economy reaches full employment, the economy experiences high demand-pull inflation. There is thus a a trade-off between the inflation rate and the unemployment rate. Referring to Figure 3.3.1, if the government could increase AD, the unemployment would reduce at the expense of higher inflation.

HL This inverse relationship between the inflation rate and the unemployment rate is shown on Figure 3.3.7. Point A may refer to an economy in a recession where 5% of the workforce is out of job. Following an increase in AD due to government intervention, the unemployment reduces to 3% but this increase in AD has increased the inflation rate from 2% to 6%. This is illustrated by the short-run Phillips curve. It follows that movements along the Phillips curve (e.g. from A to B) correspond to shifts of the AD curve on an AD/AS diagram.

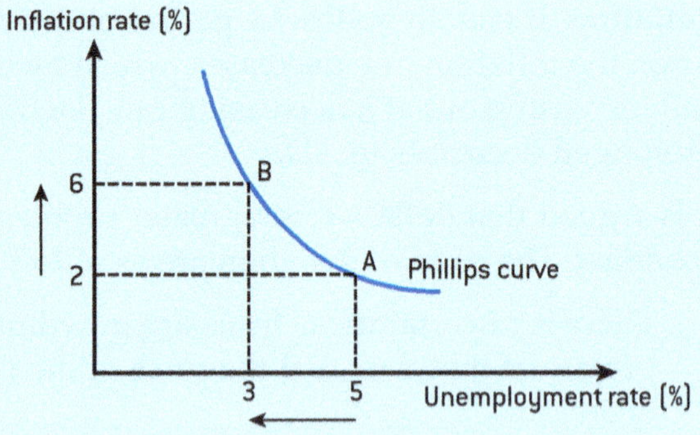

▲ Figure 3.3.7 The short-run Phillips curve

This short-run Phillips curve is aligned to the Keynesian idea that an economy may remain stuck at any level of output and thus an economy may also remain at point A on Figure 3.3.7 since there is no automatic mechanism that leads to changes in wages and prices of other factors of production. On the other hand, Monetarists believe that there is no trade-off in the long run since the economy will return to the potential output. This belief is reflected by the long-run Phillips curve, which is vertical at the potential output (LRPC on Figure 3.3.8).

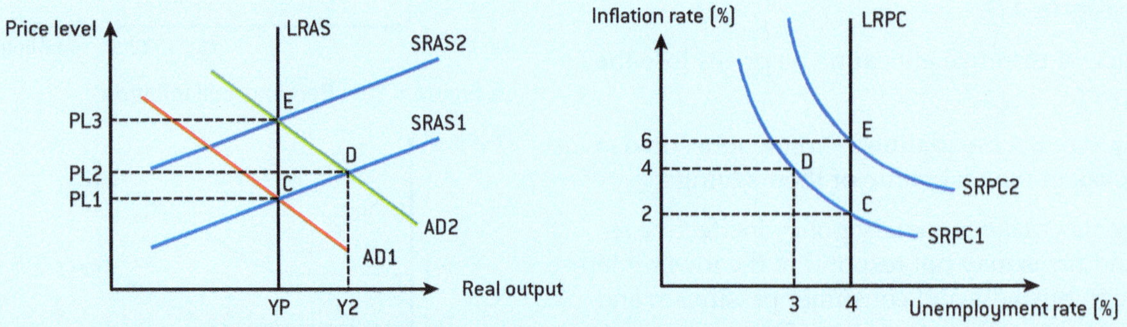

▲ Figure 3.3.8 The short-run and long-run Phillips curve

Consider Figure 3.3.8, which shows an economy operating at potential output at point C where AD1 = SRAS1. On a Phillips curve diagram, this is reflected as a situation where the unemployment rate is 4% and the inflation rate is 2%. Since the economy is at full employment, it follows that the NRU is the only form of unemployment and therefore the LRPC cuts the horizontal axis at that rate of unemployment. If the government attempts to reduce unemployment by increasing AD, the economy will move to point D where there is an inflationary gap—where unemployment is temporarily reduced to 3% but with a higher rate of inflation (which is illustrated by the higher price level, PL2). The inflationary gap will lead to higher wages in the long term and thus higher cost of production, the SRAS1 curve will shift left to SRAS2. This corresponds to a shift of the SRPC curve to the right. The economy returns to full employment at point E where unemployment is back to 4% (the NRU) but with a rate higher inflation of 6%.

Sustainable level of government (national) debt

HL **The government (national) debt** refers to what a government owes domestically (the internal debt—owed to national creditors) as well as to foreigners (the external debt). The internal debt builds up with every **budget deficit**, which is a situation that exists when government spending exceeds government revenue. A government may incur a budget deficit in order to increase AD in the economy. This will be examined in sub-unit 3.6.

The government (national) debt is expressed as a share of GDP. Comparing what a country owes to its national income (GDP) gives insights into that particular country's ability to service the debt (the amount that needs to be paid to cover the repayment of interest and principal on a debt per period). Looking at national debt in absolute terms would be misleading. For instance, in 2021, the national debt of the USA exceeded US$28 trillion while the national debt of Japan was slightly over US$12 trillion. However, the USA's national debt was about 100% of its GDP while Japan's debt was more than 250% of its GDP.

The presence of a national debt is not a bad thing, as long as the debt is incurred to finance necessary public expenditure, bring about macroeconomic stability or finance economic development. Governments should, however, make sure the national debt is manageable or sustainable as a high national debt comes with the following costs.

- **Debt servicing carries a high opportunity cost.** A high debt–GDP ratio implies that a significant share of tax revenue will go to service the debt. For less developed countries, a high debt–GDP ratio makes it difficult to finance essential goods and services such as education and healthcare.
- A **lower credit rating** is given to countries with high debt–GDP ratio by international credit rating agencies. The low rating signals to creditors that the country may not meet its debt obligations and hence makes it difficult for countries with low ratings to borrow funds to finance public expenditure and development.
- If the debt–GDP ratio is high, governments may be forced to reduce public spending and increase taxes.

Conflicting macroeconomic goals

- **Low unemployment and low inflation**—we saw earlier that there is a trade-off between unemployment and inflation. As such, governments may need to prioritize one of the two macroeconomic objectives in the short term. There is no convention on which is more important, it varies from country to country. For instance, an export-driven economy with exports that face competition from other exporting nations may prioritize a low inflation rate over a low rate of unemployment. In contrast, if a country has experienced a prolonged recession the government may prefer to focus on unemployment to prevent the social problems that tend to accompany long periods of unemployment.
- **High economic growth and low inflation**—in the short term, increases in AD may bring increases in economic growth at the cost of an increase in demand-pull inflation. The closer the economy is to its potential output, the higher the inflation rate when short-term economic growth is not accompanied by long-term economic growth. An economy with a lot of spare capacity would be likely to prioritize short-term economic growth over the management of inflation.

Content link

Refer to the impacts of economic growth on the environment, earlier in this sub-unit.

Economic growth:

- may be accompanied by pollution and environmental degradation
- in high income countries has also spurred the development of green technologies.

- **High economic growth and environmental sustainability**—governments have varying levels of commitment to sustainable growth. Some still give subsidies to high carbon-emitting industries to promote economic growth.
- **High economic growth and equity in income distribution**—to avoid a conflict between these two objectives, governments must aim for inclusive growth. The Organisation for Economic Co-operation and Development (OECD) defines inclusive growth as economic growth that is distributed fairly across society and creates opportunities for all. As mentioned earlier (page 97), higher real output may come with higher income inequality but it also provides governments with the tax revenue to finance poverty reduction policies, allowing for inclusive growth.

QUESTION PRACTICE

This question is adapted from the November 2021 examination paper.

Read the following passage and answer the question that follows.

Over the last decade, annual economic growth in Burundi has been between 4% and 5 % and is expected to remain strong in 2016. Inflation continues to decline reaching 3.9 % in July 2016, down from 24 % in March 2012, partly due to a recent decrease in the prices of imports, especially oil, which is an essential input.

Using an AD/AS diagram, explain why the "decrease in the prices of imports, especially oil" might reduce inflationary pressure. [4]

SAMPLE STUDENT ANSWER

Response 1

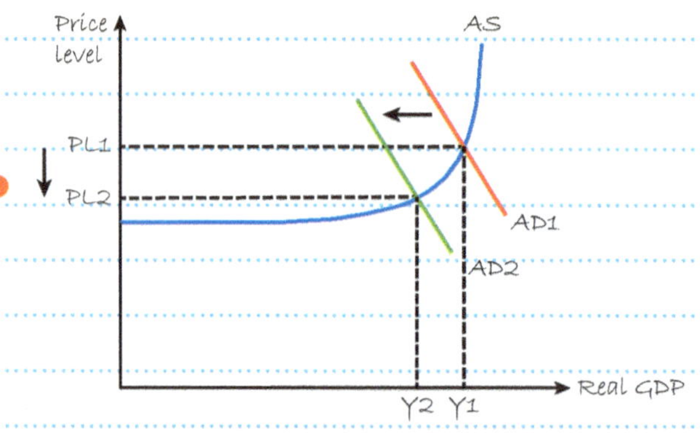

If the prices of imports decrease, the residents of the country will buy a lot more of them – especially oil because they will want to use more fuel for their cars and probably will go on more road trips. With a lot more imports, AD will decrease since AD = C + I + G + (X – M). As you can see on my diagram, the shift of AD from AD1 to AD2 will result in a lower price level and thus reduce the inflationary pressures.

▼ The diagram is fully labelled and does illustrate a decrease in inflationary pressure. However, the passage does not suggest that the lower inflationary pressure is caused by decreases in AD. This makes the diagram incorrect in this context.

▼ The response does not align with the information provided. The passage clearly indicates that oil was used as an input (a factor of production). While cheaper imports may lead to a greater spending on imports (depending on the PED for imports), the passage indicates a growth rate of 4–5%, so AD cannot be decreasing.

It is likely that this response would not be awarded a mark (0/4 marks).

Response 2

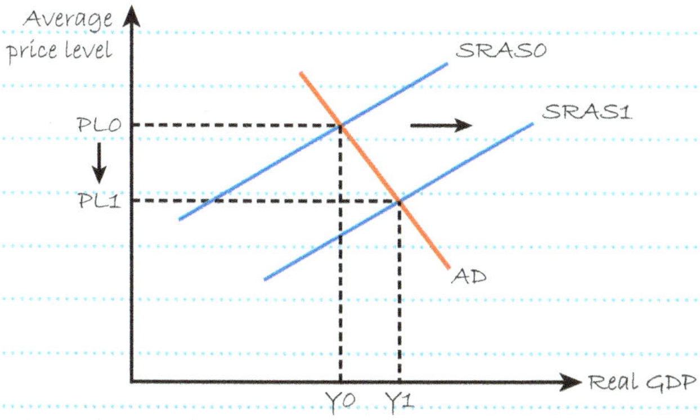

As imported factor inputs are going down, producers will enjoy lower costs of production for manufacturing goods using these materials in Burundi. This leads to an increase in the short-run aggregate supply, from SRAS0 to SRAS1, accompanied by a decrease in the average price level from PL0 to PL1, which indicates lower cost-push inflation and so the inflationary pressure would decrease.

▲ The diagram is fully and correctly labelled. The candidate correctly identifies the reduced inflationary pressure as an increase in SRAS.

This response could have achieved 4/4 marks.

QUESTION PRACTICE

This question is adapted from the May 2014 examination paper.

Distinguish between structural and cyclical (demand-deficient) unemployment. [10]

SAMPLE STUDENT ANSWER

Unemployment occurs when individuals, of legal working age, are actively seeking employment but do not have a job. There are different causes for unemployment, some short-term and others more long-term. As such, unemployment is often categorised to reflect such differences. Cyclical and structural unemployment are two of the four types of unemployment.

▲ This is a good introduction—it defines the concept of unemployment and establishes that cyclical and structural unemployment have different causes.

One of the main distinctions between the two types of unemployment is that structural unemployment will always be present in an economy as it occurs even when an economy is at its potential output, also known as the full employment output. That is, even when the economy has reached its long-term equilibrium output, some individuals will not have a job. They are part of what is called the natural rate of unemployment (NRU) – the unemployment that exists even at the full employment level of output. The NRU consists of

▲ This paragraph clearly explains the concept of structural unemployment. There is already an attempt to distinguish between (make clear the differences between) the two types of unemployment by stating that structural unemployment is part of the NRU and always present in an economy.

▼ A diagram could have been used to illustrate structural unemployment—either a diagram to illustrate the permanent drop in the demand for specific labour or a minimum wage diagram.

▲ This is a clear explanation of cyclical unemployment. The diagram is fully and correctly labelled, and adequately referenced.

frictional, seasonal, and structural unemployment – cyclical unemployment on the other hand does not contribute to the NRU. Structural unemployment occurs due to a skills mismatch in labour markets as employers (who "demand" labour) look for workers with skills that those who are structurally unemployed do not have. There is thus a demand for workers but the members of the labour force who are seeking employment are unable to join the labour markets in these industries due to a lack of suitable qualifications. There are three main origins to structural unemployment. The first is due to changes in the geographical location of industries – for example outsourcing when companies want to produce in a country with a lower labour cost. Another cause of structural unemployment is the change in the demand for particular skills due to changes in methods of production and technology such as automatic check-outs in supermarkets that result in a permanent drop in the demand for cashiers. Finally, labour market rigidities may impede adjustment in the labour market and result in structural unemployment. Minimum wage legislation can be the cause of labour market rigidities as wages in a specific labour market may not be able to adjust to changes in the demand for, or supply of, labour.

In contrast, cyclical unemployment is associated with the recessionary phase of the business cycle and thus may not always be present in an economy while the NRU exists even during periods of economic growth. A recession is the result of a fall in aggregate demand (AD) which leads to a lower real output in the short run. Since the demand for labour depends on the demand for the goods and services they produce, the fall in AD would inevitably result in a drop in the demand for labour (from firms). This is illustrated on the graph below. As real AD falls, the demand for labour also falls from DL to DL2. Since wages are sticky downwards in the short term due to the presence of strong trade unions and rigid labour contracts, the wage remains at W1 and this results in a surplus (QdQ1) in the labour market. This surplus is the cyclical unemployment.

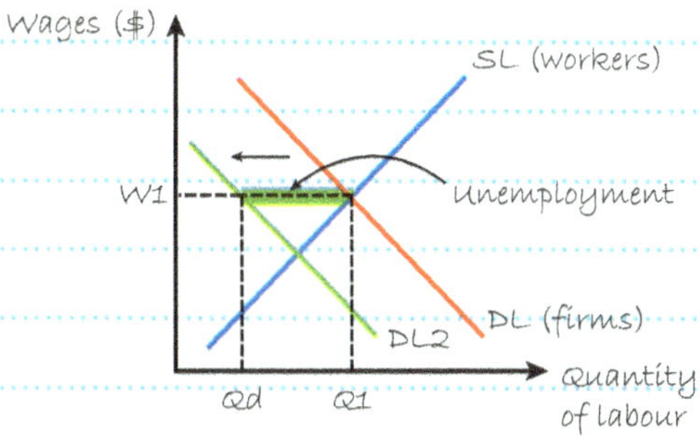

The main distinction between the two types of unemployment is that cyclical unemployment is short term, it occurs during recessions and disappears when the economy recovers. In contrast, structural unemployment is long-term in nature and will last in all phases of the business cycle.

▼ There are a few references to the AD/AS model and an AD/AS diagram could have been drawn next to the labour market diagram. This would have allowed for a clearer diagram analysis of cyclical unemployment.

▲ This conclusion helps summarize the main difference between the two types of unemployment. This reflects a good understanding of the command term, "distinguish" between (to make clear the differences between two or more concepts or items).

This response meets all of the descriptors of the highest mark band (9–10) and **could have achieved 9/10 marks.** However, there was insufficient use of diagrams to answer the question. In particular, a labour market diagram with a permanent fall in the demand for labour with a lower wage (such as Figure 3.3.2, page 99) would contrast with the cyclical unemployment diagram drawn in this response.

QUESTION PRACTICE

This question is adapted from the May 2014 examination paper.

Using real-world examples, evaluate the view that the benefits of economic growth will always outweigh the costs. [15]

SAMPLE STUDENT ANSWER

Economists distinguish between short-term economic growth and long-term economic growth. The former refers to the increase in real GDP over a period of time while the latter comes with an increase in potential output. There are many benefits to economic growth, which include an increase in economic well-being, a reduction in cyclical unemployment and greater tax revenue for the government which can be used to finance public expenditure and economic development. Unfortunately, economics growth might come with costs to society such as higher inequalities, environmental degradation if economic growth does not come with potential growth, the possibility of high inflation. With proper management of the economy, the costs could be minimized.

▲ The candidate introduces the concept of economic growth and distinguishes between short-term and long-term growth. This introduction also provides a brief outline of the body of the essay.

Short-term economic growth comes from increases in aggregate demand (AD). Depending on the existence of spare capacity, an increase in AD would result in an increase in real GDP as long as the increase in real output outstrips the increase in population and thus real GDP per capita increases. This increase in per capita GDP implies greater economic well-being as residents of the country would enjoy a higher income which reflects a greater ability to meet basic needs and financial security. For instance, China's real GDP per capita was under US$1,000 in 1990 but over US$20,000 in 2020 and thus, over one generation, the average Chinese resident can afford 20 times more goods and services. The increase in real GDP after a recession would also signal lower cyclical unemployment. For instance, on the following diagram, an economy positioned at Y1 has a lot of spare capacity and this would imply some cyclical unemployment. We could consider this to be the USA in 2020 as the COVID-19 pandemic brought about much uncertainty and the inability to travel or even go out to spend on goods and services. At that point, the increase in AD that came with an improvement in the COVID-19 situation saw an increase in AD to AD2 which led to growth in real GDP (Y1 to Y2) but a negligible increase in the price level (PL1 to PL2). Such growth was beneficial since it came with a decrease in unemployment and the end of bankruptcies for many restaurants and other businesses affected by the pandemic.

▲ This paragraph establishes some benefits of economic growth. There is evidence of economic analysis as the candidate considers other economic concepts such as economic well-being, inflation and unemployment. The real-world examples and the diagram help illustrate the arguments.

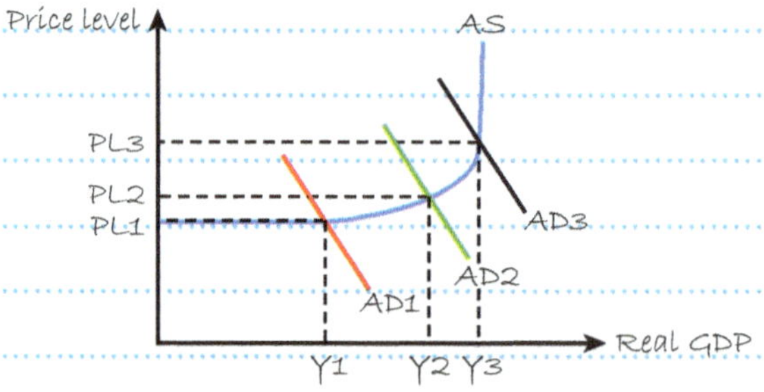

However, if the economy is near or at full employment, this increase in AD would result in high inflation, which can be negative especially for fixed income earners who tend to be low-income earners, such as unskilled workers. Referring to the diagram drawn above, an economy reaching Y3 would only overheat if AD increased further. This could be the USA in early 2022 when the inflation rate was 7% but the unemployment rate was below 4%, which was probably mostly the natural rate of unemployment. At that point any further increase in AD would result in higher inflation with minimal decrease in unemployment. Business owners who can adjust the price of their goods and professionals who can increase their fees such as lawyers and architects would be able to maintain their purchasing power. Those with fixed income would be able to afford fewer goods and services. In general, statistics such as real GDP per capita may overestimate the benefits of economic growth in terms of equity since GDP per capita is an average measure which does not consider that income will rise disproportionately. Real GDP increases also do not reflect the impact on the environment. Economic growth may be the result of the exploitation of natural resources. For example, Mexico enjoyed increases in export revenue when deposits of lithium were found in the Mexican state of Sonora. Since AD = C + I + G + (X – M), the increase in exports leads to an increase in AD and hence growth. However, mining lithium needs a lot of water, may result in chemical spills and this natural resource is being mined faster than it can be replenished. As such, growth from exporting lithium is unsustainable and would negatively affect future generations.

▲ This paragraph establishes the costs of economic growth. The candidate makes use of economic analysis (e.g. reference to the AD/AS model), real-world examples and references to the diagram.

Many of the benefits such as the increase in well-being of households who exit cyclical unemployment are short term since the individuals could lose their job again at the next recession while some of the the costs such as the impact on the environment from mining are long term since the damage is irreversible. It would thus appear that the costs could outweigh the benefits in the long term. However, many of those costs are avoidable. Inflation must be kept in check by the authorities, policies must be in place to make sure that economic growth is inclusive and the impact on the environment must be mitigated by legislation to limit negative externalities. Going back to the example of China, the 200% increase in real GDP per capita in 30 years has come with a growing income divide but the fact that tertiary education enrollment has gone from 3% to 58% over that same time period clearly indicates an increase

▲ The candidate considers the costs of economic growth relative to the benefits and hence addresses the demands of the question. The consideration of the short-term and long-term nature of those costs and benefits also demonstrates an ability to evaluate. Real-world examples are once again used effectively.

▲ This conclusion demonstrates evidence of synthesis (drawing on the key points of the essay).

in opportunities and thus that the government has made use of the increased tax revenue from economic growth to finance economic development. Economic growth has also allowed for the financing of green technologies such as solar energy and electric vehicles, which help reduce the impact of greater economic activity (real GDP) on the environment.

As long as governments intervene to mitigate the costs of economic growth brought about by unregulated markets, economic growth can come with more benefits than costs. The biggest threat comes from unsustainable growth as the damage to the environment may be irreversible while other costs and benefits seem to be a lot more short-term in nature.

This response meets all of the descriptors of the highest mark band (13–15) and **could have achieved 15/15 marks**.

QUESTION PRACTICE

This question is adapted from the May 2018 examination paper.

Population aged over 16 years	Employed	Unemployed
20.45 million	13.72 million	1.12 million

Using the information provided above, calculate the unemployment rate. [2]

SAMPLE STUDENT ANSWER

Response 1

▼ The workings are incorrect: the unemployment rate is the share of the **labour force** (and so not the entire population) that is unemployed.

$$\text{unemployment rate} = \frac{1.12}{20.45} \times 100\% = 5.47\%$$

This response would probably not be awarded a mark (0/2 marks).

Response 2

▼ The workings are correct but the unemployment rate is always expressed as a percentage of the labour force. The correct answer is 7.55%.

$$\text{unemployment rate} = \frac{\text{unemployed}}{\text{labour force}} \times 100 = \frac{1.12}{13.72 + 1.12} \times 100 = 7.55$$

This response could have achieved 1/2 marks.

QUESTION PRACTICE

This question is adapted from the May 2021 examination paper.

The following table provides data relating to Country Y.

	Unemployment rate (%)	Inflation rate (%)
2011	6.3	4.2
2012	6.8	3.5
2013	7.2	3.2
2014	6.5	3.7
2015	5.9	4.1
2016	5.5	4.8
2017	6.4	5.7
2018	7.8	7.4

(i) Identify a period in which Country Y experienced disinflation. [1]

(ii) With reference to the short-run Phillips curve, describe the relationship between inflation and unemployment in Country Y for the period 2011 to 2016. [2]

(iii) Outline how the data for the period 2016 to 2018 may reflect a change in the short-run Phillips curve for Country Y. [2]

SAMPLE STUDENT ANSWER

(i) 2011–2013

(ii) There is an inverse relationship between inflation and unemployment between 2011 and 2016. When the unemployment increased from 2011 to 2013, inflation decreased and when unemployment decreased from 2014 to 2016, inflation increased. This reflects the trade-off between inflation and unemployment illustrated by the downward sloping short-run Phillips curve.

(iii) Between 2016 and 2018, both the inflation rate and the unemployment rate increased. Since the Phillips curve is downward sloping, it must be that the curve shifted. In this case, it must be that the curve shifted to the right.

▲ Disinflation refers to a decrease in the rate of inflation. Since the inflation rate decreases from 4.2% to 3.5% and then to 3.2%, there is indeed disinflation between 2011 and 2013.

▲ The short-term trade-off between inflation and unemployment is clearly explained with reference to the data.

▲ The candidate has pointed out that both inflation and unemployment rates increased and this does not correspond to a movement along a short-run Phillips curve.

This response could have achieved 5/5 marks.

Content link

Link to your IA

The pursuit of the macroeconomic objectives is a good topic for a Unit 3 commentary. Where the information from the article allows, establish the threats to macroeconomic stability or the causes of high inflation, unemployment or recession (or economic slowdown). If you choose an article that discusses policy responses to macroeconomic problems, make sure to consider the sub-units on monetary policy, fiscal policy and supply-side policies. You are advised to choose an article that focuses on one or two macroeconomic objectives. It would be difficult to do a proper analysis of more objectives within the 800-word limit.

Concept link

- **Efficiency**—unemployment and recessions indicate spare capacity in the economy, implying that resources are not fully utilized. Even unemployment statistics may underestimate the level of inefficiency due to underemployment and discouraged workers (refer to the difficulties in measuring unemployment on page 97). An increase in AD might thus reduce inefficiencies in the use of scarce resources. However, too much of an increase in AD might lead to high inflation which, as you learned earlier, might lead to growing inequalities. As such, the goal of equity might be compromised in trying to achieve greater efficiency. If your article suggests such a conflict, you might have an opportunity to use your key concept as part of an evaluative statement (judgment).
- **Economic well-being**—the macroeconomic objectives are linked to the concept of economic well-being. High inflation, unemployment and recessions affect households in terms of lower (real) income, which will affect their present and future financial security and the ability to meet essential needs. While economic growth might seem positively related to greater well-being, it must be inclusive growth to benefit all households and sustainable growth to protect the economic well-being of future generations.

3.4 ECONOMICS OF INEQUALITY AND POVERTY

This sub-unit examines the causes and consequences of poverty and inequality.

You should be able to:

- ✔ define the terms
  - ✔ absolute poverty
  - ✔ relative poverty
  - ✔ progressive, regressive and proportional taxes
  - ✔ transfer payments
- ✔ explain how a Lorenz curve may be used to illustrate the distribution of income
- ✔ explain how the Gini coefficient (index) is derived and interpreted
- ✔ explain how poverty may be measured using single and composite indicators
- ✔ explain possible causes of economic inequality and poverty
- ✔ discuss, with the aid of real-world examples, the impact of income and wealth inequality on economic growth, economic well-being (standards of living) and social stability
- ✔ evaluate, with the aid of real-world examples, the effectiveness of direct and indirect taxes as a mechanism to redistribute income
- ✔ distinguish between progressive, regressive and proportional taxes
- ✔ evaluate, with the aid of real-world examples, the use of non-tax policies to reduce poverty, income inequality and wealth inequality.

HL In addition to the points above, for HL you should be able to:

- define the terms average tax rate and marginal tax rate
- construct a Lorenz curve from income quintile data.

Summary

Income inequality is due to an uneven distribution of national income across the population. Income includes wages, interest from savings accounts, rent from property, pensions, and so on.

Wealth inequality—wealth includes both money and assets (e.g. savings, stocks and bonds, houses) minus what a household may owe. High income earners tend to accumulate assets over time that can be passed on across generations, so wealth inequalities are more severe than income inequality.

A **Lorenz curve** illustrates the degree of income inequality in an economy. The horizontal axis displays the cumulative percentage of people in the population (usually expressed as income quintiles). From left to right, we go from the lowest to the highest income households. The vertical axis shows the cumulative percentage of national income. Looking at Figure 3.4.1, the lowest quintile (the poorest 20% of the population) receives only 8% of national income. The poorest 40% receive 20% of national income (implying that the second quintile receives 20 – 8 = 12% of national income). The poorest 80% receive 60% of national income, implying that the top quintile gets the rest, 40% of national income. The diagonal line, also known as the line of perfect equality, represents a hypothetical situation where income is distributed equally. The farther away the Lorenz curve is from the line of perfect equality, the more unequal the distribution of income.

Income inequality may also be measured by the Gini coefficient (index), which is the ratio of the area between the Lorenz curve and the diagonal line to the whole area below the line of perfect equality.

On Figure 3.4.1, it is: $Gini\ coefficient = \frac{Area\ (A)}{Area\ (A + B)}$

The **Gini coefficient (index)** can vary from 0 to 1 (0% to 100% when it is expressed as the Gini index. The greater the Gini coefficient (index), the greater the income inequality.

National income is unevenly distributed, so some households will be poorer than others. Poverty focuses on the lower quintiles of the population (the left side of the Lorenz curve). Economists distinguish between two types of poverty.

- **Absolute poverty** refers to a situation where households are unable to meet basic needs for survival. It is the income necessary for a person to afford sufficient food, housing, healthcare and education for survival.
- **Relative poverty** is a comparative measure of poverty. Individuals are said to be in relative poverty if they do not reach some specified level of income (e.g. 50% of the average or median income of the country).

Content link

Link to other sub-units

There is more on the concepts of equality and equity in sub-units 1.2 and 2.12. Equality is a positive concept, equity is a normative concept. Markets do not achieve equity, so government intervention is required.

While equity and equality mean different things, government policies often focus on reducing inequalities.

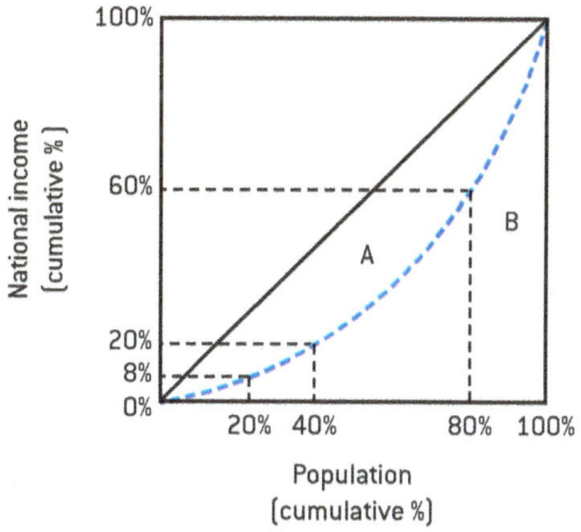

▲ Figure 3.4.1 The Lorenz curve

Poverty is usually measured in terms of income. A common single indicator of absolute poverty is determined by a minimum income level called the "**poverty line**". Most countries set their own poverty line. In addition, the World Bank has set the international poverty line as US$1.9 a day. Individuals who earn less than that amount are, according to the World Bank, living in absolute poverty. The World Bank reviews this international poverty line regularly. Another single indicator of poverty is the **minimum income standards (MIS)** developed by the Joseph Rowntree Foundation. The MIS is determined through surveys with the general population to determine the needs of different household types (e.g. single person, families) and therefore the minimum household budgets they require to function normally in society. According to the foundation, the MIS in the UK in 2021 for a single person was £20,400 a year and combined income of £34,200 for a couple with two children. Individuals with an income lower than the MIS would not reach a minimum acceptable standard of living in the UK in 2021.

The **Multidimensional Poverty Index (MPI)** is a composite indicator (a summary measure of several indicators) introduced by the Oxford Poverty and Human Development Initiative (OPHI) and the United Nations Development Programme (UNDP) to measure poverty in economically least developed countries. The MPI includes 10 indicators to reflect 3 dimensions of poverty—health, education and living standards. Each of the 10 indicators is given a weight (e.g. child mortality has a weight of $\frac{1}{6}$).

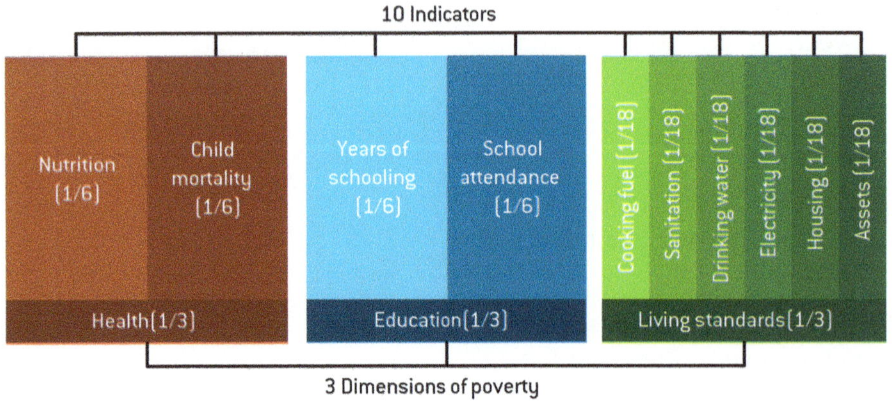

▲ **Figure 3.4.2** The MPI

The MPI reflects the deprivations (essential things that people do not have) at the individual level. If a person is deprived in 3 or more of the 10 weighted indicators, the MPI identifies them as "MPI poor".

The above single and composite indicators are some of the commonly used measures of poverty. Economists face the following difficulties in measuring poverty.

- Poverty is a normative concept. People have different understanding of what is an acceptable level of economic well-being (living standard). There are also different methods to measure poverty (as we have seen above) as different countries use different methods and indicators.
- Some information needed can only be collected from household surveys, which are not done regularly and, in some cases, hard to obtain. For example, the housing indicator of the MPI is measured in terms of deprivation of "adequate housing materials in any of the three components: floor, roof, or walls". Accurate data requires home visits as survey respondents may not answer truthfully or may misunderstand the question. Income data may also be unreliable due to omissions or undeclared income. For example, omissions include homeless people, who may not be included since they cannot be contacted for mail surveys—and yet they are, by definition, in poverty. There might be divergence in cost of living that underestimates the level of poverty. For instance, the cost of living is higher in cities so some urban residents might be unable to afford necessities despite being above the poverty line. Individuals within the same household might not face the same level of poverty. For example, in developing countries women often do not have the same access to education as men. Such inequalities may not be reflected in measures of poverty.
- Poverty is often measured based on income and may ignore inequalities in terms of wealth. Some households may earn a low income but be rich in terms of assets.

The common **causes of economic inequality and poverty** are as follows.

- **Inequality of opportunity**—individuals do not have the same opportunities in terms of education and employment. Education, even when subsidized, is an expensive experience, especially in less developed countries where parents need their children to contribute to household income (the opportunity cost of education). Parental background does not only affect the chances of obtaining a comprehensive education but also access to internships, jobs and business opportunities. Individuals whose parents work in established firms and businesses may gain employment through their parents' network or borrow the funds needed to start a business.

Content link

Link to other sub-units

Refer to sub-unit 2.12. Households receive income from providing factors of production to firms. If there is a highly unequal ownership of the factors of production, there will be a highly unequal income distribution.

- **Different levels of resource ownership**—as you learned in sub-unit 2.12, households receive income from providing factors of production to firms. If the ownership of the factors of production is highly unequal, income distribution will also be highly unequal.
- **Different levels of human capital**—workers with specialized skills and higher levels of education or work experience earn higher wages than those who are less skilled, educated or experienced.
- **Discrimination** (gender, race, religion and other forms)—workers may have difficulties in finding jobs and may be paid less than their peers with the same qualifications.
- **Unequal status and power**—individuals who live in countries where industries are controlled by large firms (which HL students may identify as monopolies and oligopolies) may face higher prices due to a lack of competition. This results in lower real income for consumers and high profits for a few large firms. Concentration of power in the hands of some members of society may lead to income inequality. Business permits, contracts and jobs may be granted to those with connection to the political or social elite.
- **Government tax and benefits policies**—governments may redistribute income by taxing proportionately more high income individuals to finance subsidies and access to necessities for low income individuals. However, some countries may impose lower rates of tax on income, profits and wealth, making their governments less able to finance such benefits. Highly indebted countries may need to divert tax revenue away from benefits for the poor to service the national debt.
- **Globalization and technological change**—these factors may result in economic inequality.
- **Market-based supply side policies**—these aim to increase potential output by reducing the level of government intervention. Privatization, deregulation and labour market reforms are some of these policies. Unfortunately, they tend to lead to lower wages, less powerful trade unions and less favourable working conditions.

  These policies will be examined in greater detail in sub-unit 3.7.

These are the impacts of income and wealth inequality.

- **Economic growth**—low income households may not be able to afford adequate education for their children and for themselves, resulting in lower productivity. Those who are trapped in poverty are often unable to save and when poverty is widespread in an economy, banks have limited funds to lend to firms and businesses who wish to purchase capital goods. The combined effect of low investment in human capital and physical capital limits long-term economic growth. It also makes increases in income difficult, which traps households in poverty. (The poverty cycle will be covered in sub-unit 4.9.) High income households, on the other hand, tend to buy more imported luxuries (especially in the least economically developed economies), spend more on holidays and invest overseas when the opportunities are limited at home (which contributes to leakages from the circular flow). The middle income class, which typically saves the most, is squeezed by the high inequality. Thus, overall savings and investment are low, resulting in low economic growth.
- **Economic well-being (standards of living)**—those trapped in poverty may not be able to afford essential goods and services and their inability to save affects their future financial security. Low income individuals may also need to take two jobs and this may lead to high stress and less leisure time.
- **Social stability**—high levels of income and wealth inequalities lead to discontent among those who are trapped in poverty or suffer from the inequalities. This may result in protests, riots and a higher crime rate.

Taxes may be used to redistribute income and so reduce income inequalities. There are two broad types of taxes.

- **Direct taxes** are are levies paid by individuals and businesses.
  - **Personal income taxes** are imposed on wages, rental income, dividends and other forms of income earned by households.
  - **Corporate income (business) taxes** are imposed on profits.
  - **Wealth taxes** are levied on personal assets (e.g. property taxes and inheritance taxes).
- **Indirect taxes** are taxes imposed on goods and services (taxes on expenditure). In contrast to

direct taxes, they are paid by consumers through the sellers—the person paying for the tax does not pay the tax directly to the government.

Content link

Link to other sub-units

Refer to sub-unit 3.3. Changes in the geographical location of industries and technological advances may lead to a permanent drop in the demand for labour. Hence, global competition and technological advances may depress wages of workers who face structural unemployment.

Taxes can be progressive, proportional or regressive.

- A tax is **progressive** if the share (%) of income paid to the tax increases when income increases. For instance, most countries have a progressive personal income tax. As their income increases, individuals pay a higher share (%) of their income as personal income tax payment to the tax authorities. Table 3.4.1 shows the 2022 income tax rates in Belgium.

  Belgian residents with an annual income of €10,000 will pay €2,500 in income tax (25% of their income). Other residents who earn €20,000 in a year will pay 25% on the first €13,870 earned and 40% on the rest since an income of €20,000 covers two income tax brackets. The total paid to income tax is 13,870 × 25% + 6,130 × 40% = €6,099.5 (which is 30.5% of these individuals' entire income). The Belgian residents with a higher income pay a higher share of their income to income tax and thus Belgium's income tax structure is progressive.

Taxable income (€)	Rate (%)
0–13,870	25
13,871–24,480	40
24,481–42,370	45
42,371 and above	50

▲ Table 3.4.1 Tax rates in Belgium (2022)

- A tax is **proportional** if the share (%) of income paid to that tax does not change with income. The island of Jersey charges a flat tax of 20% on personal income—regardless of the level of income earned, residents of Jersey pay 20% of their income to the authorities as personal income tax.
- A tax is **regressive** if the share (%) of income paid to the tax decreases when income increases. Most expenditure taxes are regressive. For example, a 20% VAT applied to a €1,000 watch implies a tax payment of €200. For individuals with an income of €20,000, that is 1% of their income paid for that tax but for someone with a higher income of €40,000, it is only 0.5% of the individual's income.

HL A tax may be identified as progressive, proportional or regressive by comparing the average tax rate (ATR), which is the proportion of income paid to tax, and the marginal tax rate (MTR), which is the additional payment to tax as a result of additional income earned.

Average tax rate (ATR)	Marginal tax rate (MTR)
$ATR = \frac{T}{Y}$	$MTR = \frac{\Delta T}{\Delta Y}$

Let's go back to the example above of Belgium's income tax structure. We saw that Belgian residents earning €20,000 a year would pay 30.5% (which is the ATR). If those residents' salary increases by €2000 a year, their additional income is taxed at 40% (the MTR) since the income tax rate for the (13,871 – 24,480) income bracket is 40%. It follows that when MTR > ATR and/or the ATR rises with income, the tax is progressive. Conversely, if MTR < ATR and/or ATR falls with income then the tax is regressive. Of course, ATR = MTR occurs when ATR does not change with income, which applies to proportional taxes.

Since regressive taxes affect low income earners more than high income earners while the latter pay a higher proportion of their income to progressive taxes, it follows that the use of progressive taxation to raise government (tax) revenue helps achieve a more equal income distribution. However, high income and corporate (businesses) taxes can create:

- disincentives to work (for example, a Belgian citizen earning €43,000 may not want to work overtime or accept a promotion with more responsibility since 50% of the additional income will be paid in tax) and this limits increases in real output
- lower productivity of labour when workers do not feel sufficiently rewarded for their work.

Countries with high tax rates also have higher occurrence of unrecorded activities as workers seek to escape taxes. Many high income economies have an ageing population, which results in a relatively smaller share of residents being of working age and thus progressive taxes cannot be the sole source of government revenue. This has led to increases in regressive taxes in countries with an ageing population.

The following are further policies to reduce poverty, income and wealth inequality.

- **Policies to reduce inequalities of opportunities through investment in human capital** may be used—unrestricted access to quality education and healthcare services increases someone's chances to gain employment, earn higher wages, and it increases the productivity of labour.
- **Transfer payments**, which are payments individuals receive without contributing to the production of goods or services, may be used. For instance, unemployment benefits and state pension payments are transfer payments allowing those who are no longer working or unable to find a job to maintain an acceptable standard of living.
- The government can subsidize or directly provide **targeted goods and services** such as education, healthcare and food vouchers. The authorities may also target areas with higher incidences of poverty. For instance, there may be provision of basic education programmes on hygiene, nutrition, farming methods or family planning in remote rural areas.
- **Universal basic income**, which is a regular cash payment given to all adult citizens, regardless of employment status, may be provided to alleviate poverty.
- **Policies to reduce discrimination** would improve access to education and employment.
- A **minimum wage** policy would increase the incomes of low skilled workers.

Content link

Link to other sub-units

Refer to sub-unit 3.3. The imposition of a minimum wage prevents the labour market from reaching an equilibrium. Such labour market rigidity may result in structural unemployment.

QUESTION PRACTICE

This question is adapted from the November 2021 examination paper.

Vanuatu is an island nation in the west of the Pacific Ocean. The government of Vanuatu is currently reforming the tax system to lower the reliance on indirect taxes and implementing a more progressive tax system to increase government revenue.

Using a Lorenz curve, explain how the tax reform could change Vanuatu's income distribution. [4]

SAMPLE STUDENT ANSWER

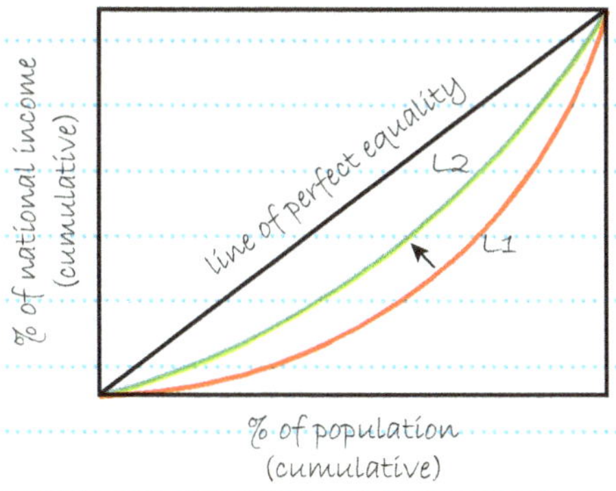

▲ The diagram is fully and correctly labelled. The inward shift of the Lorenz curve is clearly indicated and referenced in the explanation.

The Lorenz curve illustrates changes in the distribution of income. Indirect taxes such as goods services taxes are regressive. By reducing the reliance on indirect taxes, the government of Vanatu would make goods cheaper and since lower income households tend to spend most of their income, they would benefit more from lower indirect taxes than high income earners. Implementing a more progressive tax structure would mean that

▲ The candidate clearly explains the redistributive effect of lower regressive taxes and higher progressive taxes.

high income earners would pay more taxes. The combined effect would make Vanuatu's income distribution less unequal and so the Lorenz curve moves from L1 to L2, closer to the line of perfect equality.

This response could have achieved 4/4 marks.

QUESTION PRACTICE

This question is adapted from the specimen examination paper.

Table 1 below shows the income tax rates in New Zealand for the 2015–2016 tax year.

Table 1

Taxable income	Tax rate
Up to NZ$14 000	10.5%
Over NZ$14 000 and up to NZ$48 000	17.5%
Over NZ$48 000 and up to NZ$70 000	30.0%
Remaining income over NZ$70 000	33.0%

In New Zealand, the Good and Services Tax (GST) is an indirect tax charged on all goods and services at a standard rate of 15%.

Maya and Takeshi live and work in New Zealand. **Table 2** shows their annual income and tax details. Read the information in Table 2 carefully and use it to answer the questions which follow.

Table 2

	Maya	Takeshi
Income (NZ$)	28 000	88 000
Income tax paid (NZ$)	3920	
Disposable income (Yd) (NZ$)	24 080	
% of Yd spent	100	80
GST paid (NZ$)	3140.87	
Total tax paid (NZ$)	7060.87	
Average rate of tax		

(i) Calculate the annual income tax to be paid by Takeshi. [2]

(ii) Calculate the GST paid by Takeshi per year. [3]

(iii) Calculate the average rate of tax (including both direct and indirect tax) paid by Maya and Takeshi. [2]

(iv) Explain the likely impact on New Zealand's Gini coefficient if the government increased the rate of GST to 20 % in 2017. [4]

SAMPLE STUDENT ANSWER

▲ The workings are valid: the candidate has identified the correct tax rate for each income bracket.

▼ Unfortunately, the unit, $, is missing so only 1 mark can be awarded here.

(i) Tax due = (14 000 × 10.5%) + (34 000 × 17.5%) + (22 000 × 30 %) + (18 000 × 33%) = 1470 + 5950 + 6600 + 5940 = 19 960

This response could have achieved 1/2 marks.

SAMPLE STUDENT ANSWER

(ii) Takeshi's disposable income = 88 000 − 19 960 = $68 040
He spends 0.8 × 68040 = $54432

GST paid = 54 432 × $(\frac{0.15}{1.15})$ = $7099.83

▲ The candidate has calculated the disposable income (income after deduction for income tax) and the amount spent on goods and services. There is a clear understanding that, since the prices of goods and services already include GST, Takeshi's spending on goods and services of $54,432 is also inclusive of payment for GST.

This response could have achieved 3/3 marks.

(iii) Maya: $(\frac{7060.87}{28000}) \times 100 = 25.22\%$

Takeshi: $(\frac{19960 - 7099.83}{88000}) \times 100 = 30.75\%$

▲ All calculations are correct. Workings are provided and the final values are given as % values.

This response could have achieved 2/2 marks.

(iv) GST is a regressive tax as GST paid on any good/service. It constitutes a smaller percentage of income for those on higher incomes. Thus, increasing GST will make New Zealand's overall tax system more regressive, meaning that lower income individuals will be affected more than the high income earners.

▲ The candidate has identified GST as a regressive tax and explained that its increase would affect low income earners the most.

Hence, individuals in the lowest income quintile will see a relatively higher drop in real income and so the Lorenz curve will move away from the line of perfect equality. This implies a higher Gini coefficient and hence higher inequality in New Zealand.

▲ The impact of a more regressive tax structure on the Gini coefficient is explained.

This response could have achieved 4/4 marks.

Content link

Link to your IA

Even if poverty and income inequality are not the focus of the chosen article, consider the links we have established to economic growth, inflation and unemployment. Turn to the government policies introduced in this sub-unit and in sub-units 3.5–3.7. You may wish to evaluate these policies by examining their impact on the distribution of income and poverty. Economic policies, which aim to achieve the macroeconomic objectives, often affect low income individuals and high income earners differently.

Concept link

- **Equity**—we often equate government efforts to achieve a more equitable distribution of income and wealth as attempts to make things more equal. Since markets tend to lead to growing inequalities, it follows that intervention is needed to reduce inequalities. Adequate levels of intervention and acceptable degrees of inequality are closely linked issues that may divide societies. You might want to offer your own opinion on this debate but be sure to support your viewpoint. This may be done by considering the impact of a poverty-reducing policy on the macroeconomic objectives.
- **Efficiency**—progressive taxes and transfer payments help redistribute income but might create disincentives to work, which negatively impact efficiency in the utilization of the economy's resources in the long run by limiting increases in LRAS. The provision of essential services (e.g. healthcare services, education, sanitation, clean water supplies) might have the opposite impact, resulting in higher productivity of labour and hence higher potential output.

3.5 DEMAND MANAGEMENT—MONETARY POLICY

This sub-unit introduces monetary policy, which falls under the authority of the central bank (monetary authority).

You should be able to:

- ✔ define the terms
  - ✔ monetary policy (contractionary and expansionary)
  - ✔ central bank
  - ✔ real and nominal interest rates
- ✔ calculate real interest rates from given data
- ✔ explain how central banks influence interest rates to achieve macroeconomic objectives
- ✔ explain, using an AD/AS diagram(s), the mechanism through which contractionary and expansionary monetary policies can help an economy close deflationary (recessionary) and inflationary gaps
- ✔ evaluate, with the aid of real-world examples, the effectiveness of monetary policy in achieving the macroeconomic objectives.

HL In addition to the points above, for HL you should be able to:

- explain, using a demand and supply of money diagram, how equilibrium interest rates are determined
- explain how commercial banks create money
- explain the tools of monetary policy.

Summary

The policies to achieve macroeconomic objectives can be categorized into: **demand management (demand-side) policies**, which aim to either increase or decrease AD; and **supply-side policies**, which seek to increase potential output (increase AS/LRAS). This sub-unit will examine the first of two demand-side policies, monetary policy.

Monetary policy refers to changes in the money supply or interest rate, carried out by the central bank to influence AD and thus the level of economic activity, employment and price level. The central bank of a country has the following functions or responsibilities.

- It conducts monetary policy to achieve and maintain price stability.
- It serves as "lender of last resort" to commercial banks—these banks may borrow from the central bank if they do not have sufficient funds to meet their obligations. This helps prevent a banking crisis when all account holders lose faith in the banking system and try to withdraw their money at the same time.
- It regulates commercial banks to prevent excessive lending that could make it difficult to meet their obligations to depositors.
- It is banker to the government—the government borrows by selling bonds through the central bank. The central bank also manages the government's finances.
- It is the sole provider and printer of notes and coins in circulation.
- It oversees exchange rate policies (which will be examined in sub-unit 4.5).

The **real interest rate** is the interest rate that has been adjusted for inflation. The real interest rate is calculated as:

real interest rate = (nominal interest rate – inflation rate)

For instance, if banks offer an interest rate of 2.5% but the inflation rate is 2% per annum, the real interest rate is 0.5%.

Content link

Link to other sub-units

Refer to sub-unit 3.2. The interest rate is the cost of borrowing and the reward for saving. The interest rate affects both the C and I components of the AD, so manipulating the interest rates helps influence the AD.

HL The interest rate is determined by the supply of, and demand for, money in the money market. Money refers to anything generally acceptable as a means of payment. It can be cash and deposits in checking accounts (which can be withdrawn at short notice). Money does not earn interest (the interest payment on a checking account is often at or very near 0%). Holding on to money—whether in the form of cash or checking account deposit—comes with an opportunity cost, the interest rate payment people may receive by keeping their savings in bonds, or any other financial asset that offers an interest payment. Individuals *demand* money to make transactions such as buying groceries. The **demand for money** is downward sloping (see Figure 3.5.1)—as the interest rate increases, the quantity of money demanded by households and firms decreases. With higher interest rates, it becomes less attractive to hold money because of the foregone interest rates. The **supply of money** is fixed at a level decided upon by the central bank. It follows that the central bank can alter the interest rate by either increasing the money supply (from MS1 to MS2 on Figure 3.5.1, for example) or decreasing it (from MS1 to MS3).

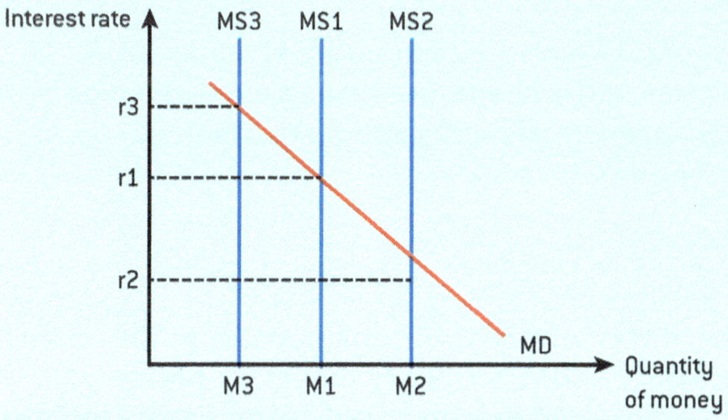

▲ Figure 3.5.1 Interest rate determination in the money market

Commercial banks contribute to the creation of money. Commercial banks are the intermediaries between "savers" and "borrowers". Banks pay savers an interest, which is lower than the interest they charge to borrowers; the difference reflects profits of commercial banks. Banks use as much of the deposits from savers to issue as many loans as they can, as this is the way they increase their profits. There is, however, a minimum reserve requirement set by the central bank. This is the minimum amount of reserves (cash held in its vaults or as deposits in the central bank) that commercial banks cannot lend out—to ensure that they have sufficient liquidity to meet their obligations to depositors.

As such, commercial banks can create money by issuing loans. The process can be illustrated with a numerical example. Let's assume there is a minimum reserve requirement of 20%. For every deposit the bank receives it can lend 80% and keep the remaining 20% as reserves. Let's consider an initial deposit of $1,000 at a commercial bank. That deposit does not affect the money supply (currency in circulation plus demand deposits). However, the $1,000 deposit allows the commercial bank to create a loan of $800 (since only 20% = $200 must be kept in reserves). The $800 will be spent by the borrower and be deposited in another bank account, which increases the money supply by $800 and allows for a subsequent loan of $640 (80% of $800). The process will go on until no additional loan can take place out of the original $1,000 deposit. As shown in Table 3.5.1, the initial $1,000deposit has in fact contributed $5,000 to the money supply.

▼ **Table 3.5.1** Bank loan example

Deposit ($)	20% required as reserves ($)	Loans issued ($)
1,000	200	800
800	160	640
640	128	512
...	...	...
Total deposits ($)	Total required reserves ($)	Total loans ($)
5,000	1,000	4,000

The increase in the money supply is given by the money multiplier:

$$\textit{Money multiplier} = \frac{1}{\textit{required reserve ratio}}$$

In this case, the multiplier $= \frac{1}{0.2} = 5$. The increase in the money supply is $5 \times \$1{,}000 = \$5{,}000$.

The central bank has, at its disposal, tools that allow for changes in the money supply.

- The central bank may alter the money supply by changing the **minimum reserve requirement**. Increasing the minimum reserve requirement would result in a smaller money multiplier so it would reduce the money supply. On Figure 3.5.1, this would be reflected by a leftward shift of M1 to M3 and hence a higher interest rate, at r3.
- The central bank may sell or buy outstanding government bonds from commercial banks—which is called **open market operations.** When the central bank purchases bonds, the payments made by the central bank enter the economy and so the money supply increases (there is a rightward shift to M2, resulting in a lower interest rate, r2).
- There may be **changes in the central bank minimum lending rate** (different countries use different terms to refer to this rate, such as the base rate, discount rate and refinancing rate). It is a special interest rate on loans that the central bank makes to commercial banks. If the minimum lending rate is lowered, commercial banks can obtain additional reserves by borrowing from the central bank. With these additional reserves, commercial banks can lend more. This increases the money supply.
- **Quantitative easing** works like open market operations but at a larger scale and includes other types of financial assets. By purchasing a wide variety of long-term (5-year or 10-year) assets that commercial banks hold, the central bank increases the reserves of commercial banks and so the money supply increases.

In times of recession or economic slowdown, the central bank may lower the interest rate (increase the money supply) in the hope of increasing AD. This is known as **expansionary monetary policy** (also known as loose or easy monetary policy). An expansionary policy could also be used to combat deflation or reduce cyclical unemployment.

In contrast, the central bank may adopt the opposite measure, a **contractionary monetary policy** (also known as tight monetary policy) by raising interest rates (decreasing money supply) when the economy is facing inflationary pressures.

Content link

Link to other sub-units

- Refer to sub-unit 3.2. Lowering interest rates may increase consumption and investment as the cost of borrowing and reward from saving are reduced and conversely when increasing interest rates.
- An expansionary policy may increase AD and close a deflationary (recessionary) gap while a contractionary policy may decrease AD and close an inflationary gap.
- The impact of the fall or the increase of AD on the real output and price level depends on the position of the economy with respect to potential output when using a Keynesian AD/AS model.
- Refer to sub-unit 3.3. Adopting a contractionary monetary policy to combat high inflation may have negative impacts on economic growth and employment. An expansionary monetary policy may have the opposite effect.
- Sub-unit 4.5 will examine how changes in interest rates may affect exchange rates, impacting inflation, growth and unemployment.

Table 3.5.2 summarizes the effectiveness of monetary policy in influencing AD.

▼ Table 3.5.2 Strengths/advantages and limitations of monetary policy in influencing AD

Strengths/advantages	Limitations
• Monetary policy is flexible. Central bank authorities can easily call for a committee meeting and rapidly adjust interest rates. In contrast, fiscal policy (which will be covered in sub-unit 3.6) requires changes in the government budget which is only adjusted once per (fiscal) year. • It is incremental. The interest rate can be adjusted by 0.25% at a time. This allows central banks to monitor the impact of changes in interest rates and further adjust the interest rate as necessary. This makes monetary policy, unlike fiscal policy, easily reversible. • Central banks are often independent from the government, so they are less subject to political pressure.	• Monetary policy is more effective in reducing inflation than in fighting a recession. Consumer and business pessimism have a stronger impact on the decision to borrow and invest than changes in the cost of borrowing. • The central bank has limited scope for expansionary monetary policy when the interest rate is near zero. • Monetary and fiscal policies are subject to time lags—it takes time for policymakers to identify economic problems, implement policy changes, and consumers and firms take time to react to changes in interest rates (for monetary policy). The implementation lag is however shorter for monetary policy as central banks can decide quickly, whereas changes to the budget needed for fiscal policy have to go through the legislative process.

QUESTION PRACTICE

This question is adapted from the November 2020 examination paper.

Outline how monetary policy is used to lower the inflation rate in an economy. [2]

SAMPLE STUDENT ANSWER

The money supply is reduced and this will lead to higher interest rates. Since the cost of borrowing is higher, consumers and firms may not be willing to take loans. There is also a greater incentive to save. As such, C and I decrease and both are components of AD and this will result in lower inflationary pressures.

▲ The candidate identifies the correct monetary policy: contractionary monetary policy. The link between higher interest rates and lower C and I is also established. An alternative or additional point is that the higher interest rate would lead to an appreciation of the currency, which reduces (X – M) and thus AD. (There is more on this in sub-unit 4.5.)

This response could have achieved 2/2 marks.

QUESTION PRACTICE

This question is adapted from the May 2016 examination paper.

Read the extract below and answer the question that follows.

In mid-2013, Indonesia's inflation rate neared 10%. In response, Bank Indonesia (the central bank of Indonesia) tightened monetary policy. This slowed down inflation, but also slowed economic growth.

Using an AD/AS diagram, explain why "tightened monetary policy" may have "slowed down inflation" and "slowed economic growth". [4]

SAMPLE STUDENT ANSWER

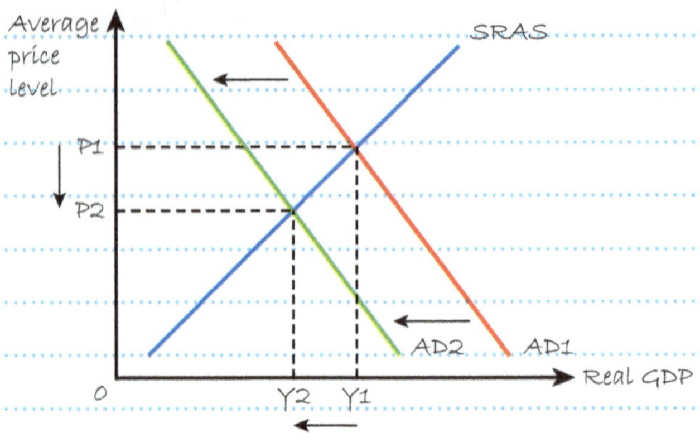

A "tightened monetary policy" refers to a contractionary monetary policy, meaning the interest rate is increased and so would reduce AD = (C + I + G + [X − M]). The higher interest rates would deter borrowing by households and firms. This would lead to lower spending by households and firms, the C and I components of AD. As AD decreases from AD1 to AD2, the average price level is reduced from P1 to P2 and this implies a lower inflation rate. Real GDP would go from Y1 to Y2 implying slower economic growth.

▲ The diagram is fully and correctly labelled, the changes in both the average price level and real GDP are clearly indicated.

▲ The response clearly explains how higher interest rates would lower AD. The candidate makes adequate references to the diagram to establish the impact both on the price level (and hence inflation) and real GDP (and hence growth).

This response could have achieved 4/4 marks.

QUESTION PRACTICE

This question is adapted from the November 2021 examination paper.

The following shows the values of the consumer price index (CPI) between 2016 and 2020 in Kanyaland.

	CPI
2016	176.3
2017	174.2
2018	172.9
2019	174.4
2020	180.2

With reference to the CPI data in the table, describe the most likely monetary policy response adopted at the end of 2018 by the central bank of Kanyaland. [1]

SAMPLE STUDENT ANSWER

The central bank would adopt an expansionary monetary policy to combat deflation. It would decrease interest rates to boost consumption and investment.

▲ The candidate identifies a fall in the CPI and hence deflation. The usual response from the central bank is to increase money supply (decrease interest rates) in an attempt to increase AD.

This response could have achieved 1/1 mark.

3.6 DEMAND MANAGEMENT—FISCAL POLICY

You should be able to:

- ✔ define the term
    - ✔ fiscal policy (contractionary and expansionary)
- ✔ explain how fiscal policy can influence the level of AD in an economy to achieve the macroeconomic objectives and other goals of the government
- ✔ explain, using an AD/AS diagram, the mechanism through which contractionary and expansionary fiscal policies can help an economy close deflationary (recessionary) and inflationary gaps
- ✔ evaluate, with the aid of real-world examples, the effectiveness of fiscal policy in achieving the macroeconomic objectives.

This sub-unit introduces fiscal policy, which unlike monetary policy is conducted by the government.

HL In addition to the points above, for HL you should be able to:

- define the terms
    - automatic stabilizers
    - marginal propensity to consume (MPC), marginal propensity to save (MPS), marginal propensity to tax (MPT) and marginal propensity to import (MPM)
- explain, with reference to the concepts of leakages (withdrawals) and injections, the Keynesian multiplier
- use the multiplier to calculate the effect on GDP of a change in an injection in investment, government spending or exports.

Summary

Fiscal policy is a demand-side policy implemented by the government. It involves changing government expenditure and/or revenue (from taxation) to influence AD.

Government expenditure includes capital expenditure (public investment on infrastructure), current expenditure (salaries on public sector employees, expenditure on health and education) and transfer payments (pensions, unemployment benefits and other cash transfers).

Government revenue mostly comes from direct and indirect tax payments.

When government expenditure exceeds government (tax) revenue (G > T), the government is running a **budget deficit**. If government (tax) revenue is higher than government expenditure (G < T), then the government has adopted a **budget surplus**.

Like monetary policy, fiscal policy can be used to increase or decrease AD. The government can make use of **expansionary fiscal policy** (also known as loose or easy fiscal policy), which is a situation where government spending exceeds tax revenue with the intention of increasing AD. Conversely, a **contractionary fiscal policy** (also known as tight fiscal policy) decreases AD, as government revenue exceeds government spending.

Fiscal policy may help achieve the following economic objectives.

- **Short-term and long-term economic growth**—expansionary fiscal policy, especially by means of increased government spending, is more effective than monetary policy during severe recessions when households and firms do not respond to decreased interest rates due to low consumer and business confidence. Increased government spending on infrastructure can also lead to an increase in AS/LRAS and hence allow for long-term growth.

Content link

Link to other sub-units

- If government spending (G) increases, then AD will *directly* increase as government spending (G) is a component of AD.
- Refer to sub-unit 3.2—lowering (increasing) personal and business taxes increase (decrease) the disposable income of households and after-tax profits of firms. This may lead to higher (lower) consumption and investment (the C and I components of AD).
- An expansionary policy may increase AD and close a deflationary (recessionary gap) while a contractionary policy may decrease AD and close an inflationary gap.
- The impact of the fall or the increase of AD on the real output and price level depends on the position of the economy with respect to potential output when using a Keynesian AD/AS model.

HL **Automatic stabilizers** are features of fiscal policy that are built into the government budget to automatically counter-balance short-term fluctuations in economic activity. For example, no legislative approval is needed to pay unemployment benefits during recessions—they are automatically paid, cushioning the drop in consumer spending (the C component of AD). Conversely, when the economy experiences high economic growth and incomes and profits rise, progressive income and business taxes lead to an increase in the share of income and profits that is paid in taxes (hence slowing the increase in C and I), reducing the risk of overheating.

Assessment tip

As fiscal and monetary policies are demand-side policies, you should specify the components of AD the policy may affect—C, I, G and/or (X – M). Note that only fiscal policy by means of changes in government spending will *directly* impact AD. The impact of changes in interest rates and direct taxes may have on consumption (C) and investment (I) expenditures depends on the response of households and firms. They may not wish to borrow more in response to lower interest rates or spend more when tax rates are lowered.

Content link

Link to other sub-units

- Sub-unit 3.3—an increase in AD leads to short-term economic growth and reduces cyclical unemployment. A reduction in AD reduces the price level and hence inflationary pressures.
- Sub-unit 3.1—a business cycle refers to the circular movement of a GDP around the potential (long-term) output.
- Sub-unit 3.4—progressive taxes and transfer payments may be used to redistribute income.

- **Low unemployment**—expansionary fiscal policy can help decrease cyclical unemployment.
- **Price stability**—although monetary policy is more commonly used to control inflation, contractionary fiscal policy may also dampen inflationary pressures.
- **Reduction in business cycle fluctuations**—fiscal policy and, in particular, automatic stabilizers, may help reduce fluctuations in economic activity.
- **Equitable distribution of income**—expansionary fiscal policy through increased transfer payments (cash handouts, unemployment benefits) and contractionary fiscal policy through increased progressive taxes help reduce income inequality.
- **External balance**—fiscal policy can be used as an expenditure-reducing method to decrease a trade (current account) deficit (HL students will be learn more about this in sub-unit 4.6.)

HL The circular flow of income model tells us that an individual's spending becomes another individual's additional income, which in turn leads to additional spending and that spending becomes another person's additional income, and so on. As such, injections into the economy—investment (I), government spending (G) or exports (X)—result in an increase in national income (Y) that is greater than the increase in the original injection. This is called the **Keynesian multiplier** effect. For instance, if the government spends $100 million on infrastructure as part of expansionary fiscal policy (the original injection), this increase in government spending (G) gives rise to an initial increase in national income equal to $100 million (the value of the infrastructure project). The income received by the firms building the infrastructure will be distributed to the workers who can spend it within the economy (but some income will be withdrawn as savings, taxes and imports). This process continues, resulting in an increase in national income that is greater than the initial injection of $100 million.

$\Delta Y = k\Delta G$ where k is the multiplier.

The size of the multiplier depends on the proportion of income earned that is spent within the circular flow. The smaller the leakages, the greater the increase in national income and therefore the greater the multiplier.

$$k = \frac{1}{(MPS + MPT + MPM)} = \frac{1}{MPM} = \frac{1}{(1 - MPM)}$$

- The **marginal propensity to save** (MPS) is the additional income that is saved by households.
- The **marginal propensity to pay tax** (MPT) is the additional income that is taken in tax.
- The **marginal propensity to import** (MPM) is the additional income that is spent on imports.
- The **marginal propensity to consume** (MPC) is the additional income that is spent on domestic goods and services.
- The **marginal propensity to withdraw** (MPW) is the sum of MPS, MPT and MPM (MPW = 1 – MPC).

Revision tip (HL)

The multiplier can be a very powerful tool for evaluating the effectiveness of expansionary fiscal policy in increasing AD. Consider how reliant the country is on imports, the magnitude of direct taxes and the attitude to save of the residents.

Table 3.6.1 summarizes the effectiveness of fiscal policy in influencing AD.

Table 3.6.1 Strengths/advantages and limitations of fiscal policy in influencing AD

Strengths/advantages	Limitations
• An increase in government expenditures is the only direct way to increase AD. The effectiveness of other demand-management tools depends on many variables and in particular on consumer and business confidence, which is often low in times of recession. • An increase in government spending will lead to multiplied increase in national income (HL only). • The government may increase expenditure on specific sectors such as education or healthcare, or infrastructure that supports industries, depending on the need of the economy. • The increase in government spending could also target specific regions where the unemployment rate is higher than the national average. • Long-term growth may result if the increased spending is on infrastructure, research and development (R&D) or retraining workers. • Tax cuts can target low income individuals and thus help achieve a more equitable distribution of income. • Automatic stabilisers do not need to go through the legislative process and are thus characterized by a shorter time lag (HL).	• Unlike monetary policy, fiscal policy is often dependent on the political agenda. Decisions to alter expenditures and tax rates may be motivated by the need to win elections. • Fiscal policy is subject to longer time lags than monetary policy. It takes time for changes in expenditures and taxes to be approved by the legislature. The implementation lag is also longer due to the time needed to disburse the funds to the relevant government agencies. • There is a risk of unsustainable government (national) debt from the accumulation of budget deficits. • Tax cuts may not induce more spending due to poor consumer and business confidence and may result in higher income inequality or less inclusive growth.

HL An expansionary fiscal policy implies that the government is running a budget deficit and will likely need to borrow to fund this deficit (a process known as "deficit spending"). This increases the demand for loanable funds (which refers to all forms of funds available for borrowing, such as savings deposits in commercial banks) and pushes interest rates up, resulting in higher borrowing costs. This deters private investment and consumption, a situation known as the "**crowding out**" effect. Since increased government spending (G) may be accompanied by a drop in investment (I) and consumption (C), AD may not increase as much as expected. This limitation is of expansionary fiscal policy is debatable because in times of recessions when economic activity is low, the demand for loanable funds by firms to make investment and by households to buy durables tends to be low, so interest rates may not increase.

QUESTION PRACTICE

Using an AD/AS diagram, explain how a country's shift from a budget surplus to a budget deficit might affect the price level. [4]

SAMPLE STUDENT ANSWER

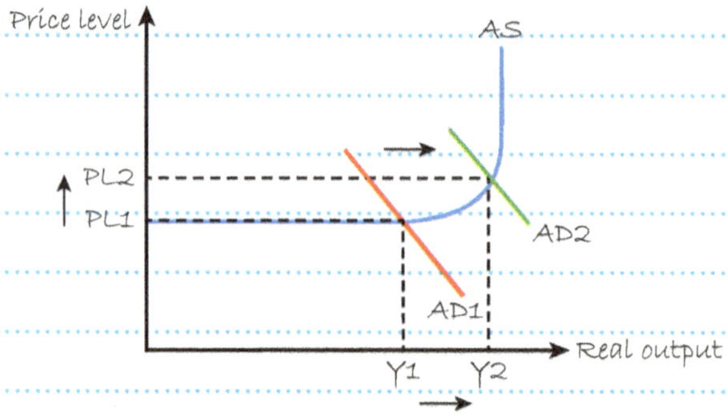

▲ The diagram is fully and correctly labelled, the changes in both the average price level and real GDP are clearly indicated. Note that the candidate uses a Keynesian AD/AS model so the impact on the price level and real output depends on the position of the economy with respect to potential output.

A budget surplus implies that the government expenditure is less than the revenue from taxes. In contrast, a budget deficit is the opposite, implying that the government is making use of expansionary fiscal policy thus increasing AD as G increases and/or C and I increase due to lower income and business taxes. As AD increases from AD1 to AD2, the average price level is increased from PL1 to PL2 and this implies a higher inflation rate.

▲ The response shows a clear understanding of expansionary effect of a budget deficit on the economy. There are adequate references to the diagram.

This response could have achieved 4/4 marks.

QUESTION PRACTICE

This question is adapted from the November 2019 examination paper.

Explain **two** reasons why fiscal policy may prove effective in lifting an economy out of a deep recession. [4]

SAMPLE STUDENT ANSWER

An expansionary fiscal policy in the form of higher government spending (G) will have a direct effect on aggregate demand (AD) since G is a component of AD. It will thus not be limited by low confidence during a deep recession.

▲ The candidate clearly explains why fiscal policy may be effective in increasing AD in times of poor consumer or business confidence, which characterizes a deep recession.

Spending by the government may decrease unemployment and thus improve confidence levels.

▼ This point lacks clarity. The link to a "recession" is missing. For example, the candidate could have mentioned that an increase in government spending leads to a multiplied increase in economic activity and so the creation of jobs.

This response could have achieved 3/4 marks.

QUESTION PRACTICE

This question is adapted from the May 2019 examination paper.

Government economists have estimated that citizens of Fairland spend 10% of any additional income on imported goods and pay a tax rate of 20% on every extra dollar of income. The marginal propensity to save for Fairland's citizens is 10%.

(i) Using this information, calculate the value of the Keynesian multiplier. [2]

(ii) Using your answer to part (i), calculate the increase in government spending necessary to increase nominal GDP by $100 billion. [2]

SAMPLE STUDENT ANSWER

(i)

$$\text{Multiplier} = \frac{1}{MPS + MPT + MPM} = \frac{1}{0.1 + 0.2 + 0.1} = 2.5$$

▲ The candidate has correctly identified the values of MPS, MPT and MPM, all of which must be expressed as decimals when calculating the Keynesian multiplier. The workings are also provided.

(ii) $\Delta Y = k\Delta G$

$100 billion = 2.5 × ΔG

ΔG = $40 billion

▲ The answer is valid. Workings are provided and the unit (billion $) is included in the final answer.

This response could have achieved 4/4 marks.

3.7 SUPPLY-SIDE POLICIES

This sub-unit examines the range of market-based and interventionist supply-side policies available to governments.

You should be able to:

- ✔ define the terms
  - ✔ (interventionist/market-based) supply-side policy
  - ✔ deregulation
  - ✔ privatization
  - ✔ trade liberalization
  - ✔ infrastructure
- ✔ explain, using an AD/AS diagram, how market-based and interventionist policies can increase the productive capacity of an economy
- ✔ explain that supply-side policies may lead to an increase in AD in the short term
- ✔ explain that fiscal policies may impact long-term economic growth
- ✔ evaluate, with the aid of real-world examples, the effectiveness of supply-side policies in achieving the macroeconomic objectives.

Content link

Link to other sub-units

- Refer to sub-units 1.1 and 3.2—supply-side policies lead to an increase in potential output. This is reflected by an increase in the PPC (Figure 1.1.3, page 4) and rightward shift of the AS/LRAS (Figure 3.2.3, page 87).
- Refer to sub-unit 3.2 for the factors leading to an increase in LRAS.

Summary

Supply-side policies are government policies that aim to increase productivity and efficiency in the economy. Supply-side policies increase the productive capacity (potential output) of the economy, resulting in long-term economic growth.

Market-based (market-oriented) supply-side policies promote competitive markets with limited or reduced government intervention. They can be grouped under three sub-categories, examined below.

Encouraging competition among firms forces them to be more efficient in production, resulting in lower costs and improved quality of goods and services. The government may achieve this in various ways.

- **Privatization** refers to the sale of state-owned enterprises. This may increase efficiency as private firms are profit-motivated and will seek to reduce costs by reducing the underutilization of resources (particularly labour). The lower costs of production may be passed on to consumers as lower prices. However, privatization may lead to job losses and higher prices if the privatized firm becomes an unregulated monopoly.
- **Deregulation** refers to the elimination or reduction of some government regulations that make it difficult for entrepreneurs to start and operate a business. Deregulation may lead to investment, reduced costs for firms (on a diagram, the SRAS curve shifts right) and greater number of businesses and overall increase in efficiency (the LRAS curve shifts right). However, the removal of some regulations such as health and safety regulations or environmental protection laws (for example to attract foreign mining companies) may negatively impact the well-being of residents and pose a threat to sustainability.
- **Trade liberalization** (the process of reducing trade barriers) increases competition domestic firms face, resulting in lower prices for consumers, product innovation and improved global resource

allocation. However, increased import penetration may result in structural unemployment and domestic markets being dominated by multinational corporations. (The benefits and disadvantages of free(r) trade will be examined in greater details in sub-units 4.1 and 4.4.)

- **Anti-monopoly regulation** may prevent anti-competitive behaviour, which limits competition. For example, governments may break up large firms that have been found to engage in anti-competitive behaviour, or prevent mergers of firms if it is feared that consumers may be negatively affected.

Labour market reforms aim to reduce labour market rigidities (increase labour market flexibility) and therefore reduce the natural rate of unemployment (NRU), which implies a higher potential output. They may also lead to lower costs for firms, which encourages investment; encourage R&D; attract foreign direct investment (FDI), which will be covered in sub-unit 4.10. However, they tend to negatively affect the well-being of workers and are considered responsible for increased income inequality. Common labour market reforms include the following.

- Minimum wages could be decreased or abolished.
- Labour (trade) unions that resist cuts in the wages of their members could have their power reduced. Reducing their power would allow for wages to adjust to market changes.
- Reducing unemployment benefits will increase the incentive to accept a lower paying job. However, this may lead to underemployment as individuals may be forced to take jobs that underutilize their skills.
- There could be reductions in labour costs such as medical and dental benefits.

Incentive-related policies could be used, especially the reduction of high (direct) taxes, which may otherwise discourage workers from working longer hours (in exchange for overtime pay) and firms from investing.

- Personal income tax rates could be decreased, with the aim to incentivize individuals to join (or return to) the labour force, encourage the unemployed to accept the earliest job offers and workers to work longer hours.
- Business (corporate) taxes could be decreased, with the aim to encourage investment by firms. Lower capital gains taxes may increase financial investments into stocks and bonds, which provide firms with funds for investment. However, empirical work suggests that such corporate tax cuts have had minimal impact accelerating investment spending and have mostly led to higher profits and increased income inequality.

In contrast, **interventionist supply-side policies** favour greater intervention by the government when free markets fail to achieve the macroeconomic objectives. They include the following.

- **Public investments in education, training and healthcare** lead to higher labour productivity (increase in human capital). The increased access to healthcare services allows for a healthier workforce, reducing the loss of output due to workers taking sick leave. As a merit good, education benefits both the individuals

Content link (HL)

Link to other sub-units

Refer to sub-unit 2.11 for information about government intervention in response to abuse of significant market power.

Content link (HL)

Link to other sub-units

Supply-side policies may also help reduce unemployment and lower inflationary pressures.

Refer to sub-unit 3.3. Labour market reforms help reduce or remove labour market rigidities that may be the cause of structural unemployment.

Policies such as trade liberalization and reduction of minimum wage legislation help decrease the costs of (imported) inputs and labour costs, which make up most of the cost of production for firms. This leads to a shift of the SRAS curve to the right and hence reduces inflationary pressures.

Content link

Link to other sub-units

Supply-side policies may have a demand-side effect (the AD curve shifts right).

Refer to sub-unit 3.2. A decrease in personal income and/or business taxes (incentive-related policies) will also result in an increase in AD.

Some of the ways supply-side policies may result in an increase in AD in the short term are: increased government spending (G) on infrastructure; increased investment (I) resulting from deregulation; incentives for R&D.

and society. This also reduces long-term income inequality and facilitates economic development.

- **Public investment in infrastructure** may take place. This refers to large-scale capital usually provided by government that is necessary for economic activity. Infrastructure includes roads, railways, ports, water supplies, sewage systems and power grids. Adequate and reliable infrastructure favours private investment and can be a major attraction for FDI in economically least developed nations.
- **Public investment in R&D** allows for the development of new technologies, resulting in new or improved capital goods and increased labour productivity. R&D generates positive externalities from production and would be insufficiently provided if left to markets. Firms may also be reluctant to invest in research due to poorly established or enforced intellectual property rights. The authorities may give tax incentives and grants to firms to invest in R&D and strengthen laws protecting firms from infringement of property rights.
- **Industrial policies** target specific sectors (e.g. manufacturing) or industries that the government see as essential to achieve structural change in the economy. For instance, economically least developed countries may adopt industrial policies to reduce dependency on the agricultural sector by providing firms (mostly) in the manufacturing sector with subsidies, low interest loans, tax cuts and allowances, and protection from foreign competition. Advanced economies also make use of industrial policies to promote high tech industries. For instance, many governments support firms developing 5G applications, services and products.

Analysing the expected impact of supply-side policies using an AD/AS diagram

Supply-side policies lead to an increase in potential output, YP to YP' and this is reflected (depending on the AD/AS model used) by the shift from LRAS1 to LRAS2 on Figure 3.7.1 and AS1 to AS2 on Figure 3.7.2. Using Figure 3.7.1, you could also illustrate the shift of the SRAS curve to the right (SRAS1 to SRAS2) to show the impact of lower production costs resulting from supply-side policies such as deregulation, labour market reforms or trade liberalization but it is not necessary (as the analysis of supply-side policies tends to focus on the long-term impact). As described above, some supply-side policies such as cuts in personal income and business taxes have a demand-side effect and so AD might shift right as well (AD1 to AD2). As shown on Figures 3.7.1 and 3.7.2, the increase in AD does not result in (significant) upward pressure on the price level when supply-side policies successfully increase productive capacity.

Table 3.7.1 summarizes the effectiveness of supply-side policies in achieving the macroeconomic objectives.

▼ Table 3.7.1 Strengths/advantages and limitations of supply-side policies in achieving the macroeconomic objectives

	Strengths/advantages	Limitations
Market-based	• There is improved allocation of resources as reduced interference by the government allows prices to provide accurate signals and incentives to consumers and producers (which you learned in sub-unit 2.3). • These policies do not incur higher government expenditure and thus do not increase the government debt.	• Increased reliance on unregulated markets leads to growing inequalities (which was covered in sub-unit 2.12). Privatization and deregulation may lead to monopolies and oligopolies, resulting in a transfer of income from consumers to producers through higher prices. • There are long time lags as gains from privatization, deregulation and labour market reforms may take years to materialize and increase potential output. • Deregulation could lead to more lax environmental protection laws and hence environmental degradation.
Interventionist	• Industrial policies may target essential infrastructure and industries with high potential for economic growth and development.	• Some policies may be very costly (public investment in infrastructure, healthcare and education), resulting in an increased government debt, which may be an issue for countries with a significant debt burden. • These policies may come with very long time lags, for example because infrastructure takes time to be built, the benefits of education may take a generation to show results. However, they may come with positive short-term demand-side effects on the economy.

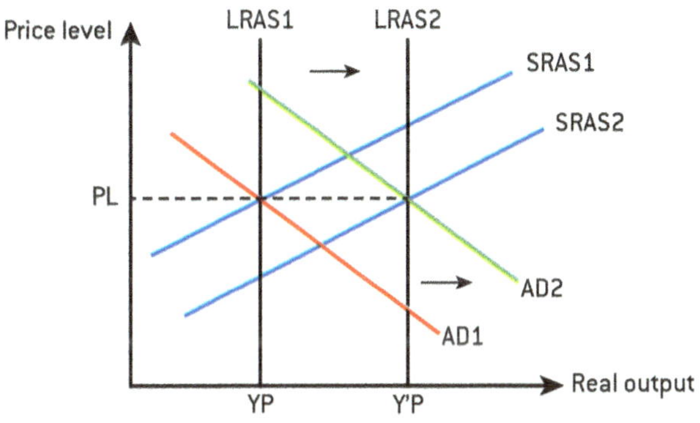

▲ Figure 3.7.1 Impact of supply-side policies (Monetarist/New Classical diagram)

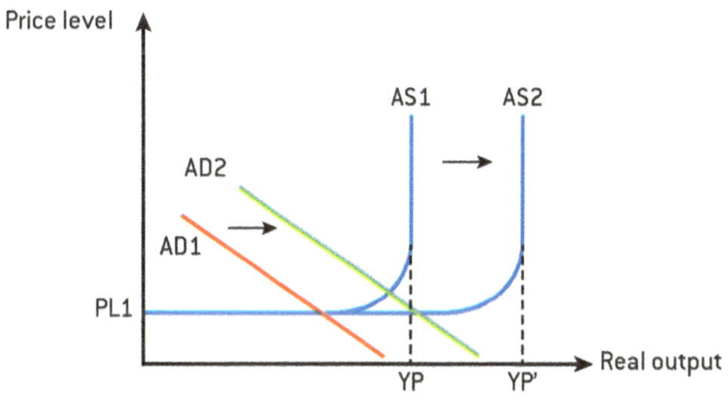

▲ Figure 3.7.2 Impact of supply-side policies (Keynesian diagram)

Revision tip

Governments often use a mix of demand-side (fiscal and monetary) policies and supply-side policies. For instance, if the unemployment rate is higher than the NRU (usually the case during a recession), a government may make use of expansionary fiscal policy to reduce cyclical unemployment *and* subsidize labour retraining programmes (an interventionist supply-side policy) to reduce structural unemployment. Similarly, demand-pull inflation (in the presence of an inflationary gap) may be addressed by contractionary monetary policy in the short term by decreasing AD. However, supply-side policies should be used concurrently to increase potential output and thus reduce the "bottlenecks" in production. A mix of demand-side and supply-side policies would also help avoid short-term conflicts between macroeconomic objectives, which you learned in sub-unit 3.3, such as economic growth and low inflation.

You have learned that some supply-side policies have a demand-side effect (AD increases). In a similar way, expansionary monetary and fiscal policies may also have a supply-side effect. For instance, increased government spending on infrastructure during a recession will lead to increases in both AD and LRAS/AS. Lower interest rates may incentivize firms to invest in physical capital and this would also increase productive capacity.

Here are a few questions to guide you when evaluating the effectiveness of demand-side and supply-side policies.

- Is a specific policy or type of policy required? For example, are demand-side policies needed in order to reduce cyclical unemployment?
- Do the circumstances make a particular policy unlikely to succeed? For instance, monetary policy may not work due to low confidence of consumers and firms.
- Does the nature of the economic problem call for a mix of policies?
- Are there additional demand-side or supply-side effects?

QUESTION PRACTICE

This question is adapted from the November 2020 examination paper.

Using real-world examples, evaluate the view that fiscal policy is the best way to reduce unemployment. [15]

SAMPLE STUDENT ANSWER

Fiscal policies are demand-management policies, carried out by the government to shift the aggregate demand (AD) by manipulating government spending and direct taxes. To combat unemployment, expansionary fiscal policies are used to bring the economy to full employment – a situation where the economy is at potential output. Unemployment refers to the members of the labour force who are without work but actively looking for a job. There are four types of unemployment: structural, frictional and seasonal unemployment, which make up the natural rate of unemployment and cyclical unemployment, which underlines a deficiency in the country's AD and typically happens during a recession. Fiscal policy would only be effective in reducing cyclical unemployment.

▲ The candidate has defined fiscal policy and unemployment, the two concepts in the question. The introductory paragraph has also identified **expansionary** fiscal policy as a tool to reduce **cyclical** unemployment. This provides a good overview of the effectiveness of fiscal policy in addressing unemployment.

Cyclical unemployment was prevalent across Canada in 2020 and 2021 as more Canadians became unemployed when AD decreased due to falls in consumption and investment throughout 2020, resulting in a fall in AD. The real GDP fell by almost 5.5% in 2020, which represents a significant recession. The Canadian government resorted to massive stimulus spending to support households and firms. This is a form of fiscal policy and its aim is to shift AD to the right.

▲ This is a valid real-world example—an illustration of cyclical unemployment and how the Canadian government has used fiscal policy in response.

▼ However, the example is underdeveloped. What did the government spend on? Which workers or industries benefited?

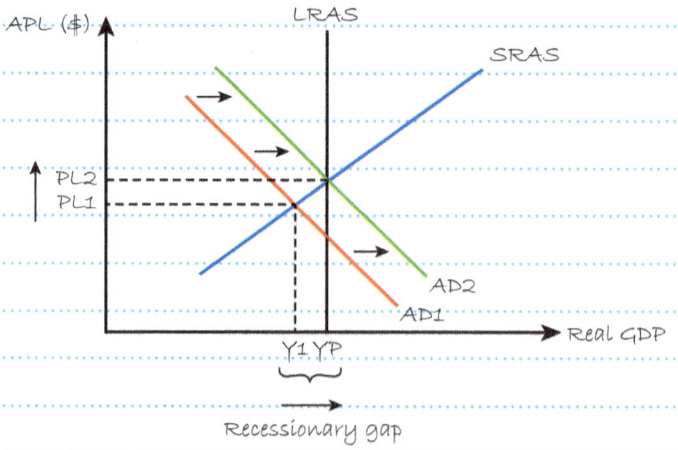

Because this significant drop in GDP implies that level of real output of the Canadian economy was below its potential output (Y1 < YP), a recessionary gap occurred. It implies that on the top of the natural rate of unemployment, which still occurs at full employment, there was also cyclical unemployment. The increase

▲ The candidate includes a relevant diagram to illustrate the workings of expansionary fiscal policy. An additional labour market diagram might be helpful in illustrating the reduction in cyclical unemployment.

in government spending was meant to push AD1 to AD2, since G is a direct component of AD, and in this way decrease the cyclical unemployment. If such expansionary fiscal policy is effective, the economy will come back to its potential output. However, the natural rate of unemployment will not be reduced.

Fiscal policy is usually more effective than monetary policy to reduce cyclical unemployment during a recession as it has a direct effect on the AD if it is done by means of increasing government spending. The effectiveness of monetary policy will depend on the level of consumer and business confidence, which is likely to be low during recessions – as it was in Canada in 2020 when many firms went bankrupt or faced high uncertainty which deterred them from borrowing. Fiscal policy may not be so effective if it is done by means of decreasing tax rates as consumers may also not respond to lower taxes due to pessimism.

▲ The question is asking candidates to consider whether fiscal policy is the *"best way"*. This implies that one of the requirements is to compare policies in the context of reducing unemployment. Here, the candidate also evaluates the relative effectiveness of fiscal policy in reducing cyclical unemployment, using the context set by the real-world example.

Fiscal policy, as a demand-management tool, would not reduce the natural rate of unemployment. While seasonal and frictional unemployment are usually not concerns of the government, structural unemployment poses more severe long-term problems. Since structural unemployment is due to a skills mismatch, increasing the demand for domestically produced goods and services would not lead to a reduction in this type of unemployment. Instead, interventionist supply-side policies like providing retraining for workers whose skills are considered obsolete – or at least in their region – may gain new skills relevant to other industries. Alternatively, market-oriented labour market reforms may help reduce rigidities such as minimum wage legislation that may contribute to structural unemployment.

▼ The candidate understands that some types of unemployment may not be solved by fiscal policies. However, no real-world example is provided. The paragraph could be improved by an example of one industry where structural unemployment is prevalent and the supply-side policy or policies implemented to address this unemployment.

To conclude, fiscal policies may be the best policies to address cyclical unemployment, especially in times of deep recessions such as the 2020 recession in Canada where consumer and business pessimism may render monetary policy ineffective. However, demand-management policies would never be the best policies to address the natural rate of unemployment, and especially structural unemployment, since a deficiency in AD is not the cause of the problem. In such cases, supply-side policies would be the "best way".

▲ This is a good synthesis of the essay. The candidate reiterates the limitation of fiscal policy during the recession in Canada. The lack of a real-world example for structural unemployment made it difficult to offer an evaluative judgment for such policies.

Note that while supply-side policies were not mentioned in the question, they had to be considered to establish the relative effectiveness of fiscal policy.

This response meets all the descriptors of the (10–12) mark band. To move to the highest mark band (13–15), the candidate must better develop the real-world examples to illustrate the analysis. You are strongly advised to build a pool of real-world examples for demand-side and supply-side policies that have addressed various types of economic problems. These will be useful for paper 1 questions.

This response could have achieved 12/15 marks.

QUESTION PRACTICE

This question is adapted from the May 2019 examination paper.

Using real-world examples, evaluate the view that inflationary pressures in an economy are best reduced using supply-side policies. [15]

SAMPLE STUDENT ANSWER

Inflation refers to a sustained increase in the price level. Inflation may come from supply-shocks or general increases in the cost of production, which decreases SRAS, and in such cases we talk of cost-push inflation. The USA has experienced much cost-push inflation in 2021 and 2022 due to supply shocks such as the blockage of the Suez Canal which disrupted the international flow of goods and services, as well as higher fuel prices, leading to decreases in SRAS. Inflation may also be the result of increases in aggregate demand (AD = C + I + G + (X – M)) when the economy is near or at full employment and the shortages of resources push up the price level, a situation referred to as demand-pull inflation. This is clearly a situation happening in the USA where economic activity has increased following a recession in 2020 and consumers and firms are more optimistic about the economy.

▲ This is a good introduction to the concept of inflation with real-world examples to illustrate the types of unemployment.

Supply-side policies are those policies which aim to increase the productive capacity of the economy and thus lead to an increase in potential output. They may be market-based where the government minimises interference to the market forces and prefers to remove existing rigidities or create incentives for economic agents. For instance, the government of Scotland has recently introduced R&D tax credits to encourage firms spending on the development of new technologies which would allow for better ways to produce and possibly increase productivity of labour thus increasing potential output. Supply-side policies may also be interventionist where governments fear free markets may not achieve desired outcomes, or not achieve them fast enough. For instance, the Serbian government is providing subsidies to those who wish to install solar panels to generate electricity at home and in their offices. This would reduce costs to households and firms and thus dampen the cost-push inflation from higher fuel prices. The 2022 US budget also saw an increase of close to $2 billion to environment-related agencies. This will allow public investments in renewable energy development, including wind farms. This will allow for an increase in the potential output and reduce cost for businesses if renewable energy is cheaper than conventional fuel.

An economy, like the USA in 2022, facing inflationary pressure as the economy is now producing beyond the potential output, at Y2, would ideally want to see an increase in LRAS from supply-side policies, which would result from LRAS1 to LRAS2 and thus prevent further inflationary pressures, and a further decrease in SRAS since the economy would no longer be in an inflationary gap. The policies I mentioned above would lead to research into, possibly, energy-reducing technology in Scotland and greater availability of windpower energy in the USA and hence they would lead to an increase in LRAS. Those policies which help reduce costs would also lead to an increase in SRAS from SRAS1 to SRAS2 thus reducing the inflationary pressure from PL1 to PL2. However, such supply-side policies have very long time lags. It will take a long time for the windpower plants to be built and incentives for R&D may not bear fruits for years. Interventionist policies also lead to increases in AD since they involve increase in government spending, which worsens demand-pull inflation. For instance, the $2 billion increase in the US budget mentioned above would significantly increase AD and also builds up the already high US government debt. As such, to prevent an increase in demand-pull inflation, interventionist supply-side policies should be accompanied by reduction in government spending in other areas to neutralise the increase in AD due to higher public spending associated with such policies. Otherwise, interventionist policies would only add to inflationary pressures.

▲ This is a good overview of supply-side policies with many examples to distinguish market-based and interventionist policies.

▲ The candidate includes a relevant diagram and explains it using the examples earlier mentioned. The policies are also evaluated in terms of time lags and costs of interventionist policies.

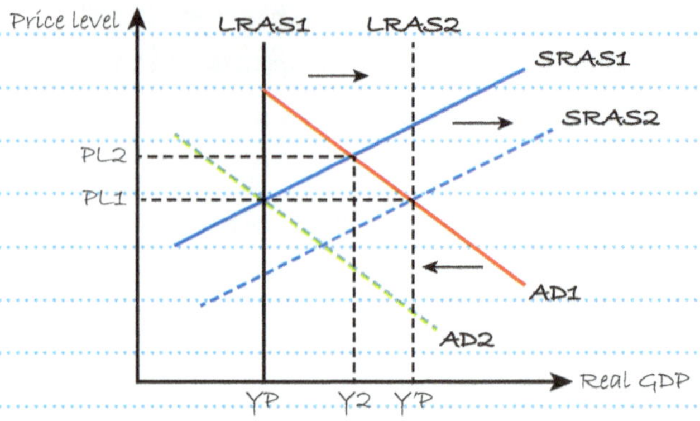

While supply-side policies would indeed be ideal to dampen the inflationary pressure, their long time lags make demand-side policies an attractive alternative, at least in the short term. Since part of the inflation in the USA is demand-pull in nature, the Federal Reserves (the US central bank) has increased the interest rates to increase incentives to save and reduce the cost of borrowing. This led to a fall of AD to AD2 and keeps the price level at PL1. Hence, the mixed approach of the US government, using both demand-side and supply-side policies, will reduce inflation in both the short term and long term.

▲ The candidate explains another policy that might be better suited to reduce inflation in the short term—the demands of the questions have been addressed.

In conclusion, contractionary demand-side policies are better suited to reduce inflation in the short-term. If supply-side policies are used, they should only be used concurrently with contractionary demand-side policies. Governments should not rely purely on supply-side policies as this would result in high inflation since such policies take a long time to bear results and may even worsen inflation through higher government spending. Special circumstances should also be considered such as the level of government debt as well as impact on equity since some supply-side policies, in particular labour market reforms, may have other side effects.

▲ This paragraph shows evidence of synthesis and evaluation.

This response meets all the descriptors of the highest mark band [12–15] and **could have achieved 15/15 marks.**

Content link

Link to your IA

A news article on government intervention (demand-side and/or supply-side policies) may be used for a commentary. Here are a few points to consider.

- Your diagrams should reflect the situation as described in the article. For example, if the economy is facing a slowdown in economic activity (and so growth rates are slowing but still positive), you should not draw an AD/AS diagram with a lot of spare capacity (with a high deflationary gap such as the horizontal section of the Keynesian AS). Similarly, if the economy is overheating, the AD should cut the Keynesian AS along or close to the vertical section where the slope is steeper, or intersect with the SRAS beyond potential output on a Monetarist/New Classical model. The magnitude of the shift of AD (AS) should also reflect the (expected) effectiveness of the demand-side (supply-side) policy described in your analysis.
- Use information and data *from the article* to evaluate the effectiveness of the policy. Was the policy timely (at the early stage of the relevant phase of the business cycle)? Can you infer the level of confidence of consumers and firms that might make lower direct taxes and interest rates less effective? (For example, if the article mentions a few interest rates cuts earlier in the year, this would signal that consumers and firms are not responding.) Is the current government debt allowing for more expansionary fiscal policy?

Concept link

While application of **intervention** is obvious, you might also want to consider these key concepts when examining the impacts of demand-side and/or supply-side policies.

- **Equity and economic well-being**—a country's residents benefit from lower unemployment, price stability and sustained economic growth. However, policies used to achieve these goals affect individuals unevenly. Progressive taxes (fiscal policy) and changes to interest rates (monetary policy) may impact the distribution of income and residents' ability to make economic choices—positively or negatively. Higher interest rates may have a redistributive effect between debtors (borrowers) and creditors (savers). Supply-side policies may also lead to such mixed impacts. Market-based supply-side policies tend to lead to non-inclusive growth. For instance, labour market reforms may result in lower worker benefits. In contrast, interventionist policies such as provision of education and healthcare may improve the standards of living of low income individuals.
- **Sustainability**—a lot of tax breaks and R&D have focused on the development of green technologies. However, industrial policies may lead to increased negative externalities, especially in economically least developed nations where weak or poorly enforced environmental protection laws have led to environmental destruction. Similarly, deregulation may remove or reduce such environmental laws, resulting in unsustainable growth.

4 THE GLOBAL ECONOMY

You should know about:

- ✔ the benefits of international trade
- ✔ types of trade protection
- ✔ arguments for and against trade control or protection
- ✔ economic integration
- ✔ exchange rates
- ✔ balance of payments
- ✔ sustainable development
- ✔ measuring development
- ✔ barriers to economic growth and/or economic development
- ✔ economic growth and/or economics development strategies.

4.1 THE BENEFITS OF INTERNATIONAL TRADE

This sub-unit introduces key terms, ideas and principles associated with international trade.

You should be able to:

- ✔ define the term
  - ✔ free trade
- ✔ explain the benefits of free trade
- ✔ illustrate the quantity of exports or imports on a trade diagram.

HL In addition to the points above, for HL you should be able to:

- define the terms
  - absolute advantage
  - comparative advantage
- calculate the quantity of exports or imports and export revenue or import expenditure on a trade diagram
- distinguish between "absolute advantage" and "comparative advantage"
- explain the sources of comparative advantage
- illustrate comparative advantage on a PPC diagram
- calculate opportunity costs to identify a country's comparative advantage
- discuss the limitations of the theory of comparative advantage with the aid of real-world examples.

Summary

Free trade refers to international exchange of goods and services that takes place without any government imposed barriers (e.g. tariffs, quotas or subsidies).

There are many benefits of free trade.

- It results in increased **competition** between domestic and foreign firms, which leads to **lower prices**, innovation and greater **efficiency in production**.
- It allows **greater choice** for consumers, who are no longer limited to domestic goods and services.
- Firms may **acquire resources (factors of production)** that may not be available locally or may be more expensive when purchased from domestic producers.

- Firms may enjoy **economies of scale** when they export goods and services to **larger markets**.
- **Foreign exchange** is earned from the sale of exports, which importing firms can use to finance imports.
- A **more efficient world resource allocation** results as countries specialize in goods and services they can produce more efficiently.

HL A country has an **absolute advantage** in the production of a good (or service) when it can be produced using fewer resources (factors of production) than another country. For example, Country B has the absolute advantage in the production of good X if it can produce it using 3 units of labour, whereas Country A must use 5 units of labour. So, Country B produces good X at a lower absolute cost.

A country has a **comparative advantage** in the production of a good (or service) when it can be produced at a *lower opportunity cost* than in another country. For example, Country B has a comparative advantage in the production of good X if producing an unit of X requires the sacrifice of 10 units of good Y whereas Country A must sacrifice 12 units of good Y. Country B can produce good X at a lower relative cost.

The following are the main **sources of comparative advantage**.

- The **quantity and quality of resources (factors of production)** —fertile land allows for higher productivity in the production of agricultural goods or a highly educated and trained labour force allows for more efficient production of knowledge-based goods.
- **Differences in technology**—greater access to capital goods and the latest technology allow for more efficient production of manufactured goods.

Some of the **limitations of the theory of comparative advantage** are as follows.

- **Resources (factors of production) are not perfectly mobile**—the principle of specialization is based on the assumption that resources are occupationally and geographically mobile but labour, for example, is often highly specialized or unable to relocate.
- **Opportunity costs may not be constant** (the PPC may not be a straight line but rather bow outward). Transferring resources from one industry to another may be increasingly costly.
- **The assumption that all firms operate in a perfectly competitive market producing homogeneous goods is not realistic**. In reality, large firms that enjoy market power and economies of scale dominate world trade. Goods are seldom perceived as homogeneous by consumers.
- **Transportation costs** may outweigh gains from exporting a good.
- **Excessive specialization** may expose a country to fluctuation in economic activity in the event of changes in world demand.
- Specialization may **impede structural change** and hence economic development for developing countries, which often have a comparative advantage in the production of agricultural goods.
- **Governments may create a comparative advantage** in an industry by investing in human and physical capital. For example, introducing IT courses in schools and investment in high-speed internet infrastructure may lead to a comparative advantage in IT-related industries.

QUESTION PRACTICE

This question is adapted from the May 2019 examination paper.

The market for oranges in Country Z is illustrated below.

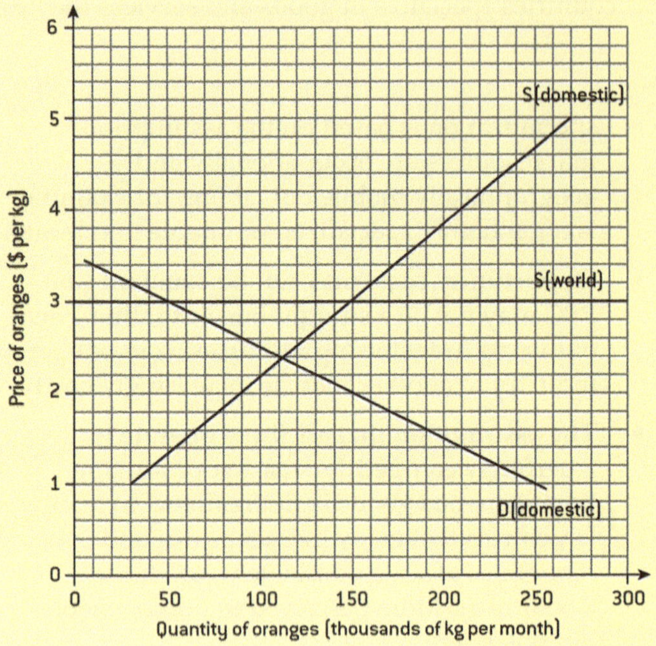

Calculate Country Z's revenue from exporting oranges. [2]

SAMPLE STUDENT ANSWER

quantity of exports = 150 − 50 = 100

export revenue = $3 × 100 = $300

This response could have achieved 1/2 marks.

▲ The candidate understands that the country is a net exporter as the world price is above the domestic price, and shows workings.

▼ Unfortunately, the candidate has not considered the unit provided on the horizontal axis. The correct answer is 100 **thousand** (100,000).

▲ Although the quantity of exports is incorrect, the working allows the examiner to award 1 mark for a correct understanding of the concept of export revenue.

Assessment tip

Do not forget to label the world supply curve or world price line. A trade diagram is not fully labelled if the "S(world)" or "World price" label is missing.

QUESTION PRACTICE

This question is adapted from the May 2018 examination paper.

The following diagram illustrates the production possibilities of two countries, Country A and Country B, in the production of cotton and bananas.

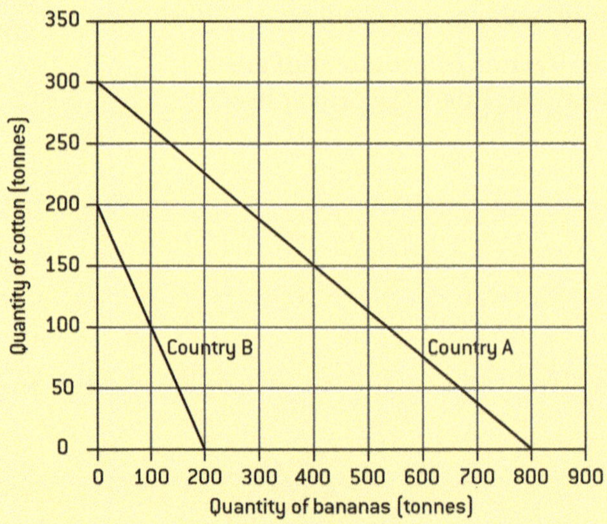

Using information provided in the diagram to support your answer, determine which country should specialize in the production of cotton. [2]

SAMPLE STUDENT ANSWER

Country B should specialize in the production of cotton since it faces a lower opportunity cost.

▲ The candidate correctly identifies the lower opportunity cost as the justification for comparative advantage.

Country A's opportunity cost of producing a tonne of cotton is $\frac{8}{3}$ tonnes of bananas while country B's opportunity cost of producing a tonne of cotton is 1 tonne of bananas.

▲ Information from the diagram is used to support the answer.

This response could have achieved 2/2 marks.

Revision tip

- The opportunity cost of producing the good on the horizontal axis is the slope of the PPC.
- The country with the flatter PPC has a comparative advantage in the good on the horizontal axis (in the diagram, Country A has a comparative advantage in the production of bananas).
- Once you have calculated the opportunity cost of producing a unit of one of the goods for a country, the opportunity cost of producing the other good is just the inverse (Country A's opportunity cost of producing a tonne of bananas is $\frac{3}{8}$ tonnes of cotton).

QUESTION PRACTICE

This question is adapted from the May 2017 examination paper.

Explain **two** limitations of the theory of comparative advantage. [4]

SAMPLE STUDENT ANSWER

Response 1

Transport costs exist.

▼ The candidate is **listing** and not **explaining** the limitations. There are 2 marks allocated for **each** limitation. Listing a point without explanation is usually only awarded 1 mark.

It would also mean that the country would not enjoy economic development.

▼ This answer is too vague. It would not be awarded a mark. There are many barriers to economic development that are not related to comparative advantage.

This response could have achieved 1/4 marks.

Response 2

Some of the assumptions of the theory of comparative advantage may not hold in the real world. One such assumption is that there is no transportation cost involved. In real life, a country might prefer not to import from a country with a comparative advantage because the difference in cost might be less than the transport costs incurred in getting the item delivered across countries.

▲ This clearly explains an assumption of the theory that may not hold in the real world—that transportation costs could offset any potential cost-reduction from comparative advantage.

▼ The lack of incentive for structural change in developing countries is a valid example. This part of the answer is more precise than the previous answer. However, the point is not adequately linked to the theory of comparative advantage so only 1 mark would be awarded for this paragraph. To achieve 2 marks, the candidate should have explained that most developing countries have a comparative advantage in agricultural goods.

The application of comparative advantage may not bring about the benefits inherent in the theory. In particular, developing countries may not pursue structural change needed for economic development.

This response could have achieved 3/4 marks.

Revision tip

Discussion topics may be tested as part (b) of essay questions (paper 1), which candidates need to illustrate with real-world examples. There's one discussion topic for this unit—the limitations of the theory of comparative advantage. Consider researching countries that may not benefit from specialization according to their comparative advantage. Build up your own list of real-world examples.

4.2 TYPES OF TRADE PROTECTION

This sub-unit introduces key terms, ideas and principles associated with trade protection.

You should be able to:

- ✔ define the terms
  - ✔ trade protection
  - ✔ tariff
  - ✔ quota
  - ✔ subsidies and export subsidies
  - ✔ administrative barriers
- ✔ discuss the effects of a tariff, quota, subsidy or export subsidy, or administrative barriers on markets and stakeholders with the aid of real-world examples
- ✔ illustrate the effects of a tariff, quota or subsidy or export subsidy on price, production, consumption, expenditures, revenues and welfare on a trade diagram.

HL In addition, for HL you should be able to:

- calculate with reference to a trade diagram, in cases where there are changes in tariff, quota or subsidy or export subsidy, the changes in
  - the quantity of exports or imports
  - export revenue or import expenditure
  - government revenue or spending
  - consumer and producer surpluses
  - welfare loss.

Summary

Trade protection refers to government policies that limit imports and/or encourage exports by setting up trade barriers.

These are the main types of trade barriers.

- A **tariff** is a duty (tax) that is placed upon imports. Tariffs serve the purposes of protecting domestic industries from foreign competition and raising revenue for the government.
- A **quota** sets a limit on the quantity of a good that can be imported.
- A **subsidy** is an amount of money paid by the government to firms to lower costs of production. Subsidies give domestic firms an advantage over foreign competition. Subsidies may be given to firms competing with imports in the domestic market. Export subsidies are given to exporting firms to increase their revenue from sales in foreign markets.
- **Administrative barriers** are the legal barriers (e.g. technical standards, health and safety requirements, environmental standards) that make it difficult and costly to import goods.

Trade protection always benefits domestic producers and leads to inefficiency (welfare loss). The effects on consumers and the government depend on the type of trade protection.

	Impacts on consumers, governments and foreign producers
Tariff	**Consumers:** higher price, lower level of consumption and hence lower consumer surplus **Government:** tax revenue collected **Foreign producers:** lower export revenue
Quota	**Consumers:** higher price, lower level of consumption and hence lower consumer surplus **Government and foreign producers:** impacts depend on the quota system. Governments may auction licenses to export, raising government revenue—this system involves a cost for foreign firms. When governments do not charge foreign firms for the right to export, foreign firms will charge a higher price, enjoying higher export revenues.
Subsidy	**Consumers:** no change in price, level of consumption or consumer surplus **Government:** spending incurred **Foreign producers:** lower export revenue
Export subsidy	**Consumers:** higher price, lower level of consumption and hence lower consumer surplus **Government:** spending incurred **Foreign producers:** lower revenue

QUESTION PRACTICE

This question is adapted from the November 2021 examination paper.

Using a tariff diagram, explain the likely effect on consumer surplus of a 25% tariff on all wooden furniture imported into the US. [4]

Test yourself

Practise drawing trade diagrams to illustrate the effects of tariffs, quotas and subsidies. Look for real-world examples of each type of trade protection.

SAMPLE STUDENT ANSWER

Response 1

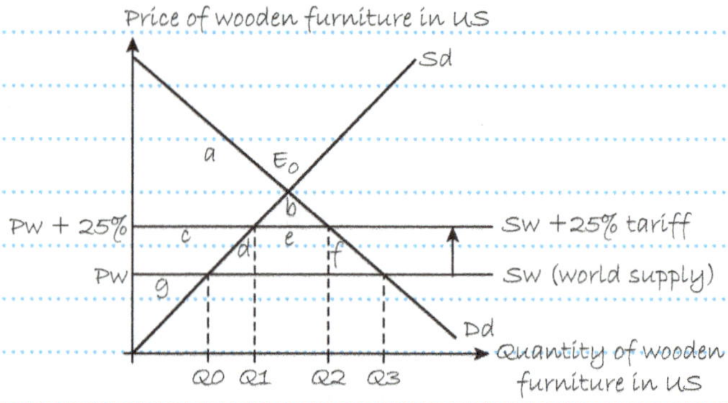

When there is a 25% tariff on wooden furniture imported into the US, the price of wooden furniture in US increases from Pw, assuming US is a price-taker, to Pw + 25%, as the tariffs lead to a shift of would supply curve upwards from Sw to Sw + 25%. Initial consumer surplus is represented by (a + b + c + d + e + f) area, and tariffs lead to a fall in consumer surplus to area (a + b).

▼ The explanation lacks clarity. Two variables need to be considered to determine the consumer surplus—price and quantity demanded. The candidate does not mention the impact on the quantity demanded and the increase in price is not identified as the cause of the fall in consumer surplus. This is not a valid answer.

▲ The candidate has drawn a correct and fully labelled diagram. The impact on the consumer surplus is identified correctly. This response could be awarded 2 marks for the diagram.

This response could have achieved 3/4 marks.

Response 2

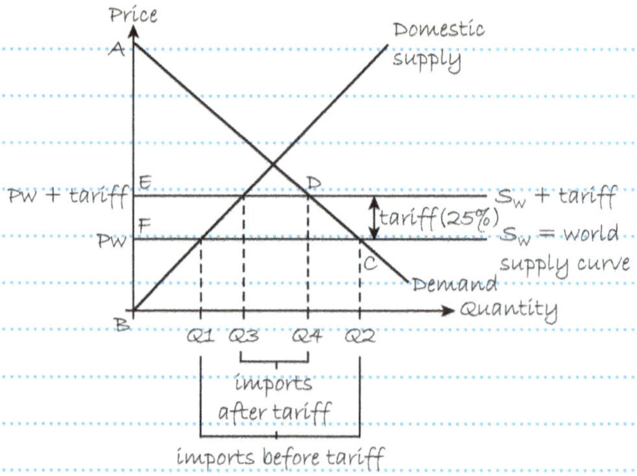

Figure 1 Tariff on wooden furniture

Due to the introduction of a tariff, consumers are required to pay a higher price from Pw to Pw + tariff and quantity demanded reduces to Q4 from Q2. This causes consumer surplus to decrease from the area denoted by AFC to AED, negatively affecting consumers (Fig. 1).

▲ The diagram is correct and fully labelled. The candidate identifies the change in the consumer surplus. The diagram could be awarded 2 marks.

There is a clear explanation that the increase in price and decrease in quantity demanded lead to a smaller consumer surplus, which could achieve 2 marks.

This response could have achieved 4/4 marks.

Response 3

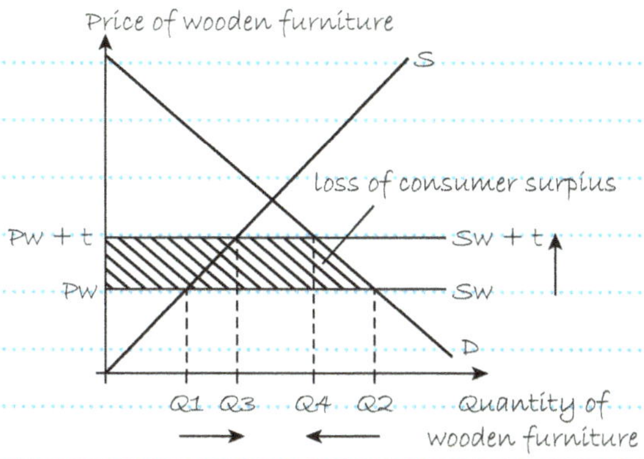

Tariff is a form of trade protection and is indirect tax on imported goods. Due to tariff, the price of wooden furniture increases from Pw to Pw + t. The quantity of domestic production of wooden furniture increases from Q1 to Q3, and the quantity of import decreases from Q1Q2 to Q3Q4. Therefore, the quantity that consumer buys decreases from Q2 to Q4. Hence, consumers are worse off and consumer surplus decreases. Consumer surplus is defined as the benefit for people who buy at lower price than that they are willing to pay for. The loss of consumer surplus is shown by the shaded area, as price increases from Pw to Pw + t, and quantity decreases.

This response could have achieved 4/4 marks.

▲ Unlike the previous two diagrams, this one does not illustrate the original consumer surplus (before the imposition of the tariff) but it does show the reduction in consumer surplus (shaded area). This approach is valid as it illustrates the effect of the tariff on the consumer surplus, answering the question. The response also clearly states that the higher price and lower quantity demanded would imply a reduction in the consumer surplus.

Assessment tip

For many questions you need to calculate or identify an area on a diagram (consumer surplus, welfare loss, for example). Responses 2 and 3 looked at the original and new consumer surpluses to determine the change. Response 3 went for a more "direct approach" by identifying the change (the shaded trapezium). Illustrating the area by shading worked well for response 3 as the candidate focused on a single area.

However, shading may make it hard to read a diagram if there are multiple areas identified, as was the case for responses 1 and 2. The annotations for those responses clearly identified the areas in the explanations.

Similarly, a change in consumer surplus can be calculated by subtracting the new consumer surplus (triangle AED in response 2) from the old consumer surplus (area AFC) **or** the change can be directly calculated from the diagram (the shaded trapezium in response 3) but attention must be paid to include the correct sign as it reflects whether the consumer surplus increased or decreased. Which approach works best for you?

QUESTION PRACTICE

This question is adapted from the November 2020 examination paper.

Country B grants rice producers an export subsidy of \$2 per kilogram of rice.

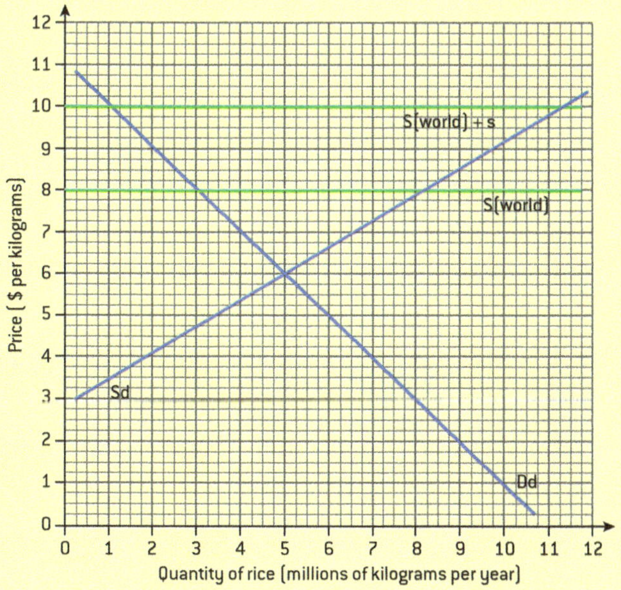

Using the diagram provided, calculate the welfare loss as a result of Country B granting the export subsidy. [2]

SAMPLE STUDENT ANSWER

▲ The candidate identifies the correct areas and notes that the quantities are in millions.

0.5 × (2 × 2) + 0.5 × (3 × 2) = $ 5 million

This response could have achieved 2/2 marks.

Assessment tip

The previous question asked you to calculate but not identify the welfare loss associated with the export subsidy on the diagram. Even if it is not a requirement of the question, shading the welfare loss or identifying the changes in quantities demanded and supplied on the diagram might make it easier for you to calculate the welfare loss and avoid missing or miscalculating an area.

Going back to the previous diagram, let's identify the welfare loss and domestic quantities demanded and supplied.

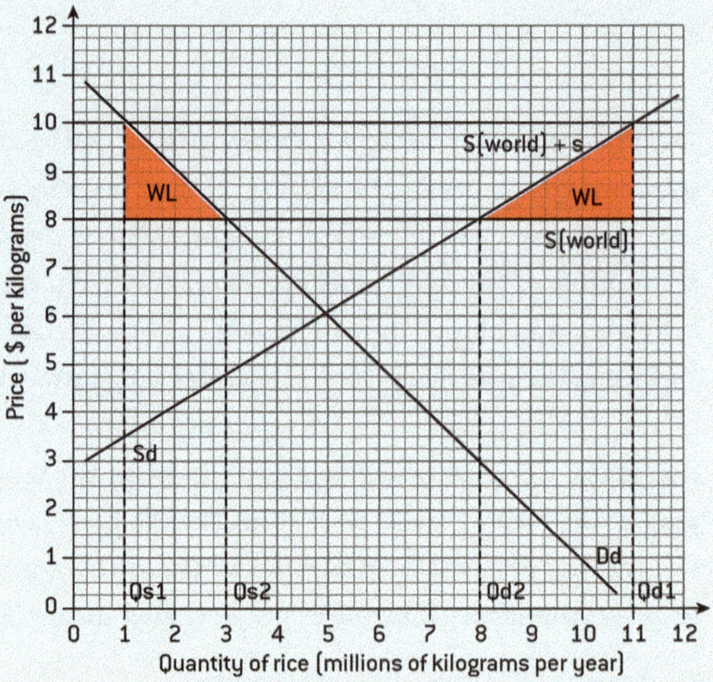

QUESTION PRACTICE

Using real-world examples, discuss the impact of tariffs on markets and stakeholders. [15]

SAMPLE STUDENT ANSWER

▲ The candidate introduces the purpose of a tariff. Some understanding of the term "stakeholders" is demonstrated.

A type of trade protection, a tariff is a tax that is placed on imports. It serves the purposes of protecting domestic industries from foreign competition and raising revenue for the government. Tariffs will directly impact the consumers and producers of goods on which they are imposed and may also impact other stakeholders indirectly especially if the tariff leads to retaliation by trading partners.

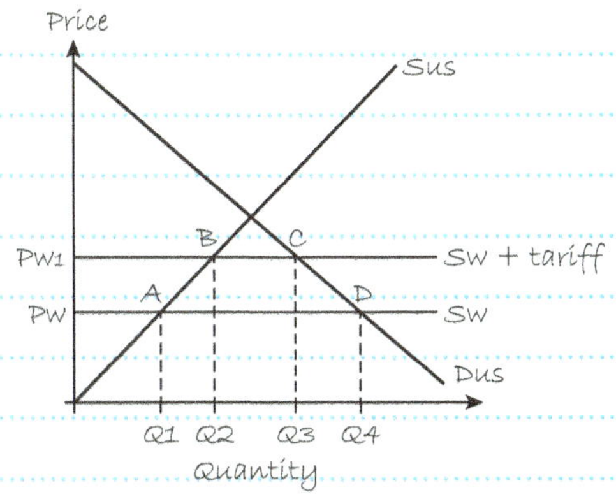

Figure 1

As can be seen in Figure 1, a 25% tariff imposed by the United States in 2018 on imported steel leads to a higher price of steel on the US market, from Pw to Pw1. This would lead to a lower quantity of steel consumed by US consumers, from Q4 to Q3 as fewer consumers are willing and able to consume at the higher price. The consumer surplus is reduced by area Pw1CDPw. Steel factories in the US would benefit as they produce a higher quantity, Q2 instead of Q1, since some firms which were previously unwilling or able to produce at price Pw are now willing and able to produce steel. They receive a higher revenue of OPw1CQ3 instead of OPwAQ1. The producer surplus is also increased by area PwABPw1. The US government also benefits through the collection of the tariff revenue, which can be used to reduce their budget deficit. From this diagram analysis, it is clear that domestic producers and the government benefit from the tariff, while consumers are disadvantaged.

▲ The tariff diagram is included and explained with adequate reference to the diagram.

▼ The candidate could have shown on the diagram the tariff revenue and the impact on foreign producers.

To increase production from Q1 to Q2, the domestic producers will need to hire more workers, and this would lead to lower unemployment. In the case of US steel, the tariff would lead to a significant decrease in structural unemployment since this industry is labour-intensive. The higher revenue earned by producers would also allow them to pay higher wages to the workers and this could lead to higher economic well-being.

▲ The candidate elaborates on the impact of tariffs on producers and related stakeholders such as employees.

▼ There is an interesting comment about the type of unemployment that is reduced, but the candidate does not explain it sufficiently.

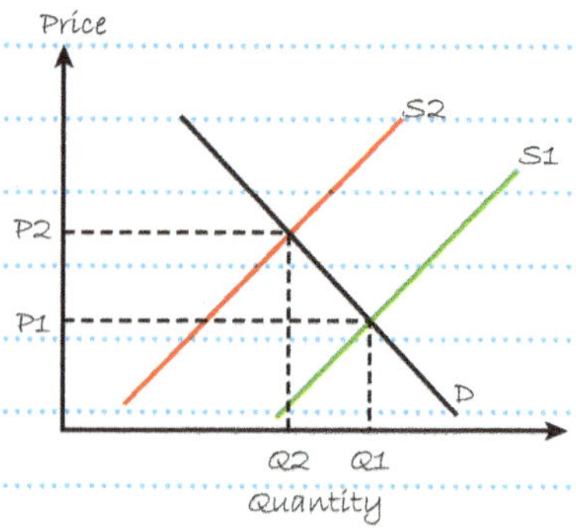

Figure 2

▲ The candidate shows awareness of the demand of the question set by the command term—"discuss"—by providing a balanced view on the impact on firms in the USA.

Some imported goods (such as steel) are also used by other firms as factors of production, the tariffs may therefore lead to higher costs of production for firms. This can be seen in Figure 2 where the supply changes from S1 to S2. Going back to our example of the 25% tariff on steel imported into the US, firms producing canned food and cars use steel and would have to pass on the higher cost of production to the consumers through higher prices (from P1 to P2 on Figure 2).

▼ Examples could be used more effectively, for example by naming the affected car, canned food or motorbike producers.

Tariffs may also lead to retaliation when trading partners also impose tariffs on US exports. This happened as a result of the US imposing tariffs on steel and other products in 2018. A series of trade wars with the EU and China led to the increase in the tariffs imposed on US-made motorbikes, for example. This means that while the producers of steel benefit from the tariffs, the motorbike makers will be disadvantaged.

▲ Here the candidate makes better use of real-world examples. The numbers quoted are not exact ("about 15%", "over 130%") but they are sufficient to show a good knowledge of the issue.

There is also evidence of evaluation and synthesis in this conclusion.

The extent of the impact on consumers and producers will depend on varying factors such as the value of the tariff, the type of industry and how easily the imported good can be substituted with domestic production. For example, the United States imposes tariffs on steel, peanuts and wool sweaters, among other goods. However, the tariff on wool sweaters is only about 15% and may not have a large impact on branded sweaters whose demand can be quite price-inelastic since consumers may show some brand loyalty and not want to buy US-made sweaters if they feel the quality is inferior to foreign sweaters. The tariff on peanuts is over 130% and would make imported peanuts more than twice the price of foreign peanuts and this would make consumers more likely to switch to local peanuts due to the significant increase in price. Finally, the US tariff on steel is 25%. While it is only slightly more than the tariff on wool sweaters, it will have a much larger impact on domestic producers because steel is a rather homogeneous product so US consumers (the US firms that require steel as factor of production) will be more willing to switch to local steel. So, it is clear that the tariff will only benefit firms who are protected by the tariff if they can easily increase production and offer products of similar or better quality to imported ones. The tariffs will disadvantage firms who need to pay for the tariff on imported factors of production and those who face the consequences of retaliation by trading partners.

This response meets all the descriptors in the second highest mark band (10–12) and **could achieve 12/15 marks.** To reach mark band 13–15, the candidate should discuss further the impact on consumers and/or foreign producers rather than focus so much on one stakeholder (the domestic producers).

Refer to Unit 5 (pages 194–195) for a full explanation of the paper 1 level descriptors.

Concept link

- **Intervention**—trade protection is a form of government intervention. The government becomes involved in the workings of markets (free trade takes place in free markets) with the aim of achieving important macroeconomic and societal goals. Can you identify the costs and benefits of intervention through trade protection in your chosen article? You may also consider some of the points learned in sub-unit 4.1, as the benefits of free trade offer possible drawbacks of intervention. The benefits of free trade that a country forgoes by opting for trade protection are the opportunity cost of trade protection.
- **Efficiency**—if the article provides insights into wastages of scarce resources (e.g. lack of scope for economies of scale, no incentive for technological improvement) then you could also consider efficiency as key concept for your commentary.

Content link

Link to your IA

You may choose an article on trade protection for your third commentary. If so, you will likely draw a diagram to illustrate the effects of the trade protection(s) mentioned in the article. Keep in mind that trade protection diagrams come with a lot of information—quantities produced and consumed domestically, quantities imported/exported, different types of expenditures and revenues as well as the resulting welfare losses. Focus on what is relevant to your article. Presenting a lengthy, generic diagram analysis may result in a lower mark on criterion C: Application and analysis).

4.3 ARGUMENTS FOR AND AGAINST TRADE CONTROL OR PROTECTION

This sub-unit builds on sub-units 4.1 and 4.2 and reviews the arguments for and against trade control or protection.

You should be able to:

- ✔ explain the arguments for and against trade protection with the aid of real-world examples
- ✔ evaluate trade policies (trade protection and free trade) for a given country

Content link

Link to other sub-units

Refer to sub-unit 3.3. Industrial jobs may be lost due to lower cost imports. This is represented on a diagram by a fall in the demand for labour for a particular country.

Summary

These are the main arguments **for** trade protection.

- It can **protect or create local jobs** and in particular **prevent or reduce structural unemployment** if the workers' skills are not transferrable to other industries.
- Trade protection can **correct a trade (current account) deficit on the balance of payments** (see sub-unit 4.6 on expenditure switching policies to reduce a persistent current account deficit).
- Domestic producers are protected from **unfair practices** such as **dumping** (the sale of goods at a price below the cost of production or below the price charged in the home market).
- A country's **strategic industries** are protected and its continued access to goods such as staples, steel and weapons is ensured. This is also known as the **national security** argument.
- Tariffs raise **government revenue.** There are often high tariffs on luxury goods in economically least developed countries (ELDCs).
- Trade protection encourages **diversification** of economic activities, by preventing specialization in agricultural goods in ELDCs.
- It protects new domestic industries, known as **infant (sunrise) industries** that lack the efficiency and economies of scale of established foreign competitors. This is often used to justify trade protection in ELDCs.
- The sale of goods that may not meet the **health and safety** standards of the importing nation is prevented.
- Production of goods is reduced in countries with lower **environmental standards** that may pose a threat to sustainability.

The reasons governments give to justify trade protection must be carefully evaluated. Trade protection is popular with industries competing with imports and governments may hide populist policies behind unfounded economic claims. Accusations of dumping may be unfounded (dumping can be hard to prove) and countries imposing trade protection on goods that do not meet environmental standards are sometimes those with poor records of environmental protection.

These are the main arguments **against** trade protection.

- Consumers pay **higher prices** and face **fewer choices** if they are unable to afford the higher-priced imports.
- Trade barriers may lead to **retaliation** and start a **trade war**.

- Trade protection leads to **misallocation of resources** as goods are not produced by countries that use the fewest resources to produce them (efficiency in production).
- Domestic firms may pay **higher costs** if they import factors of production. This may affect **export competitiveness** if exporting firms are reliant on imported resources.
- Domestic firms may **lack incentive to become more efficient.**

Test yourself

Proton Holdings Berhad (*Proton* for short) was established in 1985 in Malaysia to produce the developing country's first national car. Identified as an infant industry, Proton benefited from protection from foreign competition as Malaysia imposed tariffs as high as 300% on imported cars. Since its foundation the company also received a total of USD 3 billion in subsidies from the government. "It is a national car industry. It's not just about a car. It's about engineering. A country without engineering skill and knowledge will never become a developed country," commented the Prime Minister of Malaysia.

In the beginning, Proton was reliant on imported factors of production such as car chassis made by Mitsubishi Motors. Proton gained the technological knowledge to train workers to build cars entirely in their Malaysian factories after 15 years. In 1993, Proton cars accounted for 74% of all new cars sold in Malaysia. In 2016, a decade after the government reduced tariffs on imported cars as part of its participation in a Southeast Asian free-trade pact, Proton cars only accounted for 12.5% of new car sales in Malaysia.

Adapted from https://www.livemint.com/Industry/WfScncX72isx6B6GPCWOGL/Malaysia-eyes-sale-of-Proton-as-Mahathir-Mohamads-auto-drea.html

Read the above passage and identify at least **two arguments for** and **two arguments against** imposing tariffs on foreign cars in Malaysia.

Hint: consider the size of the tariff (as high as 300%)—would such a tariff help raise government revenue? Would it lead to a significant increase in prices for consumers? Keep in mind that the passage introduced Malaysia as a developing country. Are some of the common arguments for trade protection in ELDCs applicable?

Research other cases of infant industries. Try to find a least one industry that is now established and no longer needs protection from foreign competition (a success story). This would be a good real-world example to illustrate a part (b) essay question on this topic.

Assessment tip

Diagrams are very important in economics. The highest mark bands for the 15-mark questions in papers 1 and 2 stress the importance of diagrams—*Where appropriate, relevant diagram(s) are included and fully explained.* Note that diagrams need to be included **and fully explained** or what examiners sometimes call *effective use of diagrams.*

What does it mean to use diagrams effectively? Diagrams are meant to illustrate your arguments to convince the examiner that your point is anchored in economic theory. Your diagrams must be woven into your answers. Link the diagrams learned in sub-units 4.1 and 4.2 to the arguments for and against trade protection (where appropriate). For example, explain the argument of higher prices for consumer with reference to the *higher price on a tariff or quota diagram*. The *higher quantity supplied by domestic producers* can support the argument for *job creation*. The *welfare loss* is evidence of the misallocation of resources.

QUESTION PRACTICE

This question is adapted from the May 2012 examination paper.

Using real-world examples, discuss the view that it is never desirable for countries to resort to trade protection. [15]

SAMPLE STUDENT ANSWER

▲ This shows good understanding of the key concept, trade protection.

Trade protection is defined as the partial or complete protection of domestic industries from foreign competition in domestic markets. There are many types of trade protection such as tariffs, quotas and subsidies, and regulatory barriers. Trade protection, although aimed at benefitting domestic industries, may bring about numerous harms. For example, the US imposed a series of tariffs on Chinese imports from 2018 to 2019, such as a steel and aluminium tariff in February 2018.

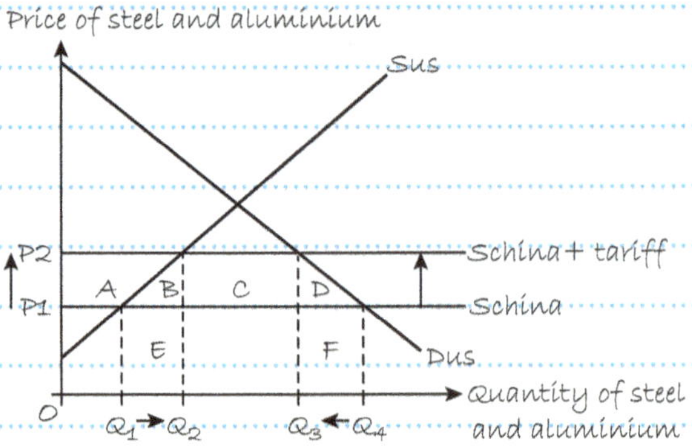

Diagram 1

▲ The candidate has included a diagram and has customized the labels to the real-world example (e.g. "S(China)" instead of "S(World)"; "Price of steel and aluminium" instead of just "Price".

▲ A full explanation of the diagram is included.

With the tariff, the prices of steel and aluminium in the US rises from P1 to P2, shifting the Chinese supply curve upwards from S(China) to S(China) + tariff (Diagram 1). At the higher price, more US domestic producers are willing and able to supply steel and aluminium, increasing quantity supplied by Q1Q2. US consumers are less incentivised to purchase at the higher price P2, causing quantity demanded to fall by Q3Q4. Thus the volume of imported steel and aluminium reduces from Q1Q4 to Q2Q3. Tariffs result in a loss of consumer surplus of areas A + B + C + D as domestic consumers consume less of the good at a higher price P2. While domestic producer surplus increases by area A as total revenue increase from (P1 × Q1) to (P2 × Q2) and the government earns tariff revenue equivalent to area C, society suffers a net welfare loss of areas B + D of consumption in efficiency is represented by area D which is a loss of consumer surplus. Area B represents production inefficiency due to the extra cost paid as the US economy shifts steel and aluminium purchases away from efficient foreign producers to relatively inefficient domestic firms.

Thus trade protectionism almost always guarantees a reduction in efficiency, especially production inefficiency which results in global resource misallocation. In addition, tariffs on Chinese steel and aluminium may breed dependency on such protection in domestic producers, reducing their incentive to innovate, lower costs and operate efficiently. Long-run efficiency thus declines as competition is effectively reduced.

Trade protection also increases the probability of a trade war occurring, where protectionism results in retaliatory protectionist measures imposed by the other country. For example, China retaliated to the tariffs set by the US by imposing higher tariffs on US soy and automobile exports in 2019. As both countries became increasingly protectionist, there was a significant reduction in the volume of trade between them, reducing the gains from free trade. Since export earnings are an injection into the global circular flow of income, and especially given that both US and China are large global economies, there may be a significant impact on world trade. With increased instability and volatility, long-term growth and investment is hindered.

However, trade protection may bring about desirable benefits in some circumstances. For example, Ecuador imposed new regulatory barriers on imported goods such as cereals in 2013, in the form of quality control measures and import licensing. It also increased tariffs on raw materials and capital equipment which are also produced in Ecuador. Such measures were aimed at protecting infant industries, new domestic industries that have not had time to establish themselves and achieve production efficiencies and may therefore be unable to compete with mature foreign industries.

By reducing the volume of imports such as through tariffs as in Diagram 1 (Q1Q4 to Q2Q3), competition is reduced, allowing infant industries to increase market share and efficiencies. Such policies may be especially necessary for developing countries such as Ecuador to expand production into new industries that give them a comparative advantage, allowing for long-term economic growth and development. For example, if Ecuador grows its cereal export industry, export earnings may increase, increasing net

▲ The candidate continues to make use of the diagram to support the argument that trade protection is not desirable.

▼ There is a real-world example but it is not fully developed. Who are the consumers of steel and aluminium? What is the impact of the higher prices for them in particular? The candidate could have mentioned US companies that use the metals in production; their goods will become more expensive.

▲ This judgement demonstrates the candidate's ability to evaluate the argument—that trade protection might have more significant impacts for some countries.

▲ The candidate is meeting the requirements set by the command term ("discuss") by providing a counter-argument to the proposition that trade protection is never desirable.

A real-world example is developed. References to the tariff and AD/AS diagrams help support the analysis.

exports (X-M) and thus AD from AD1 to AD2 (Diagram 2). Real GDP increases from Y1 to Y2, causing actual growth. If economic growth is sustained or industries gain more funds from profits, investment in physical and human capital may increase, increasing Keynesian AS from Keynesian AS1 to Keynesian AS2; potential output increases to Y4 while real GDP increases to Y3, allowing both short-term and long-term growth.

▲ There is a clear attempt at synthesis, which summarizes some of the key points raised in the essay.

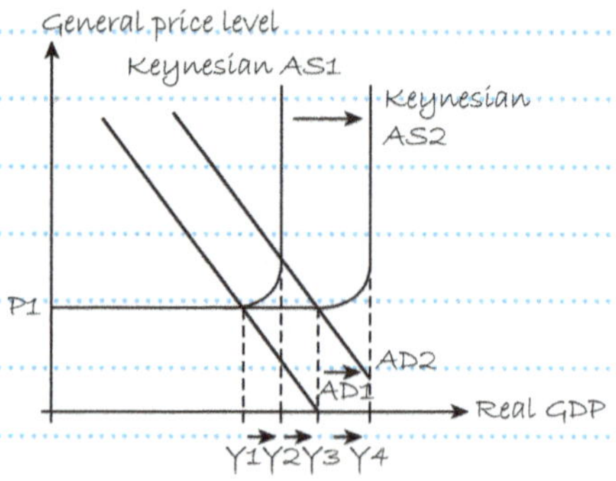

Diagram 2

In conclusion, trade protection is often deemed undesirable because of its negative implications for parties involved, not only the country on which protectionism is imposed but also the domestic economy of the country imposing trade protection. Negative repercussions also extend to countries not directly involved, having global implications. However, a country's context may decide whether the benefits of protection can outweigh its harms. Especially in economically less developed countries, trade protection may be necessary in the short-term to grow infant industries and its economy. Hence, countries may find it desirable to resort to trade protections at times, but must do so with caution.

This **response could achieve 13/15 marks**. It meets all of the descriptors for the highest mark band (13–15). However, the real-world examples are not always well developed to support the arguments.

Assessment tip

Pay attention to the command term. "Discuss" was the command term of this question practice. A discussion needs to be balanced. In the question, the balance comes in the form of considering arguments that support the idea that trade protection is not desirable, but also considering the opposite view—that trade protection can be desirable. An unbalanced answer to a discussion question would probably receive a lower mark as it would not meet the first descriptor of the highest mark bands—the specific demands of the question (which are partly determined by the command term) would not be addressed.

Content link

Link to your IA

Trade protection is covered extensively in the news and so candidates often opt for this topic for their third commentary. A good article would point to the reasons that pushed the government to impose the trade barrier. For example, a mention of job losses could signal the fear of structural unemployment; a difficulty to compete with imports from more established firms could indicate an infant (sunrise) industry that needs time to grow; a depreciating currency is often the symptom of a high current account deficit. Also pay attention to other information given in the article that could provide arguments against the implementation of trade barriers. For example, a mention of rising inflation would suggest that consumers' real income would be significantly affected by higher prices of imports. Explaining those arguments in favour and against trade protection in economic terms and with reference to the contents of the article is important (criterion C: Application and analysis) but it is important to assess the validity of the arguments in context (criterion E: Evaluation).

South Africa imposed tariffs on imported chicken meat in 2020, for example. Would the infant industry argument make a valid reason to support the tariff? Could chicken farmers be part of a new industry in South Africa?

Concept link

As mentioned in sub-unit 4.2, a commentary that allows for some debate on free trade versus trade protection may illustrate the key concepts of **efficiency** and **intervention**. Here is another key concept you may consider.

Interdependence—the focus of the article may be the impacts of trade protection on trading partners, especially in terms of lower income, unemployment and the risk of retaliation. Such an article would allow you to explore the interdependence of nations in a globalized world.

4.4 ECONOMIC INTEGRATION

You should be able to:

- ✔ define the terms
  - ✔ preferential trade agreements
  - ✔ free trade areas or agreements
  - ✔ customs unions
  - ✔ common markets
  - ✔ monetary union
- ✔ explain the arguments for and against joining a trading bloc
- ✔ evaluate a country's decision to join a trading bloc
- ✔ explain the objectives and functions of the World Trade Organization (WTO) and the common criticism of the WTO.

This sub-unit introduces the different types of trading blocs.

HL In addition to the points above, for HL you should be able to:

- define the terms
  - trade creation
  - trade diversion
- evaluate a country's decision to join a monetary union.

Summary

Economic integration refers to the process by which two or more countries cooperate on economic and other matters. The most common form of economic integration is a **preferential trade agreement** (PTA).

A PTA is a trading bloc that encourages **trade liberalization** (the process of reducing trade barriers) by giving member countries preferential access to certain goods and services (e.g. through reduced tariffs) .

PTAs may be **bilateral** (between two countries), **regional** (between many countries) or **multilateral** (agreed through the WTO) agreements.

The degree of economic integration varies with the type of PTA or trading bloc.

- A **free trade area** or **agreement** is the lowest form of economic integration—where member countries reduce or remove trade barriers against each other. Each country keeps its own trade policies with countries outside the free trade area or agreement.
- A **customs union** is an agreement between countries to reduce or remove trade barriers and adopt common external barriers against non-member countries.
- A **common market** is the highest form of economic integration—member countries agree to reduce or remove trade barriers, adopt common external trade barriers and permit free movement of capital and labour. In addition, members may adopt common policies on product regulation.

In addition to the benefits of free trade (see sub-unit 4.1), the advantages of joining a trade bloc include the following.

- (HL) When trade barriers are reduced, goods that were previously produced domestically will now be imported from producers who can produce them more efficiently (at a lower cost). This situation is known as **trade creation**.
- Membership in a trading bloc may allow for **stronger bargaining power** in multilateral negotiations. As a common market, the European Union (EU) has signed economic agreements with some of the largest economic markets, which individual EU member states may not be able to negotiate on their own. For example, the EU-China Comprehensive Agreement on Investment (CAI) "grants EU investors a greater level of access to China's market" (https://ec.europa.eu/trade/policy/in-focus/eu-china-agreement/).
- There is **greater political stability and cooperation** within the trading bloc as countries become more interdependent.
- With permitting free movement of labour, there are **greater employment opportunities** for residents of a common market.

In addition to the arguments for trade protection (see sub-unit 4.3), membership to a trading bloc may also lead to:

- (HL) **trade diversion**, a situation where a member country of a trade bloc no longer imports goods from a more efficient (lower cost) producer outside the trading bloc and instead imports them from a less efficient producer within the trading bloc
- a **loss of sovereignty** as economic decisions may no longer be taken independently, especially in customs unions and common markets where countries adopt common trade and other economic policies
- a **reduction in the incentive to participate in multilateral trading negotiations** through the WTO.

HL A trading bloc may further integrate economic activities as a **monetary union** where member countries share the same currency and have a common central bank.

Besides the advantages of a trading bloc, members of a monetary union may also benefit from:

- the **elimination of exchange rate conversion costs** and **risk associated with exchange rate fluctuations**
- greater **inflows of foreign direct investment** due to the greater stability resulting from the lower currency risk.

Members of a monetary union may also suffer a **loss of independence in implementing monetary and exchange rate policy**.

The WTO is a multilateral organization seeking to liberalize trade. The functions of the WTO are to:

- set and enforce rules for international trade
- provide a forum for negotiating trade liberalization
- monitor further trade liberalization
- resolve trade disputes
- increase the transparency of decision-making processes
- cooperate with other major international economic institutions involved in global economic management to help developing countries benefit fully from the global trading system.

The WTO has faced many **difficulties in reaching agreements on services and primary products**. Developing countries often denounce the policies of the WTO that they feel **benefit developed countries more than developing countries**.

Test yourself

A common central bank is shared by 19 members of the EU as part of a monetary union, the Eurozone. The European Central Bank is responsible for its monetary policy.

▼ **Table 4.4.1** Inflation and economic growth rates for selected Eurozone members (2018)

	Estonia	Greece	Germany	Poland	Spain	Eurozone average
Inflation (%)	3.44	0.63	1.73	1.81	1.68	1.70
Economic growth (%)	4.13	1.60	1.09	5.35	2.30	1.84

As you can see, inflation and growth rates vary across the Eurozone. Would you say all countries want the same monetary policy? As the President of the European Central Bank, would you adopt a contractionary or expansionary monetary policy?

Assessment tip

The EU is the largest common market with 27 member countries. Croatia was the last country to join the EU in 2013 but other countries such as Serbia and Turkey are currently negotiating membership to the common market. Research the (potential) benefits and problems of an EU membership for those countries. Those could be good real-world examples for paper 1 questions.

QUESTION PRACTICE

This question is adapted from the November 2021 examination paper.

List **two** functions of the World Trade Organization (WTO). [2]

SAMPLE STUDENT ANSWER

Response 1

To negotiate rules and to settle disputes.

▼ While it looks as if the candidate has highlighted two functions of the WTO, they are poorly expressed. What are the rules for? What kind of disputes does the WTO help to resolve?

This response would probably not be awarded a mark.

Response 2

1. Settles trade disputes.
2. Provides a forum for trade negotiations between countries.

▲ This response is a lot clearer. If you compare it to the previous response, here the candidate clearly states that the disputes are trade-related.

This response could have achieved 2/2 marks.

4.5 EXCHANGE RATES

You should be able to:

- ✔ define the terms
  - ✔ exchange rate
  - ✔ fixed, floating and managed exchange rates
  - ✔ appreciation and depreciation
  - ✔ devaluation and revaluation
  - ✔ overvalued and undervalued exchange rates
- ✔ explain the reasons for a change in the demand of, or supply for, a currency
- ✔ illustrate changes in exchange rates on a diagram
- ✔ calculate changes in the value of a currency from a set of data
- ✔ discuss the consequences of a change in exchange rate on economic indicators with the aid of real-world examples
- ✔ illustrate the impact of a change in exchange rate on an AD/AS diagram

This sub-unit introduces key terms, ideas and principles associated with exchange rates.

HL In addition to the points above, for HL you should be able to:

- evaluate a country's decision to change its exchange rate system.

Summary

An **exchange rate** is the price of a currency in terms of another currency.

Currencies are transacted ("exchanged") on the foreign exchange market. For example, residents of the UK who wish to visit France will need to exchange British pounds for euro since the British pound is not accepted by most hotels, restaurants and shops in France. That currency exchange is both a purchase and a sale.

- British pounds are sold—this increases the supply for the British pound on the market for British pounds.
- Euro are purchased—demand for the euro increases on the market for euro.

The exchange rate, being a price, changes with the changes in market forces. In the above example, the exchange rate for the British pound decreases and the exchange rate for the euro increases.

There are three types of exchange rate system.

- The **floating exchange rate** system—the exchange rate is determined by market forces (the demand for, and supply of, the currency on the foreign exchange market) without government or central bank intervention.
- The **fixed exchange rate** system—the value of a currency is fixed, or pegged, to the value of another currency by the central bank. In this system, constant intervention is needed to counter changes in the exchange rate resulting from movements in the demand for, and/or supply of, the currency.
- The **managed exchange rate** system—the exchange rate is allowed to change within limits. In this system, regular intervention by the central bank is required to prevent excessive appreciation or depreciation.

Appreciation (**depreciation**) refers to the increase (decrease) in the value of a currency resulting from movements in market forces. These terms are used to refer to exchange rate changes in floating and managed exchange rate systems.

These are the main reasons for changes in the demand for, and supply of, a currency.

- **Changes in the demand for exports and imports**—for example, importing electronic devices from Korea results in an increase in the demand for the Korean won since the currency is needed to pay for the electronic devices.
- **Inward or outward flow of foreign direct investment or portfolio investment and remittances**—shares issued by a company in Norway can only be purchased with Norwegian krones. Foreigners will need to sell their currency to purchase the Norwegian krone to pay for the shares. The purchase of shares represents an inward flow of portfolio investment for Norway and hence an increase for the demand for Norwegian krones.

  When Mexican workers in the USA send money back to their families (an inward flow of remittances for Mexico), they convert US dollars to Mexican pesos. In doing so, they sell US dollars (the supply of US dollars increases) to purchase pesos (the demand for Mexican pesos increases).
- **Speculation**—when a currency is expected to appreciate, foreigners may wish to purchase it ahead of the higher exchange rate. This would lead to an increase in the demand for the currency. If the Indonesian rupiah is expected to appreciate next year, speculators may decide to buy it now at the lower exchange rate to sell the currency at a higher price next year. This would lead to an increase in the demand for the Indonesian rupiah.
- **Changes in relative inflation rates**—if inflation in Canada exceeds the US inflation rate, US goods may become cheaper than Canadian goods over time. This would lead to greater imports of US goods in Canada, and reduced Canadian exports to the USA. Both the demand for, and supply of, the Canadian dollar would change as a result, leading to a depreciation of the Canadian dollar.
- **Changes in growth rates**—economic growth leads to increases in income. With higher income, residents of a country may buy more goods and services, some of which will be imported. Also, the higher economic growth may attract foreign investment. This would lead to increases in the supply of, and demand for, the currency. The overall impact on the currency would depend on the magnitude of the changes in demand and supply.
- **Changes in interest rates**—a higher interest rate in Australia implies higher return on bank deposits at Australian banks. Foreigners may want to convert their savings to Australian dollars, and hence increase the demand for the Australian dollar, to transfer savings to an Australian bank account.
- **Central bank intervention**—under fixed and managed exchange rate systems, central banks buy and sell currencies. To counter a downward pressure in the currency, the central bank of Vietnam may need to sell some of its foreign currency reserves to purchase the excess of Vietnamese dong on the foreign exchange market (this results in an increase in demand for the Vietnamese dong). When it needs to counter an increase in the value of the Vietnamese dong, the central bank may purchase foreign currencies using Vietnamese dong. This would increase the supply of the Vietnamese dong.

Revaluation (**devaluation**) refers to the increase (decrease) in the value of currency through intervention by the country's central bank. Thus, these two terms describe changes in exchange rates resulting from intervention in fixed exchange rate systems.

When the central bank tries to maintain the value of a currency lower (higher) than what it would be in a floating exchange rate system, the currency is said to be **undervalued (overvalued)**.

The central bank maintains the value of a currency mostly through the sale and/or purchase of its currency in the foreign exchange market, and/or changes in interest rates.

HL These are the advantages of a floating exchange rate.

- A balance of payment disequilibrium is automatically corrected.
- Monetary policy can be used to achieve domestic objectives (e.g. higher economic growth). Under a fixed or managed exchange rate, interest rates may need to be adjusted to maintain or influence the exchange rate.
- There is no necessity to hold foreign reserves.

These are the advantages of a fixed exchange rate.

- Uncertainty caused by fluctuation in exchange rates is reduced. Prices of imports, revenue from exports, foreign debts and return from foreign investment will not fluctuate.
- A fixed exchange rate encourages fiscal discipline. A fixed exchange rate regime may not be sustainable with relatively high inflation rates, which would lead to changes in demand for, and supply of, the currency. As such, governments are less likely to adopt expansionary fiscal policy.
- Firms will not benefit from a currency depreciation, which makes exports cheaper in foreign currency terms. It forces firms to remain efficient to keep the prices of their goods competitive.
- There is higher export revenue and economic growth if the exchange rate is fixed below the market value of the currency (it is an undervalued currency).

Changes in exchange rates will impact the economy through changes in the prices of export and imports.

- A change in the (X – M) component of aggregate demand will affect **demand-pull inflation**, **economic growth** and **unemployment**.
- There will be changes in the price of imported resources, which will affect **cost-push inflation**.
- More (less) affordable imported goods and services would lower (increase) the cost of living and improve (worsen) residents' **standard of living**.

Assessment tip

One descriptor of the highest mark band for questions carrying at least 10 marks is the *appropriate use of economic terms*. A lot of terms are introduced in this sub-unit, and some may seem to describe a similar phenomenon. For example, devaluation and depreciation both refer to a fall in the value of a currency. However, a devaluation is the result of the central bank's intervention, while a depreciation is the result of changes in market forces.

QUESTION PRACTICE

This question is adapted from the May 2021 examination paper.

Define the term depreciation. [2]

SAMPLE STUDENT ANSWER

A depreciation is the fall in the value of a currency expressed in terms of another currency.

▼ This could also apply to a devaluation. If a definition can apply to two different economic terms then it is vague. The candidate should have specified that this fall in the currency's value is the result of a change in market forces (or that it takes place in a floating exchange rate system).

This response could have achieved 1/2 marks.

Assessment tip

An *exchange rate* diagram may look like a *demand and supply* diagram, but the vertical axis should not be labelled as just "price". An exchange rate is the **price** of a currency **in terms of another currency**. Therefore, the label for the exchange rate for the euro in terms of the US$ may be "price of euro in US$" or "exchange rate $\frac{\text{US\$}}{\text{euro}}$".

Note that if you use a currency pair (such as $\frac{\text{US\$}}{\text{euro}}$) for your vertical axis label, the currency on the denominator is the currency listed on the horizontal axis (it is the currency that is bought and sold).

QUESTION PRACTICE

This question is adapted from the November 2021 examination paper.

Using an exchange rate diagram, explain the effect on the South Korean won's exchange rate of South Korea's central bank selling US dollars. [4]

SAMPLE STUDENT ANSWER

Response 1

By selling US dollars, the demand for won increases, since the South Korean central bank is demanding won in exchange for US dollars. This shifts demand for won from D to D1, increasing the exchange rate of won from ERe to ER1.

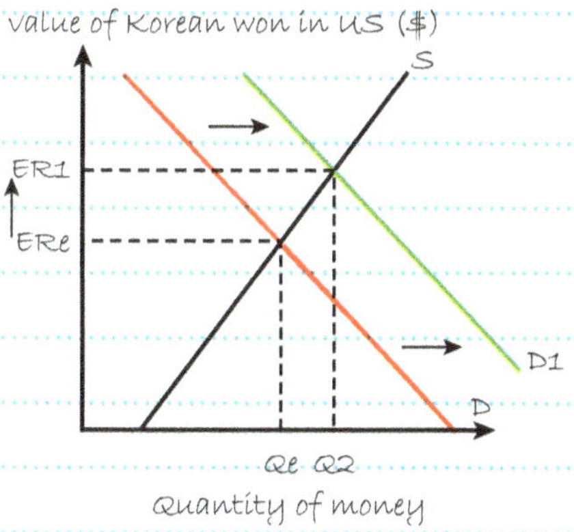

▲ The explanation establishes a link between the sale of US$ and the demand for Korean won.

▲ The candidate clearly indicates the rightward shift of the demand curve and the increase in the exchange rate with arrows.

▼ However, the vertical axis is not labelled correctly—it should be "*price* of Korean won in US$" and not "*value* of Korean won in US$". It is likely that this diagram would only be given 1 mark.

This response could have achieved 3/4 marks.

Response 2

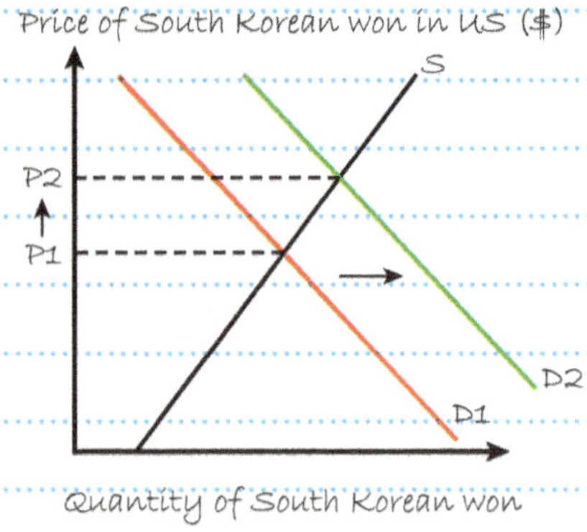

The South Korean won appreciates from P1 to P2 as the central bank is selling its foreign currency reserves to buy (demand) South Korean won. This has the effect of decreasing the demand for the won and thus there is a rightward shift from D1 to D2.

▲ The candidate explains that by selling US dollars, the central bank buys Korean won and this causes an increase in demand. The diagram is correctly labelled and the changes in the demand curve and exchange rate are clearly shown.

This response could have achieved 4/4 marks.

QUESTION PRACTICE

This question is adapted from the November 2021 examination paper.

Using an exchange rate diagram, explain how a decrease in the interest rate in Thailand might influence the value of the Thai baht. [4]

SAMPLE STUDENT ANSWER

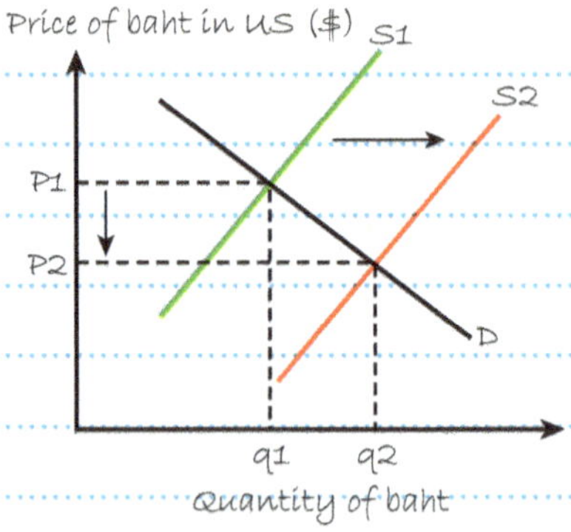

▲ The candidate clearly indicates the rightward shift of the supply curve and the decrease in the exchange rate with arrows.

As seen in the figure above, a decrease in interest rates disincentivises saving in Thailand by domestic and foreign savers, as the return on savings falls. Thus, savers sell Thai baht to buy other currencies to save in other countries with higher interest rates, increasing the supply of baht S1 → S2, thus decreasing the value of the baht in terms of US$, P1 → P2.

▲ The response clearly establishes the link between the lower interest rate and the sale of the Thai baht as savings are converted to another currency. There are adequate references to the diagram to explain the depreciation.

This response could have achieved 4/4 marks.

QUESTION PRACTICE

This question is adapted from the November 2020 examination paper.

Read the following passage and answer the question that follows.

The depreciation of the Argentinian peso causes imported oil prices to go up, further raising inflation. The falling real incomes of households combined with higher interest rates will affect the economy negatively, possibly leading to a recession. Interest rates will remain high for some time, discouraging investment. Economists expect Argentina to fall into recession, for the fifth time in a decade.

Using an AD/AS diagram, explain how the peso's weakness is "raising inflation". [4]

SAMPLE STUDENT ANSWER

Response 1

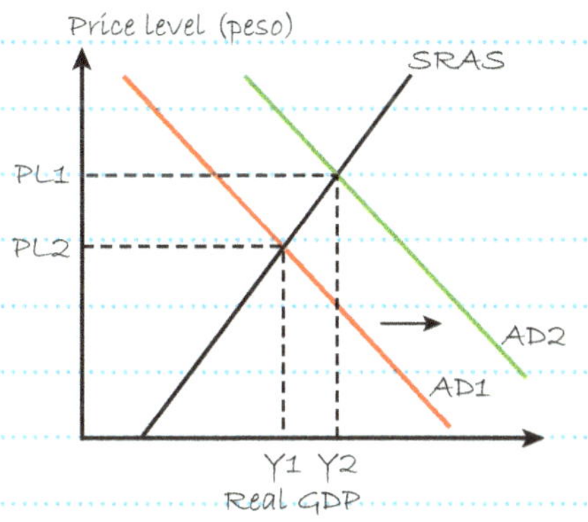

A weaker peso will make imports more expensive and exports cheaper. This can increase the exports from Argentina with an increase in export quantity and export revenue. At the same time, as imports become more expensive, domestic consumers will turn to cheaper alternative domestic products, decreasing consumption of imports. Together, the weaker peso can increase net export (X-M) in the country by raising export (X) and reducing imports (M), shifting aggregate demand from AD1 to AD2. As such, the general price level increases from PL1 to PL2. Hence, the peso's weakness raises inflation.

▼ While a depreciation could lead to an increase in aggregate demand if export revenue increase due to the lower prices of exports in foreign currency terms and/or lower import spending due to more expensive imports, that is not what the passage describes. On the contrary, the mention of a recession in the passage points to a decrease in aggregate demand so this response is incorrect. Paper 2 questions always refer to text and/or data provided and must be answered in context.

It is likely that this response would not be awarded a mark.

Response 2

A deprecation of the peso means that imports become more expensive, leading to cost-push inflation. This is shown in the diagram below.

▲ In contrast to response 1, this response clearly points to the higher price of imported factors of production, which lead to cost-push inflation as suggested by the text. The diagram is correctly and fully labelled with a leftward shift of the SRAS and the corresponding increase in the price level to reflect the higher inflation rate. Arrows clearly indicate the changes in SRAS and the price level.

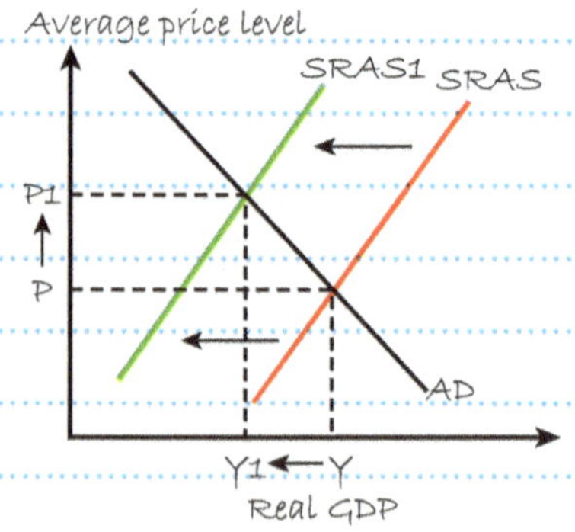

Aggregate supply is the total amount of goods and services produced in an economy at a given price level over a period of time. Increased import prices causes costs of production to increase, shifting the SRAS curve left to a new equilibrium at P1. The average price level of the economy has increased, therefore, imported inflation has occurred due to the weakness of the peso.

▼ There is no reference to the specific imported factor of production that leads to higher production costs (oil).

This response could have achieved 3/4 marks.

Content link

Link to your IA

News articles on the impact of a change in exchange rate on economic indicators are a good choice for a commentary—in particular, if the article provides the reason for the change in the currency (e.g. fall in demand due to lower export revenue). This allows you to apply economic theory to explain both the change in the price of the currency and the impact on the economic indicator (on inflation, for example).

However, be mindful that there are a few ways a change in currency may affect the rate of inflation—as we saw in the previous practice question. The article may establish that the higher inflation rate is due to a significant increase in export revenue, which would point to demand-pull inflation. It could also be that the higher price of imports following a depreciation has led to cost-push inflation. Make sure you explain the correct impact to achieve the highest mark on criterion C: Application and analysis.

Concept link

- **Change**—a change in an economic variable can have very different impact on different stakeholders. For example, the price of the traditional Peruvian staple food, quinoa, increased significantly when it became popular as a superfood in overseas markets. The resulting increase in the value of Peruvian exports led to the appreciation of Peru's currency, the sol. This was good news for quinoa producers who enjoyed higher income cheaper imports in domestic currency terms. Firms who had taken foreign loans benefited from smaller repayments in domestic currency after the appreciation of the sol. In contrast, it was not good news for the residents of Peru who were not quinoa producers and had to spend so much more on food that they had little income left to enjoy cheaper imports. This impact of the change in trend for superfood on the exchange rate of the sol and the differing impact of that exchange rate appreciation on the welfare of the people of Peru is an apt illustration of the concept of change.

4.6 BALANCE OF PAYMENTS

This sub-unit examines the different accounts (and their components) of the balance of payments and the interdependence between those accounts. The relationship between the current account and the exchange rate is another important feature of this sub-unit.

You should be able to:

- ✔ define the terms
  - ✔ balance of payments
  - ✔ current, capital and financial accounts
- ✔ list and explain the components of each of the accounts in the balance of payments
- ✔ calculate the deficit/surplus in any one of the accounts of the balance of payments
- ✔ explain that the sum of the current, capital and financial accounts equals zero.

HL In addition to the points above, for HL you should be able to:

- explain why a deficit (surplus) in the current or financial account of the balance of payments may result in downward (upward) pressure on the exchange rate of the currency
- discuss, with the aid of real-world examples, the implications of a persistent current account deficit
- explain the methods a government can use to correct a persistent current account deficit
- evaluate the effectiveness of expenditure switching policies, expenditure reducing policies and supply-side policies as measures to correct a persistent current account deficit with the aid of real-world examples
- apply the Marshall-Lerner condition to the effect of a currency devaluation or depreciation on the current account
- explain the J-curve effect, with reference to the Marshall-Lerner condition
- discuss, with the aid of real-world examples, the possible consequences of a persistent current account surplus.

Summary

The balance of payments is a record of all the transactions between the residents of a country and the residents of all other countries over a year.

The transactions in the balance of payments are categorized into three accounts.

- The **current account** includes the funds related to the trade in goods and services (export revenue minus import expenditure), net investment income flows (profit, interest and dividends) and net current transfers (foreign aid, grants and remittances).
- The **capital account** includes all capital transfers (e.g. debt forgiveness, payment for inheritance taxes), and transactions in non-produced assets (e.g. land rights such as land sold to embassies) and non-financial assets (e.g. patents and copyrights) between countries. The capital account is usually the smallest of the three accounts on the balance of payments.
- The **financial account** includes flows of funds related to foreign direct investment (FDI) and portfolio investment, the purchase and sale of a country's reserve assets (official assets) and funds related to official borrowing (by governments).

Credits (+) are inflows of funds and *debits (–)* are outflows of funds. There is a surplus (deficit) in an account of the balance of payment when the credits exceed (fall short of) the debits for that account.

Content link

Link to other sub-units

Refer to sub-unit 4.5 as a reminder of the reasons for changes in the demand for, and supply of, a currency.

HL Credits (such as the export revenue) lead to an increase in the demand for the currency on the foreign exchange market. This puts an upward pressure on the exchange. Debits (e.g. FDI outflows) increase the supply for the currency. This leads to a downward pressure on the exchange rate.

More on the reserve assets (official assets)

A central bank keeps reserve assets to settle urgent international transactions, intervene in the foreign exchange market to influence the exchange rate or finance balance of payments deficits (see the next point on financial account surplus compensating for current account deficit). Reserve assets include foreign currency deposits and government bonds (e.g. US Treasury Bills). Note that the use (spending) of reserve assets will be recorded as a credit (+) on the balance of payments account whereas the accumulation (purchase) of official reserves is recorded as a debit (–). For example, if the People's Bank of China (the central bank of China) spends some of its US$ reserves, the transaction will be recorded as an inflow or credit on China's balance of payments.

An account may be in deficit or surplus, but the balance of payments *should* always "balance"—the sum of all the accounts in the balance of payment *should* always be zero:

$$\text{current account} + \text{capital account} + \text{financial account} = 0$$

The sum of credits should balance with the sum of debits across all accounts. As the capital account is usually small (almost insignificant), an imbalance in the current account is mostly compensated by the financial account. If portfolio investment and FDI inflows are insufficient to finance the current account deficit then, to ensure that the balance of payment balances:

- either the Central Bank uses its official reserves to finance the deficit (and we saw earlier that using reserve assets is recorded as a credit (+))
- or the country must resort to official borrowing, (which will also appear as a credit (+) on the balance of payments).

HL A current account deficit may become a concern if it is persistent and represents a significant proportion of the country's GDP. A persistent deficit in the current account may lead to these situations.

- A **depreciation** of the currency may help decrease the current account but may lead to cost-push inflation and foreign investors losing confidence in the economy.
- **Higher interest rates** may be set, to attract financial investment to increase the financial account inflows. This may have a contractionary impact on the economy.
- There may be **sales of sale of domestic assets to foreigners** to increase inflows into the financial account.
- The country will experience **indebtedness** if the current account deficit forces the government to borrow from abroad to finance the deficit. The increase in foreign debts worsens the economic standing of the country and leads to **a poor credit rating by international agencies.**
- **Contractionary demand-side policies** may be used to reduce lower import spending (see the next point on expenditure reducing policies). This may, however, lead to an economic slowdown.
- The combined effect of a lower (X – M) component of the aggregate demand, lack of investment due to poor confidence and inability of the government to finance infrastructure due to high government debt will likely lead to **lower economic growth prospects**.

To reduce a persistent current account deficit, governments may consider these measures.

- **Expenditure switching policies** may be used, such as trade protection and/or a currency devaluation (or sharp depreciation if the currency operates in a managed exchange rate system). A devaluation (sharp depreciation) will only be effective in reducing a current account deficit if the Marshall-Lerner condition (explained below) is satisfied.
- **Expenditure reducing policies** may be used, such as contractionary fiscal policy and contractionary monetary policy, to reduce

consumers' willingness and ability to spend on all goods, inclusive of imports. Such policies may also help decrease inflationary pressures (which could be the root cause of the current account deficit) but could worsen an economic slowdown or recession.

- **Supply-side policies** may be used to promote efficiency and reduce firms' costs to raise export competitiveness, but these policies are often difficult to implement and only yield results in the long term.

A currency devaluation or depreciation implies that the foreign price of exports decreases and the domestic price of imports increases. The impact the changes on the prices of exports and imports have on the current account depend on the PED for exports and the PED for imports.

The **Marshall-Lerner condition** states that a currency devaluation (or a sharp depreciation) will improve the current account balance only if the sum of PED for exports and PED for imports is greater than 1. That is:

$$PEDx + PEDm > 1$$

Content link

Link to other sub-units

Consider the advantages and limitations of the policies learned in:

- sub-unit 4.3 for additional arguments in favour and against trade protection
- sub-units 3.5 and 3.6 for additional notes on the effectiveness of demand-side policies
- sub-unit 3.7 on supply-side policies and their effectiveness.

The Marshall-Lerner condition usually does not hold in the short run as price elasticities are low. Exporters and importers need time to adjust to price changes following the devaluation or depreciation. As a result, a current account will initially widen and only after a period of time will it narrow. This is known as the **J-curve effect**.

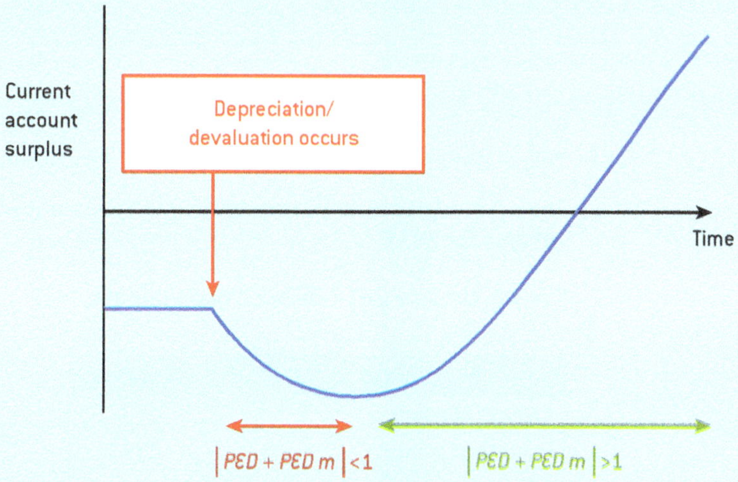

▲ Figure 4.6.1 The J-curve effect

A persistent surplus in the current account may lead to these situations.

- There may be an **appreciation** of the currency and hence **reduced export competitiveness**.
- There may be **lower cost-push and demand-pull inflation** due to lower prices of imports and lower (X – M) component of aggregate demand.
- A higher rate of **employment** may result as jobs are created in export and import-competing industries.
- The current account surplus implies greater production (exports) than consumption (imports) and thus relatively **low levels of domestic consumption** (the residents of the country could enjoy a higher standard of living by consuming more imports).
- The current account surplus is likely to be compensated by a financial account deficit (since the capital account is usually a small part of the balance of payments). Portfolio and FDI outflows imply that domestic investors favour foreign markets over the domestic markers, leading to less **domestic investment**.

Test yourself

There are debits (outflow of funds) and credits (inflow of funds) associated with each component of the balance of payment. Can you provide a real-world example for each component—credit and debit—on your country's current and financial accounts? Can you explain each flow's impact on the exchange rate? (Remember that credits lead to an increase in the demand for the currency and debits lead to an increase in the supply of the currency.)

▼ **Table 4.6.1** Examples of credits and debits on specific countries' balance of payments

Account	Component	Country	Real-world examples	Impact on the exchange rate diagram
Current account	balance of trade in goods	India 	*credit:* revenue from the exports of rice	demand for Indian rupees ↑
			debit: expenditure on imports of petrol	supply of Indian rupees ↑
Financial account	portfolio investment	USA 	*credit:* payments for the purchase of Uber (a US company) shares by Canadian residents	demand for the US dollar ↑
			debit: payments for the purchase of Japanese government bonds by US residents	supply for the US dollar ↑

You may not find examples for all components but try to at least have examples for the balance of trade in goods, balance of trade in services, FDI and portfolio investment flows.

QUESTION PRACTICE

This question is adapted from the May 2018 examination paper.

Table A provides information relating to the balance of payments for Urbania for 2017.

Table A: Urbania 2017 balance of payments

Item	$ million
Exports of goods	1527
Imports of goods	1393
Exports of services	**V**
Imports of services	954
Net income	−35
Net current transfers	−49
Net capital transfers	11
Net transactions in non-produced, non-financial assets	6
Net direct investment	−196
Net portfolio imvestment	285
Reserve assets	**W**

Urbania has a current account deficit of $125 million in 2017.

(a) Using the information in Table A, calculate the value of V (exports of services) for Urbania in 2017. [2]

SAMPLE STUDENT ANSWER

$1527 + V - 1393 - 954 - 35 - 49 = -125$

$V = \$779$ million

This response could have achieved 2/2 marks.

▲ The candidate identifies all the components of the current account. Workings are given and the units (millions of $) are included in the final answer.

QUESTION PRACTICE

(b) Using the information in Table A, calculate the financial account balance. [2]

SAMPLE STUDENT ANSWER

Current account + capital account + financial account = 0

− 125 + (6 + 11) + financial account = 0

Financial account = $108 million

This response could have achieved 2/2 marks.

▲ The candidate demonstrates a clear understanding that the balance of payment must always balance (equal 0). The workings are correct and the units (millions of $) are included in the final answer.

QUESTION PRACTICE

(c) Using your answer to part (b), calculate the value of **W** (reserve assets) in Table A. [1]

SAMPLE STUDENT ANSWER

Net portfolio + net direct investment + W = financial account

285 − 196 + W = 108

W = $19 million

This response could have achieved 1/1 mark.

▲ All relevant components of the financial account are identified. As the table does not include any data on "official borrowing", it is assumed the government from Urbania is neither borrowing from abroad nor lending money to other governments.

QUESTION PRACTICE

(d) Using your answer to part (c), describe how the level of reserve assets in Urbania has changed in 2017. [1]

SAMPLE STUDENT ANSWER

The level of reserve assets has decreased.

This response could have achieved 1/1 mark.

▲ The previous answer was (+) $19 million. As long as the answer is a positive value (a credit item), it means that reserve assets have decreased. Official reserves are considered to be assets residing outside the country or economy. A positive value (as in this case) means that the reserves have left the central bank to flow into the country or economy.

QUESTION PRACTICE

With the aid of real-world examples, evaluate the view that expenditure switching policies are the most effective methods to correct a persistent current account deficit. [15]

SAMPLE STUDENT ANSWER

▲ This is a good introduction of the first concept mentioned in the question, the current account. The candidate has also brought in one real-world example.

The current account is one of the three accounts of the balance of payments. The current account is in deficit when there are more debits than credits on all international transactions related to the trade in goods and services, income flows and current transfers. A current account deficit is often the result of expenditure on imports exceeding the revenue from exports. For example, the USA is a country which usually suffers from a current account deficit due to its trade deficit.

Expenditure-switching methods include trade protection and currency devaluation. Trade protection methods such as tariffs and quotas help make imports more expensive and therefore lead to a reduction in the current account. For example, the USA increased its tariffs on imports of aluminum and steel. A tariff is a tax on imports which protects domestic producers from foreign competition. The higher price of aluminum and steel incentivized US producers of these goods to increase production. The amount of steel purchased by domestic consumers decreases due to the higher price but a higher share of the aluminum and steel purchased comes from local firms. Trade protection is especially appropriate for countries with the combined problems of a persistent current account deficit and low economic growth or high unemployment. As the import expenditure reduces but other components of aggregate demand are not affected, unlike for expenditure-reducing methods, the aggregate demand will increase, and this leads to higher economic growth and reduced unemployment.

▲ The candidate demonstrates a good understanding of the main forms of expenditure methods—trade protection and devaluation. The answer considers some of the factors that affect the effectiveness of such policies. There is a real-world example of trade protection and a diagram to illustrate the limitations of a devaluation.

▼ There is no diagram to illustrate how tariffs work, although that is chosen as the real-world example. The J-curve is included but not used effectively. There is also no example of countries opting for a devaluation to reduce their current account deficit. Even the real-world example for trade protection is not precise—when did the US impose a higher tariff on steel?

If the country is on a fixed exchange rate system, the central bank may consider a devaluation to make exports cheaper in terms of foreign currency and imports more expensive in terms of domestic currency. This would also increase aggregate demand, but it would lead to other problems such as imported inflation and increase the value of foreign debts. A devaluation is also only effective in reducing a current account deficit when the Marshall-Lerner condition holds. That is when PEDx + PEDm > 1. The Marshall-Lerner condition usually does not hold in the short-term and hence a devaluation often worsens the current account deficit before it improves it. This can be seen in the following diagram.

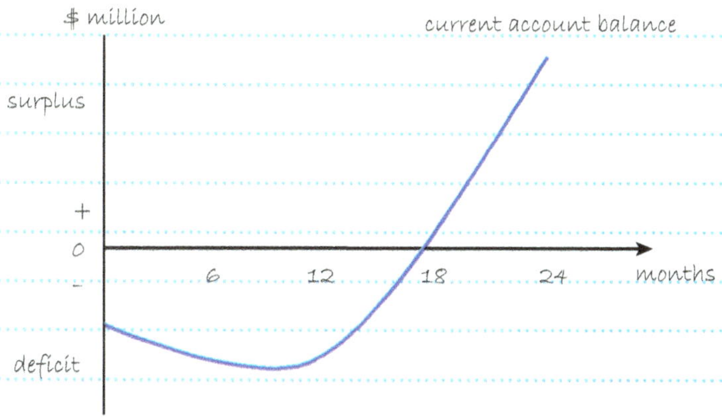

The main reason countries may not want to use expenditure switching methods is that they often lead to retaliation by trade partners. This was especially the case in the USA which saw the EU and China impose tariffs on US goods. Alternatively, expenditure reducing policies such as contractionary monetary and fiscal policies may be used to reduce a current account deficit. They are demand-side policies which are conducted by the central bank and the government respectively. The central bank may opt for contractionary monetary policy through an increase in interest rates in order to create incentives for consumers to save more and reduce their consumption on goods and services, and some of those would be imported goods. The higher interest rates may also attract foreign savings into local banks and so increase the financial account, which would help increase the value of the balance of payments. Contractionary fiscal policy, through increases in direct taxes, may also reduce consumers' disposable income. With a lower disposable income, consumers would be less able to afford goods and services and hence would buy less of imports.

▲ The candidate offers an alternative to expenditure switching methods and this helps establish the relative effectiveness of expenditure switching methods to reduce a current account deficit. A sufficient understanding of the policies and their workings is demonstrated.

A contractionary monetary policy may not be effective if consumers do not respond to the higher interest rate maybe due to high confidence in the economy. Contractionary fiscal policy may also not be effective if the majority of imports are necessities which consumers would still purchase when their disposable decrease. Furthermore, the main problem with using contractionary policies is that they lead to a fall in AD and this may not be advisable for countries which are facing an economic slowdown or a recession. Ideally, a country which faces high economic growth and high demand-pull inflation would use contractionary demand-side policies to reduce its current account deficit and at the same time reduce inflationary

▲ The candidate considers the effectiveness of the alternative policies and evaluates those policies.

pressures – especially since a high rate of inflation is often the root cause of a current account deficit and so targeting inflation may help maintain export competitiveness.

▲ Supply-side policies are a valid alternative to expenditure switching policies. The argument helps establish the relative effectiveness of expenditure switching policies and so it answers the question. There is also a real-world alternative to illustrate the argument.

Moreover, both expenditure-reducing and expenditure-switching methods are short-term measures in nature as they do not target the root of the problem, which is that domestic consumers prefer to buy imported goods. Supply-side policies may be a good alternative. They help improve export competitiveness and make local products more attractive than imports. Singapore is a country with a good record of use of supply-side policies to increase export revenue. The Singapore authorities have invested a lot in infrastructure to facilitate the growth of the bio-medical industries which now contribute significantly to the country's export revenue. Supply-side policies are more long-term in nature and have the great advantage of also leading to reduced cost-push inflation and higher long-term growth.

▼ The example and the workings of supply-side policies are underdeveloped. The candidate might have run out of time to explain this point. It would have been more strategic to elaborate on this method to reduce the current account deficit instead of expenditure reducing methods since an example could be provided for this argument. One alternative method would have been sufficient to answer the question.

To conclude, expenditure switching methods may be more effective than expenditure reducing methods to help reduce a persistent account deficit but they lead to trade wars. Governments should also consider the impacts policies may have on other macroeconomic variables such as economic growth in deciding on which would be the most desirable and effective policy to reduce a current account deficit.

▲ There is evidence of synthesis in this concluding paragraph.

This response meets some but not all the descriptors of the second highest mark band (10–12). The candidate demonstrates a good understanding of the requirements of the question—all arguments are relevant and help to answer the question. The economic theory is explained, economic terms are used appropriately and there is evidence of evaluation and synthesis. However, although there are real-world examples, they are often underdeveloped and sometimes missing. A second diagram to illustrate the workings of a tariff should also be included.

This response could have achieved 10/15 marks.

4.7 SUSTAINABLE DEVELOPMENT

This sub-unit introduces the concepts of economic development and sustainable development.

You should be able to:

✔ define the terms
  ✔ economic development
  ✔ sustainable development

✔ explain how a country's population would benefit from the pursuit of (any of) the Sustainable Development Goals (SDGs) and their contribution to sustainability.

HL In addition to the points above, for HL you should be able to:

- explain that the existence of poverty in economically least developed countries (ELDCs) creates negative externalities through over-exploitation of land for agriculture, and that this poses a threat to sustainability.

Summary

Economic development is a process leading to improvements in standards of living, reduction in poverty, improved health and education along with increased freedom and economic choice.

Sustainable development is the economic development that meets the needs of the present generation without compromising the ability of future generations to meet their own needs.

To achieve sustainable development, governments must strike a balance between three major goals.

- **Economic development**—the improvements in the standards of living, both material (more goods and services) and non-material (e.g. better healthcare and education)
- **Social progress**—the improvements in well-being must not be limited to economic gains but also include social improvements (e.g. empowerment of women, freedom of expression and the rule of law)
- **Environmental protection**—the use of resources must be sustainable to ensure that future generations continue to enjoy the same improvements in standards of living.

The United Nations introduced the 17 Sustainable Development Goals (SDGs) in 2015. The SDGs guide both developed and developing countries on their path to achieving sustainability by addressing economic development, social progress and environmental protection.

HL Low incomes in developing countries often do not permit farmers to adopt sustainable farming methods, forcing them instead to employ intensive methods. The use of **unsustainable farming methods** leads to pollution and the loss of land fertility, which will affect future generations.

Content link

Link to other sub-units

- Development is closely related to sub-unit 2.8 on market failure relating to externalities and common pool (common access) resources.
- Environmental degradation in less developed countries is often the result of the poor management of common pool (common access) resources such as forests.
- The threat to sustainability is a global problem, unsustainable activity in a (less developed or developed) country will affect citizens of all other countries and it calls for international cooperation.

Test yourself

Visit the United Nations' dedicated website to find out more about the 17 SDGs (https://sdgs.un.org/goals). In particular, find out how the World Bank and governments are working towards meeting the SDG(s) in specific countries. Paper 2 questions may cover sustainable development issues. You should be able to identify the SDG(s) that specific policies or programmes help to achieve.

Some of the SDGs may be very obvious (for example, a development programme providing women greater access to healthcare and family planning services will help achieve SGD 3–good health and well-being and SGD 5–gender equality); others may not come to mind immediately. For instance, world bank funds could be used to finance access to electricity in rural areas. Since poverty levels are often higher in rural areas in developing countries than in industrial areas, such a programme may help the transition from agricultural to manufacturing activities, reducing poverty and inequalities (SGDs 1 and 10).

QUESTION PRACTICE

This is a sample paper 2/3 question.

Using an externalities diagram, explain how poverty in less developed countries poses a threat to sustainability. [4]

SAMPLE STUDENT ANSWER

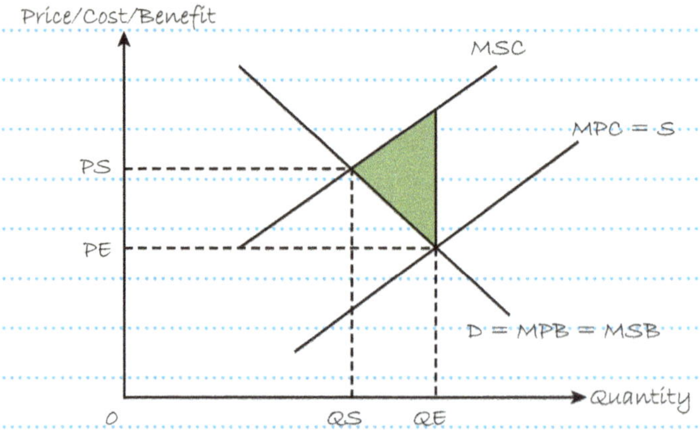

▲ The diagram is fully labelled and shows that the social costs are greater than the private costs, leading to a welfare loss.

In less developed countries, farmers who do not have access to funds for modern tools may clear forests and land for farming using unsustainable methods such as slash and burn. Such methods lead to the emission of large amounts of carbon dioxide and affect the ozone layer. This induces climate change, destroys the natural habitat of many species and indigenous people. Using slash and burn methods will also remove nutrients that forests had, leading to infertility of the soil in the future. Hence, the use of these unsustainable methods which come about from poverty leads to external costs and the MSC is greater than the MPC on the diagram. There is thus market failure as seen by the overproduction (QS QE) and the resulting welfare loss, shaded on the diagram.

▲ The explanation establishes a clear link between poverty in less developed countries and external costs. The candidate also refers to the diagram.

This response could have achieved 4/4 marks.

4.8 MEASURING DEVELOPMENT

You should be able to:

- ✔ explain the multidimensional nature of economic development
- ✔ explain how economic development may be measured using single and composite indicators
- ✔ discuss the strengths and limitations of using single and composite indicators to measure economic development
- ✔ distinguish between economic growth and economic development
- ✔ discuss the relationship between economic growth and economic development.

This sub-unit looks at the various indicators of economic development.

Summary

Economic growth can easily be measured by calculating the increase in real GDP, but economic development has multiple dimensions. It may come with changes in many variables such as higher income, reduced poverty and inequalities, better access to healthcare and education, and increased employment opportunities. As such, there are many possible ways to measure economic development.

A **composite indicator** is a summary measure of several indicators of development and so it aims to capture different aspects of economic development. The most famous is the Human Development Index (HDI), which looks at improvements made by a country in terms of healthcare, education and income. However, economists often use **single indicators** such as GDP/GNI per person (per capita) at PPP for ease of comparison since higher income implies greater access to goods and services, so it is often accompanied by greater well-being.

Other single indicators may focus on specific aspects of economic development (e.g. life expectancy at birth or access to healthcare and the Gini coefficient for determining the degree of income inequality in the country).

Economic growth often leads to economic development. Economic growth implies rising incomes and thus greater household spending on goods and services and greater tax revenues that a government may use to finance access to healthcare and education. However, economic growth may not lead to economic development if it is not inclusive and only a small proportion of households (such as business owners or government officials) see their incomes increase. It is also possible for a country to achieve economic development without growth in the short term if resources are diverted towards the production of merit goods.

Content link

Link to other sub-units

- Refer to sub-unit 3.1 on measuring economic activity where GDP/GNI per person (per capita) and the Happy Planet Index are covered.
- Many of the strengths and limitations of GDP/GNI statistics in measuring economic well-being also apply to the use of such indicators in comparing levels of development across nations.

Table 4.8.1 Strengths and limitations of indicators used to measure economic development

	Strengths	Limitations
Single indicators: • GDP/GNI per person (per capita) at PPP • health and education indicators • economic or social inequality indicators • energy indicators • environmental indicators	• Single indicators are easily accessible as data such as GDP/GNI and population size are available for most countries. • These indicators allow comparison on specific aspects of economic development. For example, primary school enrolment data provide a better indication of access to education than the HDI.	• Single indicators cannot adequately reflect the multidimensional aspects of development. • Increases in GDP/GNI per capita may reflect economic growth but not development if the increase in income is not enjoyed by all households—GDP/GNI per capita reflects "average income" but the increase in the "average" may come with a greater variation in income). The higher GDP/GNI per capita may come from the production of goods that leads to environmental degradation. Hence growth would not lead to sustainable development.
Composite indicators: • the Human Development Index (HDI) • the Inequality adjusted HDI (IHDI) • the Gender Inequality Index (GII) • the Happy Planet Index	• Composite indicators capture multiple dimensions of economic development. • Composite indicators are more reliable indicators than GDP/GNI statistics for countries that achieve growth without development.	• Not all dimensions of development can be captured by a single indicator. For example, the HDI does not provide insights on women's empowerment—although the IHDI and GII try to reflect such inequalities. • Data is not always available for many indicators in less developed nations, making comparisons between countries difficult.

Assessment tip

The last question on paper 2 may ask candidates to look at the impact of economic policies on economic development. Here is an example.

Using information from the text or data and your knowledge of economics, evaluate the impact on economic development of the Tanzanian government's policy of spending on infrastructure projects.

Sometimes, because candidates cannot identify sufficient arguments to respond, they write about the impact of policies on economic *growth*—rather than *development* (which is the requirement of this question). Indeed, for this question some candidates wrote about the increase in aggregate demand and the resulting increase in real GDP, which come from increased government spending. Looking at the impact on economic growth would not be answering the question **unless** the link between growth and development is established in the response, for instance by using the example of greater tax revenue to finance infrastructure. Also keep in mind that growth may not always lead to development. For example, the construction of infrastructure may lead to environmental degradation, or the infrastructure may only benefit a small group of people.

QUESTION PRACTICE

This question is adapted from the November 2018 examination paper.

List two components of the Human Development Index (HDI). [2]

SAMPLE STUDENT ANSWER

Education and healthcare.

Education and healthcare are some of the dimensions of economic development the HDI considers but they are not *components* or *indicators*. Any two of the following would have answered the question:

- life expectancy at birth
- mean years of schooling
- expected years of schooling
- GNI per person (per capita) at PPP.

This response would likely not be awarded a mark.

QUESTION PRACTICE

This question is adapted from the May 2016 examination paper.

Using data from Table 1 with reference to Rwanda and Nigeria, explain why higher gross national income (GNI) per capita may not lead to higher scores on the Human Development Index (HDI). [4]

Table 1 Selected economic data for Rwanda and Nigeria. (Source: adapted from www.hdr.undp.org accessed 29 September 2014.)

	Rwanda	Nigeria
Life expectancy at birth	64.1	52.5
Expected years of schooling	13.2	9.0
Gross national income (GNI) per capita (2011 purchasing power parity (PPP) US$)	1403	5353
Human Development Index (HDI) value (2013)	0.506	0.504
HDI rank (2013)	151	152

SAMPLE STUDENT ANSWER

From the data, we can see that both countries have similar HDI scores, but Nigeria has a much higher national income per capita (US $5353) than Rwanda (US $1403). As GNI per capita is one of the components of the HDI, it must be that the other components of the HDI (life expectancy at birth, mean years of schooling and expected years of schooling) have pulled down Nigeria's score (life expectancy at birth and expected years of schooling are shown to be higher in Rwanda in table 1).

▲ The candidate explains that the HDI is a composite indicator that includes more than just GNI per capita.

While average income is higher in Nigeria, it does not mean that all residents of Nigeria have access to education and healthcare services. It highly likely that income inequality is much higher in Nigeria than Rwanda and that has prevented poorer households in Nigeria from having access to education and healthcare, which would add to economic development as reflected by a higher score on the HDI.

▲ The candidate provides a possible reason to justify the two countries' similar scores for the HDI despite their significantly different GNI per capita scores.

This response could have achieved 4/4 marks.

4.9 BARRIERS TO ECONOMIC GROWTH AND/OR ECONOMIC DEVELOPMENT

This sub-unit looks at the factors that may lead to a low level of economic development and/or a low economic growth rate in less developed nations.

You should be able to:

- ✔ define the terms
  - ✔ poverty trap (poverty cycle)
  - ✔ informal economy
  - ✔ property rights
  - ✔ capital flight
  - ✔ infrastructure
- ✔ explain how some individuals or communities may be caught in a poverty trap (poverty cycle)
- ✔ explain the economic, social and political barriers to economic growth and/or economic development
- ✔ discuss the significance of specific barriers to economic growth and/or economic development using real-world examples.

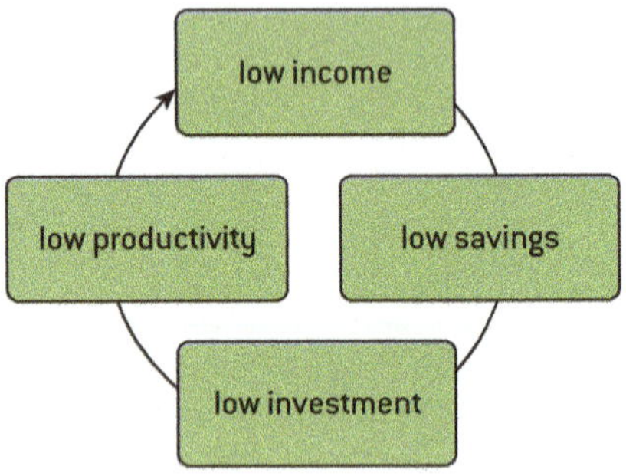

Summary

A poverty trap (poverty cycle) is a circular chain of events starting and ending in poverty. Poor communities are unable to invest in physical, human and natural capital due to low or no savings; poverty is therefore transmitted from generation to generation.

The **economic barriers** to economic growth and/or economic development include the following.

- High levels **of income and wealth inequalities** —these result in a significant number of residents being unable to afford healthcare and education. This leads to **low levels of human capital** , which does not allow communities to break the poverty trap (poverty cycle), as they are unable to overcome the "low productivity" segment of the trap (cycle).
- The **lack of access to infrastructure and appropriate technology** makes it difficult for structural change to take place, often keeping communities in low productivity agricultural activities. **Infrastructure** refers to the large-scale physical capital typically financed by governments that is essential for economic activity to take place (e.g. roads, utilities, telecommunications, sanitation).
- Another economic barrier is **dependence on the primary sector**, which is often characterized by low and fluctuating prices.
- The **lack of access to international markets** due to protectionist measures in developed countries makes diversification of economic activities difficult.
- The **high share of workers employed in the informal economy**, which refers to the part of an economy where activity is not officially recorded, regulated or taxed, forms an economic barrier. It makes it difficult for governments to raise funds to finance development.

- **Indebtedness** often leads to tax revenue being diverted from the provision of merit goods to service debts and this means that investment in human capital remains low.
- **Capital flight** occurs, which is when assets flow out of a country to seek a "safe haven" in another country. The financial capital that flows out of the country cannot be used to finance domestic investment, which could help break the poverty cycle.
- You will see in the sub-unit 4.10 that trade strategies may help to achieve economic growth and development. However, the **lack of sea access for landlocked countries** increases the shipping cost of exports and imports and makes such strategies difficult to implement.
- **Tropical climates** may result in low or fluctuating yields and **endemic diseases** affect labour productivity.

The **political and social** barriers to economic growth and/or economic development include the following.

- A country's institutional framework refers to the system of laws, regulations and procedures that govern socio-economic activities. Economic activity can be hindered by a **weak institutional framework**, which could be caused by:
    - an **inadequate legal system** where laws are not applied and enforced fairly
    - an **ineffective taxation structure**, which limits the ability of the government to raise funds to finance pro-development expenditures—for example, the prevalence of informal markets makes it difficult for the authorities to collect tax payments
    - an **underdeveloped banking system** that fails to provide poor and small-scale producers with the access to the funds needed to invest in physical, human and/or natural capital
    - **poorly established property rights** (the exclusive, legal, authority to own property and determine how that property is used, whether it is owned by the government or by private individuals)—well-defined and legally protected property rights permit the poor to use their land or property as collateral against a loan to start a business.
- **Gender inequality** is an economic barrier in a country where women have limited access to education and work opportunities. This leads to lower rates of economic growth as the country is deprived of the skills, talents and efforts of approximately half of the population.
- **Lack of good governance or corruption** often lead to public funds being diverted away from economic development.
- **Unequal political power and status** permits certain groups to influence the government into adopting policies that advance their own narrow economic and political interests and not the interests of the economy.

Content link

Link to other sub-units

You learned about PED and YED in sub-unit 2.5.

- The PED for primary commodities is generally lower than the PED for manufactured products. As the production of agricultural commodities is subject to supply shocks (e.g. changes in weather), the changes in supply coupled with the low PED lead to wide price fluctuations.
- Agricultural products have a low YED so economic growth will not lead to significant increases in demand over time and thus prices of agricultural products do not increase as much as prices of manufactured goods.

Content link

Link to other sub-units

Refer to sub-unit 4.2.

- Trade protection leads to low export revenue as less developed nations are unable to export manufactured goods that offer a more stable source of income.
- Use tariff and quota diagrams to illustrate the reduction in export revenue when developed countries impose trade protection on goods from less developed countries.

Test yourself

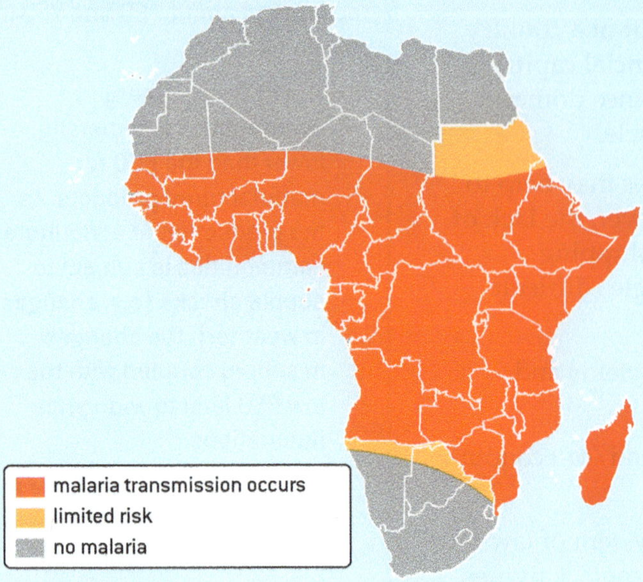

▲ Figure 4.9.1a

▲ Figure 4.9.1b

Figure 4.9.1 shows two maps of the African continent. Figure 4.9.1a shows the regions where the temperature, precipitation and relative humidity drive the abundance of mosquitoes, which transmit the debilitating tropical disease of malaria. Figure 4.9.1b illustrates the railway network of African nations. Try to identify countries where economic growth and development might be limited by the lack of infrastructure, lack of sea access and easy spread of tropical diseases. You may also consider doing some research on the growth rates and development indicators of those countries. Those would be good real-world examples to illustrate your essays.

QUESTION PRACTICE

This question is adapted from the May 2017 examination paper.

Define the term poverty trap (poverty cycle). [2]

SAMPLE STUDENT ANSWER

Response 1

The poverty cycle takes place when low incomes lead to low savings, resulting in low investment which keeps productivity low.

▲ This response explains why low incomes make it difficult to increase productivity.

▼ However, the candidate does not establish that the low income will self-perpetuate (there is no notion of a cycle or trap).

This response could have achieved 1/2 marks.

Response 2

The poverty cycle is a self-perpetuating circular chain of events starting and ending in poverty. A low income would imply difficulties in saving and this would likely lead to low capital accumulation or investment in human capital (e.g. education), which are necessary to increase productivity. Without an increase in productivity, income will not increase and thus individuals remain trapped in poverty.

▲ This candidate clearly explains why low income would make it difficult to escape poverty.

This response could have achieved 2/2 marks.

QUESTION PRACTICE

This question is adapted from the May 2017 examination paper.

Explain **two** reasons for which a highly unequal income distribution may prove a barrier to economic development. [4]

SAMPLE STUDENT ANSWER

A highly unequal distribution of income implies that the poorest might not be able to afford education. This would make it difficult for them to gain skills for increased labour productivity. As low productivity leads to low income, they are unable to break the poverty cycle.

▲ The lack of access to education is indeed a barrier to economic development. The candidate establishes a clear link between the low levels of education and low levels of economic development through the poverty trap.

A highly unequal distribution of income may lead to lower consumption and thus lower AD (because the rich have a lower propensity to consume) leading to slower growth.

▼ Economic growth is indeed needed for economic development but the candidate does not establish a link to economic development. That link could have been established by mentioning the difficulties in funding education and healthcare due to lower tax revenue, or by pointing out that income would remain low and keep people trapped in poverty.

The first reason given by the candidate could be awarded 2 marks; the second reason is only a partial answer and as such would only be rewarded with 1 mark.

This response could have achieved 3/4 marks.

QUESTION PRACTICE

This question is adapted from the November 2009 examination paper.

Using real-world examples, evaluate the view that, to achieve greater economic growth and development, countries must lessen their dependence on the production of primary commodities. [15]

SAMPLE STUDENT ANSWER

Firstly, it is important to distinguish economic growth from economic development. While economic growth is a more quantitative concept (increase in income/production), economic development is a more qualitative concept which comes with multiple dimensions. One of the barriers to economic growth and development in less developed countries (LDCs) is the over-reliance on primary commodities, which refer to the resources of natural origin. Commodities include minerals such as coal, copper, iron ore, rough diamonds and crude oil, and agricultural products such as wheat, coffee beans or cotton.

▲ The main concepts that appear in the question are clearly introduced and the candidate establishes the idea of over-reliance on the primary sector as a barrier to economic growth and development.

Economic growth is the sustained increase in economic activity, often measured by the increase in real GDP over time. It usually comes from increases in aggregate demand (AD). As expenditure on domestically produced goods increases,

▲ Relevant economic theory (economic growth) is explained. A diagram is also included.

firms respond by producing more goods and services. This is illustrated on the diagram below where the increase in AD (AD1 to AD2) leads to a new equilibrium (E2) with real GDP, Y2 is greater than the initial real GDP, Y1. To be sustained, economic growth must also be accompanied by long-term growth, which is an increase in productivity capacity. This happens with the financing of infrastructure or investment in physical, human and/or natural capital and is reflected by an increase in the LRAS.

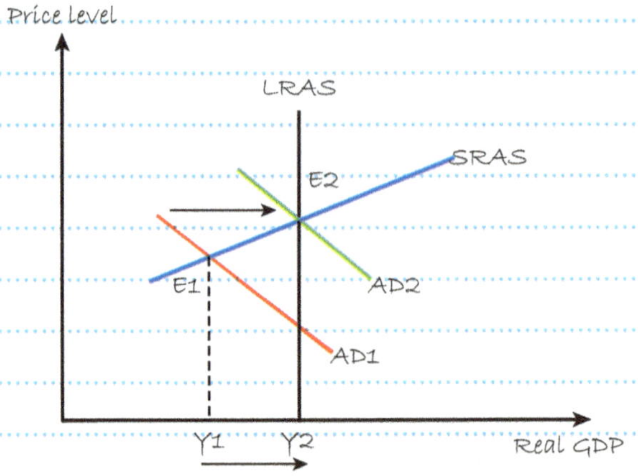

▲ The candidate explains why the over-reliance on agricultural products is a barrier to economic growth. The argument is illustrated by a real-world example. There are also adequate references to the diagram to illustrate the argument.

In many LDCs, the majority of workers are employed in agriculture and the production of other commodities depending on the resource endowment of the country. The sale of commodities also makes up a large proportion of export revenue – for example, Bolivia's main exports are natural gas, zinc ore, gold and soybeans. As such, changes in AD are largely correlated to changes on expenditure on commodities. Unfortunately, many commodities, especially agricultural products, are subject to wide price fluctuations. Agricultural products are subject to weather conditions. When good weather allows for a bountiful harvest, the supply for agricultural products will increase. Similarly, the supply will decrease with floods or drought. For example, the world price of soybeans had increased a lot in 2012 and 2013 due to dry soil conditions and hot temperatures – this is shown by the shift from S1 to S2 on the next diagram which illustrates the market for soybean. Bad weather conditions and increased production in South America, motivated by the previous increase in price, led to an increase in supply of soybean (from S1 to S2 on the diagram) from 2014 and the price of soybeans dropped by 50% (from P1 to P3) between 2014 and 2019. The wide fluctuation in prices (P2 to P3) which come from the changes in supply are due to the demand for most agricultural products like soybean being price-inelastic as they are necessities. The plunge in the price of soybeans, coupled with the price-inelastic demand, led to smaller export revenue from soybeans for Bolivia over the years – P3Q3 is smaller than P1Q1. This means that Bolivia's falling export revenue put downward pressure on the country's AD and hence limited economic growth. In addition, the demand for agricultural products tend to be income-inelastic so there is limited scope for growth over time.

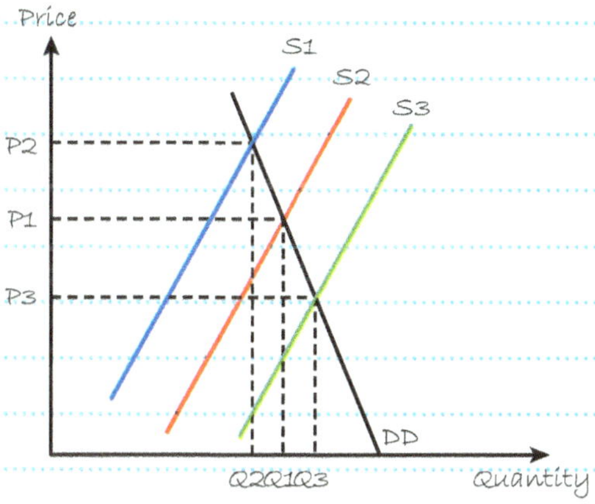

Economic development takes place when the residents of a nation enjoy higher standards of living. Economic growth is required for economic development to take place in the long-run. Economic growth leads to higher income and this allows access to healthcare and education. It also leads to higher tax revenue which may finance infrastructure and the provision of merits goods. Without economic growth, the prospects for higher income are limited. On the contrary, farmers involved in traditional agricultural often live in poverty. Their low income is reinforced over time due to the poverty cycle as farmers do not have the means to invest into capital goods to raise productivity. Even when prices of agricultural products increase, the increase in income in the community may be offset by higher spending on food for residents who are not involved in the production of those crops. It would wrong to dismiss the contribution of commodity production to economic growth and economic development. Some countries have enjoyed considerable export revenue from the production of minerals which are less prone to supply shocks. A country like Australia enjoyed high economic growth rates thanks to high export revenue from iron ore. Bolivia also enjoyed

▲ The candidate explains why over-reliance on the primary sector may be a barrier to economic development. (A diagram is used to explain the poverty cycle.)

▲ The candidate builds on previous arguments to establish the need for diversification to lessen dependence on primary commodities. This paragraph addresses the specific demands of the question as it evaluates some of the arguments brought forward earlier, such as the lack of investment in the agricultural sector. More real-world examples are also used as illustrations.

some economic growth due to growth in the export revenue of petroleum, iron ore and gold. It would also be incorrect to state that no investment takes place in agriculture. The Bolivian government approved the use of some genetically engineered seeds for soybeans in 2019. It is also considering approving the use of biotechnology for corn and cotton. The new technology would increase production of those crops and hence supply, further depressing prices. However, the issue is not that the production of commodities does not lead to economic growth and economic development but that the over-reliance on primary products does pose a barrier to economic growth and development. A country like Australia is highly diversified with a high share of its workforce employed in the secondary and tertiary sector. When the export revenue from commodities dropped due to lower demand from China, revenue from other sectors was able to help mitigate the drop in economic growth and continue to contribute to government tax revenue to finance infrastructure, merit and public goods.

To conclude, communities which are over-reliant on primary commodities are often trapped in poverty due to low fluctuating prices and a lack of scope for growth due to the income-inelastic demand, especially for agricultural crops. While there is evidence of some investment in agricultural production, it may be difficult for farmers with low income to afford improved capital. Governments should seek to diversify their economies. Diversification to reduce the reliance on one sector is one of the strategies available to governments to overcome the barrier to economic growth and development posed by the over-reliance of the economy on a narrow range of commodities.

▲ There is evidence of synthesis and evaluation in the conclusion. The candidate has presented some judgments and summarized the main arguments given in the response.

This answer meets all of the descriptors for the highest mark band (13–15) and **could achieve 15/15 marks**.

Assessment tip

Paper 2 text materials may depict the problems faced by less developed countries. The specific barriers to economic growth and/or development may not be stated in the text but they are implied. For example, a table showing a high proportion of workers employed in the primary sector suggests that the country faces the economic barrier of dependence on primary sector production. A passage from the text might mention that women are less likely to attend primary school and that would point to the social barrier of gender inequality.

Identifying the barriers faced by a country in your response demonstrates greater use of economic terminology and understanding of economic concepts. It also helps you suggest appropriate policies and strategies to overcome those barriers to growth and/or development.

4.10 ECONOMIC GROWTH AND/OR ECONOMIC DEVELOPMENT STRATEGIES

This sub-unit introduces the policies and strategies available to governments to promote economic growth and/or economic development.

You should be able to:

- ✔ define the terms
  - ✔ import substitution
  - ✔ export promotion
  - ✔ economic integration
  - ✔ foreign aid
  - ✔ development aid
  - ✔ humanitarian aid
  - ✔ official development assistance (ODA)
  - ✔ non-governmental organizations (NGOs)
  - ✔ multilateral development assistance
- ✔ explain the strategies used by governments and/or multilateral institutions to promote economic growth and/or economic development
- ✔ evaluate the effectiveness of strategies and policies in promoting economic growth and/or economic development with the aid of real-world examples
- ✔ discuss the strengths and limitations of government intervention in contrast to market-oriented approaches to achieve economic growth and/or economic development with the aid of real-world examples
- ✔ evaluate the effectiveness of policies or strategies in meeting specific SDGs.

Summary

The governments of less developed countries (LDCs) may aim to promote economic growth and development using the following strategies.

Trade strategies

- **Import substitution**—this advocates replacing imports with domestically produced goods and services. This strategy requires the use of trade protection and is better suited to countries with large domestic markets allowing local firms to enjoy sufficient economies of scale to offer domestic consumers low prices.
- **Export promotion**—this is a strategy targeting the expansion of export industries. In contrast to import substitution, export promotion focuses on the external rather than internal demand for goods and services. This policy is more suitable for countries with smaller markets that may not achieve sufficient economies of scale should firms focus on production for the domestic market. Note that countries with large markets may still prefer export promotion over income substitution for reasons such as avoiding tensions with trade partners resulting from trade protection.

Content link

Link to other sub-units

Many of the strategies and policies aim to overcome the barriers to growth and development introduced in sub-unit 4.9.

- Trade strategies try to overcome the lack of access to international markets and diversify economic activities.
- Diversification of economic activities may reduce a dependence on the primary sector.
- Market-based policies require less government spending than interventionist policies and thus help overcome high indebtedness.
- Increased access to healthcare and education allows higher productivity, breaking the poverty cycle.
- Multinational corporations (MNCs) bring expertise and technology, and guarantee an export market.

Content link

Link to other sub-units

Refer to sub-units 4.1, 4.3 and 4.4 for the strengths and limitations of free trade, trade protection and economic integration.

Content link

Link to other sub-units

Review sub-unit 3.7 for the strengths and limitations of supply-side policies.

- **Economic integration**—LDCs can form larger markets through regional free trade agreements. Protectionist measures from developed nations may also be reduced through free trade agreements.

Diversification

Diversification of economic activities can:

- reduce vulnerability to price fluctuations of commodities
- allow for structural change.

Market-based policies

- **Trade liberalization** can be used to encourage the growth of export industries, attract foreign firms and increase competition and efficiency in domestic markets.
- **Privatization** of public enterprises allows public funds to be redirected to merit goods. The profit-driven private firms will try to cut costs and decrease inefficiencies, leading to lower prices.
- Reducing red tape and unnecessary bureaucracy through **deregulation** of markets leads to higher efficiency and thus lower prices.

Interventionist policies

- **Redistribution policies** such as progressive tax structures, transfer payments and minimum wage regulations help to reduce inequalities, which tend to be high in LDCs.
- **Provision of merit goods** through education and health programmes may be used to increase labour productivity. Greater access to (improved) education and healthcare services also improves the living standards of the population and so it directly promotes economic development.
- There may be **provision of infrastructure** including energy, transport, telecommunications, clean water and sanitation that decreases the overall cost of economic activity. This will attract foreign investment and promote local entrepreneurship.

Multinational corporations

Multinational corporations (MNCs) can be attracted by facilitating **foreign direct investment (FDI) inflows**. Refer to Table 4.10.1 for the strengths and limitations of FDI as a source of growth and, it is hoped, development.

Aid

Aid is an important policy tool that developed countries can use to promote economic development in poorer countries. **Foreign aid** refers to grants, concessional loans and/or technical assistance from developed to developing countries to promote economic development. Refer to Table 4.10.1 for the strengths and limitations of aid in promoting growth and/or development.

- Aid may come as **official development assistance (ODA)**—from governments and multilateral organizations such as the World

Bank. Aid may also come from **non-government organizations (NGOs)**, which are private organizations that promote economic development and/or humanitarian ideals and/or sustainable development (Amnesty International is one example).

- There are different types of aid. **Humanitarian aid** is given to meet short-term needs (food aid, medical aid and emergency relief aid in the event of natural catastrophe or war). **Development aid** refers to the long-term assistance provided to developing countries in their development efforts (project aid, programme aid and debt relief).
- High indebtedness implies large debt repayments. The opportunity cost of debt servicing is the provision of infrastructure, education, healthcare and other public programmes. **Debt relief** refers to measures to reduce or refinance the high debt of LDCs to allow for the financing of growth and development strategies.
- **Multilateral development assistance** is the aid provided by international organizations such as the **World Bank** and the **International Monetary Fund** (**IMF**). They help channel financial contributions from developed countries to LDCs.
  - The main aims of the World Bank are to provide aid and advice to LDCs, as well as reducing poverty levels and encouraging and safeguarding international investment.
  - The IMF is an organization working to foster global monetary cooperation, secure financial stability, facilitate international trade and reduce poverty.

Social enterprises

Governments may choose to facilitate the growth of **social enterprises**. These organizations are not profit-motivated and instead prioritize the welfare of local producers (e.g. farmers).

Institutional change

- **Improved access to banking**, including microfinance and mobile banking, allows farmers and small business owners to borrow funds to finance investment and break the poverty cycle.
- **Women's empowerment is increased** through increased access to education, job opportunities or funds to start small businesses. (Evidence suggests that the majority of microfinance scheme recipients are women. Some microfinance institutions issue loans exclusively to women.)
- In many counties an important aim is **reducing corruption** that often leads to higher transaction costs and deters FDI.
- Establishing **property rights** and in particular **land rights** provides legal recognition and protection of assets (e.g. land for farmers). Assets may then be used as collateral to borrow funds for investment.

▼ Table 4.10.1 Strengths and limitations of different strategies or policies to achieve economic growth and development

Policy/strategy	Strengths	Limitations
FDI	• This is direct spending by foreign firms (MNCs) on physical capital (the I component of AD increases). • FDI contributes to the host country's exports earnings and reduces balance of payments deficits. • Technological transfer and training of workers lead to higher productivity. • A result of FDI is more jobs and higher income than in the agricultural sector, helping to break the poverty trap. • There is diversification of economic activities. • FDI is a source of foreign exchange.	• FDI may lead to the depletion of natural resources and threaten sustainability. • FDI may lead to future balance of payment deficits as profits are repatriated. • MNCs may put political pressure on governments. • The tax contribution may not be significant because business tax rates are kept low to attract MNCs. • Not all jobs created will be given to locals. Some MNCs may not train local workers and give higher skill positions to foreign workers.
Foreign aid	• Project aid may lead to the building of infrastructure to attract investment and diversify economic activities away from agriculture. • Programme aid in the areas of education and healthcare may help increase productivity and income and break the poverty cycle.	• Aid may lead to indebtedness, with future public funds diverted away from development spending to service the debt. • Receiving aid may lead to dependency. • Aid may be political. • Funds may not be channelled to development due to corruption. • Aid may come with strict conditions, which the recipient country may not be able to meet.

QUESTION PRACTICE

This question is adapted from the November 2019 examination paper.

Outline **one** possible disadvantage of foreign direct investment (FDI) for economically less developed countries. [2]

SAMPLE STUDENT ANSWER

Response 1

MNCs may repatriate profits.

▼ The candidate has not explained why the repatriation of funds is a concern for economically less developed countries—for example, the repatriation of profits may lead to a deficit in the balance of payments. Attention must be given to the command term, "outline" (to give a brief account or summary).

This response could have achieved 1/2 marks.

Response 2

Domestic firms may not be able to compete with MNCs and this could lead to bankruptcies. This is especially the case for infant industries and small firms, which may not reap sufficient economies of scale to offer prices as low as MNCs.

▲ A clear cause for concern for economically less developed countries is established.

This response could have achieved 2/2 marks.

QUESTION PRACTICE

Using real-world examples, evaluate the view that foreign aid is an effective means to achieve economic growth and development in less developed countries (LDCs). [15]

SAMPLE STUDENT ANSWER

Economic growth consists of short-term and long-term growth. Short-term growth refers to an increase in real GDP. Long-term growth refers to an increase in productive capacity. Economic development refers to a sustained improvement in living standards.

▼ Instead of listing all relevant terms at the beginning of the essay, the candidate should define them as they are used in the essay.

Explaining the relationship between economic growth and economic development (that economic growth is necessary for economic development, but that economic growth may not necessarily lead to economic development) might allow for a more effective introduction.

Foreign aid refers to the assistance received by a country, typically a less-developed country (LDC), by a donor country or multilateral organisation.

▼ Aid is a broad concept. Assistance from donor countries and/or multilateral organizations may come in many forms—grants, concessional loans and/or technical assistance. A good essay on foreign aid needs to acknowledge that aid may come in various forms.

Foreign aid can promote economic growth and development in LDCs. Papua New Guinea (PNG) has received AU$477 million from Australia to promote economic development, specifically to help women and children. The money was spent on providing free education for women and children as well as the provision of vaccines to protect young children from diseases such as polio.

▲ A valid link is established between aid and economic development (that is, access to healthcare and education). A real-world example is also provided.

▼ The paragraph starts by stating that aid can promote both economic growth and economic development. However, no link to growth is established.

The candidate could have specified the type of aid received by Papua New Guinea (development aid).

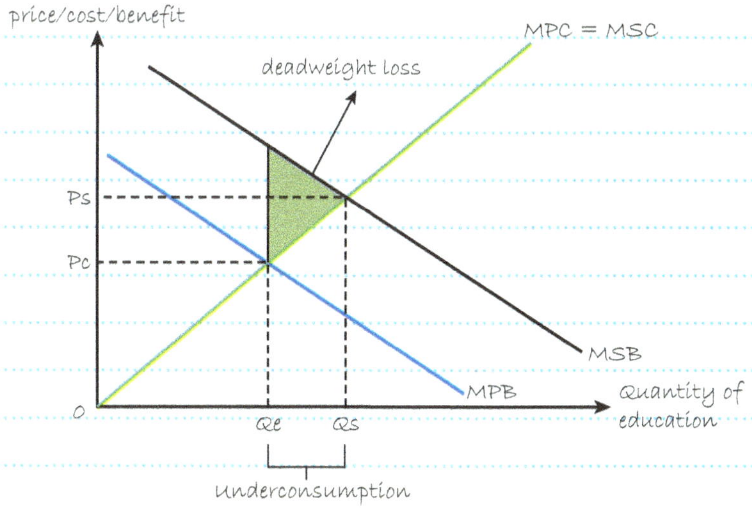

Looking at the market for education and assuming that marginal private cost (MPC) = marginal social cost (MSC), the marginal social benefit (MSB) is greater than the marginal private benefit (MPB). Not only will individuals receive an education, these educated individuals tend to be more enterprising, which would lead to them bringing more efficiency to the economy when they enter the workforce. Hence, because benefits are enjoyed by third parties who are not involved in the consumption or production of education, the market equilibrium is found where MPB intersects with MPC, at Qe but the social optimum is found where MSB intersects MSC, at Qs. The foreign aid money spent by PNG on education will help reduce the underconsumption of education by increasing the supply of education in PNG.

▼ While this analysis and the accompanying diagram are theoretically correct, market failure is not directly relevant to this question. The focus should be on economic growth and development. It is important not to drift away from the focus of the essay question because it signals to the examiner that you do not understand the specific demands of the question.

Moreover, foreign aid could help communities break the poverty cycle, illustrated below. A higher level of education and healthcare in PNG would result in a higher level of human capital and thus productivity. This would increase the level of income. Stop the self-perpetuating poverty cycle allows for a sustained increase in living standards.

▲ This is another valid argument to support the claim that foreign aid may lead to economic development. The poverty cycle diagram is relevant to the question.

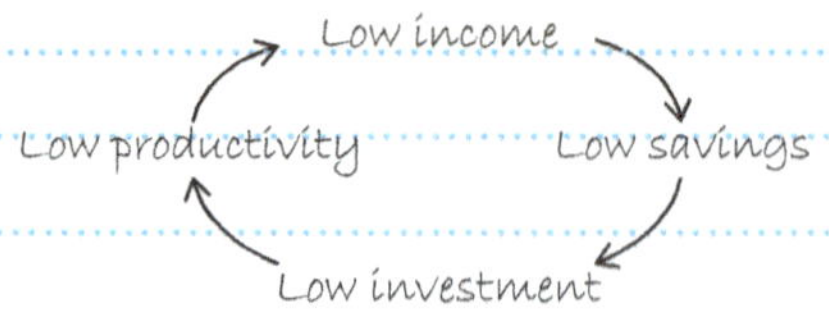

However, there are some factors that may affect the effectiveness of foreign aid as a tool to promote economic growth and development. The prevalence of corruption may lead to parts of financial aid being diverted to the pockets of government officials. Foreign aid may also lead to dependency and the over-reliance on aid may make it difficult for governments to continue to finance economic growth and development if aid is discontinued.

▲ The candidate considers some of the factors that could limit the effectiveness of aid. This reflects some understanding of the specific demands of the question.

▼ No real-world examples are provided to illustrate this argument.

This response meets most of the descriptors of the (7–9) mark band. Here are some pointers to push this response to a higher mark band.

- The response does not address all the demands of the question—no link is established between foreign aid and economic growth. This could have been done by considering the contribution of aid in the form of debt relief to greater government spending on domestically produced goods and services (higher aggregate demand), leading to short-term growth. The contribution of project aid to finance infrastructure would also lead to long-term growth.

- Economic theory is not fully explained. The candidate should have explained that aid may come in various forms (e.g. debt relief, project aid, concessional loans, technical assistance) and that economic growth is needed for economic development to take place but that economic growth may not necessarily lead to economic development.
- The diagrams are not all relevant to the question. The poverty cycle is an adequate diagram, but the market failure diagram is not necessary to answer the question. An AD/AS diagram to illustrate the contribution of foreign aid to economic growth would have been more appropriate.
- One real-world example is provided but more variety is needed. Examples could have illustrated different types of aid (one example of a debt relief programme could have been given) or the limitations of foreign aid (e.g. countries with high level of corruption).

This response could have achieved 7/15 marks.

Concept link

- **Economic well-being**—economic development and sustainable development come with improvements in the economic well-being of the residents of a country. Using the different aspects of economic well-being could also help you establish whether a policy or project promotes economic development or sustainable development.
- **Interdependence**—policies in developed countries (e.g. trade protection, provision of aid) affect LDCs. Some practices in LDCs pose a threat to sustainability, which affects all nations.
- **Intervention**—what type of policies are described in the article? Are they market-based or interventionist? Consider the strengths and limitations of government intervention in the context set in the article.
- **Sustainability**—poverty often leads to unsustainable practices and the over-exploitation of natural resources. Policies that help reduce economic well-being often help LDCs on their path to sustainability.

Content link

Link to your IA

Few candidates opt for a commentary on economic development or sustainable development for Unit 4. After all, there are plenty of news articles on trade-related issues and currency fluctuations. However, many of the past topics (international trade, supply-side policies, for example) can be examined in the context of LDCs. Sub-units 4.7–4.10 also provide you with links to some of the key concepts (see "Concept link").

Assessment tip

Always draw your diagrams using a 2B pencil. This will mean that you draw dark lines or curves and make clearer diagrams. Using a ruler is always a good practice as it makes your diagrams more presentable. In this book, many diagrams in sample answers are given in colour, but bear in mind the following. Your exam scripts are scanned in black and white, so do not use coloured pencils to distinguish between lines or curves on a diagram—the examiner will not be able to distinguish between colours on the scanned script. You may continue to use colours for digitally assessed work submitted as PDF files.

5 PAPER 1

5.1 PAPER 1: STRUCTURE AND TIPS

The paper 1 questions require extended responses (essays).
The structure of this paper is the same for SL and HL.

Duration: 1 hour 15 minutes

Weighting: 30% (SL)/20% (HL) of the final grade

Syllabus coverage: questions are drawn from the four units of the syllabus (HL extension topics are included for the HL paper 1). However, each question focuses on a specific unit of the syllabus.

Format: answer _one_ question from a choice of three. Each question is subdivided into two parts, (a) and (b). The paper carries a total of 25 marks—10 marks for part (a) and 15 marks for part (b).

Part (a)

This part of a paper 1 question tests your ability to explain relevant economic theory using economics terms and, where appropriate, illustrate your explanation with diagrams. The command terms associated with part (a) questions are almost invariably "explain" or "distinguish". Refer to the Introduction, page vi, for a detailed explanation of these command terms. Any of the topics associated with these command terms in the "You should be able to" sections of each sub-unit could be the tested as a part (a) question.

Examiners use mark bands to assess your answers, so it is important that you are familiar with the descriptors for the highest mark bands to understand the expectations of this task.

Marks	Level descriptors
1 –2	• The response indicates little understanding of the specific demands of the question. • The economic theory is stated but it is not relevant. • Economic terms are stated but they are not relevant.
3–4	• The response indicates some understanding of the specific demands of the question. • Relevant economic theory is described. • Some relevant economic terms are included.
5–6	• The response indicates understanding of the specific demands of the question, but these demands are only partially addressed. • Relevant economic theory is partially explained. • Some relevant economic terms are used appropriately. • Where appropriate, relevant diagram(s) are included.
7–8	• The specific demands of the question are understood and addressed. • Relevant economic theory is explained. • Relevant economic terms are used mostly appropriately. • Where appropriate, relevant diagram(s) are included and explained.
9–10	• The specific demands of the question are understood and addressed. • Relevant economic theory is fully explained. • Relevant economic terms are used appropriately throughout the response. • Where appropriate, relevant diagram(s) are included and fully explained.

Part (b)

This part of the question tests the higher-order thinking skills of synthesis and evaluation. The command terms used are usually "discuss" or "evaluate". Refer to the Introduction, page vi, for a detailed explanation of these command terms. Part (b) questions always start with the instruction "Using real-world examples". Therefore, you must illustrate your response with real-world examples to reach the higher mark bands for this part of a paper 1 question. These examples should be explained in relation to the question asked rather than simply stated.

The mark bands used by examiners to assess part (b) responses are included below. If you compare the descriptors for the highest mark band for both parts of a paper 1 question, you may notice that part (b) includes two additional descriptors. These descriptors relate to the use of **real-world examples** and evidence of **synthesis** or **evaluation**. It is therefore essential that these elements feature prominently in this part of a paper 1 response.

Marks	Level descriptors
1–3	• The response indicates little understanding of the specific demands of the question. • Economic theory is stated but it is not relevant. • Economic terms are stated but they are not relevant. • The response contains no evidence of synthesis or evaluation. • A real-world example(s) is identified but it is irrelevant.
4–6	• The response indicates some understanding of the specific demands of the question. • Relevant economic theory is described. • Some relevant economic terms are included. • The response contains evidence of superficial synthesis or evaluation. • A relevant real-world example(s) is identified.
7–9	• The response indicates understanding of the specific demands of the question, but these demands are only partially addressed. • Relevant economic theory is partly explained. • Some relevant economic terms are used appropriately. • Where appropriate, relevant diagram(s) are included. • The response contains evidence of appropriate synthesis or evaluation but lacks balance. • A relevant real-world example(s) is identified and partly developed in the context of the question.
10–12	• The specific demands of the question are understood and addressed. • Relevant economic theory is explained. • Relevant economic terms are used mostly appropriately. • Where appropriate, relevant diagram(s) are included and explained. • The response contains evidence of appropriate synthesis or evaluation that is mostly balanced. • A relevant real-world example(s) is identified and developed in the context of the question.
13–15	• The specific demands of the question are understood and addressed. • Relevant economic theory is fully explained. • Relevant economic terms are used appropriately throughout the response. • Where appropriate, relevant diagram(s) are included and fully explained. • The response contains evidence of effective and balanced synthesis or evaluation. • A relevant real-world example(s) is identified and fully developed to support the argument.

Here are some guidelines to help you do well when answering paper 1 questions.

- Research real-world examples as you go through the syllabus. All possible part (b) topics are listed in the "You should be able to" sections with the command terms "discuss" and "evaluate".

You need to compile more than a simple list of examples. For each example, identify causes, consequences and any other information that will help you illustrate the relevant concept. For instance, an effective real-world example of a price floor should be developed to include the method used by the authorities to deal with the surplus of a good, possible storage problem when the government buys the surplus or the supporting policies to make sure low income individuals may still be able to access the good on which the price floor is imposed.

- Examples are not expected for part (a) but sometimes they can help you explain your economic analysis. If so, do not hesitate to use examples, even if generic or theoretical, in part (a). For instance, a question asking you to explain the difference between merit and demerit goods might be more easily explained using examples—in this case, the generic examples vaccines and cigarettes may be used to explain why some goods are deemed socially desirable or undesirable.
- Make effective use of your five-minute reading time to choose your question. Part (a) is easier, so candidates tend to choose their question based on that part but it only carries 40% of the entire marks for this paper. Instead, consider part (b) and make sure you can develop good real-world examples for that part. You should also make sure you understand the requirements of both parts.
- Use your time effectively. Candidates often spend as long on part (a) as they do on part (b). You should spend no more than 25–30 minutes writing your response to part (a) because part (b) is more demanding and carries more marks. However, you are advised against writing your response straight away. Instead, spend about five minutes planning your answers to both parts to give your answer logical progression and avoid unnecessary repetition.
- Do not repeat what you have already explained in part (a). It is not uncommon for part (b) to test on a concept explained in part (a). For instance, part (a) might ask you to distinguish between *merit goods* and public goods while part (b) asks you to evaluate the effectiveness of subsidies in increasing the consumption of *merit goods*. In such a case, you do not need to explain again in part (b) what economists call merit goods. Similarly, you might want to refer to a diagram you have drawn in part (a). Refrain from explaining the same concept or drawing exactly the same diagram twice as examiners will not award marks the second time. Instead, you may state "as explained in part (a)" or "as illustrated by diagram 1 in part (a)". This being said, candidates sometimes realize as they write their response to part (b) that some of their part (a) response belongs to part (b) and does not address the demands of the part (a) question. This shows the need to plan your responses to both parts of the question before you start writing.
- A good way to end a part (b) answer is to provide a brief summative evaluation. This should not merely repeat the response, but should consider, for example, whether subsidies are effective in increasing consumption of all merit goods. For instance, do they work equally well for tertiary education and vaccination?

5.2 SAMPLE PAPER 1 QUESTION AND RESPONSE

You will find part (a) and part (b) practice questions throughout Units 1–4. A full paper 1 question is also included in this section.

QUESTION PRACTICE

This question is adapted from the May 2021 examination paper.

(a) Explain how the price mechanism reallocates resources when there is a decrease in the supply of a good. [10]

(b) Using real-world examples, evaluate the effectiveness of legislation in achieving a reduction in the consumption of demerit goods. [15]

SAMPLE STUDENT ANSWER

a) The price mechanism is a system where the forces of demand and supply determine the prices of goods and services. By bringing consumers (demand) and firms (supply) together, the market mechanism allocates society's scarce resources. A change in supply would affect the price of the good and this would act both as signal and incentive to consumers and firms, which would alter the allocation of resources. Supply refers to the quantities that firms are willing to produce at various prices.

▲ The notion of price serving as a signal and an incentive, a central theme in the answer, is introduced.

When the supply of a good decreases (maybe due to higher costs of production), (from S1 to S2 on the following diagram on the left) a shortage (Q*Q1) is created at the existing price, P1. The shortage places upward pressure on the price of the good. The higher price sends a signal to consumers that the good is less affordable and an incentive to search for substitutes (similar goods such as ice-cream and popcorn that are interchangeable) and so the quantity demanded for this item decreases. The higher price also sends a signal to firms that production of the good is now becoming more profitable and incentivises them to produce more. This leads to a higher quantity supplied. This process carries on until a new equilibrium is achieved with a higher price (P2) and lower equilibrium quantity (Q2).

▲ The candidate explains relevant theory (signal and incentive functions of price) with reference to a diagram. Adequate economic terms (e.g. "quantity demanded", "quantity supplied") are also used.

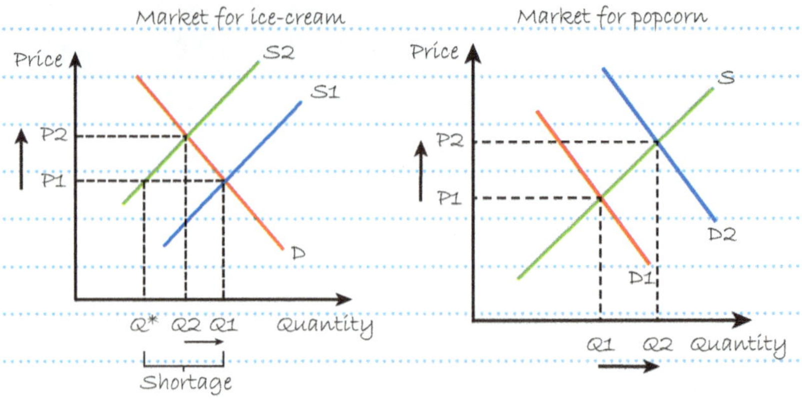

For example, in the market for ice-cream, a decrease in supply (maybe due to higher storage cost) leads to a shortage of Q*Q1, resulting in a higher price (P2). Consumers such as moviegoers may not be willing to pay the higher price and thus switch to popcorn because ice-cream and popcorn are substitutes. This increase in the price of a substitute, a non-price determinant of demand, leads to an increase in the demand for popcorn (from D1 to D2 on the diagram on the right). The higher price serves as signal and incentive in the market for popcorn, leading to a higher price and higher quantity (P2, Q2). Firms produce less ice-cream (Q1 to Q2 on the left-side diagram) and more popcorn (Q1 to Q2 on the right-side diagram). The producers will allocate fewer resources such as labour and sugar to ice-cream production and more to popcorn production.

▲ The candidate continues to explain relevant theory to establish that the change in price leads to reallocation of resources, as required by the question. (The specific demands of the question are understood and addressed.) Real-world examples are not required for part (a) of paper 1 questions but this hypothetical example demonstrates the candidate's understanding of economic theory. The diagram is also fully explained.

Looking at the level descriptors on page 194, this answer meets all the descriptors of the highest mark band (9–10).

- The specific demands of the question are understood and addressed—the candidate understood that the signalling and incentive functions of price had to be explained to answer the question.
- Relevant economic theory is fully explained—the mechanism by which a change in price, due to a decrease in supply, leads to a change in the allocation of resources is explained.
- Relevant economic terms such as "quantity demanded", "quantity supplied", "demand" and "supply" are used appropriately throughout the response.
- Diagrams are clearly needed to illustrate the impact of the change in price on resource allocation. These diagrams are adequately explained with multiple references ("changes in supply", "change in price") included and fully explained. While the diagrams are correct, it would be wise to use different annotations for the prices and quantities across both markets to avoid confusion (e.g. P3, P4, Q3, Q4 for the market for popcorn).

This response could have achieved 10/10 marks.

(b) Demerit goods refer to goods which generate significant negative externalities from consumption and are deemed socially undesirable by the government. Because consumers and producers only consider their own benefits and costs, a free market transaction – one where the price mechanism determines resource allocation as explained in part (a) – ignores the external costs (on third parties) generated in the consumption of demerit goods. The free market outcome will always be one where demerit goods are over-consumed. The authorities must intervene to alter the allocation of resources to try to achieve allocative efficiency. However, economics being a social science deals with individuals and so it is not possible to make an accurate estimation of the impact of government tools in achieving an exact outcome where MSB = MSC or even estimate the external cost with certainty. Hence this essay does not attempt to judge the effectiveness of legislation in achieving the social optimum outcome but rather get closer to it by reducing consumption.

▲ This is an effective introduction—it introduces relevant economic theory (market failure) and clearly establishes the difficulties in reaching a socially optimum level of output. Relevant economic terms such as "allocative efficiency" are used.

Legislation refers to the set of laws and rules set by the government and public agencies and which individuals are expected to follow, otherwise they face legal consequences. They may help reduce the consumption of demerit goods and/or reduce the third party costs. The need for such intervention can be illustrated on the following diagram, which depicts the market for cigarettes. As mentioned earlier, the interaction of consumers and producers determines the market equilibrium quantity, QE, ignoring the external costs on third parties (those who neither consume cigarettes nor produce/sell cigarettes). As such the marginal social benefit (MSB) curve is lower than the marginal private benefit (MPB) curve which is also the demand curve. The socially optimum level of output is where the MSB is equal to the marginal social cost (MSC), QS. Governments therefore aim to bring the market closer to QS.

▲ The candidate clearly establishes the need for government intervention with reference to a diagram.

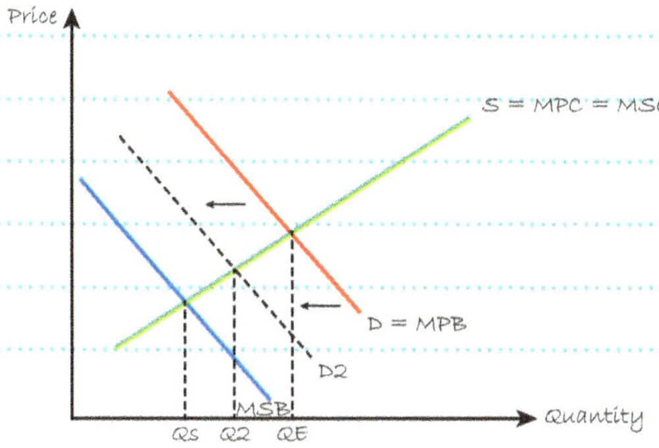

▲ The diagram is fully and correctly labelled. The candidate has not shaded the welfare loss associated but since the question is about the effectiveness of legislation in reducing demand, the welfare loss is not relevant to the discussion—but it would have been relevant had the question asked about effectiveness in "reducing the misallocation of resources".

Legislation may help reduce the demand for a demerit good. In the case of cigarettes, most countries have laws that prohibit the sale of cigarettes to young people and this cuts away an entire consumer group. Hawaii raised the minimum age for buying cigarettes from 18 to 21 in 2017. This effectively led to a fall in demand for cigarettes since people aged 18 to 20 could no longer buy cigarettes. Hence the demand on the above diagram shifts from D=MPB to the left, possibly to D2 and hence and probably closer to MSB where the new quantity, Q2 is closer to QS. Some laws may also help reduce the external cost. For example, most European nations have banned smoking in restaurants while Hong Kong has banned smoking in most bus stations. This reduces the third-party exposure to second-hand smoke and thus MSB shifts closer to MPB.

Legislation and regulation can be more effective than alternative policies such as taxes because the demand for cigarettes is price-inelastic and as such consumers may still be willing to pay a higher price for cigarettes but they are obliged to follow the laws and rules put in place by the authorities. Legislation is a more targeted approach than other tools of the government such as taxes and education campaigns. For instance, increasing the minimum legal age for smoking targets young smokers who may develop a long-term addiction when they are less mature to make decisions impacting their health. Legislation is also a more appropriate tool for demerit goods which come with such significant external cost that their use needs to be strictly controlled and possibly banned for public use. For example, guns are deemed to be socially undesirable in most nations because of the high external cost in terms of lives and accidents when they are used recklessly. Alternative policies such as taxes and awareness campaigns may not reduce the demand significantly enough. Instead, most countries simply keep the use of weapons to law enforcement agencies.

▲ This paragraph explains the workings of legislation and regulation with reference to the diagram and with the aid of real-world examples.

The effectiveness of legislation may depend on two important criteria – the ability to enforce laws and strong deterrents to ensure that individuals follow them. Indeed, enforcing laws requires police officers in sufficient number and many nations are unable to increase their police budget to allow for sufficient control and checks. It is well known that before it was legalised in many US states, the ban on cannabis led to illegal trade. Because police could not control homegrown production, it weakened the effectiveness of the ban. The punishment for not following the laws may also vary considerably. Those caught with illicit drugs risk the death penalty in Malaysia whereas in Luxemburg, the consumption of such drugs can be punished by a fine of no more than €2500 and/or a prison sentence not exceeding 6 months. As such, the laws on illicit drugs are a more effective deterrent in Malaysia than Luxemburg.

▲ This paragraph establishes the strengths of legislation in reducing the demand for demerit goods and thus helps address the specific demands of the question set by the command term.

▲ This paragraph evaluates the effectiveness of legislation by establishing the limitations of such policy. Real-world examples are used to illustrate the arguments.

It is clear that legislation is an effective tool in limiting the consumption and production of demerit goods especially considering the limitation of alternative policies such as taxes given the addictive nature of most demerit goods (cigarettes, alcohol, illicit drugs). However, they come with limitations such as the high cost of enforcement. As such, legislation may be more effective if used in tandem with other policies, as is often the case. For instance, high taxes on tobacco-related products help finance law enforcement agencies.

▲ This is a good synthesis. It establishes the main strengths and limitations of legislation, as established in the body of the essay.

Looking at the level descriptors on page 195, this response meets all the descriptors of the highest mark band (13–15).

- The specific demands of the question are understood and addressed—the candidate understands that the effectiveness of policies addressing market failure is determined by their ability to reach allocative efficiency.
- Relevant economic theory is fully explained—the workings of legislation in changing market outcomes are explained.
- Relevant economic terms such as “allocative efficiency”, “external cost” and “demerit goods” are used appropriately throughout the response.
- Diagrams are used to illustrate the workings of legislation in achieving allocative efficiency. There are multiple references to the diagrams in the explanation.
- The candidate establishes the strengths and limitations of policies (evaluation) and ends the response with an overall judgment on the relative effectiveness of legislation (synthesis).
- The real-world examples are fully developed to illustrate the effectiveness and limitations of legislation.

This response could have achieved 15/15 marks.

6 PAPER 2

6.1 PAPER 2: STRUCTURE AND TIPS

The economics paper 2 task tests your ability to apply economic theory to unseen texts and data. The structure of this paper is the same for SL and HL.

Duration: 1 hour 45 minutes

Weighting: 40% (SL)/30% (HL) of the final grade

Syllabus coverage: questions are drawn from the four units of the syllabus (HL extension topics are included for the HL paper 2).

Format: answer *one* question from a choice of two. Each question is subdivided into seven parts, (a), (b), (c), (d), (e), (f) and (g). Parts (a) and (b) both have subparts.

The paper carries a total of 40 marks, which are distributed across the 7 subparts. The questions are designed to have an incline of difficulty. The initial subparts are intended to be comparatively easy and carry only a few marks. The last subpart carries the most marks and tests the higher-order thinking skills of synthesis and evaluation.

	Part (a)	Part (b)	Part (c)	Part (d)	Part (e)	Part (f)	Part (g)	Total
Maximum marks	4	5	4	4	4	4	15	40

Part (a)

This part is divided into two subparts, (i) and (ii). Part (a) usually requires candidates to define two economic terms, but candidates may also be asked to list the functions of an institution (e.g. central bank, WTO) or components of a composite indicator (e.g. HDI).

Here are some points to keep in mind.

- Definitions should be precise. A statement that could apply to two different concepts is considered too vague to be awarded 2 marks. For example: "the responsiveness of quantity in response to a change in price" could apply to both PED and PES—specifying "quantity *demanded*" or "quantity *supplied*" would narrow the response down to the right concept. Similarly, "an increase in the price of a currency in terms of another currency" can be applied to both appreciation and revaluation—specifying the type of exchange rate system is needed to be awarded full marks for the definition of appreciation or revaluation.
- Definitions should also be concise. As a general rule, definitions should not exceed two sentences. Marks are not deducted for over-elaborating on a concept but you may self-penalize by having less time for other subparts, especially part (g), which carries a lot more marks. Use the mark allocation as a guide of the time you should spend answering a subpart.
- Diagrams and examples are not required.

Part (b)

This part may also be divided into subparts and tests your ability to draw or sketch relevant diagrams and/or calculate economic figures (e.g. PED, GDP) from data (and/or from an area from a diagram for HL candidates).

Here are some guidelines for answering part (b).

- You are allowed to use a calculator for this paper. All part (b) subparts can be answered using a four function (plus, minus, multiply, divide) calculator but graphic display calculators (GDCs) are also allowed. Note that you may not use other electronic devices such as mobile phones to perform calculations.
- Always show your workings for calculation questions. You may not be awarded full marks if workings are not shown, even if your final answer is correct. You may receive parts of the marks if your final answer is incorrect but your workings reflect some understanding of the steps required to reach the answer.
- Unlike parts (c)–(f), which may require you to draw and explain diagrams, you are not required to explain diagrams for part (b).

Parts (c)–(f)

These subparts carry 4 marks each and require candidates to apply economic theory to explain a situation described in the text or reflected in the data, almost invariably with the aid of a diagram. The responses are usually awarded 2 marks for the explanation and 2 marks for the diagram.

Here are some guidelines and tips on answering parts (c)–(f).

- Most questions refer you to a specific text and passage, or a table or chart. Make sure you use the information provided in answering the question. Candidates sometimes provide theoretically sound answers that do not reflect the information in the text/data—and so cannot be awarded marks—because the candidate ignored the stimulus material. For instance, a question asking you to explain the impact of currency depreciation on inflation may *theoretically* come with two possible answers—demand-pull inflation if we consider the impact on the (X – M) component of AD and/or cost-push inflation if the country relies on imported inputs. If the text/data only suggests **one** of those two *theoretical* causes of inflation, then only **one** explanation is valid.
- Take time to draw clear—and sufficiently large—diagrams, preferably using a ruler. Make sure all curves and axes are fully and correctly labelled. Any one missing or incorrect label will lead to a loss of marks.
- Where a diagram is required, you should explain the diagram by making references to it in your response. Refer to the movements in curves (e.g. AD) and the changes in variables (e.g. price, quantity, real GDP). Use dotted lines to project variables along the axes (e.g. P1, P2) for easy referencing. In particular, make sure you have projected and referred to the variable tested in the question. For instance, if the question is asking you to explain the impact of higher interest rates on economic growth, then you must refer to the changes in real GDP on your diagram (e.g. Y1, Y2).
- The answer should focus on the question's requirements and avoid giving additional (unnecessary) diagram analysis. This often happens with trade protection diagrams (e.g. tariffs) where candidates provide a full welfare analysis (consumer surplus, producer surplus, government revenue, welfare loss) when the question does not call for it. There is no penalty for over-elaborating but it leaves you less time for the 15-mark question.

Part (g)

Unlike previous subparts, which only require you to apply economic theory to a specific passage or table, part (g) requires you to use information from all texts and data to formulate reasoned economic arguments with evidence of evaluation and/or synthesis. The command terms testing synthesis and evaluation are given in the Introduction (pages vi–vii). The most common command terms are "discuss" and "evaluate". Refer to the "You should be able to" sections, especially those throughout Unit 4, for topics associated with these command terms, which could be tested for part (g).

The descriptors for the highest mark band are given below for reference.

Mark	13–15
Descriptors	• The specific demands of the question are understood and addressed. • Relevant economic theory is fully explained. • Relevant economic terms are used appropriately throughout the response. • Where appropriate, relevant diagram(s) are included and fully explained. • The response contains evidence of effective and balanced synthesis or evaluation. • The use of information from the text/data is appropriate, relevant, and is used to formulate a reasoned argument supported by analysis/evaluation.

Here are some guidelines to help you do well when answering part (g).

- Read the question carefully. It is not uncommon for candidates to answer a slightly different question from the one asked, possibly to fit a rehearsed response to a similar practice question. Consider these two questions: "evaluate the role of FDI in promoting *economic growth* in Ethiopia" and "evaluate the role of FDI in promoting *economic development* in Ethiopia". They may look similar but their specific demands are clearly different.
- Make sure you refer to the text/data. Some candidates approach this question as if it was a paper 1 (b) question and are awarded a low mark for providing responses that are mostly theorical—"no use of text/data" is a descriptor for the lowest mark band (1–3). However, do not simply repeat the text/data, without analysis or evaluation—"limited use of text/data" only takes you into the second lowest mark band (4–6).
- Consider building on your answers to previous subparts. Parts (b)–(f) may hint at information that is relevant and useful when answering part (g). For instance, you might have been asked to illustrate the impact of a tariff on domestic production in a 4-mark question. You could refer to that earlier diagram and analysis if you wanted to elaborate on the benefits of trade protection in part (g). Even calculation questions in part (b) may have useful information—a question asking you to calculate GNI from GDP might suggest the extent of profit repatriation by MNCs, for example.
- Illustrate your arguments with the aid of diagrams, as long as the explanation of the diagram fits what the question requires and/or the information in the text/data. For instance, an AD/AS diagram may help explain the impact of an economic policy on economic growth or the inflation resulting from currency depreciation. If you have drawn a diagram in parts (b)–(f) that is relevant, you may refer to that diagram in part (g)—do not redraw exactly the same diagram in part (g) as you will not be awarded marks twice for the same diagram.
- A good way to end a part (g) answer is to provide a brief summative evaluation. This should not merely repeat earlier sections, but should consider, for example, whether foreign aid is, overall, effective in achieving economic development, or the short-run and long-run impacts of increased use of trade protection.

6.2 SAMPLE PAPER 2 QUESTION AND RESPONSE

Instructions

- You are allowed to use a calculator for this paper.
- Unless otherwise stated in the question, all numerical answers must be given exactly or correct to two decimal places.
- You must show all your workings.
- Use fully labelled diagrams and references to the text/data where appropriate.
- The maximum mark for this examination paper is **[40 marks]**.

Sample paper 2

Read the extracts and answer the questions that follow.

Text A: An overview of Papua New Guinea

1. Papua New Guinea (PNG) is a country in the Pacific Ocean with a population of 9 million. The population is young (one third is aged 14 and below) and grows at an annual rate of 2%.

2. Economic activity is dominated by the primary sector and in particular:

- the agricultural, forestry and fishing industries, which employ 57% of PNG's labour force
- mining and energy extraction, which attract most of the country's foreign investment funds and accounted for 77% of export earnings in 2019.

The manufacturing sector remains largely underdeveloped due to the limited public infrastructure, skills shortage and lack of access to finance.

3. The rise in commodity prices in the early 2010s led to the expansion of mining and energy extraction activities. PNG quickly became a large exporter of liquified natural gas. The economic growth rate was 15.4% in 2014, at the height of the commodity boom.

4. The economy's reliance on petroleum and gas-related activities made it vulnerable to external commodity-price shocks and natural disasters. Indeed, economic activity slowed after 2014 as a result of sharp falls in energy prices due to a decrease in global demand. Energy prices remained low until 2017 when the economy grew by just 2.8%.

5. Economic growth decreased further to 0.3% in 2018 when the country was hit by a devastating earthquake, which caused extensive damage to basic infrastructure. The production of liquefied natural gas and other mining activities were also disrupted. The resulting contraction in the mining sector almost fully offset growth in other sectors of the economy.

6. There are limited employment opportunities outside of the agricultural sector. Mining and energy extraction are capital-intensive activities and thus generate fewer jobs than agriculture. Agricultural production is dominated by small farms and mostly takes place in the informal economy.

7. The authorities decided to reduce the dependency on the mining and energy sector after the poor economic performance in 2018. They planned for a budget deficit with increased government spending on infrastructure and education to address the skills shortage. Government efforts now target agriculture, fisheries and tourism, which offer ample employment opportunities for women and young people.

8. To finance their development policies and address the shortage of foreign exchange, the government successfully raised 1.7 billion kinas (the currency of PNG), the equivalent of US$500 million, through the sale of a 10-year bond on the international market. The bonds carry an **interest rate** of 8.4%.

Text B: Foreign direct investment (FDI) in PNG

1. PNG is home to many multinational corporations (MNCs), many of which come from Australia. The two countries have enjoyed a close relationship, which goes beyond investment projects. Australia is also a contributor of development aid to PNG.

2. This close relationship may change as new taxes and stricter environmental protection are threatening the profitability of foreign firms. The government has vowed to put an end to the unsustainable exploitation of primary resources by MNCs. Taking advantage of PNG's inadequate taxation system, Australian mining companies have paid little or no corporate tax. In 2018, economic activities in mining and energy extraction contributed to almost 90% of PNG's export revenue but to less than 10% of government revenue.

3. The recent change in regulations and higher taxes have however not deterred foreign investors, who hope to benefit from the recent pick up in global demand for energy. A French MNC has just signed an agreement with the PNG government for a US$13 billion project which will double the country's liquified natural gas exports by 2024. Under the deal, the government will own 22.5% of the project but it will also need to contribute US$900 million to the initial investment cost.

4. To reduce the economy's reliance on foreign investment, the authorities will continue to facilitate local investment in agriculture and small-scale manufacturing. Farmers will be taught the use of sustainable practices and natural fertilizers to export organic coffee and rice, which sell for higher prices than traditional foodstuffs in developed nations. The higher revenue could allow poverty-stricken farmers to purchase modern farming tools. Progress is also seen in the development of small manufacturing centres. Compasses and surveying equipment are already finding export markets in the Netherlands and in Australia.

Text C: Malnutrition and lack of food security

1. Almost half the children of PNG suffer from stunting due to malnutrition. A child is stunted if his or her physical development is hindered, resulting in lower productivity when the person reaches working age. The economic cost of malnutrition is estimated to be 8.45% of gross domestic product (GDP). Malnutrition is also the main cause of PNG's high infant mortality.

2. The country has sufficient fertile soil and natural resources to feed its people. The issue is not the quantity but quality of food. Mothers need education about sanitation and an understanding of essential protein, fats, vitamins and minerals needed for the physical growth of their children. The authorities are conscious of this problem but lack the financial means to provide nutrition education programmes that would improve human capital in the long term.

▼ **Table 1** Selected components of PNG's balance of payments (2018)

Exports of goods and services (US$ million)	10 597
Imports of goods and services (US$ million)	5 492
Net income (US$ million)	-616
Net current transfers (US$ million)	382

▼ **Table 2** Selected national income data for PNG

	2018	**2019**
Nominal GDP (US$ million)	24 110	24 751
GDP deflator	126	128

Table 3 Indicators of health (2019)

	PNG	World average
Under-5 mortality rate (per 1000 lives born)	45.3	37.7
Prevalence of stunting (% of children under 5)	48.3	22.44

QUESTION PRACTICE AND SAMPLE STUDENT ANSWER

(a) (i) Define the term *interest rate* indicated in bold in the text (**Text A**, paragraph 8). [2]

The interest rate is the cost of borrowing and the reward for saving.

▲ This is a precise definition of interest rate.

This response could have achieved 2/2 marks.

(ii) List **two** single indicators of economic development other than the *under-5 mortality rate* and *prevalence of stunting* (**Table 3**). [2]

The Gini coefficient and the HDI.

▲ The Gini coefficient is a social indicator of economic development; it gives us some understanding of the level of inequality.

▼ The HDI is not a single indicator, it is a composite indicator.

This response could have achieved 1/2 marks.

(b) (i) Using information in **Table 1**, calculate the current account balance in 2018. [2]

Current account = exports – imports + net income + net current transfers

= 10 597 – 5 492 – 616 + 382

= 4 871

▼ The workings are correct but the final answer does not give the unit. The correct answer is US$4871 million.

This response could have achieved 1/2 marks.

(ii) Using information in **Table 2**, calculate PNG's economic growth rate in 2019. [3]

Real GDP in 2018 = $\left(\frac{24110}{126}\right) \times 100$ = \$19134.92 million

Real GDP in 2019 = $\left(\frac{24751}{128}\right) \times 100$ = \$19 336.72 million

Economic growth rare in 2019 = [(19 336.72 – 19 134.92)/(19 134.92)] × 100 = 1.54%

▲ All figures are correct and calculated to two decimal places. The workings are also shown.

This response could have achieved 3/3 marks.

(c) Using an AD/AD diagram, explain how PNG achieved a high rate of economic growth in 2014 (**Text A**, paragraph 3). [4]

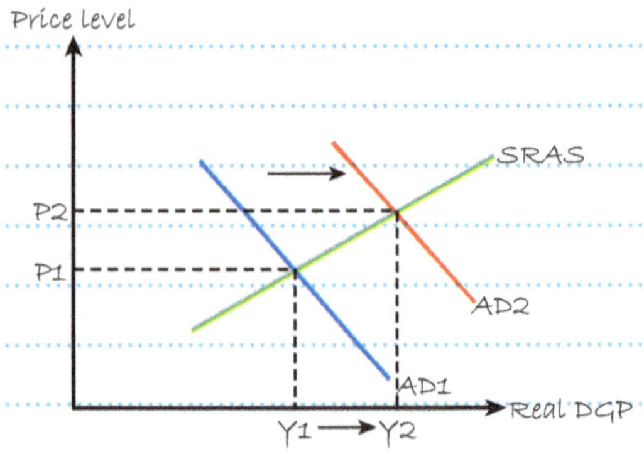

PNG is an exporter of liquefied natural gas, the country benefitted from higher export revenue during the commodity boom. Since export revenue is a component of AD, the rightward shift of AD from AD1 to AD2 led to an increase in real GDP, Y1 to Y2 and hence economic growth.

▲ All figures are correct and calculated to two decimal places. The workings are also shown.

▲ The candidate has identified relevant information from the passage—PNG is an exporter of liquefied natural gas—and applied this to the AD/AS model adequately. There are also adequate references to the diagram to establish that real GDP is increasing.

This response could have achieved 4/4 marks.

(d) Using an exchange rate diagram, explain the likely impact of the sale of government bonds on the exchange rate for the kina (**Text A**, paragraph 8). [4]

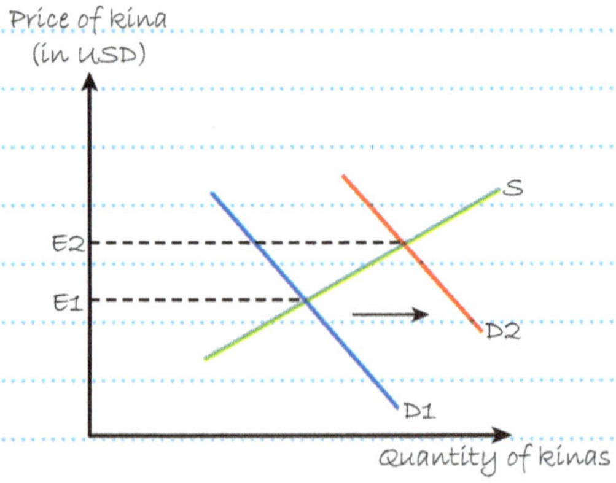

The bonds are sold on the international market and so foreigners who want to purchase those bonds will need to pay for them using PNG kinas. Since they very likely do not hold the kina, the interested bond buyers will first need to purchase the kina and hence it increases the demand for kinas from D1 to D2.

▲ The diagram is correct and fully labelled.

▲ The candidate has clearly established the link between the sale of bonds to foreigners and the increasing demand for the currency.

▼ Unfortunately, the response does not answer the question—what happens to the exchange rate? The candidate should have pointed out that the exchange rate would appreciate (preferably with a reference to the diagram, (e.g. from E1 to E2).

This response could have achieved 3/4 marks.

(e) Using a poverty cycle diagram, explain how exports of organic food may help farmers break the poverty cycle (**Text B**, paragraph 4). [4]

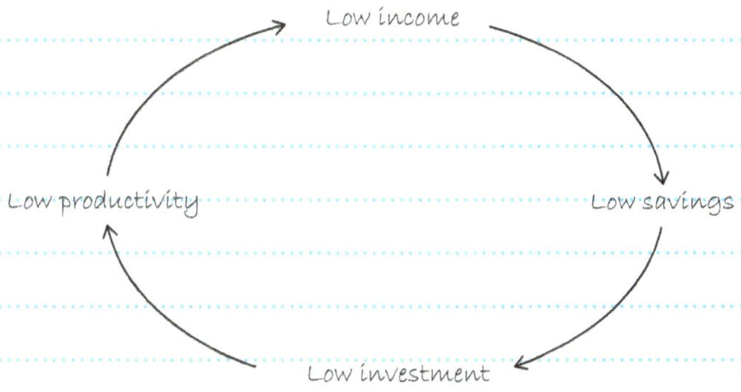

Farmers are trapped in poverty because of their low income which does not allow them to save and invest into capital equipment. The higher revenue they get from the sale of the more lucrative organic food will allow them to purchase modern tools which may lead to higher productivity and hence higher income.

▲ The poverty cycle includes all required elements—"low income", "low savings", "low investment" and "low productivity".

▲ The candidate has clearly explained how the higher revenue from the export of organic food would help break the poverty cycle.

This response could have achieved 4/4 marks.

(f) Using a PPC diagram, explain the likely impact of greater provision of nutrition education programmes on the potential output of PNG (**Text C**, paragraph 2). [4]

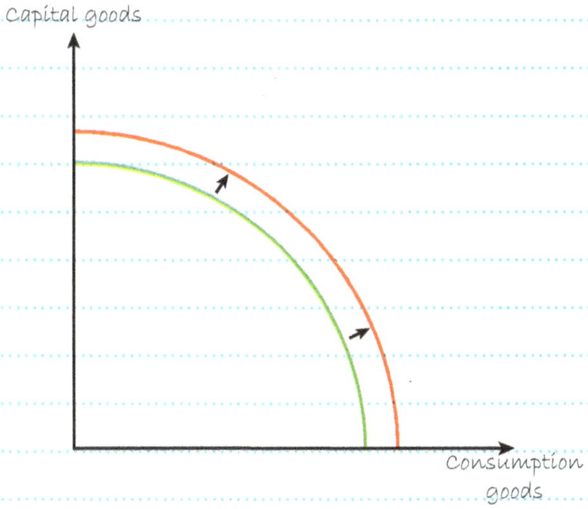

The provision of nutrition education programmes would help mothers prepare healthy meals for their children. Fewer children would suffer from malnutrition and be stunted. This would mean healthier and hence more productive workers in the future. This increase in the quality of human capital would lead to an increase in potential output, represented by an outward shift of the PPC.

▲ The diagram is correct and fully labelled. The arrows clearly indicate the direction of the change in the PPC.

▲ This clearly establishes that the PCC would shift outward due to an improvement in factors of production.

This response could have achieved 4/4 marks.

(g) Using information from the text/data and your knowledge of economics, evaluate the contribution of foreign direct investment inflows and diversification strategies to economic development in Papua New Guinea. [15]

SAMPLE STUDENT ANSWER

PNG has a small population of nine million and given that one third of the population is below the age of 14, it means it is a small market with a limited number of consumers to generate growth without trade. Focusing on export revenue is a good way for the country to enjoy an increase in AD since AD = C + I + G + (X - M). Economic growth does not imply an improvement in the quality of life, which is economic development. However, economic growth may allow for economic development if increases in income allow farmers to break the poverty cycle and greater tax revenue allows for the provision of public healthcare and education. Theoretically, FDI inflows and diversification can lead to growth and hence development. Indeed, FDI refer to the long-term investment by MNCs who would operate in PNG with the intention to export commodities. Diversification also allows for a greater variety of exports and hopefully higher value exports. With higher export revenue, AD would increase thus leading to growth – as illustrated on the diagram in (c) – and hopefully development.

▲ This is an effective start. The candidate establishes a link between FDI inflows, diversification strategies and economic development—which is the exact requirement of the question. The text is used and the candidate also refers to a diagram drawn previously instead of redrawing it (showing effective use of time). The paragraph is a good overview of the rest of the response.

It is clear that the economy of PNG is not sufficiently diversified. Most workers are employed in the primary sector, which is also the main source of export revenue (Text A, paragraph 2). This is a problem because the dependence on the primary sector is a barrier to economic development. We saw that the economy of PNG suffered from the price volatility of commodities which is their main – almost their only – export source (Text A, paragraphs 4 and 5). The fact that MNCs are once again investing in the primary sector in PNG to take advantage of the increase in global demand (Text B, paragraph 3) means the economy is again being too reliant on the primary sector and maybe heading to another fall in economic growth if another commodity boom ends in the future.

▲ The candidate makes use of the text to establish the need for diversification. Note that information is not just lifted from the text but it is enriched with economic analysis (e.g. the risk of further fluctuations in economic activity is explained).

Thus, diversification strategies would be very good to ensure that the economy is no longer subject to substantial fluctuations

▲ This paragraph considers the strengths and limitations of the diversification strategies in achieving economic development (which is part of the demands of the question). There is effective use of text/data. There is also effective evaluation (e.g. judgment on the effectiveness of the promotion of organic farming).

in AD and to focus on goods which have a more income elastic demand such as manufactured goods. Manufacturing may also offer more jobs which are not in the informal sector. There are too many agricultural workers in the informal sector (Text A, paragraph 6) where there is no protection of workers and no tax revenue generated for the government to finance development expenditure. Unfortunately, most foreign direct investment flows into mining and energy extraction and it seems that the government is diversifying within the agricultural sector with organic farming as much as trying to diversify away from the primary sector with small-scale manufacturing. This is a mistake because even if organic rice and coffee are more expensive than traditional crops, they are still subject to fluctuations due to changes in weather. When prices of coffee and rice drop, the income of farmers may drop and make it difficult to break the poverty cycle. If income for farmers or workers in commodity-related industries falls because of a supply shock, they may not be able to save to invest in physical capital (such as modern farming tools) and human capital through the education of their children – this would prevent them from breaking the poverty cycle at point A and/or B.

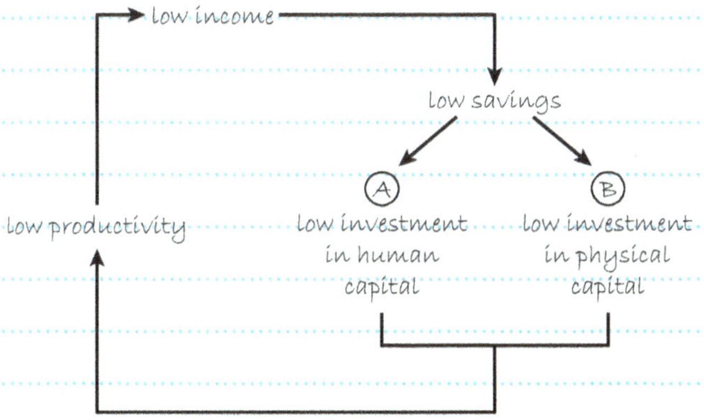

▲ The diagram is relevant as it illustrates an important economic development concept. A poverty cycle appears in part (e) but this one includes more information. Redrawing it here is justified.

While MNCs help generate government revenue now that they pay higher taxes, mining and energy extraction generate few jobs since the activities are mostly capital intensive (Text A, paragraph 6) and so few residents of PNG would benefit in terms of employment and income from more activities by MNCs and so their material quality of life may not increase directly from more FDI. It is also likely that most of the proceeds from the sale of liquified natural gas will be repatriated as profits. That may be why the net income component of the current account is negative in table 1. However, the government is now demanding

▲ The discussion remains focused on the impact on the standard of living of residents of PNG and hence economic development. This paragraph is focused on the strengths and limitations of FDI inflows—so the response consistently addresses the question's specific demands.

a 22.5% share of the mining and energy extraction projects of close (Text B, paragraph 3) and this could provide a steady flow of government revenue to finance development projects such as the nutrition education programmes which would have a good impact on the well-being of PNG residents. However, given the important government commitment of $900 million to the investment projects, it might take a few years before the government breaks even and have funds to finance development. It seems that diversification is the way forward especially given that mining and energy extraction are likely unsustainable if the resources are extracted faster than they can be replenished. However, the government revenue generated from the activities of MNCs may help finance more diversification efforts in the long term and exports can be diversified away from the export of liquified natural gas towards more manufactured goods such as compasses and other equipment (Text B, paragraph 4).

▲ This is an effective synthesis of the response.

This response meets all the descriptors of the highest mark band and **could have achieved 15/15 marks.**

Test yourself

Use these additional questions as practice for answering paper 2 questions.

1. Define the term *informal economy* indicated in the text (**Text A**, paragraph 6). [2]
2. Define the term *human capital* indicated in the text (**Text C**, paragraph 2). [2]
3. Using a demand and supply diagram, identify the cause of the sharp fall in the price of energy (**Text A**, paragraph 4). [4]
4. Using an exchange rate diagram, explain the likely impact of the inflows of development aid from Australia on the exchange rate for the kina (**Text B**, paragraph 1). [4]
5. Using information from the text/data and your knowledge of economics, evaluate the challenges to economic development faced by Papua New Guinea. [15]

7 PAPER 3 (HL)

7.1 PAPER 3: STRUCTURE AND TIPS

HL The economics paper 3 task includes both quantitative and qualitative questions. The last subpart of each question tests your ability to select and use economic data to make policy recommendations. This paper is not part of the SL assessment.

Duration: 1 hour 45 minutes

Weighting: 30% of the final grade (HL only)

Syllabus coverage: questions are drawn from the four units of the syllabus including the HL extension topics.

Format: the paper carries a total of 60 marks, which are distributed across <u>*two compulsory*</u> questions. Each question is subdivided into two parts, (a) and (b). Part (a) has subparts, many of which require the use of a calculator.

Part (a)

Many of the subparts are quantitative questions, which are associated with command terms such as "calculate", "construct", "identify", "plot", "sketch". Some may be qualitative questions with command terms such as "define", "describe", "list", "outline", "state", "comment" or "explain". Familiarize yourself with the requirements of these command terms, which are defined in the Introduction on pages v–viii. The subparts will carry from 1 to 4 marks each. Unlike papers 1 and 2, responses are not written on a separate answer booklet but directly on the question paper in answer boxes. Indeed, one of the instructions on the cover page of the paper will read "Answers must be written within the answer boxes provided". The command term should guide you on the expectations of each subpart and how much to write, especially for the qualitative questions. You may also check the number of marks allocated and the size of the answer boxes as a rough guide. Questions earning 1 mark usually have much smaller boxes than the 4-mark question or the 10-mark question. However, if you find the space provided in the answer box insufficient, especially for part (b), you may request an answer booklet during the examination.

Here are some things to keep in mind.

- Consider the command term carefully. Unlike paper 1 and paper 2 questions, paper 3 uses a wide range of command terms. You may face a combination of command terms such as "sketch", "calculate", "state", "outline" and "explain" across the (a) subparts. It is not uncommon for candidates to miss marks because they have misinterpreted the command term. For instance, one may *state* factors rather than *explain* them simply because the previous subpart had "state" as a command term.
- Always show your workings for calculation questions. You may not be awarded full marks if workings are not shown, even if your final answer is correct. You may receive parts of the marks if your final answer is incorrect but your workings reflect some understanding of the steps required to reach the answer.
- Remember to show the units. Units are not required for intermediate workings but must be accurate for final answers.
- Round correctly for calculations. Although there is no requirement for rounding at any particular stage in a calculation, you should be aware that rounding at intermediate stages may produce a different answer from that derived from a final rounding only. Examiners will reward both ways equally as long as the workings are given and the final figure is rounded to two decimal places (dp).
- Advice on definitions and 4-mark questions given in Unit 6, which covered the paper 2 assessment, remain applicable. (Refer to pages 202 and 203 for tips on how to do well when answering parts (a) and (c)–(f) of paper 2 questions.)

Part (b)

This subpart is worth 10 marks and requires an extended response. The command term for part (b) questions is "recommend". Candidates are required to present an advisable policy that is supported by economic theory **and** the information from the text/data provided. There is no right or wrong policy—your policy is valid as long as you can support it. Note that you should only recommend **one** policy—a second policy, if needed, should only be included as a complementary policy (for example "legislation may be required to enforce the price floor and prevent the establishment of a parallel market") or to establish the relative effectiveness of your policy (for example "legislation is more effective than a tax since demand is very price-inelastic"). Your recommendation must reflect evaluation of the policy—that is, you must establish its strengths (possibly in comparison to other policies) but also show awareness of its limitations in the context given in the materials provided.

The highest mark band (9–10) for part (b) includes the following descriptors.

9–10	• The response identifies and fully explains an appropriate policy. • The response uses relevant economic theory effectively to support the recommendation. • Relevant economic terms are used appropriately throughout the response. • The use of information from the text/data is appropriate, relevant and supports the analysis/evaluation effectively. • The response contains evidence of effective and balanced synthesis or evaluation.

Here are some guidelines to help you do well when answering part (b) questions.

- Make sure to refer to the text/data in formulating your recommended policy. Candidates might be tempted to approach this 10-mark question as if it were a paper 1 (a) question and explain all possible *theoretical* strengths and limitations of the policy rather than consider those in the context given in the question. Such a response may not be awarded more than 6/10 marks—"the response includes some relevant information from the text/data to support the recommendation" is one of the descriptors for the (5–6) mark band. However, make sure you do not simply repeat the text/data without analysis or evaluation.
- Consider all information provided throughout the question, including your answers to part (a). For instance, you might have been asked to calculate the price elasticity of demand for a good in part (a). A low magnitude would indicate that a tax may need to be high to be an effective policy to reduce consumption of this good.
- Diagrams are not required but they may be included if they help support your recommendation.
- Do not only focus on the strengths of your recommended policy and fail to address its limitations or its advantages over other policies. Providing a "mostly balanced" response is necessary for entering the (7–8) mark band.
- Your response to part (b) could end with a summative evaluation of the policy recommended. For instance, you might conclude "the government should choose a price ceiling since, as it was established, this policy comes with multiple long-term benefits and most of its limitations may be addressed in the short term. In particular, it has the advantage of not requiring the government spending associated with a subsidy, which this government cannot afford".

7.2 SAMPLE PAPER 3 QUESTION AND RESPONSE

Instructions

- You are permitted access to a calculator for this paper.
- Unless otherwise stated in the question, all numerical answers must be given exactly or correct to two decimal places.
- You must show all your workings.
- The maximum mark for this question is **[30 marks]**.

QUESTION PRACTICE

A minimum unit pricing (MUP) on alcohol was introduced in the Republic of Ireland. The introduction of this price floor on alcohol pushed up prices of wine and spirits (strong alcoholic drinks such as whisky) in shops and supermarkets throughout the country.

The following table presents the price (per litre) of a specific type of wine and the quantity sold by retailers in Ireland before and after the MUP was introduced.

	Price in € (per litre)	**Quantity of litres** (thousands/week)
Before MUP	5.75	27.2
After MUP	6.15	26.4

(a) (i) Define the term *price elasticity of demand*. [2]

(ii) Calculate the price elasticity of demand for this specific type of wine in Ireland. [2]

(iii) Using your answer to part (a) (ii), sketch an appropriate demand curve to show the impact of the MUP on revenues collected by Irish wine retailers. [2]

SAMPLE STUDENT ANSWER

(i) The responsiveness of the quantity of a good to a change in its price, ceteris paribus.

▼ This definition could also apply to PES—it lacks precision. PED measures the responsiveness of quantity *demanded*.

This response could have achieved 1/2 marks.

(ii) $\text{PED} = \dfrac{\%\,\Delta \text{ in quantity demanded}}{\%\,\Delta \text{ in price}} = \dfrac{\left[\frac{26.4 - 27.2}{27.2}\right]}{\left[\frac{6.15 - 5.75}{5.75}\right]}$

$= \dfrac{-0.03}{0.07} = -0.43$

▲ While only the final answer needs to be rounded to 2 dp, this candidate decided to also round the intermediate results to 2 dp (e.g. –0.03 instead of –0.02941176) which is fine, as long as it is clearly indicated in the workings. Note that the minus sign is not required for PED calculations. An answer of 0.43 would be accepted.

▲ The candidate has drawn a steep demand curve to reflect that the increase in price from €5.75 to €6.15 has resulted in a less than proportionate fall in quantity demanded, so total revenue (P × Q) has increased. Note that since the command term is "sketch", the demand curve need not be drawn to scale.

(iii)

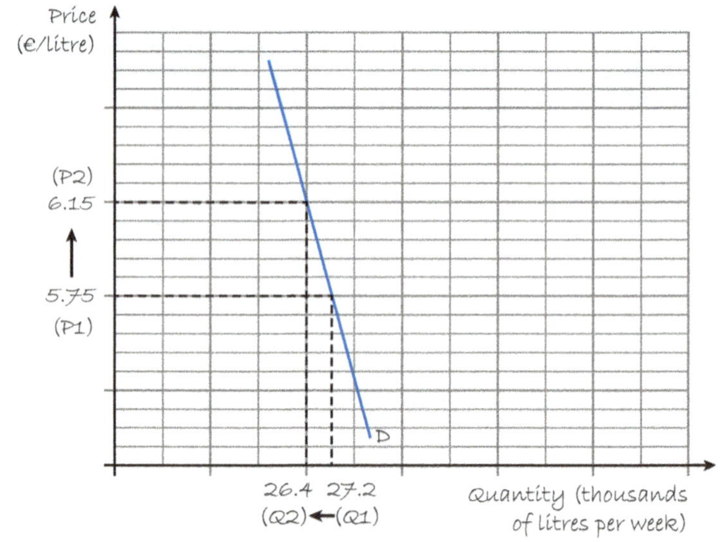

This response could have achieved 2/2 marks.

QUESTION PRACTICE

- Three out of five Irish people aged 15–17 drink alcohol.
- Youths tend to be ill-informed of the risks associated with consuming inexpensive but high-alcohol content drinks. An Irish mother, whose 16-year-old daughter died in her sleep after drinking at a party, welcomed the introduction of the MUP.
- Alcohol misuse impacts society by causing a greater burden on the criminal justice system, and health and social work services.

(iv) Using an appropriate diagram, explain why the free market leads to an inefficient allocation of resources in the market for alcohol. [4]

SAMPLE STUDENT ANSWER

▼ This diagram illustrates a case of negative externality from production but it is the *consumption* of alcohol that generates negative externalities—so no mark can be awarded for this diagram.

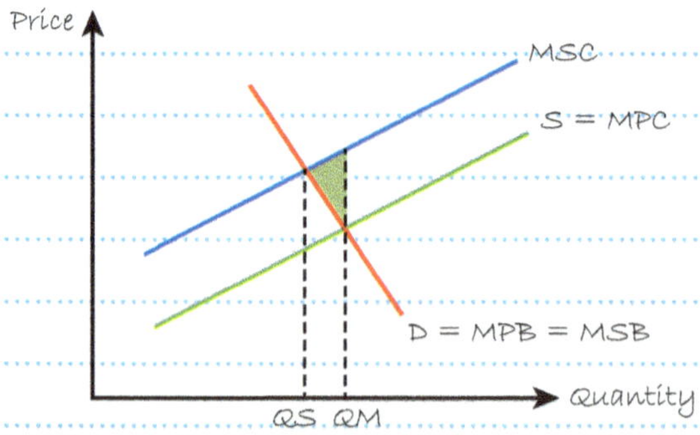

Consumers and producers of alcohol do not consider the third-party costs from excessive drinking of alcohol. The external costs incurred include overcrowded hospitals, with fewer beds available because of accidents due to drink driving. If we consider these external costs, the social optimum is QS (where MSB = MSC), which is less than the market equilibrium, QM. The market for alcohol leads to allocative inefficiency as it has over-allocated resources and there is a welfare loss (shaded).

▲ The candidate establishes that since the market quantity is higher than the social optimum quantity, resources are over-allocated.

This response could have achieved 2/4 marks.

QUESTION PRACTICE

Some argue that the greatest burden of alcoholism on society is the loss in productivity. Close to 73% of working men's deaths in Ireland are alcohol-related (e.g. traffic accidents, liver and heart diseases, strokes).

(v) Using a PPC diagram, explain the impact of excessive alcohol consumption on the economy. [4]

SAMPLE STUDENT ANSWER

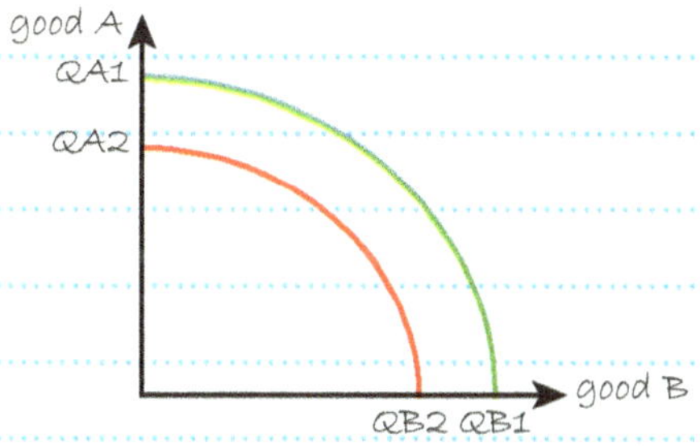

▲ The diagram is correct and fully labelled, although an arrow could help to indicate clearly the direction of the change in the PPC.

Excessive drinking leads to a reduction in the number of workers due to death from alcohol-related diseases and accidents. Some workers may also be less productive at work since they are impaired by liver and heart diseases. There is a reduction in the quantity and quality of human capital. This results in a reduction in potential output, represented by an inward shift of the PPC from QA1QB1 to QA2QB2.

▲ The response clearly establishes the link between excessive drinking and the potential output, with reference to the diagram.

This response could have achieved 4/4 marks.

QUESTION PRACTICE

The following table provides information on government expenditure and revenue for the Republic of Ireland.

	Government revenue (€ billion)	Government expenditure (€ billion)
2016	74.7	76.6
2017	77.9	78.8
2018	83.9	83.4
2019	89.1	87.6

(vi) Calculate the government budget in 2019. [2]

▲ Workings are provided and the unit (€ billion) is included in the final answer.

SAMPLE STUDENT ANSWER

The government budget = government revenue – government expenditure

= 89.1 – 87.6 = €1.5 billion

This response could have achieved 2/2 marks.

QUESTION PRACTICE

(vii) Identify **one** year in which the government ran a budget deficit. [1]

▲ Note that 2017 is also a valid answer since government expenditure also exceeded government revenue in that year.

SAMPLE STUDENT ANSWER

2016.

This response could have achieved 1/1 mark.

QUESTION PRACTICE

Irish households earning less than €36,800 a year pay an income tax of 20%. The current VAT rate (an indirect tax on all goods and services) is 23%.

(viii) Calculate the average tax rate (ATR) (including both direct and indirect tax) for a household earning €20,000 a year, assuming that all disposable income is spent (no savings). [3]

▲ All workings were provided and the final answer is correct. *Be careful here*: the total spending includes the VAT payment so indirect tax paid = amount spent on goods and services × [t/(1 + t)] where t is the tax rate.

SAMPLE STUDENT ANSWER

income tax paid = 0.2 × €20000 = €4000

disposable income = €20000 – €4000 = €16000

amount paid to VAT = €16000 × $\frac{0.23}{1.23}$ = €2991.87

ATR = $\frac{T}{Y}$ = $\frac{4000 + 2991.87}{200000}$ = 0.384 = 34.96%

This response could have achieved 3/3 marks.

QUESTION PRACTICE

- Expenditure on healthcare in Ireland increased by 6% from 2018 to 2019. Ireland spent 6.7% of its GDP, or €23.8 billion, on healthcare in 2019. The majority of health expenditure (74%) is funded by the government.
- In Scotland and Wales, where an MUP had been implemented earlier, the households that bought the most alcohol were most likely to reduce the amount they bought by at least 7%. However, the households that bought the most alcohol and also fell into the lowest income bracket (€20,000 a year and below) did not appear to buy any less.

(b) Using the data provided and your knowledge of economics, recommend one policy *other than* an MUP (price floor) that the Irish government could introduce to reduce the overconsumption of alcohol. [10]

I recommend that the Irish government uses a tax on alcoholic drinks instead of the MUP. A tax has the same impact as an MUP, it increases the price of drinks with some alcohol content. The tax can be based on the content of alcohol so a drink with 40% alcohol content would be taxed more than a drink with just 5% alcohol – the higher the alcohol content, the higher the tax.

▲ The candidate has identified a policy, an indirect tax on alcohol, and briefly explained how the policy would work.

Unlike the MUP, the tax will not increase the revenues of producers, as we saw in part (a) (iii). Instead, the producers of alcohol will see their revenue decrease and the impact should be greater for higher alcohol-content drinks. This would incentivize producers to reduce the alcohol contents of their drinks or even produce more alcohol-free party drinks such as mocktails. Hence the external costs would be reduced with lower alcohol content in drinks consumed. Another advantage of a tax over the MUP is that the tax would increase government revenue. Since the Irish government ran a budget deficit for 2 of the past 4 years, the revenue could help pay back some of the past deficits (i.e. reduce the government debt). The revenues would also help finance the cost of law enforcement. With more police, they might be able to conduct more road checks for drunk drivers and reduce the number of accidents, which lead to a loss of productivity. The tax revenue can also help finance the cost of social work and healthcare services, which have been increasing from 6% to 6.7% of GDP. In this way, the revenue can help mitigate some of the external costs of excessive drinking. The tax would thus help internalize the externality.

The government can also use the tax revenue to finance awareness campaigns and school programmes to inform the public, especially youths, of the dangers associated with alcohol.

▲ The candidate establishes some of the benefits of a tax in comparison to another policy, the MUP. The information provided is used to support the arguments and the candidate also uses relevant economic terms such as "internalize the externality".

A tax would be a good long-term solution since it would address future increases in healthcare costs and change the habits of consumers.

▲ The candidate evaluates the effectiveness of the tax by considering the long-term benefits of the policy.

One limitation is that since the tax would be based on the alcohol content, it will be lower for drinks such as wines, which have typically less alcohol content than spirits. Since the demand for wines can be price-inelastic, as calculated in (a) (ii), then the consumption of alcohol may not drop significantly for such drinks. Another concern is that the

ATR for low-income consumers is already very high and so, since this tax is regressive, low-income consumers would be badly affected.

A tax seems to an advisable policy given that it comes with more advantages than disadvantages. Many of the latter can be mitigated if the tax revenue is spent wisely. Besides the awareness campaign mentioned above, it could also be used to increase the number of social work services, which may help low-income individuals or even finance retraining programmes to help them get higher paying jobs. This would thus help meet other objectives of the government.

▲ The candidate has considered the limitations of the policy, based on evidence from the materials and previous sub-parts (e.g. the ATR).

▲ This is a good summative statement (synthesis) and it addresses some of the limitations of the policy (evaluation).

The response meets all the descriptors of the highest mark band (9–10).

- The response identifies a tax as a policy and explains why a tax would be an appropriate policy.
- The response uses relevant economic theory such as market failure and the need for a sustainable level of debt to support the policy recommendation.
- Relevant economic terms such as "government debt" and "regressive" are used appropriately throughout the response.
- Information from the text/data is used to support the analysis (why a tax would be appropriate) and for evaluation (looking at the strengths and limitations, especially in comparison to other policies).
- The response contains evidence of effective and balanced synthesis and evaluation since both strengths and limitations of a tax are considered. The conclusion also provides a good summary of the response.

This response could have achieved 10/10 marks.

Test yourself

Recommend another policy to answer part (b), such as legislation. Check your response against the level descriptors for the 9–10 mark band (page 214).

8 INTERNAL ASSESSMENT

8.1 THE ECONOMICS COMMENTARIES

The economics internal assessment (IA) task requires you to produce a **portfolio of three commentaries** on published extracts from the news media. Each of the three commentaries should be no longer than **800 words**, be based on **different units of the syllabus** (excluding Unit 1: Introduction to economics) and demonstrate the application of a **different key concept** (scarcity, choice, efficiency, equity, economic well-being, sustainability, change, interdependence, intervention).

The IA is very different from the external assessment (papers 1, 2 and 3). It is not performed under timed examination conditions and allows you to demonstrate the application of economic concept to topics of your choice. The IA requirements are the same for SL and HL students but the IA portfolio contributes 30% to the final grade for the SL course and 20% to the final grade for the HL course.

It is recommended that you discuss your choice of article with your economics teacher before writing a draft commentary—some articles may be very interesting but may not have enough scope for an economics commentary. The first step of selecting a suitable article is arguably the most important in the process of writing a good commentary. It is not uncommon for commentaries that reflect a good understanding of economic theory to be awarded low marks on a few criteria due to a lack of application to the article.

Your economics teacher can provide feedback on **one** draft for each of your three commentaries. After reworking your draft, you submit the final commentary file (cover page, article and commentary) to your teacher for submission on the IB portal. It is recommended that you submit all final documents in PDF format to avoid a loss of formatting when uploaded—IA documents are submitted in digital format.

Choosing an article

What makes an appropriate article?

Source	Your news article may be from printed press (newspaper, journal) or from the internet—you will need to provide a *clear* scan of printed articles so internet sources might be more convenient (most candidates use articles from internet sources). The following **are not** valid sources: • video and audio files (e.g. podcast) • opinion pieces from social media accounts (e.g. blogs and Facebook pages) • advertisements • government reports. **Each article must be taken from a different source.**
Contents	Your article must have sufficient content for analysis and evaluation. **Try to focus only on what the article is about unless some information that is not in the article is mentioned briefly as part of an evaluation**. For example, if the article covers an increase in cigarette purchases but does not mention government policies to reduce consumption of cigarettes, you should not elaborate on the use of policies such as taxes or legislation in your commentary. Including references to other news articles or sources in a bibliography would be inappropriate (as a general rule, commentaries should not need a bibliography).

	Avoid articles that are heavy in economic analysis as you may end up summarizing the article. In such a case, the credit for economic analysis will not go to you but to the author of the article. Candidates who do an internet search using economic terms such as "externalities", "expansionary fiscal policy" or "current account deficit" will probably end up with an article that already contains economic analysis because those are technical terms—"cigarette tax", "stimulus package" or "trade deficit" are layman terms and thus more likely to return suitable articles on a web search. Finally, **keep in mind that one key concept needs to be linked to the article**. Go back to the concept links in Units 2–4 for suggestions. Unit 2 commentaries are often easier to link to efficiency, interdependence and sustainability; Unit 3 to intervention and equity; Unit 4 to economic well-being, change, interdependence, intervention and efficiency. An article may have a lot of scope for application of economic theory but offer no easy link to one of the key concepts.
Date of publication	Articles used must have been published **no earlier than one year before the writing of the commentary**. You may need time to discuss the article with your teacher then write the commentary so it is advisable to select an article no more than 10 months old.
Length	Avoid articles that are too brief as there will not be enough content in the article to base the commentary on. Lengthy articles are not advisable either as it becomes difficult to write an effective commentary when there is a lot to analyse. **As a general rule, articles should be at least one printed page long but not exceed three pages**. You are advised to highlight the section(s) of the article upon which your commentary is based. This will help you focus on relevant content and it directs the assessor's attention to the sections of the article you are commenting on.

Presentation

Each commentary should be submitted with a cover page and a copy of the news article.

The cover page should reflect:

- the title of the article
- the source of the article
- the article's publication date
- the date the commentary was written
- the commentary's word count
- the relevant unit of the syllabus
- the key concept being used.

You are advised to place the copy of the news article before the commentary since the assessor must read the article, or at least the sections of the article you highlighted, before assessing your commentary.

Summary

Figure 8.1 summarizes the process of writing each of your economics commentaries.

Select article
- Choose a news article that illustrates the application of economic concepts from Unit 2, 3 or 4 and one of the key concepts
- Discuss your choice of article with your teacher before writing your draft commentary

Submit draft commentary
- Write a commentary that does not exceed 800 words
- Your teacher may only provide feedback once per commentary so invest time and effort into your draft
- Submit your draft to your teacher for feedback

Submit final commentary
- Revise your commentary based on your teacher's feedback
- You cannot revise your commentary once submitted so check the document carefully, especially diagrams for missing or incorrect labels (see sub-unit 8.2 for a more comprehensive checklist)
- Submit the final version of your commentary, preferably in PDF format

▲ Figure 8.1 Writing your economic commentary: a three-stage process

8.2 THE IA ASSESSMENT CRITERIA

Each of your three commentaries will be assessed using five criteria, A–E.

Criterion	Commentary section	Marks
A	Diagrams	3
B	Terminology	2
C	Application and analysis	3
D	Key concept	3
E	Evaluation	2
Total		**14**

There is one additional criterion for the whole portfolio.

Criterion	Commentary section	Marks
F	Rubric requirements	3

The maximum for the portfolio is 45 marks: (14 marks × 3 commentaries) + 3 marks = 42 + 3 marks.

Criterion A: Diagrams

This criterion assesses your ability to construct and explain diagrams.

Marks	Descriptor
0	The work does not reach a standard described by the descriptors below.
1	Relevant diagram(s) are included but not explained, or the explanations are incorrect.
2	Relevant, accurate and correctly labelled diagram(s) are included, with a limited explanation.
3	Relevant, accurate and correctly labelled diagram(s) are included, with a full explanation.

The table below sets out what is required for your diagrams to be awarded 3 marks on criterion A.

Your diagrams must be:	
relevant	• Your diagram(s) should relate to the article. For example, you should only draw an AD/AS diagram to illustrate the impact of expansionary fiscal policy if the article mentions an increase in government spending and/or reduction in direct taxes. • Note that the criterion A descriptors state diagram**(s)**—it is possible to be awarded 3 marks with a single diagram. If there are no obvious other diagrams to illustrate your economic analysis, then keep to one diagram. If you only use one diagram it should be *dynamic*—more on this later. Adding unnecessary diagrams will probably lead to a lower mark on this criterion as the diagrams used must be relevant and fully explained (within the 800-word limit). • Statistical tables and charts are not considered to be diagrams.
accurate	• Your diagrams must be adapted to *precisely* describe the contents of the article. For example, if your article describes both an increase in cost-push and demand-pull inflation but it is made clear that most of the increase in the price level comes from higher costs of production, then the leftward shift in SRAS must be greater than the rightward shift in AD. • Do not use diagrams downloaded from the internet or scanned from a textbook. They are not your own diagrams and since they are not adapted to the article, they are generic. If you have difficulties constructing your diagram(s) using software, it is preferable to draw them by hand, scan them and insert them at the appropriate part of the commentary.

correctly labelled	These are common reasons for candidates losing marks on criterion A. • Missing labels—make sure all axes and curves are labelled. Candidates tend to forget to label the world supply/price line on international trade diagrams. • Incorrect labels—in particular, candidates sometimes mix microeconomic and macroeconomic labels (e.g. they include an AD/AS diagram with axes incorrectly labelled as "price" and "quantity"). • It is always a good idea to customize the labels of your diagrams. For example, use the label "Price of oil" instead of just "price"; "SChina" instead of 'SWorld" if imports are only coming from China; "$7" instead of "P1" if the article states that the price is $7. • Only include labels next to curves and axes. Do not add brief explanation notes on your diagram to go around the 800-word limit. Note that the word count does not include: ◦ labels on diagrams—*of 5 words or fewer* ◦ headings on diagrams—*of 10 words or fewer.* ◦ Labels and headings that exceed these word limits must be included in the word count of your commentary.
fully explained	• Diagrams need to be sufficiently referenced in your explanation. The best way to make sure your diagrams are effective is to: draw *dynamic* diagrams (ones that illustrate movements in curves—static diagrams have limited scope for referencing); refer to the changes in curves and variables in your explanation (e.g. "price increases from P1 to P2", "aggregate demand decreases from AD1 to AD2"). • Position your diagrams judiciously. Diagrams tend to be more effective when their explanation appears on the same page. You are strongly advised against placing all your diagrams together at the end of your commentary.

Criterion B: Terminology

This criterion assesses the extent to which appropriate economic terminology is used.

Marks	Descriptor
0	The work does not reach a standard described by the descriptors below.
1	Economic terminology relevant to the article is included in the commentary.
2	Economic terminology relevant to the article is used appropriately throughout the commentary.

The table below shows what is required to be awarded 2 marks on criterion B.

The economics terms you use must be:	
relevant	• Economic terms, learned as part of the IB course, must be included in your analysis. It is a test of your ability to convert layman terms used in the article to economic terms. For example, if the article mentions the "medical costs borne by the family members of smokers", you need to identify those as "third-party costs" or "external costs"; "cash handouts during a recession" are "transfer payments", which are part of "expansionary fiscal policy". • Try to be as specific as possible—"negative externalities from production", "direct taxes", "structural unemployment" and "cost-push inflation" are more precise terms than "externalities", "taxes", "unemployment" and "inflation".
used appropriately	• Do not misuse terms or include terms that are not relevant to the article or analysis. • Note that you are not required to define the economic terms you use. This criterion assesses your ability to use economic terms, not to define them. However, to reach the highest mark on criterion C, you might need to explain the concepts central to your economic analysis and sometimes a definition may help with the economic analysis. For example, if the article is about carbon taxes imposed in Canada, you would probably need to explain that the taxes are necessary to internalize negative externalities from production. To be effective, you would probably establish the external costs incurred. In such a scenario, you might find it useful to define negative externalities from production. In short, you should only define terms if it makes your analysis more effective; do not define terms indiscriminately.

Criterion C: Application and analysis

This criterion assesses the extent to which you apply and analyse economic theory in the context of the article.

Marks	Descriptor
0	The work does not reach a standard described by the descriptors below.
1	Relevant economic terminology is applied to the article with limited analysis.
2	Relevant economic terminology is applied to the article throughout the commentary with appropriate economic analysis.
3	Relevant economic terminology is applied to the article throughout the commentary with effective economic analysis.

To be awarded 3 marks on criterion C, the commentary must demonstrate both application and effective analysis.

Application is the identification of the correct economic concepts and theories applicable to the context set in the article. Examples would be identifying the correct type of market structure, unemployment, demand-side policy or trade protection. Discussing structural unemployment when the article is describing cyclical unemployment would not be applying relevant economic theory to the article.

Analysis is the detailed examination of the economic issue(s). For instance, you might examine the sources of inflation or the consequences of higher income tax. **Analysis is effective** when it is consistently applied to the context set in the article. A purely theoretical analysis (as presented in textbooks) without adaptation to the article's contents will not reach the highest mark on this criterion.

Criterion D: Key concept

This criterion assesses the effective application of one of the nine key concepts to the article (scarcity, choice, efficiency, equity, economic well-being, sustainability, change, interdependence, intervention).

Marks	Descriptor
0	Either the work does not reach a standard described by the descriptors below **or** the key concept identified has already been used in another commentary.
1	A key concept is identified and there has been no attempt to link it to the article.
2	A key concept is identified and the link to the article is partially explained.
3	A key concept is identified and the link to the article is fully explained.

To be awarded 3 marks on criterion D, you need to do the following.

- Choose a different key concept for each commentary.
- Choose a key concept that can be applied to the issue(s) discussed in the article. If the link to the article is superficial, it is likely that only 1 mark will be awarded. Consider the "Concept link" suggestions in Units 2, 3 and 4.
- Make explicit references to the key concept in your commentary. It is advisable to write the key concept in bold type whenever you mention it. This will remind the assessor that you have applied the key concept. Note that the key concept should not be mentioned just once in the introduction and/or once in the conclusion. The link to the article must be **fully explained**, not briefly mentioned. That is why when choosing an article, you must make sure there is an appropriate key concept to use that hasn't yet been used.

Criterion E: Evaluation

This criterion assesses the extent to which your judgments are supported by reasoned argument.

Marks	Descriptor
0	The work does not reach a standard described by the descriptors below.
1	Judgments are made that are supported by limited reasoning.
2	Judgments are made that are supported by appropriate reasoning.
3	Judgments are made that are supported by effective and balanced reasoning.

Evaluation is demonstrated when you reach judgments based on economic analysis and the information provided in the article. Some ways to demonstrate evaluation follow.

- Establish the most and least likely causes or consequences of an economic problem. For example, inflation may lead to a loss in export competitiveness and greater inequality. Is there evidence in the article that the country is reliant on exports or that the distribution of income is highly unequal? Then you could establish the *most serious consequence* of inflation for the country under study. Phrases such as "the *most effective* policy ..." or "*the weakest argument* in favour of ..." are helpful in introducing evaluative statements.
- Distinguish between the short-term and long-term benefits and/or costs of policies. For instance, stricter environmental protection laws introduced in Papua New Guinea may reduce the profitability of firms engaged in mining activities. This may lead to a *short-term cost* to the economy as fewer MNCs invest in Papua New Guinea, but the policy comes with a *long-term benefit* as the laws reduce the threat to sustainability.
- Discuss the validity of the author's arguments, using economic rationale. The author might not have considered all perspectives on the economic issue(s) discussed.
- Establish the limitations of economic theory in the context of the article. Many economic concepts and models come with assumptions that may not hold. For instance, trade protection may not be effective in protecting domestic producers if consumers do not see imports and local products as close substitutes.
- Discuss the likely effectiveness of policies or strategies. For example, would expansionary monetary policy be effective in boosting consumers' and firms' spending if the article suggests poor business and consumer confidence?

To be awarded 3 marks on criterion E, judgments must be as follows.

- **Your own**—the article's author might give a personal opinion and summarizing it is not evaluation (but finding flaws in the author's economic reasoning is clearly good evaluation).
- **Supported**—it is not sufficient to state that reduced export competitiveness is the biggest threat from inflation. Why is export competitiveness so important in this case? Similarly, stating that green taxes come with a short-term cost must also be supported. What is the cost and what is the *short-term* impact?

Judgments must be supported by **effective and balanced reasoning**. Your reasoning is effective if it is based on two components: information from the text—for example, you might say that reduced export competitiveness is the biggest threat from inflation *since the article states that* 20% of workers are employed in export industries; and economic theory—for instance, you can logically deduce that the loss of jobs in export industries might lead to structural unemployment. Balanced reasoning implies that all relevant information and perspectives are considered. For example, ignoring a statement that the country's inflation is at very nearly the same level as inflation in other economies would reduce the validity of the claim that inflation is a threat to export competitiveness.

Criterion F: Rubric requirements

Under this criterion, 3 marks are awarded for meeting the following requirements for your commentaries.

- Each article is based on a different unit of the syllabus.
- Each article is taken from a different and appropriate source.
- Each article was published no earlier than one year before the writing of the commentary.

Marks	Descriptor
0	The work does not reach a standard described by the descriptors below.
1	One rubric requirement is met.
2	Two rubric requirements are met.
3	Three rubric requirements are met.

8.3 THE IA CHECKLIST

Use this list to check that your commentaries have all the elements required for the highest scores.

Item	Check?
Article selection	
The article was published less than a year ago.	☐
The article is taken from an appropriate source (e.g. not a blog or Facebook page) and the source was not used for any other commentaries.	☐
The article illustrates economic theory learned in Unit 2, 3 or 4.	☐
The article allows for a clear link to one key concept (which has not been used for any other commentaries).	☐
The relevant sections of the article are highlighted.	☐
Cover page	
The cover page indicates the sequence of the commentary in the portfolio (that is, commentary 1, commentary 2 or commentary 3).	☐
The cover page states the title of the article.	☐
The cover page states the source of the article.	☐
The cover page states the date the article was published.	☐
The cover page states the date the commentary was written.	☐
The cover page states the word count of the commentary.	☐
The cover page states the unit of the syllabus.	☐
The cover page states the key concept.	☐
Commentary	
The diagrams are fully labelled (axes and curves) and the labels are correct.	☐
All labels on diagrams meet the 5-word limit and diagram headings meet the 10-word limit. Labels and headings that exceed these word limits are included in the word count.	☐
The diagrams are fully explained and references are made to them in the commentary.	☐
The diagrams are adapted to the context of the article where possible (e.g. they have customized labels).	☐
The commentary focuses on the issues or policies mentioned in the article and these are explained using economic theory.	☐
Relevant economic terms are used throughout the analysis.	☐
The key concept was not used in other commentaries.	☐
The link to the key concept is explained.	☐
The key concept is written in bold type every time it is mentioned in the commentary.	☐
Judgments are supported by information from the article and economic theory.	☐
Portfolio	
Each article is based on a different unit of the syllabus.	☐
Each article is taken from a different and appropriate source.	☐
Each article was published no earlier than one year before the writing of the commentary.	☐
All files are in PDF format.	☐

8.4 SAMPLE IA COMMENTARY 1

Cover page

Commentary number	1
Title of the article	Indonesia parliament tells government to tax a wider range of plastic products
Source of the article	https://www.reuters.com/article/us-indonesia-economy-tax-idUSKBN20D0DH
Date of publication	19 February 2020
Date the commentary was written	15 May 2021
Number of words	692
Section of the syllabus (Unit)	Unit 2: Microeconomics
Key concept	Economic well-being

▼ The article is too old. The commentary was written more than a year after the article was published so the portfolio will not achieve 3 marks on criterion F.

▲ The candidate has highlighted the sections of the article relevant to the commentary.

Article

Indonesia parliament tells government to tax a wider range of plastic products

JAKARTA (Reuters) - Indonesia's parliament on Wednesday told the government to tax a wider range of plastic products than it had proposed, but held off on the administration's plans to levy sweet drinks and polluting vehicles.

The government had at first proposed to impose excise taxes on plastic bags, sweetened beverages and vehicles that emit carbon dioxide, to discourage their use, cut waste and reduce pollution in Southeast Asia's largest economy.

The government proposal came amid weak tax collection after the economy grew at its slowest pace in three years in 2019. Indonesia had a nearly $15 billion revenue shortfall last year due to weak company profits and falling exports.

Finance Minister Sri Mulyani Indrawati said after the parliamentary hearing that she would have to redesign her policy, as lawmakers' approval was for duties on a wider range of products than originally asked for.

The Indonesian Olefin, Aromatic and Plastic Industry Association rejected parliament's move, with its secretary general, Fajar Budiyono, suggesting the government should apply duties only on imported plastic goods.

"It will be very difficult to apply excise on end products made of plastic . . . Too many small players," Budiyono said, adding that he predicted smuggling of plastic products would increase.

Indrawati had also asked to levy taxes ranging from 1,500 rupiah to 2,500 rupiah ($0.11 to $0.18) per litre on sweetened beverages to control the rise of diabetes and obesity levels, which have steadily increased in Indonesia over the past decade.

Some 2% of Indonesians aged 15 and above suffered from diabetes in 2018, up from 1.1% in 2007, while the number of obese adults rose from 10.5% in 2007 to 21.8% in 2018.

Another proposal was to impose duties on new vehicles that emit carbon dioxide as part of efforts to control pollution.

Parliament wants the finance minister to provide further explanation of the plans to implement excise taxes on sweet drinks and vehicles, said Dito Ganinduto, chairman of parliament's finance commission.

The total additional revenue expected from Indrawati's original proposal per fiscal year was 23.56 trillion rupiah ($1.72 billion).

https://www.reuters.com/article/us-indonesia-economy-tax-idUSKBN20D0DH

Commentary

This article recounts the effort of the Indonesian government to fight the rise in the rates of obesity and diabetes, as well as pollution in Indonesia. A series of taxes were proposed to reduce the use of plastic bags, polluting vehicles and consumption of sugar. The article also points out the Indonesian economy grew at its slowest pace in three years and that tax revenue has fallen.

The Indonesian government deems consumption of sweet drinks undesirable due to the negative effects of the excessive consumption has on health, which can cause diseases such as diabetes and obesity.

The consumption of sweet drinks generates negative externalities such as added burden on a country's healthcare system, resulting market failure as resources are overallocated to the market for sweet drinks. To mitigate this, Indonesia has adopted taxes on sweet drinks.

Negative externalities refer to costs borne by third parties who are not involved in the consumption of production activity, for which there is no compensation. Market failure is defined as failure of the market to achieve efficiency in the allocation of society's resources, resulting in an over-allocation or under-allocation of resources in the absence of government intervention.

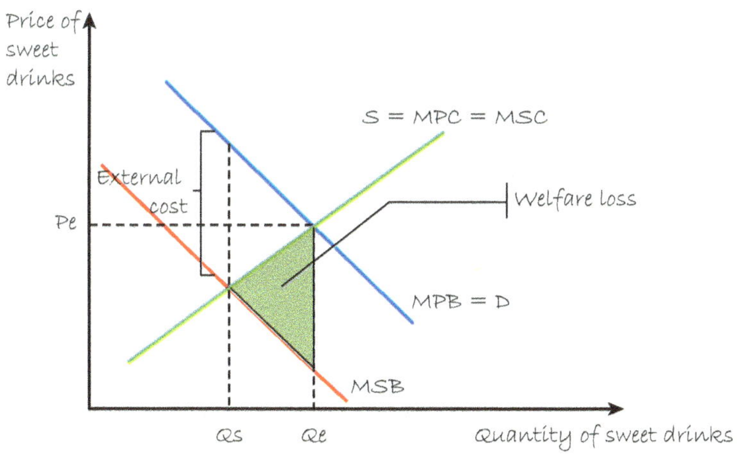

Figure 1

With reference to Figure 1, those who consume sweet drinks tend to consider only private benefit and not take into account negative externalities, which include effects such as pressure on the national healthcare system due to "prevalence of diabetes and obesity levels". Because of this, the marginal social benefit (MSB) is less than the marginal private benefit (MPB).
The analysis that follows assumes no externalities generated from the production of sweet drinks, thus marginal private cost (MPC) equals marginal social cost (MSC). Without government intervention, the diagram shows that

▼ The candidate summarizes the article, which is unnecessary since the assessor must read the article, or at least the highlighted sections. As neither economic analysis nor economic terms are applied, this paragraph does not contribute to any of the A–E criteria.

▼ The candidate should have used the term "demerit good" here.

▲ The candidate makes good use of terms to establish the economic issue discussed in the article.

▼ The tax on sweet drinks was proposed but not implemented. It is the tax on plastic that was implemented. The commentary should reflect the exact contents of the article to achieve 3 marks on criterion C.

▼ Definitions do not contribute to marks on criterion B. There is limited value in defining negative externalities and market failure here. The definition of externalities might have been more adequate as part of the analysis in the next paragraph.

▼ The diagram is correct but not fully explained. What is the difference between MPB and MSB? What is the socially optimal quantity and what is the market quantity on the diagram? Hardly any reference is made to the diagram and this would affect the mark awarded on criterion A.

▼ The candidate refers to "overproduction" when this is a case of negatively externality from consumption. The correct economic term is "overconsumption".

▲ The welfare loss is correctly identified and explained.

▲ There is good use of information (data) from the article. This diagram is better explained than the previous diagram with effective references to the annotations made.

▼ However, the candidate continues to state that the tax was imposed when it was only proposed.

the socially optimal quantity is less than the market quantity, resulting in overproduction.

This overproduction results in social costs being greater than social benefits, causing a welfare loss, as represented by the shaded area in the graph. This results in social inefficiency and market failure, as scarce resources are being over-allocated to producing sweet drinks.

To reduce market failure by reducing consumption of sweet drinks, the Indonesian government has imposed a "levy excise taxes of 1,500 rupiah to 2,500 rupiah (US$0.11–US$0.18) per litre on sugar- and artificial sugar-sweetened beverages". Ideally, this tax would be equal to the external cost, shifting the MPC curve upward to the MPC + tax curve, as shown in Figure 2. This causes the price per unit of sweet drink to increase from Pe to Pe1, thereby reducing quantity demanded from Qe to Qs, the socially optimal level.

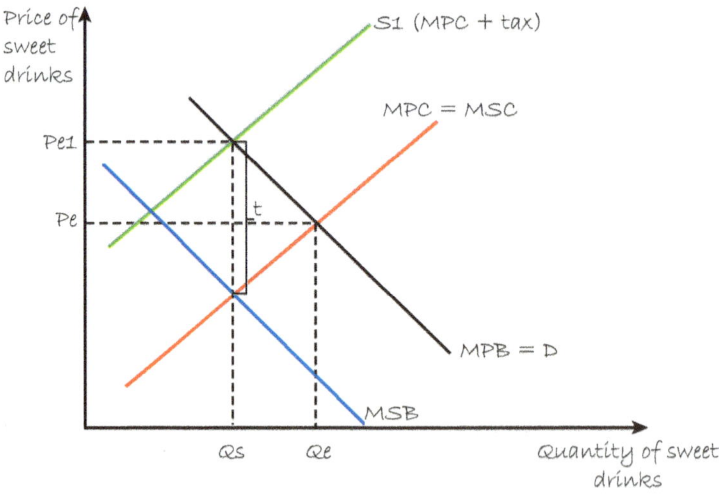

Figure 2

▼ This judgment is not supported. Why will it help in the short term?

The immediate increase in price would likely discourage consumption in the short term.

▲ The candidate establishes a link to the key concept, which is written in bold to attract the assessor's attention.

▼ The key concept is mentioned late in the commentary and the link superficial. Is economic well-being only about health?

It is a good policy because it will improve the health of the people in Indonesia and hence improve their **economic well-being**. The government can utilise the tax revenue generated for on medical services, especially if pre-existent impacts of heavy consumption of sweet drinks have placed a strain on the healthcare system. Tax revenue can also be used to support funding for information provision to advocate against high consumption of sugar, such as low-sugar drink campaigns in schools.

▼ The difficulty in establishing the amount of the tax is a theoretical judgment but the notion that it could cause damage to firms is supported by the article. However, there is no evidence that the producers of sweet drinks are exporters. The argument would have been more effective had it considered the tax on plastic, as production of many goods uses plastic.

However, there are also disadvantages. It would be difficult for the government to measure the marginal external cost and set the tax at exactly the correct value. Should the tax be too light, overproduction would still occur. Should the tax be too hefty, underproduction would occur. This would be particularly harmful in Indonesia, which has already been experiencing "weak company profits and falling exports".

In conclusion, a reduction in consumption cannot be accomplished through a tax alone. Though an increased price in sweet drinks may help to reduce consumption in the short run, Indonesia's heavy entrenchment in the culture of consuming sweet drinks may cause citizens to adapt to the higher prices in the long run and still consume the initial quantity. The increase in prices may merely hurt the purchasing power of individuals.

▼ The conclusion makes an interesting point but the article does not suggest it. The candidate could explain this point with some economic terminology. It seems that the suggestion is that demand is price inelastic. The observation that the higher prices would affect purchasing power was another opportunity to link to the key concept.

Marks awarded

Criterion	Mark	Justification
A	2	The diagrams are fully and correctly labelled but not always fully explained. In particular, the first diagram was hardly explained. More effective referencing, especially for Figure 1, would likely see the grade increase to 3 marks.
B	1	Relevant economic terms were used in the commentary, but some terms were missing (e.g. "demerit goods") or used incorrectly (e.g. "overproduction").
C	2	There is valid analysis that relates to the article, but the analysis is not always effective. The tax on sweet drinks was only proposed but the commentary suggest it was implemented. On the other hand, the tax on plastic, which is mentioned multiple times in the article, is not considered in the commentary.
D	2	A link to the key concept is established but it is rather superficial. There are a lot of dimensions to economic well-being. Considering the impact of the tax on plastic on producers of affected products, and the risk of informal employment (smuggling is mentioned in the article, would have allowed for a fuller discussion).
E	1	Judgments are not always supported or they are supported by limited reasoning (e.g. theoretical arguments). The article has scope for effective evaluation, especially in considering the difficulties in implementing the tax on plastic. There is also a mention of parallel markets that could affect the effectiveness of the tax.
TOTAL	**8**	

As the article is more than a year old, the portfolio will be awarded a maximum of 2 marks on criterion F.

8.5 SAMPLE IA COMMENTARY 2

Cover page

Commentary number	**2**
Title of the article	New Zealand unveils $8,600 subsidy for electric vehicles to reduce emissions
Source of the article	https://www.theguardian.com/environment/2021/jun/14/new-zealand-unveils-8600-subsidy-for-electric-vehicles-to-reduce-emissions
Date of publication	14 June 2021
Date the commentary was written	02 March 2022
Number of words	789
Section of the syllabus (Unit)	Unit 2: Microeconomics
Key concept	Intervention

Article

New Zealand unveils $8,600 subsidy for electric vehicles to reduce emissions

The New Zealand government is introducing subsidies to make electric vehicles thousands of dollars cheaper and new petrol and diesel cars more expensive, as the country tries transition to an emissions-free fleet.

▲ The candidate has highlighted the sections of the article relevant to the commentary.

The changes follow New Zealand's Climate Commission recommendations which laid out sweeping changes required to get the country closer to its emissions targets.

The subsidies for electric and some hybrid vehicles would be up to NZ$8,625 (£4,360) for new vehicles and NZ$3,450 (£1,744) for used cars. They will start next month.

Transport now makes up almost 33% of long-lived greenhouse gas emissions in Aotearoa, and last week, the Climate Commission laid out new benchmarks for the country to transform the makeup of its fleet. The commission's recommended plan included banning imports of petrol and diesel cars by 2032, and that road transport be almost completely decarbonised by 2050. To meet its goal for transport emissions, the commission concluded electric vehicles would need to make up half of all light vehicle registrations by 2029, and 100% by 2035.

"Our transport emissions are the fastest growing source of greenhouse gas emissions in New Zealand, so we need to start taking action now if we are going to meet our 2050 targets," transport minister Michael Wood said in a written statement.

"New Zealand is actually lagging behind on the uptake of EVs, so we are playing catch up internationally," he said. He said the policy would prevent up to an estimated 9.2m tonnes of carbon dioxide emissions.

The subsidies would be funded by introducing new charges on imports of high-emission utility vehicles and SUVs. For example, an imported Toyota Hilux – one of New Zealand's more popular utes – could incur a fee of NZ$2,900. Those fees would kick in at the start of January 2022.

New Zealand is one of the world's worst performers on emission increases, and hitting its climate goals will require a reversal of its current trajectory. The country's emissions rose by 57% between 1990 and 2018 – the second greatest increase of all industrialised countries. Earlier this year, data showed that New Zealand's emissions had increased by 2% in 2018–19.

Climate change minister James Shaw said that at present, low emissions vehicles were financially out of the reach of many New Zealanders.

"As technology develops and more manufacturers decide to stop making petrol and diesel cars, the cost of low emissions vehicles will come down. However at the moment they are still more expensive to buy. Today's announcement helps to address that," he said.

The policy has sparked some criticism. Centre-right opposition party National said tying the rebates to fees on higher-emissions vehicles meant it amounted to a "reverse Robin Hood" strategy – imposing fees on lower and middle-income New Zealanders while subsidising those wealthy enough to afford a new electric vehicle. The policy would "unfairly hurt farmers, tradespeople and low-income earners for whom low-emission vehicles will still be too expensive or unsuitable for their lifestyle," said shadow transport spokesperson Michael Woodhouse.

Woodhouse said National supported incentives for people to buy EVs but disagreed with financially punishing those who didn't.

Wood said that the policy "only applies to new and used cars arriving in New Zealand, so the existing secondhand market of cars that lower income families tend to purchase from will not be affected".

Shaw said the policy "will also stimulate the second-hand market, so in the years to come even more people can access low carbon transport options".

Many other nations already have subsidies for electric vehicles. Germany introduced a €4,000 (NZ$6,785) subsidy for electric vehicles back in 2016. Slightly less-generous subsidies exist in the UK, where buyers can get a grant for an electric cars of £2,500 (nearly NZ$5,000) – reduced from £3,000 in March.

Other countries have taken more radical steps. In Norway, electric cars now make up 54% of market share, after the country exempted fully electric vehicles from taxes imposed on those relying on fossil fuels. That move made new electric models cheaper than some comparable petrol cars for Norwegians.

https://www.theguardian.com/environment/2021/jun/14/new-zealand-unveils-8600-subsidy-for-electric-vehicles-to-reduce-emissions

Commentary

Electric vehicles (EVs) are substitutes for conventional cars, which will be referred to as high-emission vehicles. While EVs contribute as much to traffic congestion as high-emission vehicles, they help to reduce greenhouse gas emissions and hence reduce some of the costs incurred to society from the use of high-emission vehicles such as air pollution and global warming. High-emission vehicles also generate additional costs to those who may have to deal with health impacts from pollution due to the excessive greenhouse gas emissions. Hence, the use of high-emission vehicles brings about negative externalities. They impose costs on third parties such as those who suffer from poor health due to pollution and the future generations as global warming reduces results in the loss of biodiversity. Moreover, "New Zealand is one of the world's worst performers on emission increases", implying that the external costs are rapidly increasing as the country's emissions rose by 57% between 1990 and 2018 – the second greatest increase of all industrialised countries". The threat to sustainability is a global concern, international cooperation is needed, and New Zealand must do its part. Vehicle markets will to be regulated hence the **intervention** through subsidies for electric vehicles and higher tax on some high-polluting vehicles.

▲ The candidate has introduced the economic issue presented in the article (threat to sustainability) which is explained using economic concepts from Unit 2. The key concept is also introduced and linked to the article.

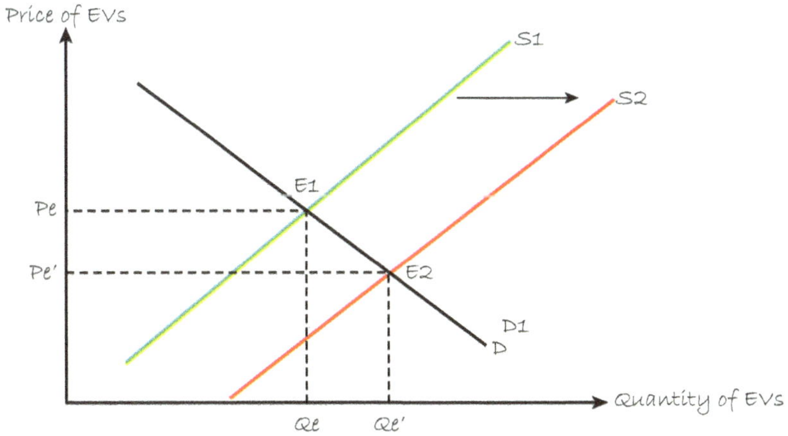

▲ Figure 1 Effect of a subsidy on EVs

▲ The diagram is fully and correctly labelled. The labels for axes are customized to the relevant market.

▲ The candidate makes effective references to the diagram to explain it. Evaluation is also evident through acknowledgment of the limitations of the analysis (that there is no consideration of externalities from EVs).

The subsidy on EVs decreases the costs of production, hence the supply curve shifts downwards and increases as shown by the new supply curve, S2 on Figure 1. The subsidy results in a new equilibrium at E2 and a reduction in price by NZ$8,625 for new vehicles from Pe to Pe', which incentivizes consumers to increase the consumption of EVs, resulting in the quantity demanded moving to Qe'. This analysis does not consider the third-party impact of EVs (such as traffic congestion) or the impact of the production of their batteries on the environment. This analysis is limited to the impact of lower prices of a substitute to high-emission vehicles.

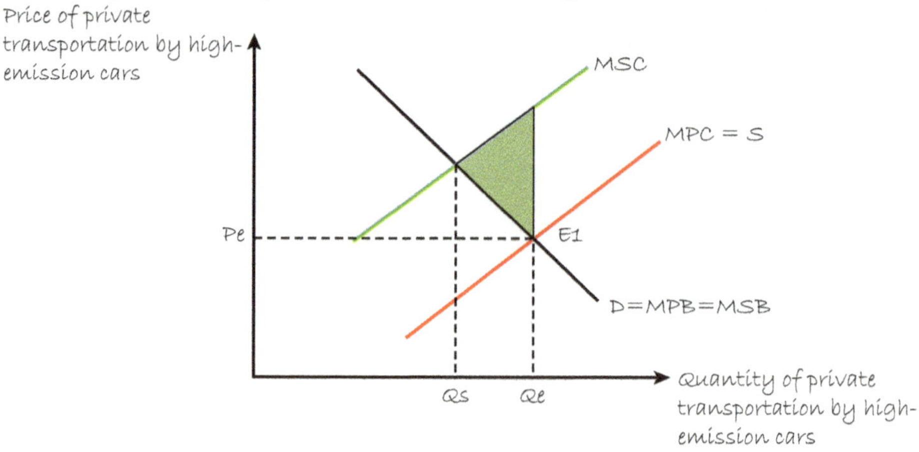

▲ **Figure 2** The market for private transportation by high-emission cars

▲ The diagram is fully and correctly labelled. The labels are customized, where applicable. (Note that the labels for each axis exceed five words so they must be included in the word count.)

Figure 2 illustrates the market for private transportation by high-emission cars before **intervention**. By driving high-emission cars, drivers incur costs on third parties. The Marginal Social Cost (MSC) is thus greater than the Marginal Private Cost (MPC). However, the market only considers private costs and benefits and will settle at E1 (Pe, Qe). At Qe, there is allocative inefficiency since MSC > MSB, and private transportation is overproduced in relation to the socially optimum amount (Qs). This suggests an over-allocation of resources in the production of private transportation by high-emission cars, resulting in market failure and hence a welfare loss (shaded area). To achieve Qs, the New Zealand government opted for **intervention** through the subsidy of NZ$8,625 and NZ$3,450 for new and used EVs respectively and taxes on the most polluting cars (SUVs).

▲ The analysis remains focused on the context set in the article. The second diagram is explained. The candidate has also made effective use of information from the article (the price of EVs).

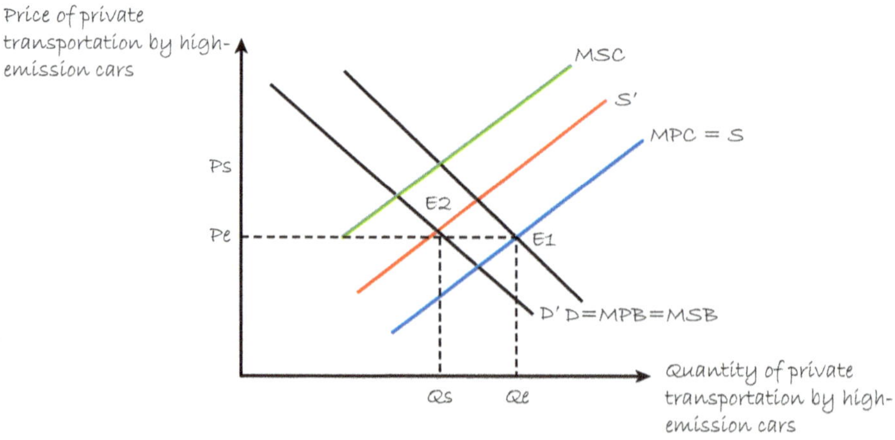

▲ **Figure 3** Impact of intervention

▲ The diagram is fully and correctly labelled. The labels were customized, where applicable. (Note that the labels for the axes will count to the word count as they exceed the five-word limit.)

In the market for high-emission vehicles, the EV subsidy leads to a change in a non-price determinant of demand. The demand for private transportation by high-emission cars decreases from D to D' on figure 3, due to the lower price of a substitute – EVs. The supply also decreases, from S to S', due to the higher tax (for SUVs). The market for high-emission cars will settle at E2 where D' = S'. At this new equilibrium, Qs is reached, and the welfare loss is eliminated. Although it is unlikely that **intervention** is precise enough to reach E2. The change in prices due to subsidies and taxes create incentives to consumers but their impacts are hard to estimate. Consumers also need time to react, especially in the short-term as cars are long time commitments and it is likely that residents who recently purchased a vehicle will take time to react to the lower-priced EVs. That may be why the New Zealand authorities set a long-term target "to meet its goal for transport emissions... by 2035".

▲ The analysis continues to be anchored on the contents of the article. There is apt use of information from the article (the long-term target). Evaluation is evident in the form of consideration of limitation and effectiveness of **intervention** (which is also the key concept).

While governments may struggle to fund the subsidies, the imposition of an indirect tax simultaneously on high-emission vehicles helps generate revenue to fund the subsidy. This ensures that the **intervention** does not incur an opportunity cost as the government does not need to forgo expenditure elsewhere. Furthermore, over time, there will also be more second-hand EVs which are more affordable options. More importantly, with improvements in technology, firms can increase the supply of EVs in the market and eventually decrease the price of EVs. This can help to reduce the need for a subsidy since a subsidy is not a sustainable policy. With a gradual increase in the supply of EVs, the price of EVs for consumers will reduce, resulting in an increase in consumption and achieving the target set by the government to have all cars being EVs in 2050.

▲ The candidate formulates some judgments that are supported by economic theory and the contents of the article.

Marks awarded

Criterion	Mark	Justification
A	3	The diagrams are fully and correctly labelled. They are also fully explained.
B	2	Relevant economic terms (e.g. "substitutes", "non-price determinant of demand", "market failure") are used throughout the commentary.
C	3	There is valid analysis that relates to the article—every paragraph contains economic analysis that is based on the contents of the article.
D	3	A link to the key concept is established and many attempts are made to bring the key concept into the analysis as well as the evaluation.
E	3	Judgments are made and supported both by the article and economic analysis.
Total	**14**	

9 PRACTICE EXAMINATION PAPERS

By this point, you will have refreshed your understanding of the content from the four units of the IB economics syllabus. Additionally, you will have picked up some key techniques and skills to refine your examination skills. It is now time to put these skills to the test; in this unit you will find original examination questions for each paper. After you have written your answers, you can check them using the mark schemes that are available at www.oxfordsecondary.com/ib-prepared-support.

9.1 PAPER 1

This sub-unit presents two sample paper 1 examinations. The first sample paper tests common SL and HL topics. The second sample paper focuses on HL extension topics. However, HL papers may also test common SL and HL content.

Instructions

- Duration: 1 hour 15 minutes
- You are not permitted access to a calculator for this paper.
- Answer *one* question.
- Use fully labelled diagrams where appropriate.
- The maximum mark for this examination paper is **[25 marks]**.

Sample paper 1 (SL and HL)

1 (a) Explain **two** reasons why governments might intervene in agricultural markets. [10]

(b) Using real-world examples, examine the consequences of price controls in agricultural markets. [15]

2 (a) Explain two government policies which might cause economic inequality and poverty in an economy. [10]

(b) Using real-world examples, evaluate the view that government policies which aim to achieve a more equal distribution of income will inevitably lead to a slower rate of economic growth. [15]

3 (a) Explain how gender inequality and the prevalence of informal activities are barriers to economic development in economically least developed countries (ELDCs). [10]

(b) Using real-world examples, discuss the impact of an openness to foreign direct investment (FDI) on economic development in economically least developed countries (ELDCs). [15]

Sample paper 1 (HL)

1 (a) Explain how a natural monopoly may arise. [10]

(b) Using real-world examples, evaluate the view that industries with a large number of small firms are more desirable than industries dominated by a few large firms. [15]

2 (a) Using the concept of the multiplier, explain how an increase in government spending might affect aggregate demand. [10]

(b) Using real-world examples, evaluate the view that there is always a trade-off between inflation and unemployment. [15]

3 (a) Explain how membership to a preferential trading bloc may lead to trade diversion. [10]

(b) Using real-world examples, evaluate the view that membership to a trading bloc will create winners but also losers. [15]

9.2 PAPER 2

Instructions

- Duration: 1 hour 45 minutes
- You are permitted access to a calculator for this paper.
- Answer _one_ question.
- Unless otherwise stated in the question, all numerical answers must be given exactly or correct to two decimal places.
- You must show all your working.
- Use fully labelled diagrams and references to the text/data where appropriate.
- The maximum mark for this examination paper is **[40 marks]**.

Sample paper 2 (SL and HL)

1. Read the extracts and answer the questions that follow.

Text A: An overview of Australia

1. Australia is a large country in terms of land area but its population size of 25.7 million makes it a relatively small market. An open economy with minimal trade protection on imports of goods and services, Australia has signed free trade agreements (FTAs) with multiple countries in Asia, New Zealand and the USA.
2. The country's openness to trade has kept Australian firms competitive, increasing productivity and keeping inflation low. The majority of Australia's imports are manufactured goods from low wage countries. This has resulted in job losses in manufacturing, especially in textile, clothing, footwear and leather manufacturing industries.
3. Australia's abundant natural resources attract high levels of **foreign direct investment (FDI)**. The significant revenue from the exports of minerals, metals, energy and food have allowed for two decades of high economic growth.
4. However, economic activity slowed considerably in 2018. A sharp fall in commodity prices and slower economic growth in Asia reduced export revenue significantly. Political tensions with China, the world's largest consumer market, had a significant impact on the economy. The value of the Australian dollar decreased by 9.85% against the US dollar in 2018.
5. Although Australia and China signed an FTA in 2015, the two nations have engaged in a trade war since 2019. Despite being members of an FTA with Australia, China imposed tariffs on imports from Australia, in particular beef, barley, coal, cotton, seafood and wine. Iron ore, a major Australian export and a critical input for China's massive steel sector, has been spared.
6. Australian wine producers were most affected by the trade sanctions as China imposed high tariffs on Australian wine following allegation of dumping. Sales to China represented 39% of the total export value of Australian wine in 2020, followed by the USA (15%) and the UK (13%).

Text B: Greater economic integration with India and the UK

1. Australia signed two trade agreements in 2022, one with India and the other with the UK. They will result in the removal of tariffs on more than $17 billion worth of Australian exports to the two nations. Some tariffs will be removed immediately while others will be progressively removed over 10 years. In return, Australia will remove tariffs on almost all imports from India and the UK.
2. Australian agricultural producers are especially anxious to gain greater market access to India, the world's second most populous nation, in light of increased trade protection by China. Exports of Australian wines to India, however, will be subject to a reduced tariff of 75% instead of the current rate of 150%. This tariff will be reduced to 25% over 10 years. The agreement with the UK will result in the immediate elimination of UK tariffs on wine.

3. The Australian government will also issue more visas for young people from India and the UK to participate in working holidays. It is hoped that this scheme will not only provide Australian businesses with a source of short-term workers but also boost the tourism industry, which suffered from a decline in demand in recent years.

4. The agreements will also ease labour market rigidities by making it easier for businesses to hire skilled workers from the three countries. Australia will especially facilitate the employment of Indian and UK workers in high value industries such as research and development, artificial intelligence, renewable energy and engineering. Australian trade unions are concerned the FTAs may result in **structural unemployment**.

Text C: Australia's commitment to reduced carbon emissions

1. Australia, the world's top coal and a major gas exporter, has been criticized for having one of the biggest carbon emissions per capita. Following the 2021 United Nations Climate Change Conference, Australia set a target of net zero carbon emissions by 2050 but activists say that date is too distant.

2. The Australian authorities had initially declined to join the multilateral pledge to curb fossil fuels, which account for a major part of Australia's export revenue. Mining and agricultural industries, which are the main contributors of carbon emissions, are a main source of jobs in rural areas.

3. However, Australia faced the threat of higher tariffs on its exports if it did not agree to commit to the reduction in emissions. The EU had planned to charge EU-based businesses that import Australian carbon-intensive products such as cement, iron, steel, aluminium and fertilizer.

▼ **Table 1** Selected national income data, Australia

	2017	2018	2019
Nominal GDP (US$ billion)	1,330	1,430	1,390
GDP deflator	112.22	114.29	118.19

(a) (i) Define the term *foreign direct investment (FDI)* indicated in bold in the text (**Text A**, paragraph 3). [2]

(ii) Define the term *structural unemployment* indicated in bold in the text (**Text B**, paragraph 4). [2]

(b) (i) Using the information in **Table 1**, calculate the economic growth rate in Australia in 2018. [3]

(ii) Illustrate the impact of the change in FDI inflows on Australia's production possibilities on a PPC diagram (**Text A**, paragraph 3). [2]

(c) Using an exchange rate diagram, explain the change in the value of the Australian dollar in 2018 (**Text A**, paragraph 4). [4]

(d) Using an international trade diagram, explain the change in the revenue of Australian wine producers as a result of trade sanctions from China (**Text A**, paragraph 6). [4]

(e) Using an AD/AS diagram, explain the likely impact of the working holiday scheme on Australia's real output (**Text B**, paragraph 3). [4]

(f) Using an externalities diagram, explain why the market for steel might be a source of market failure (**Text C**, paragraph 3). [4]

(g) Using information from the text/data and your knowledge of economics, evaluate the economic consequences of Australia's openness to trade. [15]

2. Read the extracts and answer the questions that follow.

Text D: An overview of Indonesia

1. Indonesia is the largest economy in Southeast Asia. High rates of economic growth have allowed for a reduction in the number of people living below the international poverty line, which the World Bank sets at $1.90 (PPP) a day. However, one fifth of Indonesia's population still lives on $3.20 (PPP) or less a day, an additional poverty line set by the World Bank for lower–middle income countries.
2. One source of poverty is the quality of **human capital**. While most Indonesians have access to basic primary education, the quality of education varies significantly across provinces. Enrolment in vocational education programmes is low, particularly among women. The low participation rate of women in the labour force and a gender wage gap have prevented households from breaking the poverty trap.
3. Access to essential health services remains limited in rural areas because of a shortage of qualified workers, healthcare infrastructure and medical supplies. However, Indonesia achieved notable success in reducing the child stunting rate from 37% in 2013 to under 24.4% in 2021. Stunting is associated with improper nutrition in children and affects their future work productivity.
4. High reliance on mining and agricultural exports makes the economy vulnerable to supply shocks and price fluctuations. Export revenues of agricultural crops such as palm oil tend to decrease with good harvests. Manufacturing exports have remained competitive thanks to Indonesia's low labour costs.
5. The government introduced a ban on the export of unprocessed minerals in January 2014 to diversify economic activities. The aim of the ban is to force mining companies to build domestic processing plants and export processed minerals that fetch higher prices. The ban on the export of unprocessed nickel, which is used in the production of stainless steel and batteries for electric vehicles, was successful in attracting Chinese foreign direct investment (FDI).

Text E: An overview of Thailand

1. Thailand, a country in Southeast Asia, has enjoyed four decades of economic growth, which has pulled millions of people out of poverty. Public investments have brought universal access to primary school education, child nutritional health and a national healthcare programme for all Thais. However, social assistance schemes are unevenly accessible between urban and rural areas. Ethnic tensions have led to some instability in the southern part of Thailand, where conflicts have claimed 6,000 lives since 2004.
2. Thailand's ageing population will also put a strain on government finances through rising public pension and healthcare costs. In 2018, the number of elderly persons exceeded the number of youths for the first time. This will result in a continuous reduction in the labour force.
3. The growth prospects from **export promotion** that financed much of Thailand's economic development seem to have diminished significantly, owing to a stagnation in productivity. Private investment declined from more than 40% in 1997 to 16.9% of GDP in 2019. FDI inflows have also stagnated.
4. The manufacturing sector faces increasing competition from regional neighbours. Travel and tourism, the country's main service industries, present relatively few diversification prospects when compared to the rest of the service sector.
5. Greenhouse gas emissions have risen markedly with Thailand's rapid economic growth. In July 2021, a fire at a chemical factory producing polystyrene foam in the outskirts of Bangkok, the capital of Thailand, forced nearby residents to evacuate their homes for a week. It is feared that the incident caused air and water contamination, which may have severe effects on health. The accident underscored the need for better safety regulations and urban planning in Thailand. Thailand is also a major marine plastic polluter on land, in river systems and along coastlines.

Text F: Development policies in Indonesia and Thailand

1. The Indonesian government is working with the World Bank on a programme to bring health and nutrition services to millions of pregnant women and children across the country. In addition, the programme provides women with basic financial management skills. The World Bank is also helping to improve the quality of education in Indonesia's remote areas and supports efforts to reduce deforestation.
2. To facilitate sectoral transformation from agricultural to manufacturing activities, the Indonesian authorities are helping micro, small and medium-sized enterprises to gain access to finance.
3. The World Bank is also supporting peacebuilding efforts in Thailand's south and assists Thai industries to reduce the use of unsustainable technologies. The government has also established training programmes that equip workers with the skills needed by industries. Moreover, tax benefits are granted to firms that invest in research and development.
4. The government of Thailand has imposed a minimum wage of 313 Thai baht (about US$9.20) per day and has designated standardized pay for 83 specific professions. This has allowed those who have passed standardized tests for each profession to receive between 345 and 825 Thai baht (US$10.20–24.40) per day. Thailand also issues multiple scholarships to students to help them enter the workforce with adequate skills.

Table 2 Selected national income data for Indonesia and Thailand

	Indonesia		Thailand	
	2000	**2019**	**2000**	**2019**
GNI per capita, purchasing power parity (PPP) (current international $)	4,430	11,940	7,160	18,530
Gini coefficient	0.29	0.37	0.43	0.35
Population living $1.90 (PPP) a day (% of population)	34.9	2.7	2.4	0.1
Population living $3.20 (PPP) a day (% of population)	77.2	19.9	18.3	0.3
Population (million)	211.51	270.63	62.95	69.63
Population growth (%)	1.38	1.10	1.04	0.28
Urban population growth (%)	4.30	2.29	2.40	1.76
Life expectancy at birth (years)	66	72	70	77
Expenditure on education, public (% of government expenditure)	11.59*	20	28.34	14.49
Expenditure on health, public (% of government expenditure)	3.59	8.68	12.67	13.87

*2001 data

Table 3 Current account data for Indonesia and Thailand (2019)

	Indonesia	Thailand
Exports of goods and services (current US$, billion)	206.43	323.77
Imports of goods and services (current US$, billion)	212.66	272.92
Net income (current US$, billion)	−34.02	−20.05
Net current transfers (current US$, billion)	7.63	7.2

(a) (i) Define the term *human capital* indicated in bold in the text (**Text D**, paragraph 2). [2]

(ii) Define the term *export promotion* indicated in bold in the text (**Text E**, paragraph 3). [2]

(b) (i) Using the information in **Table 2**, sketch a Lorenz curve diagram to illustrate the change in the income distribution of Indonesia between 2000 and 2019. [2]

(ii) Using the information in **Table 3**, calculate the current account balance in Indonesia and Thailand in 2019. [3]

(c) Using an exchange rate diagram and your answer to b (ii), explain the likely impact of Thailand's current account balance on the exchange rate for the Thai baht. [4]

(d) With reference to the concept of price elasticity of demand (PED), explain the possible magnitude of the PED for palm oil (**Text D,** paragraph 4). [4]

(e) Using an AD/AS diagram, explain the likely impact of unprocessed commodity export ban on Indonesia's potential output (**Text D**, paragraph 5). [4]

(f) Using an externalities diagram, explain the external costs associated with the production of polystyrene foam (**Text E**, paragraph 5). [4]

(g) Using information from the text/data and your knowledge of economics, compare and contrast factors that may contribute to Indonesia and Thailand achieving the following sustainable development goals:

- SDG 8 Promote sustained, inclusive and sustainable economic growth
- SDG 10 Reduce inequalities. [15]

9.3 PAPER 3 (HL)

Instructions

- Duration: 1 hour 45 minutes
- You are permitted access to a calculator for this paper.
- Answer *all* the questions.
- Unless otherwise stated in the question, all numerical answers must be given exactly or correct to two decimal places.
- You must show all your working.
- The maximum mark for this paper is **[60 marks]**.

Sample paper 3 (HL)

Answer **all** the questions.

1.

- Export revenues contributed to 18% of Japan's GDP in 2018.
- Japan saw its exports increase at a slower rate from 2017 to 2019, partly due the rise in trade protection by one of its major trading partners.
- A global recession in 2020 resulted in Japan's export revenue decreasing by more than 11%.

2017	2018	2019	2020
1.68	0.56	0.27	−4.59

Table 1 Japan's GDP growth (%)

(a) (i) With reference to the expenditure method used to calculate GDP, explain the likely reason for Japan's negative growth rate in 2020. [4]

(ii) Using the information in **Table 1**, illustrate the short-term fluctuations in real output between 2017 and 2020 on a business cycle diagram. [3]

- Japan is one of the most indebted industrialized countries with a debt to GDP ratio of over 200%.
- The government has been running large and rising budget deficits in 2021 and 2022 to support the economy.

(iii) Define the term *real GDP*. [2]

(iv) Using an AD/AS diagram, explain the likely impact of Japan's fiscal policy on real GDP. [4]

- Income inequality is high in Japan where the Gini coefficient is 0.54 since 2010.
- The recent increase in the sales tax from 8% to 10% has also affected real income.

	2021
lowest 20%	2.7
second 20%	8.6
third 20%	12.1
fourth 20%	17.7
highest 20%	V

Table 2 Share of national income held by Japanese households (% of national income)

(v) Calculate the share of national income held by the highest 20% (**V** in **Table 2**). [1]

(vi) Using the information in **Table 2** and your answer to (v), construct Japan's Lorenz curve in 2021. [3]

- Japan's labour ministry recommended that the minimum wage be raised around 3% to almost $8.50 per hour.
- Manufacturing firms are concerned this will make their exports less competitive.
- Japan's minimum wage is low compared to other industrialized economies such as France and Germany where the minimum wage is at least $12.0 but it is higher than the minimum wage of $7.3 in the USA, Japan's main trading partner.

(vii) Explain the likely impact of the increase in the minimum wage on Japan's Gini coefficient. [3]

- Japan has experienced two decades of poor economic performance, which has led to a stagnation of wages.
- Government efforts have focused on business incentives and labour market reforms to revive the economy. This has helped increase the profits of large firms and the income of the richest 10% of earners.
- Low income individuals are the most prone to cyclical and structural unemployment. They also tend to fall into hidden unemployment. Market-based labour rigidities have resulted in manufacturing firms cutting costs by relying more on part-time and temporary workers who are paid less benefits.
- In 2019, Japan introduced a work permit scheme to encourage foreign workers with the relevant skills to enter the Japanese labour market and address the issue of skills mismatch.

(b) Using the data provided and your knowledge of economics, recommend one policy the Japanese government could implement to reduce income inequality. [10]

2. Sri Lanka, a small island in the Indian Ocean, is a less developed country.

	2019	2020
Real GDP (US$ billion)	92.12	88.83
Real GNI (US$ billion)	89.45	86.44
Consumer price index (CPI)	155.5	165.1
Current account balance (US$ billion)	–1.84	–1.08

Table 1 Selected national income data, Sri Lanka

(a) (i) Explain why the real GNI of Sri Lanka is lower than the country's real GDP. [2]

(ii) Calculate the real GDP growth rate in 2020. [2]

(iii) Calculate the inflation rate in 2020. [2]

(iv) Ignoring the capital account, outline why the financial account must be in surplus. [2]

- Sri Lanka imposes a tariff of 10% on imported milk powder.
- The domestic price of milk powder, after tariff, was 880 rupees per kg in 2018.
- The following are the estimated quantities of milk powder produced and consumed in Sri Lanka in 2018:

	Quantity (million kg)	
	produced by domestic producers	**consumed by domestic consumers**
without tariff	40	190
with tariff	62	160

(v) Using the information provided, draw an international trade diagram illustrating the impact of the tariff on the price, domestic consumption and production in Sri Lanka. [3]

(vi) Calculate the tariff revenue collected by the government. [2]

(vii) Calculate the change in consumer surplus resulting from the imposition of the tariff. [2]

- To reduce its persistent current account deficit, Sri Lanka's central bank devalued the Sri Lankan rupee (SLR) against the United States dollar (USD) by 15% in 2022. The exchange rate before the devaluation was USD 1 = SLR 287. The weaker rupee is expected to lead to significantly higher prices of food and result in an inflation rate of 20%.
- With more than USD 50 billion in total external debt, the government of Sri Lanka faces a high annual debt servicing cost of USD 7 billion, the equivalent of 79% of GDP. Sri Lanka has among the highest debt servicing costs in emerging markets.

(viii) Using an AD/AS diagram, explain the impact of the devaluation of the Sri Lankan rupee on the rate of inflation. [4]

(ix) Calculate the annual debt servicing obligations in Sri Lankan rupees after the devaluation. [1]

- The country's main industries are tourism, textiles and clothing, tea, rice and other agricultural products.
- The importation of food and beverages accounts for 10% of all imports. Sri Lanka's other main imports include fuel, medicine and inputs for production.
- Around 80% of agricultural production comes from small farms where productivity is low. Farmers lack knowledge of modern farming methods, and access to finance to purchase capital goods and diversify into higher-value products.

(b) Using the data provided and your knowledge of economics, recommend one policy, other than a currency devaluation, that the Sri Lankan government could implement to reduce the persistent current account deficit. [10]

Index